Whitworth College Library
0 0068 00117227 8

S0-BTL-386

CREATING CONNECTIONS
BOOKS, KITS, AND GAMES FOR CHILDREN

GARLAND REFERENCE LIBRARY
OF SOCIAL SCIENCE
(Vol. 280)

CREATING CONNECTIONS
BOOKS, KITS AND GAMES FOR CHILDREN
A Sourcebook

Betty P. Cleaver
Barbara Chatton
Shirley Vittum Morrison

GARLAND PUBLISHING, INC. • NEW YORK & LONDON
1986

Library of Congress Cataloging-in-Publication Data

Cleaver, Betty P.
Creating connections.

(Garland reference library of social science ;
vol. 280)
Includes indexes.
1. Children's literature—Bibliography.
2. Elementary school libraries—Book lists. 3. Teaching
—Aids and devices—Catalogs. 4. Educational games—
Catalogs. 5. Interdisciplinary approach in education.
I. Chatton, Barbara. II. Morrison, Shirley Vittum,
1927– . III. Title. IV. Series: Garland
reference library of social science ; v. 280.
Z1037.C64 1986 [PN1009.A1] 011′.62 86-581
ISBN 0-8240-8798-4 (alk. paper)

Cover Design by Bonnie Goldsmith

Printed on acid-free, 250-year-life paper
Manufactured in the United States of America

CONTENTS

PART ONE: CREATING CONNECTIONS: THE PROCESS

PART TWO: CREATING CONNECTIONS: THE MATERIALS

ILLUSTRATIONS

FIGURES: CHARTS OF CONNECTIONS

Acknowledgments

The authors recognize the debt they owe to the work of two leaders in the field of education, Charlotte Huck and Edgar Dale. Dr. Huck's teaching has contributed significantly to our own understanding of the connections children can make through literature to the world of knowledge and ideas. Dr. Dale consistently espoused the notion of integrating all the forms in which knowledge is recorded into all areas of the curriculum. The influence of these educators, their expansive views of integrated learning experiences, and their respect for the child, are reflected in our own work.

We are indebted to Trenna Barlow, Kelly Hughes, Betty Lawson, Patricia Mason, Linda Pearson, and Angie Van Meter in the typing and word processing chores; also, we deeply appreciate the help and support of all our Edgar Dale Media Center staff, especially Ty, Christtine, Norio, Tina, Vahid, and Bill. Thank you all!

Introduction

This bibliography, CREATING CONNECTIONS, is intended to serve both as a resource and a model. It shows how a wide range of subjects and curriculum areas, as well as various formats of audiovisual and print resources, can be incorporated into a field of study. To assist teachers and librarians in making these relationships we have provided a selected list of materials on topics which are generally found in the elementary curriculum. We have also included suggestions for establishing a pattern of relationships which weaves together books and other media for use across the curriculum.

The book is organized into two parts which we call the process and the materials.

Chapter 1 examines several approaches to using materials across the curriculum and points out how these are grounded in curriculum theory. Chapter 2 identifies some reference books which might be useful to the teacher or librarian who wants to expand the concepts presented here. The list is not intended to be anything more than a sampling of the rich resources available, resources not always discovered in methods and literature classes. Chapter 3 is a detailed description of the process of elaborating a seemingly simple thematic concept so that all areas of the curriculum, from writing to science, can be used to expand and support all other areas. This is the process we used in developing the networks of resources which form the second part of the book.

Part two presents six topics: Bodies, Cities, Monsters, Mountains, Oceans, and Sound. For each of these topics we present a diagram which indicates major ideas and subordinate ideas to be examined. If a strand of the diagram is followed vertically, it will lead to more detailed knowledge, while the horizontal path emphasizes the relationship of ideas generally categorized in subject areas.

Each chapter starts with an explanation of one way the topic might be expanded. We want to stress the point that you might develop a different network or pattern of connections. The outlines and the subjects followed here are neither comprehensive nor prescriptive -- they simply say to you -- "Here's one way you might create connections." You will choose those elements most appropriate for your particular setting and needs.

After presenting a pattern of curriculum connections for each chapter topic, we have selected some of the subtopics and provided an annotated list of resources. We have been selective in this, so we feel that all of these materials are, indeed, useful. You could list many more, and to make this book really useful, you should probably consider it a beginning for your own list. The grade levels are only approximate guides; as you know, some fifth graders need third grade materials, and some first graders can read at a third grade level!

We have included out of print books which are generally available in libraries. Books go in and out of print so quickly that this is unavoidable. For the most part we have emphasized materials published in the last ten years, but we have included some of the classics, too. Most of the resources listed include a brief annotation, but there are some we list whose titles are as descriptive as any phrases we could write.

In the back of the book are an author/title index and a list of related subject headings based on LIBRARY OF CONGRESS SUBJECT HEADINGS and SEARS LIST OF SUBJECT HEADINGS. These may aid you in your search for more books and kits. Although this is a subject bibliography, a more detailed subject index has been included.

Finally, we hope this book will be useful as a finding tool, a teaching tool, and a model. It provides a resource for the selection and use of curriculum related materials for elementary students, a resource for teachers, school library media specialists, and public librarians responsible for children's services. And it provides a pattern for the integration of books and media, a pattern which extends the child's experience, making connections between fiction and non-fiction and between subject areas of the curriculum.

PART ONE

CREATING CONNECTIONS: THE PROCESS

Chapter 1

Creating Connections: A Rationale

Creating connections is, perhaps, a misnomer. The connections are already there, if we can but discover them -- connections of ideas and experiences which begin at a set point and lead to new understandings.

The process of making connections between the known and the unknown, or between several known facts, is natural to children. They structure their experiences by fitting an experience or observation into a framework of things known. A child may see an interesting looking plant in the yard and call it a flower. It fits known criteria for flower: it comes up out of the ground, the long green shoot has a colored, round shape at the top, and it looks pretty. Mother sees it and says, "Oh that's just a dandelion. It's a weed." The child is still sure it's a flower. Mother and child have different ideas about "flower" based on their own experiences. They have each made their own connections, but because they are fitting their observations into different frameworks of experience, they have reached different conclusions. This process of connecting or associating is the way we elaborate on experience and knowledge; we continue the process throughout our lives.

Making connections between ideas and seeing the relationship of one event to another ties knowledge and experience together, fitting them into the continuum of our lives. How strange, then, that we organize our schools and libraries in patterns which are based on the separation of ideas and groups of ideas! We teach language arts, social studies, science, literature, art, and music as separate subjects. We find music books in one section of the library, history books in another. In many libraries the films, audiotapes, games, and other instructional materials are in yet another section.

Of course we know that these patterns of separation are chosen to make the teaching of a subject manageable, or the retrieval of information possible. Unfortunately, the pattern of separation may become a barrier which encourages the compartmentalization of knowledge. For example, we may forget that the study of oceans, a proper subject for science, could be brought to life with John Masefield's poem,

> "I must go down to the sea again
> To the lonely sea and the sky,
> And all I ask is a tall ship
> And a star to steer her by."[1]

Lonely sea? Steer by a star? What's the connection?

Finding the connection serves to link the concepts of two or more separate areas of study. This can happen fortuitously, but teachers can plan for the linking by the questions they ask and the materials of instruction they make available. The process of finding links can be a cooperative effort in which students and teacher play with ideas, setting free their imaginations.

Northrup Frye defined imagination as "the power of constructing possible models of human experience."[2] These models can be experienced vicariously in literature and examined in the light of information from other sources. "Everything man does that's worth doing," he said, "is some kind of construction, and the imagination is the constructive power of the mind set free...."[3]

The idea of linking various curriculum areas is not new. There have been many efforts to establish an integrated approach to curriculum planning, ranging from the core curriculum to the project method to the unified arts curriculum. These rely on the integration of ideas, materials, and experiences, a method of organization which Ralph Tyler called horizontal.

"When we examine the relationship between the experiences provided in fourth-grade arithmetic and in fifth-grade arithmetic we are considering vertical organization, whereas when we consider the relationship between the experiences in fourth-grade arithmetic and fourth-grade social studies, or between the experiences in fourth-grade arithmetic and the fourth grader's learning experiences outside of school, we are considering the horizontal organization of learning experiences."[4] Both the horizontal and vertical organization are important; in the first instance the child develops the ability to associate ideas, while in the second there is an emphasis on the unfolding and elaboration of a single subject.

The charts presented in this book are models which can be followed vertically and horizontally. They are intended to serve as examples which show how teachers and librarians can create their own connections as they plan for learning experiences.

The variety of instructional resources -- books, games, films, etc. -- forms the glue which will hold these experiences together. The materials of instruction are many and varied: they include books, magazines, and other print materials as well as films, filmstrips, sound recordings, games and the like. Jerome Bruner called them "devices" which aid in the teaching process. Through them, he said, children can experience events vicariously, or discover the basic structure of a natural phenomenon. The materials enrich and extend experience, and "such enrichment is one of the principal objectives of education."[5] The proper, planned use of audiovisual materials, Edgar Dale reminded us, can: heighten motivation for learning: provide freshness and variety; appeal to students of varied abilities; encourage active participation; give needed reinforcement; widen the range of student experience; assure order and continuity of thought; and, improve the effectiveness of other materials.[6]

Using literature and instructional materials across the curriculum can be very liberating for a teacher. No longer does a filmstrip on birds and their young have to be used only in the science class; it might provide a frame of reference for McCloskey's MAKE WAY FOR DUCKLINGS.[7] On the other hand, a study of the Quakers could certainly be more interesting if Turkle's THY FRIEND, OBADIAH were read.[8] Books written to inform and instruct, sometimes called information books, can be used to complement literature, which is "the language of the imagination."[9]

Literature can be used in all areas of the curriculum; it can illuminate by allowing vicarious experience, by evoking emotion and imagination. However, we need to protect the interests of the child by allowing an enjoyment which is not dampened by pedagogic questions and the ferreting out of facts. We can ask for facts when information books are read. "Almost everything a child learns in school today is concerned with facts -- literature is concerned with feelings, with the quality of life," Charlotte Huck told us. "Literature is a kind of golden string that can place us in contact with the best minds in every period of history, the wisest, the tenderest, the bravest of all who have ever lived. And it can do this for children if only we can help them to grasp hold of it."[10]

The process of creating connections across the curriculum is exemplified in several ways: in a unified science or art curriculum, in using or building "jackdaws," and in the "webbing" of children's literature.

In Jefferson County, Colorado, a unified program was established called "Jefferson County's Primary Integrated Curriculum." It included science, social studies, health, environmental education, and career education. The units used three basic teaching techniques: 1) the informative approach (presentation of facts); 2) the discovery approach (students discover predetermined answers); and 3) the experiential approach (students experience problems whose solutions are unknown). Melle and Wilson reported that these techniques and the content of the units have proved to be highly motivating; they establish relationships and connections. In one unit, Sidewalk Safari, students made excursions in the school neighborhood, observing the houses, interviewing neighbors, and studying the environment.[11]

Jackdaws are sometimes purchased but more often are developed by teacher and students. A jackdaw is a bird, one that picks up brightly colored objects or anything else that attracts its attention and takes these back to its nest. Jackdaws, then, "are collections of interesting artifacts that help to provide information about a particular subject, period, or idea."[12] A teacher would use a jackdaw to provide a comprehensive background for the reading of a book, for "within the jackdaw concept is a commitment to the use of literature in the reading program."[13] Readers gain knowledge about a topic and this leads to greater interest in it, and therefore, greater interest in reading and exploration of the topic. A jackdaw might contain real objects, facsimiles of documents, photographs, sound recordings, newspapers, maps, and clothing. The contents provide concrete information which may help students interpret and better understand the books they are reading. For example, a Civil War jackdaw might be developed while Janet Hickman's ZOAR BLUE was being read.[14] It could contain letters, a diary, a cornhusk doll, facsimiles of newspaper articles, maps, and a daguerreotype of a Union soldier. The jackdaw documents the events of the book by providing a context for them.

Encouraging children to read, to enjoy reading, and to talk about books is often accomplished by webbing, a concept first introduced by Charlotte Huck, a concept which has become an integral part of the children's literature program at The Ohio State University. "Every book has multiple possibilities for discussion," said Huck. "A way of planning for the various directions a discussion might take, or the possibilities for interpretations, or extended reading can be shown in a diagram called 'a web'."[15] A quarterly publication, THE WEB, has been established with the purpose of "entangling ...children with Wonderfully Exciting Books."[16] Each issue has a theme, reflected in the book reviews and a diagrammed web. These themes range from Dragons to Life Stories, from Laughter to Magic to Playing with Language.

Becker has defined webbing as "a form of organizing brainstorming efforts" with the purpose of expressing what is known and broadening ways to think about a topic. It is "an integrated, connected picture of the knowledge, processes, resources, and learning experiences ... associated with a given topic."[17]

This webbing process is a good way to tie together literature and information books, promoting the integration of language arts and reading skills. Norton emphasized the importance of getting children to read, and she found it useful to start by selecting a topic that might be enhanced through children's literature, then having a group brainstorm ideas and draw a web which would identify the ideas that might branch off from the central theme. One theme, Survival on Islands, led to a web whose principal headings included Geography, Food, Clothing, Shelter, Seasonal Weather, and Medical Care. Fiction and nonfiction, trade books and textbooks became the resources the children consulted to find information or to vicariously experience an aspect of survival.[18] Just as one idea leads to another, so does success in reading one book lead the student to further reading. In the webbing process, the teacher is promoting the use of literature across the curriculum.

Summary

Developing literature units by webbing and enhancing the understanding of literature through the use of jackdaws both serve the primary purpose of encouraging children to read. The focus is on literature, on making connections through literature. In this respect they differ from the approach of "creating connections."

Creating connections is done to link the subject areas of the curriculum, linking them by following various strands of ideas and by using all available resources in the exploration of an idea.

No particular form of material is most important in this scheme; the instructional problem determines which resources are most appropriate. Literature and information combine to provide knowledge and experiential learning. A topic is divided and subdivided, vertically and horizontally. Then strands are attached and the search for materials begins. In this way we help children learn by association.

In speaking of the ways children learn, John Holt said, "They see the world as a whole, mysterious perhaps, but a whole none the less. They do not divide it up into airtight little categories, as we adults tend to do. It is natural for them to jump from one thing to another, and to make the kinds of connections that are rarely made in formal classes and textbooks. They make their own paths into the unknown, paths that we would never think of making for them... Their learning does not box them in; it leads them into life in many directions. Each new thing they learn makes them aware of other new things to be learned. Their curiosity grows by what it finds to feed on. Our task is to keep it well supplied with food."[19]

In A VISIT TO WILLIAM BLAKE'S INN, we find the poet leading a walk on the Milky Way.

> He hurried us to the horizon
> where morning and evening meet.
> The slippery stars went skipping
> under our hapless feet.
>
> "I shall garland my room," said the tiger,
> "with a few of these emerald lights."
> "I shall give up sleeping forever," I said.
> "I shall never part day from night."[20]

Creating connections will lead, so we hope, to a seamless curriculum, a curriculum which never parts day from night.

REFERENCES

1. John Masefield, "Sea Fever" in SALT-WATER POEMS AND BALLADS (New York: Macmillan, 1916).
2. Northrop Frye, THE EDUCATED IMAGINATION (Bloomington, IN: Indiana University Press, 1969), 22.
3. Frye, 119
4. Ralph Tyler, in THE INTEGRATION OF EDUCATIONAL EXPERIENCES, Fifty-seventh Yearbook of the National Society for the Study of Education, Part II, ed. Paul L. Dressel (Chicago: University of Chicago Press, 1958), 107-108.
5. Jerome Bruner, THE PROCESS OF EDUCATION (Cambridge, MA: Harvard University Press, 1960), 81.
6. Edgar Dale, AUDIOVISUAL METHODS IN TEACHING, 3rd ed. (New York: Holt, Rinehart, and Winston, 1969), 150-156.
7. Robert McCloskey, MAKE WAY FOR DUCKLINGS (New York: Viking Press, 1941).
8. Brinton Turkle, THY FRIEND, OBADIAH (New York: Viking Press, 1969).
9. Frye, 134.
10. Charlotte Huck, "I Give You the End of a Golden String," THEORY INTO PRACTICE 21 (Autumn 1982): 315

11. Marge Melle and Fern Wilson, "Balanced Instruction Through an Integrated Curriculum," EDUCATIONAL LEADERSHIP 41 (April 1984): 59-63.

12. Timothy V. Rasinski, "Using Jackdaws to Build Background and Interest for Reading." Paper presented at the Annual Meeting of the International Reading Association, Anaheim, CA, May 1983. ERIC, ED 234 351, 1.

13. Rasinski, 3

14. Janet Hickman, ZOAR BLUE (New York: Macmillan, 1978).

15. Charlotte S. Huck, CHILDREN'S LITERATURE IN THE ELEMENTARY SCHOOL, 3rd ed. rev. (New York: Holt, Rinehart and Winston, 1979), 717.

16. THE WEB, Center for Language, Literature, and Reading, College of Education, The Ohio State University, Columbus, Ohio 43210.

17. Rhoda McShane Becher, "I Know What I'm Doing, I Just Don't Know What to Call It." Paper presented at the Spring Curriculum Workshop of the St. Louis Association for the Education of Young Children, April 1983. p. 11, ED 237 190.

18. Donna E. Norton, "Using a Webbing Process to Develop Children's Literature Units," LANGUAGE ARTS 59 (April 1982): 348-356.

19. John Holt, HOW CHILDREN LEARN (New York: Dell, 1970), 139-140.

20. Nancy Willard, A VISIT TO WILLIAM BLAKE'S INN, illustrated by Alice and Martin Provensen (New York: Harcourt, Brace Jovanovich, 1982), 33.

Chapter 2

Developing the Process

Developing connections across the curriculum begins with the brainstorming process. Brainstorming as a process for solving problems was developed in the late thirties by Alex F. Osborn.[1] It follows a specific structure which is used to generate large quantities of ideas. Four basic rules of brainstorming were identified by Gorman and Baker. They are:

1. No criticism of ideas.
2. No compliments of ideas.
3. No questions or discussion regarding ideas.
4. Combination and improvement are sought.[2]

One of the key elements which leads to success in the brainstorming process is that more than one person contributes ideas and suggestions to a pool, thus increasing the number of possible ideas and connections. More and better ideas are generated in the planning process if a number of people are included in the session. In developing the session for planning thematic units planners should consider including people with some expertise in the following areas: persons with knowledge of the objectives of the school curriculum; persons with knowledge of the objectives of the given unit to be developed; persons with knowledge of books and media materials; and persons who are widely-read in the field of children's literature. To this end, it would be useful to include several teachers (perhaps all of the teachers within a certain grade level within a building), the school or district library/media specialist, and subject specialists, if they are available.

The brainstorming process mandates that there be no criticism and no compliments. This means that for the initial sessions of the planning process no judgement is passed on the worth or effectiveness of any idea or material which is suggested by participants. Members simply throw out to the group any or all connections which they can make to the topic. Each of these may lead to something which will be helpful in the later stages of planning when the combining and improving of ideas takes place.

Previous to the first scheduled planning session each participant should be notified of the major area of the thematic planning. If the theme is "Oceans," for instance, each member is invited to attend the session, is given the topic and is asked to come up with some ideas, suggestions, questions, materials or connections which could be made with that topic. Members of the group then meet and unrestrainedly offer suggestions for the topic.

These suggestions might include ways to tie the topic to areas of the curriculum, questions they have, titles of books, folk literature, or poetry which seems to fit with the topic, titles of informational materials which apply to the topic, suggestions for films, sound recordings, programs and other forms of media which relate to the topic, and aspects of the topic to be considered. Three participants in a brainstorming session on "Oceans," for example, might come together and the session might proceed in this manner:

> "This topic will include areas we study in science this year, such as fishes and the tides, as well as the material in our social studies unit on explorers."
>
> "I love the children's book by George Mendoza called AND I MUST HURRY FOR THE SEA IS COMING IN.[3] It's about a boy who daydreams about being a ship's captain. It's like a poem."
>
> "Lee Bennet Hopkins has those anthologies of poetry about various subjects. I wonder if there is a collection about the sea."
>
> "I thought about Paterson's JACOB HAVE I LOVED because it's set on the Chesapeake Bay and talks so much about the island and about crabbing."[4]
>
> "Didn't she cite an informational book at the beginning which she used as a resource? We'll have to check that and try to find it."
>
> "National Geographic has that set of filmstrips about SEA LIFE which would work with that.[5] And wouldn't Holling's PAGOO work nicely here?"[6]
>
> "How about including those recordings of the whales and other sea life?"
>
> "Yes, I'd love to do a lot on the creatures of the sea. Especially the research on whales and dolphins."
>
> "I've used that book MIND IN THE WATERS with my students.[7] There are some poignant articles in there about sea creatures."
>
> "There is so much you could do with conservation in connection to this topic: endangered species, and oil spills, and using up of the ocean's resources.

> "I've always wanted to know how oil rigs work. You know, how they float, how many people are on them, where the oil goes, and so on."

(Discussion continues)

As this process of brainstorming is taking place, one member of the group records the ideas presented in a format which all members can clearly see (on chart paper or a blackboard). The recorder tries to organize the information into loose categories as they emerge. This organizational format may take the form of a web, an outline, or a chart, depending on the form with which the group is most comfortable. For the above segment of the discussion the recorder might have listed the ideas in this manner:

OCEANS

Subject areas:	Poetry:	Fiction:
Fishes	AND I MUST HURRY...	JACOB MAVE I LOVED
Tides	Hopkins book?	Chesapeake Bay (Informational book?)
Explorers		
		Sea Life: National Geographic Filmstrips

Conservation:

- Endangered species
- Oil spills   Oil rigs?
- Ocean's resources

Crabs   PAGOO

Whales and dolphins

- Sound recording
- MIND IN THE WATERS

This organizational format will in turn prompt more ideas as people begin to see connections between topics, to expand upon the areas mentioned, and to remember titles of materials they have used effectively in the past. In many cases there will be holes in the areas of the chart. Brainstormers will remember using some materials but not their titles. They may be fairly sure that something exists although they haven't used it. They may recognize a whole area which needs to be explored but not know of materials or literature which would help in the area. They may have questions they would like to see answered. All of these pieces of information and questions are added to the chart to be pursued at a later point.

After the initial brainstorming period, a copy of the chart is made for each member of the group, and members return to other tasks. At this point members of the group may choose to consult bibliographies, catalogs, class reading lists, curriculum objectives and their own shelves of materials for further ideas and materials to add to the chart. Since library catalogs don't always give subject access to books, chapters of books, filmstrips from sets, songs, poems, tales or other materials which could be useful in a unit, bibliographic tools are extremely valuable in this next phase of the planning process. (See Chapter 2, "Widening the Search" for a list of bibliographic tools.) Because many of the bibliographic tools include cross references, the members of the group may also find other areas of study, further connections, and other titles which would expand the unit. In addition, library/media specialists can use these lists to add to the school's collection of materials which would enrich a thematic unit. After a period of time in which people can think further about the ideas presented, the books they know and the materials available, the group re-convenes.

When the group re-convenes, other materials which have been located, along with other ideas and suggestions are incorporated into the chart. Then the organization of the chart is scrutinized. Have all of the areas which should be covered been covered? Are some areas too thin or weak? Are there other materials or questions or topics which would flesh these areas out? Is there too broad an emphasis here? Will children not see the connections among topics and ideas because we have not clearly linked them? Are there questions we can ask, materials we can use which can help to provide these links? Are we trying to cover too much? Have we used a good balance of media in various formats, informational books, picture books, fiction, poetry and folk literature in this unit or have we stressed one area too heavily?

A second, more complete chart is then formulated which organizes the subjects and materials into a logical format. The chart (without titles of materials) might look something like this:

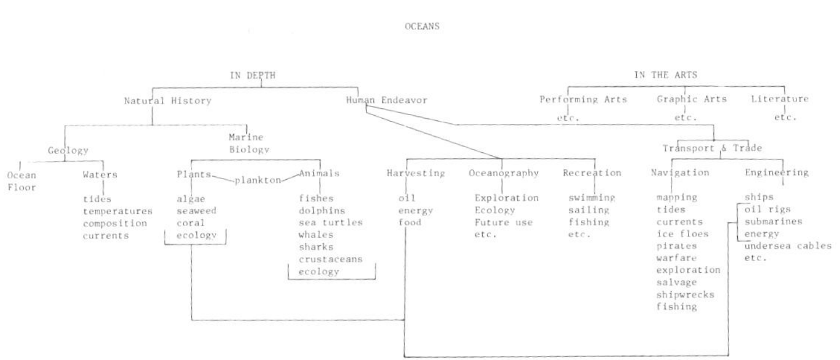

(See chapter on "Oceans" for the complete list of materials.)

Once members of the planning committee have formulated a chart showing major and minor areas which can be highlighted in any theme, then the process of materials collection begins. For many teachers this is the most frustrating part of the planning process. A good school library collection is invaluable in simplifying the job of collecting of materials for thematic units.

When a good school or district library is not available, teachers and librarians must spend time checking the holdings and loan policies of local public libraries, other community agencies, and film rental services which might provide resources. Ideally, planning for units will be done enough in advance that librarians and teachers can allocate school funds for purchase of materials which will support a variety of thematic units within the school.

The most significant member of the planning team can be the school library media specialist. This person can provide expertise in the selection of materials, and in the best use of various forms of materials as well as in the development of a plan for allocation of funds for purchasing these materials.

Once the planning process has taken place for thematic units, then the basic chart of the possibilities for the unit, an annotated list of materials, and the objectives for the unit should be retained and made available for use by all. The lists of materials should include the location of each resource and costs involved in procuring it, if applicable. Teachers across a school or district could use all or parts of the plans for these units, for other activities in their classrooms or for other thematic units. Just as, for example, the area of sharks and other strange creatures of the ocean appear in the plans for both the "Oceans" and the "Monsters" units in this text, certain areas of each plan might well be used in several different contexts. In addition, teachers and librarians can continue to watch for materials which could be added to these units as they read professional journals, order materials, attend conferences and so on. Further ideas and questions for use in the curriculum may occur as the unit is used or as other areas are added to the curriculum, and these can be added to the planning packet.

This planning process can also be used very effectively in the classroom. Students who participate in brainstorming in a free association of ideas will become more involved with the ensuing study and will be encouraged to use more creative approaches. Brainstorming nay be done by teachers and students working together as a team. This can lead to an exciting unit rich in its diversity of resources and experiences.

CREATING CONNECTIONS contains a collection of six broad thematic units as designed by three library/media specialists. The units include a chart of the vertical and horizontal possibilities for connections across a topic and a bibliography of books and media which would be most helpful in sharing this topic with children. As would be true in any school setting, these lists and charts are not comprehensive. Each school program includes ideas, materials and curriculum areas which may not have been included here. It is hoped that these plans will provide teachers and library/media specialists with a beginning place from which to work on thematic units and that they will feel free to elaborate upon or eliminate pieces from these plans which do not fit with their objectives and concerns.

REFERENCES

1. Alexander Faickney Osborn, THE APPLIED IMAGINATION (New York: Scribner, 1953).
2. Ronald H. Gorman and H. Kent Baker, "Brainstorming your way to problem-solving ideas" PERSONNEL JOURNAL (August, 1978): 438-440.
3. George Mendoza, AND I MUST HURRY FOR THE SEA IS COMING IN (Englewood Cliffs, NJ: Prentice-Hall, 1969).
4. Katherine Paterson, JACOB HAVE I LOVED (New York: Harper and Row, 1980).
5. SEA LIFE (Washington, D.C.; The National Geographic Society, 1973).
6. Holling Clancy Holling, PAGOO (Boston: Houghton Mifflin, 1975).
7. Joan McIntyre, ed., MIND IN THE WATERS (New York: Charles Scribner's Sons, 1974).

Chapter 3

Widening the Search

This resource list will provide additional sources of materials and techniques for implementing some of the ideas in this book. Most are standard reference materials available in public libraries if not in the school/library media center.

We encourage the user to refer to them and to similar materials in order to expand the lists provided in this book or to develop new curriculum connections to fit the needs of individual schools, students and situations.

<u>Guides</u>

1. Baker, Augusta. STORYTELLING: ART AND TECHNIQUE.
   New York: Bowker; 1977.
   A manual emphasizing storytelling as an oral art. Written primarily for public and school librarians.

2. Baskin, Barbara. NOTES FROM A DIFFERENT DRUMMER.
   New York: Bowker; 1977.
   A guide to juvenile fiction which portrays the handicapped.

3. Bauer, Caroline Feller. HANDBOOK FOR STORYTELLERS.
   Chicago: American Library Association; 1977.
   Discusses how to use a wide variety of media--film, music, crafts, puppetry, magic--with the storytelling experience.

4. Bramscher, Cynthia S. TREASURY OF MUSICAL MOTIVATORS FOR THE ELEMENTARY CLASSROOM. Illustrated.
   West Nyack, NY: Parker Pub.; 1979.
   Music-based classroom activities to be used for language arts, social studies, science, mathematics, physical education, and visual arts. Grade levels and instructional goals are noted.

5. Bryant, Sara. HOW TO TELL STORIES TO CHILDREN. Boston: Houghton Mifflin; 1973.
Details techniques and resources for telling stories to children.

6. Carpenter, Humphrey, and Mari Prichard. THE OXFORD COMPANION TO CHILDRENS LITERATURE. New York: Oxford University Press; 1984.
Contains information on virtually all aspects of children's books and elements of children's popular culture.

7. CREATIVE STORYTELLING TECHNIQUES [Videorecording]. Chicago: American Library Association; 1979; 1 videocassette.
Mixing the media with Caroline Feller Bauer, this program presents a variety of methods of telling stories, using books, puppets, and props.

8. Dreyer, Sharon Spredemann. THE BOOKFINDER: A GUIDE TO CHILDREN'S LITERATURE ABOUT THE NEEDS AND PROBLEMS OF YOUTH AGED 2-15, Circle Pines, MN: American Guidance Service; 1977.
Describes and categorizes current children's books according to psychological, behavioral and developmental topics.

9. Dreyer, Sharon Spredemann. THE BOOKFINDER, VOLUME 2: A GUIDE TO CHILDREN'S LITERATURE ABOUT THE NEEDS AND PROBLEMS OF YOUTH AGED 2-15: ANNOTATIONS OF BOOKS PUBLISHED 1975 THROUGH 1978. Circle Pines, MN: American Guidance Service; 1981.
Describes and categorizes current children's books according to psychological, behavioral and developmental topics.

10. Dreyer, Sharon Spredemann. THE BOOKFINDER: WHEN KIDS NEED BOOKS: ANNOTATIONS OF BOOKS PUBLISHED 1979 THROUGH 1982.
Circle Pines, MN: American Guidance Service; 1985.
Describes and categorizes current children's books according to psychological, behavioral and developmental topics.

11. FESTIVALS SOURCEBOOK, Detroit: Gale Research; 1977.
A guide to fairs, festivals, and celebrations.

12. Forcucci, Samuel L. A FOLK SONG HISTORY OF AMERICA: AMERICA THROUGH ITS SONGS. Englewood Cliffs, NJ: Prentice Hall; 1984.

Includes a description of the historical context, the music and words of songs for regions of the United States and periods of history.

13. Glazer, Joan I. LITERATURE FOR YOUNG CHILDREN. Columbus, OH: Charles E. Merrill; 1981.
A guide for teachers and parents working with preschool and primary age children. It relates concepts of child development to children's books and includes suggestions for their use.

14. Hatch, Jane M., ed, THE AMERICAN BOOK OF DAYS. 3rd edition. New York: Wilson; 1978.
Events, birthdays of important Americans, festivals and other observances for every day of the year.

15. Huck, Charlotte. CHILDREN'S LITERATURE IN THE ELEMENTARY SCHOOL. 3rd edition. New York: Holt, Rinehart, & Winston; 1979.
A children's literature textbook which focuses on the integration of literature throughout the curriculum. Extensive bibliographies are provided.

16. Koch, Kenneth. WISHES, LIES AND DREAMS: TEACHING CHILDREN TO WRITE POETRY, New York: Harper & Row; 1980.
A classic account of how one poet-teacher inspired children in a New York city grade school to write poetry. Students wrote noise poems, comparison poems, color poems, and many other concept-related poems.

17. Lamme, Linda, ed. LEARNING TO LOVE LITERATURE: PRESCHOOL THROUGH GRADE 3, Urbana, IL: National Council of Teachers of English; 1981.
Presents strategies and specific materials for implementing a literature based curriculum for young children.

18. Leonard, Charlotte. TIED TOGETHER: TOPICS AND THOUGHTS FOR INTRODUCING CHILDREN'S BOOKS. Metchen, NJ: Scarecrow Press; 1980.
Examples of presentations a teacher or librarian might use to introduce books to children, organized around more than 60 themes, from Being Different to Pancakes for Everyone.

19. Paulin, Mary Ann. CREATIVE USES OF CHILDREN'S LITERATURE. Hamden, CT: Library Professional Pub.; 1982.
    A comprehensive sourcebook which includes books and media to introduce literature to children, as well as suggested activities and guidelines for selection.

20. Pellowski, Anne. THE WORLD OF STORYTELLING. New York: Bowker; 1977.
    A detailed history of storytelling. Includes a multilingual dictionary of storytelling terms.

21. Polette, Nancy. CELEBRATING WITH BOOKS. Metuchen, NJ: Scarecrow Press; 1977.
    Suggests activities and books to use with children to celebrate major holidays.

22. PRELUDE: SERIES 1 [Sound Recording]. New York: Children's Book Council; 1975; 3 cassettes.
    Mini seminars on using books creatively by A. Baker, V. Ried, G. Blough, L. Alexander, R. Gans, and A. Pellowski.

23. PRELUDE: SERIES 2 [Sound Recording]. New York: Children's Book Council; 1976; 3 cassettes.
    Mini seminars on using books creatively by C. Huck, L. Russ, L. Jacobs, S. Sebseta, Z. Sutherland, J. Fraenkel.

24. Russell, Helen Ross. TEN-MINUTE FIELD TRIPS, USING THE SCHOOLGROUNDS FOR ENVIRONMENTAL STUDIES: A TEACHER'S GUIDE, Illustrated by Klaub Winckelmann. Chicago: Ferguson; 1973.
    How to use the school grounds, no matter how barren, for environmental studies which emphasize the interrelationships of the natural world. Field trip and classroom activities are included.

25. Smith, Ron, MYTHOLOGIES OF THE WORLD: A GUIDE TO SOURCES. Urbana, IL: National Council of Teachers of English; 1981.
    A guide to mythology, organized by geographical area.

26. Sutherland, Zena; Monson, Dianne L. Arbuthnot, May Hill. CHILDREN AND BOOKS, Illustrated by Charles Mikolaycak. Glenview, IL: Scott, Foresman; 1981.
    A children's literature text which examines the needs of children and explores the various types of literature as ways to help satisfy those needs. Includes extensive bibliographies.

Indexes and Bibliographies

27. ADVENTURING WITH BOOKS: A BOOKLIST FOR PRE-K--GRADE 6. Edited by Mary Lou White and the Committee on the Elementary School Booklist of the National Council of Teachers of English, Urbana, IL: The Council; 1981.

28. Arbuthnot, May Hill, CHILDREN'S BOOKS TOO GOOD TO MISS. New York: University Press; 1979.
An annotated listing of books for children, through age 14.

29. Bernstein, Joanne. BOOKS TO HELP CHILDREN COPE WITH SEPARATION AND LOSS. New York: Bowker; 1983.
Annotations for more than 400 books which might help children in coping with loss. Death, divorce, illness, stepparents, and adoption are some of the areas covered. Age and reading levels are noted.

30. BOOKS FOR THE TEEN AGE, 1983. New York: New York Public Library; 1983.
Lists titles on subjects which appeal to teens. All titles have been reviewd by libraians--some by New York teenage readers.

31. BOOKS FOR YOU. Urbana, IL: National Council of Teachers of English; 1976.
A booklist for senior high students prepared by a committee of the National Council of Teachers of English.

32. Brewton, John E, G. Merdith Blackburn, and Lorraine A. Blackburn. INDEX TO POETRY FOR CHILDREN AND YOUNG PEOPLE, 1976-1981, New York: Wilson; 1984.
A title, subject, author and first line index to poetry in collections for children and young people. See also earlier editions, from 1942.

33. Brown, Lucy Gregor, and Betty McDavid. CORE MEDIA COLLECTION FOR ELEMENTARY SCHOOLS. New York, Bowker; 1978. Audio-visual materials and catalogs.
A "core" collection of instructional materials for the K-6 curriculum is organized alphabetically by title under various subject headings. Complete bibliographic information, including review sources for each citation.

34. Chambers, Joanna. HEY, MISS! YOU GOT A BOOK FOR ME? Austin, TX: Bilingual Language Editions; 1981.
A model multicultural resource collection annotated bibliography.

35. CHILDREN'S CATALOG. Edited by Richard H. Isaacson and Gary L. Bogart. New York: Wilson; 1981.
A classified catalog of children's books with author, title, subject, and analytical indexes. Hardbound copy issued every five years. Prepared to coordinate with: JUNIOR HIGH SCHOOL LIBRARY CATALOG, 3rd edition.

36. CHILDREN'S BOOKS IN PRINT, 1969--. New York: Bowker; 1985.
An author, title, and illustrator index to children's books, updated annually.

37. Coughlan, Margaret N., comp. FOLKLORE FROM AFRICA TO THE UNITED STATES. Washington, D.C: Library of Congress; 1976.
A bibliography of collections of African folklore, giving original sources and tracing relationships of these stories to stories found in the West Indies and the southern United States. Titles are grouped geographically and divided into lists appropriate for adults and lists for children.

38. THE ELEMENTARY SCHOOL LIBRARY COLLECTION: A GUIDE TO BOOKS AND OTHER MEDIA, PHASES 1-2-3. Edited by Lois Winkel, Mary Virginia Gaver and others. Williamsport, PA: Brodart; 1984.
A guide to books and other media with suggested acquisition phases, 1-2-3.

39. Flemming, Carolyn Sherwood, and Donna Schatt, eds. CHOICES: A CORE COLLECTION FOR RELUCTANT READERS. Evanston, IL: John Gordon Burke; 1983.
Approximately 360 books described and indexed by reading level, grade level, interest level, and subject.

40. Gallivan, Marion. FUN FOR KIDS: AN INDEX TO CHILDREN'S CRAFT BOOKS. Metuchen, NJ: Scarecrow Press; 1981.
A guide to more than 300 books containing information about crafts. Suggestions for craft projects, with grade levels and nation of origin noted.

41. Haviland, Virginia. CHILDREN & POETRY, Washington, D.C: Library of Congress; 1979.
A selective annotated bibliography of old and new poetry originating in English, as well as translations from all over the world.

42. Higgins, Judith H. ENERGY: A MULTIMEDIA GUIDE FOR CHILDREN AND YOUNG ADULTS. Santa Barbara, CA: American Bibliographical Center-Clio Press; 1979.
A list of audiovisual materials for use in studying various energy concepts.

43. Hunt, Mary Alice, ed, A MULTIMEDIA APPROACH TO CHILDREN'S LITERATURE. 3rd edition. Chicago: American Library Association; 1984.
A selective list of films, filmstrips, and recordings based on children's books. Arranged by title so that several audiovisual versions of a book are found together.

44. Ireland, Norma Olin. INDEX TO FAIRY TALES. Westwood, MA: Faxon; 1979.
An index to fairy tales, folklore, legends and myths. Continues earlier editions compiled by Mary Huse Eastman, 1915-1952, and N.O. Ireland, 1973--.

45. Lima, Carolyn W. A to ZOO: SUBJECT ACCESS TO CHILDREN'S PICTURE BOOKS. New York: Bowker; 1982.
An alphabetical list of subject headings provides access to children's picture books; bibliographic information is given for approximately 4,000 books.

46. Lynn, Ruth Nadelman. FANTASY FOR CHILDREN: AN ANNOTATED CHECKLIST AND REFERENCE GUIDE. 2nd edition, New York: Bowker; 1983.
A comprehensive annotated bibliographic guide to more than 2,000 recommended fantasy novels for children in grades three through eight. Also includes Ph.D. dissertations on children's fantasy and a bibliograpby of critical and biographical books.

47. MacDonald, Margaret R. THE STORYTELLER'S SOURCEBOOK. Detroit, MI: Neal-Schuman; 1982.
A subject, title, and motif index to folklore collections for children.

48. Matthias, Margaret, and Diane Thiessen. CHILDREN'S MATHEMATICS BOOKS: A CRITICAL BIBLIOGRAPHY. Chicago: American Library Association; 1979.

Reviews of children's books for use in teaching counting, geometry, measurement, number concepts, and time. Recommended grade levels are noted.

49. THE OXFORD DICTIONARY OF NURSERY RHYMES. Edited by Iona and Peter Opie, New York: Oxford University Press; 1980.
Includes "Index of notable figures" and "Index of first lines". Describes different types of rhymes, the earliest collections made of them, and theories about their origins, over 500 rhymes are mentioned.

50. Peterson, Carolyn Sue, and Ann D. Fenton, comps. INDEX TO CHILDRENS SONGS: A TITLE, FIRST LINE, AND SUBJECT INDEX, New York: Wilson; 1979.

51. READING FOR YOUNG PEOPLE: KENTUCKY, TENNESSEE, WEST VIRGINIA. Edited by Barbara Mertins. Chicago: American Library Association; 1985.
An annotated bibliography of fiction, history, biography, poetry, drama, folklore, and music from and about the adjacent states ot West Virginia, Kentucky, and Tennessee.

52. READING FOR YOUNG PEOPLE: THE GREAT PLAINS. Edited by Mildred Laughlin. Chicago: American Library Association; 1979.
An annotated bibliography of fiction and nonfiction dealing wlth life in the Great Plains region of the United States.

53. READING FOR YOUNG PEOPLE: THE MIDDLE ATLANTIC. Edited by Arabelle Pennypacker. Chicago: American Library Association; 1980.
An annotated bibliography of fiction, folktales, poetry, drama, music, biography, informational books, and audio-visual materials focusing on the Middle Atlantic region of the United States, compiled for readers from the primary grades through the 10th grade.

54. READING FOR YOUNG PEOPLE: THE MIDWEST. Edited by Dorothy Hinman and Ruth Zimmerman. Chicago: American Library Association; 1979.
An annotated bibliography of fiction, history, and biography dealing with the Midwest, for use by students in grades 4 to 10.

55. READING FOR YOUNG PEOPLE: THE MISSISSIPPI DELTA. Edited by Cora Matheny Dorse. Chicago: American Library Association; 1983.
An annotated bibliography of fiction and nonfiction dealing with life in the Mississippi Delta, for grades 4-10.

56. READING FOR YOUNG PEOPLE: THE NORTHWEST. Edited by Mary Meacham. Chicago: American Library Association; 1980.
An annotated bibliography of fiction, folktales, poetry, drama, music, biography, informational books, and audio-visual materials focusing on the northwestern United States, compiled for readers from the primary grades through the 10th grade.

57. READING FOR YOUNG PEOPLE: THE ROCKY MOUNTAINS, Edited by Mildred Laughlin. Chicago: American Library Association; 1980.
An annotated bibliography of fiction, poetry, history, song and drama dealing with the southeast region of the United States, for grades 4-10.

58. READING FOR YOUNG PEOPLE: THE SOUTHEAST. Edited by Dorothy Heald. Chicago: American Library Association; 1980.
An annotated bibliography of fiction, poetry, history, song and drama dealing with the southeast region of the United States, for Grades 4-10.

59. READING FOR YOUNG PEOPLE: THE SOUTHWEST. Edited by Elva A. Harmon and Anna L. Milligan. Chicago: American Library Association; 1982.
An annotated bibliography of fiction, history, biography and folktales emphasizing the history and character of the southwest region of the United States, for grades 4-10.

60. READING FOR YOUNG PEOPLE: THE UPPER MIDWEST. Edited by Marion Fuller Archer. Chicago: American Library Association; 1981.
An annotated bibliography of fiction and nonfiction titles, designed to focus on the history and character of the Upper Midwest, i.e. Michigan, Minnesota, and Wisconsin.

61. READING LADDERS FOR HUMAN RELATIONS. Edited by Eileen Tway and others: NCTE Committee on Reading Ladders for Human Relations, Washington, D.C.: American Council on Education; 1981.

Books categorized by four themes: Creating a Positive Self-Image; Maturity--Living with Others; Appreciating Different Cultures; Coping with Change.

62. SELECTING MATERIALS FOR CHILDREN AND YOUNG ADULTS. Chicago: American Library Association; 1980. By the Association for Library Service to children and Young Adults. List of bibliographies and review sources useful to those who select materials for children/YA.

63. Spirt, Diana, INTRODUCING MORE BOOKS: A GUIDE FOR THE MIDDLE GRADES. New York: Bowker; 1978.
An expanded bibliography listing themes, discussion materials, and related materials for each entry.

64. SUBJECT GUIDE TO CHILDREN'S BOOKS IN PRINT, 1970--. New York: Bowker; 1985.
A subject index to children books in 6,742 categories, updated annually.

65. Wilkin, Binnie. SURVIVAL THEMES IN FICTION FOR CHILDREN AND YOUNG PEOPLE. Metuchen, NJ: Scarecrow Press; 1978.
A directory of sources of materials for children, covering ages preschool through grade 8--films, picture books, magazines, T.V. shows,

66. YOUR READING: A BOOKLIST FOR JUNIOR HIGH AND MIDDLE SCHOOL STUDENTS. Urbana, IL: Committee on the Junior High and Middle School Booklist of the National Council of Teachers of English; 1983.
More than 3100 annotations of books, written by teachers, librarians, and students. Organized by subject.

Writings About Children's Literature

67. THE ARBUTHNOT LECTURES, 1970-1979. Chicago: American Library Association; 1980.
Lecture series on children's literature presented annually in honor of May Hill Arbuthnot.

68. Bader, Barbara. AMERICAN PICTURE BOOKS FROM NOAH'S ARK TO THE BEAST WITHIN. New York: Macmillan; 1976.
A historical study of American picturebooks. Includes many reproductions of illustrations from children's books.

69. BOOKS I READ WHEN I WAS YOUNG. New York: Avon; 1980.
A project of the NCTE. Recollections of favorite childhood reading of famous American entertainers, authors and political and sports figures.

70. Broderick, Dorothy. IMAGE OF THE BLACK IN CHILDREN'S FICTION. New York: Bowker; 1973.
Surveys books from 1927-1967, discussing stereotypes of the Negro which have emerged, based on the author's thesis.

71. Cameron, Eleanor. THE GREEN AND BURNING TREE. Boston: Little, Brown; 1985.
An Atlantic Monthly Press book. Essays on the writing and enjoyment of children's books - a resource for parents and teachers.

72. Carr, Jo, comp. BEYOND FACT: NONFICTION FOR CHILDREN AND YOUNG PEOPLE. Chicago: American Libraray Association; 1982.
Essays on nonfiction writing for children, suggesting it should be read as literature as well as for facts. Books exemplifying approach are discussed in detail.

73. CELEBRATING CHILDREN'S BOOKS: ESSAYS ON CHILDREN'S LITERATURE IN HONOR OF ZENA SUTHERLAND. Edited by Betsy Hearne and Marilyn Kaye. New York: Lothrop; 1981.
Thoughts about children's literature from 23 authors, illustrators, publishers and critics.

74. CHILDREN'S LITERATURE. Columbus, OH: Ohio State University; 1982.
Issue of THEORY INTO PRACTICE (periodical) containing papers given at the May 1982 Conference on Children's Literature at O.S.U.

75. Donelson, Kenneth. LITERATURE FOR TODAY'S YOUNG ADULTS. Glenview, IL: Scott, Foresman; 1980.
A survey of the issues, trends and history of literature for adolescents. Includes bibliographies and indexes.

76. Dorson, Richard M. AMERICAN FOLKLORE. Chicago: University of Chicago Press; 1959.
Survey of American folklore from colonization to mass culture.

77. Egoff, Sheila. THURSDAY'S CHILD. Chicago: American Library Association; 1981.
Discusses trends and patterns in contemporary children's literature.

78. Egoff, Sheila, ed. ONLY CONNECT: READINGS ON CHILDREN'S LITERATURE. 2nd edition. New York: Oxford University Press; 1980.
Essays relating to the field of children's books and literature. Attempts to bring into focus Youth and Age. Discusses trends of the 60's and 70's.

79. Fader, Daniel N. THE NEW HOOKED ON BOOKS. New York: Berkley; 1981.
Expands earlier editions, with emphasis on the teaching of writing, and research on Fader's methods for getting kids to like to read and write. With contributions by James Duggins, Tom Finn, and Elton McNeil.

80. Holtze, Sally, ed. FIFTH BOOK OF JUNIOR AUTHORS & ILLUSTRATORS. New York: Wilson; 1983.
Short biographical sketches of authors and illustrators. Continues earlier editions: FOURTH BOOK OF OF JUNIOR AUTHORS AND ILLUSTRATORS, THIRD BOOK OF JUNIOR AUTHORS, MORE JUNIOR AUTHORS, JUNIOR BOOK OF AUTHORS.

81. Jones, Dolores Blythe. CHILDREN'S LITERATURE AWARDS AND WINNERS: A DIRECTORY OF PRIZES, AUTHORS, AND ILLUSTRATORS. Detroit, MI: Neal-Schuman in association with Gale Research; 1983.
Provides a comprehensive reference source containing information on awards granted in English-speaking countries for excellence in children's literature. Also included are several international awards.

82. Kingman, Lee, comp. ILLUSTRATORS OF CHILDREN'S BOOKS, 1967-1976. Boston: Horn Book; 1978.
Short biographies of prominent illustrators of this period.

83. Kingman, Lee, ed. THE ILLUSTRATOR'S NOTEBOOK. Boston: Horn Book; 1978.
Essays which originally appeared in THE HORN BOOK (a periodical).

84. Leach, Maria, ed. FUNK & WAGNALLS STANDARD DICTIONARY OF FOLKLORE, MYTHOLOGY, AND LEGEND. New York: Funk & Wagnalls; 1972.
Includes "key" to countries, regions, cultures, culture areas, peoples, tribes, and ethnic groups.

85. Meek, Margaret, Aidan Warlow, and Griselda Barton, ed. THE COOL WEB: THE PATTERN OF CHILDREN'S READING. New York: Atheneum; 1978.
Collection of 50 essays written by both English and American authors and critics. Also includes an annotated bibliography.

86. Meyer, Susan E. A TREASURY OF THE GREAT CHILDREN'S BOOK ILLUSTRATORS. New York: Abrams; 1983.
The development of children's picture books as seen in the work of thirteen classic illustrators, from Edward Lear to N.C. Wyeth.

87. Paterson, Katherine. GATES OF EXCELLENCE: ON READING AND WRITING BOOKS FOR CHILDREN. New York: Elsevier/Nelson Books; 1981.
A collection of essays relating to the author's experience as a writer of novels for children, and her ideas on children's literature.

88. RACISM AND SEXISM IN CHILDREN'S BOOKS [Kit]. New York: Council on Interracial Books; 1978; 2 filmstrips; 2 cassettes. Illustrates the characteristics of sex and racial discrimination found in contemporary and classic children's literature.

89. Sale, Roger. FAIRY TALES AND AFTER: FROM SNOW WHITE TO E.B. WHITE. Cambridge, MA: Harvard University Press; 1978.
Literary criticism of many classic children's stories and sketches of their authors' lives.

90. Stott, Jon C. CHILDREN'S LITERATURE FROM A TO Z: A GUIDE FOR PARENTS AND TEACHERS. New York: McGraw Hill; 1984.
Informative short essays on authors, illustrators, themes, and folklore in children's literature.

91. Vandergrift, Kay. CHILD AND STORY: THE LITERARY CONNECTION. New York: Neal-Schuman; 1980.
Uses various theories of literary criticism to look at stories for children, explores complex issues, and "invites" shared ideas by the reader.

Anthologies

92. Butler, Francella. SHARING LITERATURE WITH CHILDREN. New York: David McKay; 1977.
A thematically arranged anthology of folklore, myths, fiction, poetry, biographies, and essays.

93. Carlson, Bernice. LET'S PRETEND IT HAPPENED TO YOU. New York: Scholastic; 1975.
Presents eleven folk tales with directions for organizing dramatic improvisations of each story.

94. Carlson, Bernice. PICTURE THAT. Nashville, TN: Abingdon; 1977.
Folk tales and stories are introduced by related dramatic activities and followed by art projects.

95. Haviland, Virginia. YANKEE DOODLE'S LITERARY SAMPLER OF PROSE, POETRY & PICTURES. New York: Crowell; 1974.
Facsimiles of writing in schoolbooks, magazines, and storybooks for young readers, published in America before 1900. Selected from the rare book collections of the Library of Congress.

96. Kamerman, Sylvia, ed. CHILDREN'S PLAYS FROM FAVORITE STORIES. Boston: Plays, Inc.; 1970.
50 royalty-free plays for children in the lower and middle grades. Includes dramatizations of fables, fairy tales, folk tales, and legends.

97. Kamerman, Sylvia, ed. DRAMATIZED FOLK TALES OF THE WORLD. Boston: Plays, Inc; 1971.
50 royalty-free one-act plays adapted from folk tales of many countries.

98. Korty, Carol. PLAYS FROM AFRICAN FOLKTALES. New York: Scribner; 1975.
Gives ideas for acting, dance, costumes, and music.

99. Moore, Lilian, comp. GO WITH THE POEM: A NEW COLLECTION. New York: McGraw Hill; 1979.
A collection of 90 poems written by outstanding 20th century poets. Also includes bibliographical references.

100. Pellowski, Anne. THE STORY VINE. New York: Macmillan; 1984.
A collection of stories which require the storyteller to use objects such as dolls, string, or musical instruments.

101. Prelutsky, Jack, comp. THE RANDOM HOUSE BOOK OF POETRY FOR CHILDREN. Illustrated by Arnold Lobel. New York: Random House; 1983.
Poems with appeal for elementary schbol children have been arranged by fourteen themes; Prelutsky has written a poem to introduce each section.

102. Robinson, Herbert. MYTHS AND LEGENDS OF ALL NATIONS. Totowa, NJ: Littlefield, Adams; 1976.
A collection of the world's most famous myths presented by culture and geographic area (22 sections). Also includes indexes.

103. Sutherland, Zena, and Myra Cohn Livingston. THE SCOTT, FORESMAN ANTHOLOGY OF CHILDREN'S LITERATURE. Glenview, IL: Scott, Foresmen; 1984.
Introduces the work of authors, new and old, as well as introducing the broad spectrum of contemporary and traditional literature.

Review Sources

104. BOOK WAVES. San Francisco, CA: Bay Area Young Adult Librarians; 1982.
A compilation of reviews of books for teenagers.

105. THE BOOKLIST. Chicago: American Library Association; 1969-present. Semimonthly, except monthly for July, August, and September.
Reviews of books with a section for audiovisual media. Inclusion of a title means a positive recommendation. Grade level and call number given.

106. THE HORN BOOK MAGAZINE. Boston: Horn Book, Inc; 1975-present.
Articles about children's literature, and also reviews of books.

107. MEDIA REVIEW. Pleasantville, NY: Media Review; 1979-present. Monthly, September-June.
Professional evaluations of instructional materials, including microcomputer software.

108. SCHOOL LIBRARY JOURNAL, New York: Bowker; 1953-present. Monthly, September-May.
Books and audiovisual media reviewed with recommendation for purchase; includes negative comments. Grade level given.

109. THE WEB: WONDERFULLY EXCITING BOOKS. Columbus, OH: Center for Language, Literature, and Reading, College of Education. The Ohio State University; 1976-present.
A quarterly publication of book reviews organized around a theme and including a WEB of resources and activities.

PART TWO

CREATING CONNECTIONS: THE MATERIALS

Chapter 4

Cities: Alternative Views

When people meet for the first time, whether they are children or adults, one of the first questions asked is "Where do you live?" Where we live may define our values, our daily activities, our family, and our culture. Children may live in an ethnic neighborhood whose traditions are so strong the area becomes its own "city." If we were to ask five people who said they "came from Chicago" to tell us about the city, it is likely that five different cities would be described, ranging from the opulence of Michigan Avenue to the cultural life of orchestra and opera to the tough neighborhoods of the south side; from the architecture of a city whose skyscrapers set a pattern for other cityscapes to the recreation of a lake front to the universities and museums which abound; from MacArthur Park, the scene of student unrest and revolt in the 60's to the Water Tower, a historical landmark, or to the Loop, the center of business and industry defined by the loop of the elevated transit system -- the "el" -- which serves it. They might also speak of its baseball team, the Chicago Cubs, of the Picasso and Henry Moore sculptures, the stockyards and meatpacking industry, the social settlement houses, the Chicago fire, the city government and the political scene.

The history, the physical environment, the culture, the people of this city are seen through its many aspects. Our five friends would all describe a different Chicago, but they would share many memories and would probably share a common loyalty.

Can we draw from this discussion some hints for the study of cities? What makes a city? How can we sensibly approach such a broad topic? Shall we be general or specific?

The study of cities is most commonly associated with social studies. Cities are compared to towns, townships and states. They are seen as political entities in which people have a government and such municipal services as fire protection, law enforcement, provision for water and sewer, electricity, gas, and street building and repair, as well as federal courts and postal services.

But cities can also be examined in terms of their history; for instance, how their location on a river or in a valley influenced the development of trade, business and industry. The histories of individual cities can be studied to discover why each was established where it was, and why it thrived or failed. The cyclical decline and rejuvenation of a city such as Rome would show what aspects of life and government make successful cities. A study of cities lost through disaster, such as the destruction of Pompeii by the action of a volcano, would provide a parallel to modern problems with volcanic activity.

The many skills of the builders of a city could lead to a discussion and study of career choices. It might also be interesting to trace various careers back to their origins in medieval guilds. A study of surnames connected to various occupations (such as "Smith" and "Baker") might emerge from this study.

A museum may have been established to keep a record of a city's history, and to hold the paintings and photographs collected by its citizens. This could lead to a study of art and local history. Or students might design a museum for their own city and decide what kinds of items should be included in it which reflect the art, architecture and history of their city. Students could develop oral history accounts of their own families or neighborhoods; some students might paint their stories while others might record them in photographs. Students might want to explore their own city, describing through art, photography, and writing the various aspects of life in the city. They might also want to explore the work of local artists and photographers displayed in city museums and galleries to discover what these artists have recorded of their city.

This might lead to a study of artists in various media who have come to be associated with city-scapes. Who are the painters who have captured the look and feel of famous cities like Paris, London, or Rome? A study of painters such as Turner, Utrillo and El Greco who have captured the feeling of various cities would be interesting.

Just as artists have been associated with cities, so have writers shared their feelings for certain places. Students might enjoy reading novels and poems, or sharing picture books which describe city life. ROUND TRIP by Ann Jonas takes young children on a trip to the city. When the children turn the book upside-down, they go back home again. Lanthe Thomas describes a city street seen on the way to school in MY STREET'S A MORNING COOL STREET, while Rachel Isadora illustrates an alphabet book of city scenes, CITY SEEN FROM A TO Z. Nancy Larrick has collected poems about the city in ON CITY STREETS as has Lee Bennett Hopkins in A SONG IN STONE: CITY POEMS.

STONE AND STEEL: A LOOK AT ENGINEERING might interest the older child with its pictures and explanations of how some well known buildings and bridges were built. David Macaulay reverses the approach in UNBUILDING. He imagines that the Empire State Building is being torn down and he carefully peels back layers of structure as he describes how it will be demolished. Tunnels, bridges, and other city structures are fascinating to study. Anne MacGregor not only talks about the construction of bridges, she gives instructions for making models in BRIDGES: A PROJECT BOOK.

A city can seem overwhelming to a visitor; people often get lost in cities. Students might study maps and bus or subway routes in their city. They might develop maps of their own neighborhoods or routes to take to get to school, deciding which landmarks should be included. Students should be able to explain the maps or routes they sketch. They might imagine this map was for a visitor. Giving directions calls for the ability to explain, to order and prioritize the steps needed to get to a destination, and to describe the landmarks along the way. Florian Douglas writes for young children, telling them about the landmarks one woman notices as she walks home in THE CITY.

We have moved horizontally on our cities' chart from the cultural context to the physical world of man made structures. Structures exist within many city systems. A brief look at city planning would lead us to consider water and sewage systems, drainage, and refuse disposal. Again, David Macaulay makes complex systems understandable as he details in pictures and words the water and sewage systems and the foundations for buildings in UNDERGROUND. From these city systems we might move to the need for city planning. PLANNING THE CITY OF GREENVILLE is a simulation game which would give older students a chance to role play and should help them understand the complexity of urban planning.

From city planning we can move quite naturally to city government, city services, and work in the city. There are many services provided by a community. For young readers we might choose to read about firemen in LADDER COMPANY, THE FIRE STATION BOOK, BY HOOK AND LADDER or WHO KEEPS US SAFE? Fourth graders might view filmstrips about city services and be encouraged to compare what they learn from a kit like YOUR COMMUNITY IN ACTION with their own firsthand observations. With older children city services could be used as an introduction to occupations. Several kinds of work are described in AND WHAT DO YOU DO? A BOOK ABOUT PEOPLE AND THEIR WORK. Other books consider such varied careers as dental hygienist, telephone operator, piano tuner, scientist. An interesting way to examine occupations is to arrange for parent participation, with mothers and fathers meeting with a group of children to answer questions about where they work and what they do.

The next connection might be with the study of families -- family life in a city, the kinds of houses or housing for families, the religious or ethnic traditions of families, the holidays they celebrate, the neighborhoods they live in. So many stories have been written about life in the city. Fiction and fact both add to our understanding; fact tells us "what is," and fiction allows us vicarious experiences.

In making connections, seeing relationships across the curriculum, we are helping children integrate their learning with their experience. Sometimes we take a horizontal view, skimming across and tying together several subjects. At other times we work vertically, adding knowledge in depth about one subject.

Use this chart on cities as a starting point. Add to it. Spin your own threads!

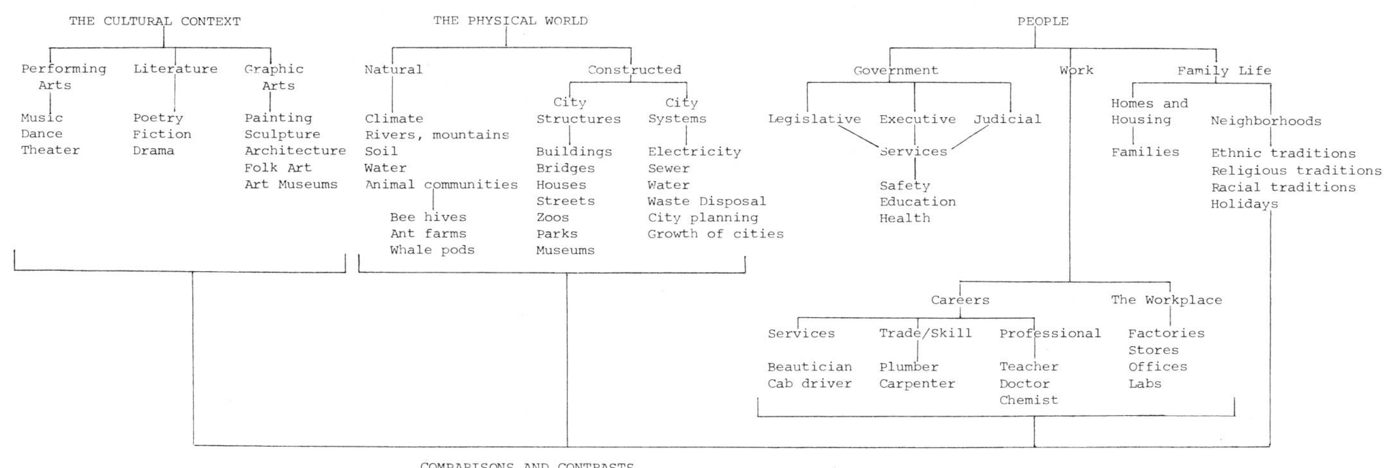
CITIES
THE CULTURAL CONTEXT
Performing Arts
Music
Dance
Theater
Literature
Poetry
Fiction
Drama
Graphic Arts
Painting
Sculpture
Architecture
Folk Art
Art Museums
THE PHYSICAL WORLD
Natural
Climate
Rivers, mountains
Soil
Water
Animal communities
Bee hives
Ant farms
Whale pods
Constructed
City Structures
Buildings
Bridges
Houses
Streets
Zoos
Parks
Museums
City Systems
Electricity
Sewer
Water
Waste Disposal
City planning
Growth of cities
PEOPLE
Government
Legislative
Executive
Judicial
Services
Safety
Education
Health
Work
Careers
Services
Beautician
Cab driver
Trade/Skill
Plumber
Carpenter
Professional
Teacher
Doctor
Chemist
The Workplace
Factories
Stores
Offices
Labs
Family Life
Homes and Housing
Families
Neighborhoods
Ethnic traditions
Religious traditions
Racial traditions
Holidays
COMPARISONS AND CONTRASTS
Cities in other regions
Cities in other countries
City life and country life

THE CULTURAL CONTEXT

The Performing Arts

110. Barlin, Paul; Barlin, Anne. DANCE-A-STORY ABOUT BALLOONS. [Sound Recording]. Illustrations by Lois Zener Spector. Incidental music by Paul Schoop. New York: RCA Records; 1964; 1 sound disc; 1 storybook.
Gr. K-3. Designed to encourage free movement and to help develop beginning dance techniques, rhythm skills, and pantomiming skills.

111. Barlin, Paul; Barlin, Anne. DANCE-A-STORY ABOUT THE BRAVE HUNTER [Sound Recording]. Illustrations by Lois Zener Spector. Incidental music by Clarence Bernard Jackson: New York: RCA Records; 1964; 1 sound disc; 1 storybook.
Gr. K-3. Designed to encourage free movement, to develop beginning dance techniques, and to interest boys in dance.

112. Barlin, Paul; Barlin, Anne. DANCE-A-STORY ABOUT THE MAGIC MOUNTAIN [Sound Recording]. Illustrated by Lois Zener Spector. New York: RCA Records; 1964; 1 sound disc; 1 storybook.
Gr. K-3. Side 1: Narration with music. Side 2: Music only. May be performed as a ballet. Designed to encourage children to express a story through movement and pantomime.

113. Chappell, Warren. THE NUTCRACKER. Illustrated. New York: Knopf; 1958.
Gr. 2-5. Text and excerpts from the music of the Tschaikovsky ballet.

114. Collard, Alexandra. TWO YOUNG DANCERS: THEIR WORLD OF BALLET. Photographs by Frank Dunand and others. New York: Messner; 1984.
Gr. 5-8. Shane and Melissa talk about their ballet training and their hopes for the future.

115. Currell, David. THE COMPLETE BOOK OF PUPPETING. Boston: Plays; 1974.
Gr. 6-up. How to construct and use puppets, marionettes, and shadow figures.

116. Diagram Group. THE SCRIBNER GUIDE TO ORCHESTRAL INSTRUMENTS. New York: Scribner; 1976.
Gr. 6-up. Musical instruments of the world, pictured and explained.

117. Diamond, Donna. SWAN LAKE. Illustrated. New York: Holiday House; 1979.
Gr. 2-6. A prince's love for a swan queen is thwarted by an evil sorcerer in this fairy tale adaptation of the classic ballet.

118. English, Betty Lou. YOU CAN'T BE TIMID WITH A TRUMPET: NOTES FROM THE ORCHESTRA. Drawings by Stan Skardinski. New York: Lothrop; 1980.
Gr. 5-up. A well-known conductor and seventeen men and women from nine well-known orchestras discuss their individual instruments.

119. Goulden, Shirley. THE ROYAL BOOK OF BALLET. Illustrated by Maraja. Chicago: Follett; 1964.
Gr. 5-up. Contents: Swan Lake, The Sleeping Beauty; Giselle; The Nutcracker; Petrushka; Coppelia.

120. Hanford, Robert TenEyck. THE COMPLETE BOOK OF PUPPETS AND PUPPETEERING. Illustrated by Ted Erik. New York: Sterling; 1981.
Gr. 6-up. How to buy or build puppets and puppet theaters; how to manipulate puppets; script writing.

121. Hoffman, E.T. NUTCRACKER. Illustrated by Maurice Sendak. Translated by Ralph Manheim. New York: Crown; 1984.
Gr. 4-up. A new translation of The Nutcracker and the Mouse King, with Sendak's illustrations and the costume and set designs he did for the Pacific Northwest Ballet Company's production.

122. Isadora Rachel. MY BALLET CLASS. New York: Greenwillow; 1980.
Gr. K-3. A young girl describes her ballet class which meets twice a week. Background drawings illustrate exercises and positions.

123. Krementz, Jill. A VERY YOUNG DANCER. New York: Knopf; 1977.
Gr. 4-up. Black and white photographs allow us to go with ten year old Stephanie to ballet class, tryouts, rehearsals, and on to the performance in the Nutcracker.

124. Kuskin, Karla. THE PHILHARMONIC GETS DRESSED. Illustrations by Mark Simont. New York: Harper & Row; 1982.
Gr. K-3. The 105 members of the Philharmonic Orchestra get ready for a performance.

125. Lasky, Kathryn. PUPPETEER. Photographs by Christopher E. Knight. New York: Macmillan; 1985.
Gr. 3-7. Black and white photographs reveal the magic of puppets and trace the puppet production from script writing to the final performance.

126. Miorano, Robert, and Rachel Isadora. BACKSTAGE. New York: Greenwillow; 1978.
Gr. K-3. A young girl watches her ballerina mother in a rehearsal.

127. Montresor, Beni. CINDERELLA. New York: Knopf; 1965.
Gr. 2-4. A retelling of the Rossini opera illustrated by the designer of the Metropolitan Opera Production.

128. MUSIC MAESTRO: A GAME OF MUSICAL INSTRUMENTS, PAST AND PRESENT [Game]. Illustrated by Pamela Rave. Ann Arbor, MI: Aristoplay; 1982; 5 games: 1 cassette; 1 game board; 3 card decks; 1 instruction sheet.
Gr. 3-up. For 2-6 players. Introduces students to the orchestra.

129. Reiniger, Lotte. SHADOW THEATERS AND SHADOW FILMS. New York: Watson-Guptill; 1975.
Gr. 6-up. The history of the shadow theater and directions for making shadow figures and a theater.

130. Robison, Nancy. BALLET MAGIC. Illustrated by Karen Loccisano. Chicago: Whitman; 1981.
Gr. 3-7. Stacey's sudden spurt of growth makes her feel unfit for ballet, until she learns that it is possible to be both tall and graceful, and that attitude is the most important element of dance.

131. STRAVINSKY'S FIREBIRD [Filmstrip]. Illustrated by John Cadel. Lakeland, FL: Imperial Film; 1968; 1 filmstrip; 1 cassette.
Gr. 4-up. Depicts the firebird, a ballet choreographed by Michael Fokine to the music of Igor Stravinsky played in its entirety by a full symphony orchestra.

132. Streatfeild, Noel. A YOUNG PERSON'S GUIDE TO BALLET. Drawings by Georgette Bordier. New York: Warne; 1975.
Gr. 3-up. A dance teacher explains ballet steps to her young pupils, and talks about famous ballet dancers.

133. Swope, Martha. THE NUTCRACKER: THE STORY OF THE NEW YORK CITY BALLET'S PRODUCTION. New York: Dodd, Mead; 1975.
Gr. 3-up. A story told in pictures, emphasizing the many elements which make up this production of the Nutcracker.

134. Zeck, Gerry. I LOVE TO DANCE. Minneapolis: Carolrhoda; 1982.
Gr. 3-5. Story of a young man heading for a professional career in dance - a student at the School of the Minnesota Dance Theater.

Literature

135. Brewton, Sara Westbrook and John E. Brewton, eds. AMERICA FOREVER NEW: A BOOK OF POEMS. Drawings by Ann Grifalconi. New York: Crowell; 1968.
Gr. 4-up. Poetry about places in America.

136. Brooks, Gwendolyn. BRONZEVILLE BOYS AND GIRLS. Illustrated by Ronni Solbert. New York: Harper & Row; 1956.
Gr. 3-6. Poetry about children of the city.

137. Hopkins, Lee Bennett, ed. CITY TALK. Photographs by Roy Arenella. New York: Knopf; 1970.
Gr. 3-7. A collection of poems by children about their experiences in the city from season to season.

138. Hopkins, Lee Bennett, ed. A SONG IN STONE: CITY POEMS. Illustrated by Anna Held Audette. New York: Harper & Row; 1983.
Gr. 2-6. Twenty short poems reveal city life.

139. Larrick, Nancy, ed. ON CITY STREETS: AN ANTHOLOGY OF POETRY. Photos by David Sagarin. New York: Evans; 1968.
Gr. 5-8. A collection of tragic and light--hearted poems about city scenes.

140. Lenski, Lois. CITY POEMS. Illustrated. New York: Walck; 1971.
Gr. 4-6. A collection of poems describing life in the city.

141. Moore, Lillian. I THOUGHT I HEARD THE CITY. New York: Atheneum; 1969.
Gr. 4-8. Seventeen poems about the sights and sounds of a city.

142. Prelutsky, Jack. THE NEW KID ON THE BLOCK. Illustrated by James Stevenson. New York: Greenwillow; 1984.
Gr. 4-8. Collection of poems about homework, strange creatures such as Gloopy Gloper, and the new kid on the block.

143. Schick, Eleanor. CITY GREEN. Illustrated. New York: Macmillan; 1974.
Gr. 3-6. A collection of poems describing the experiences of two children growing up in the city.

144. Streich, Corrine, ed. GRANDPARENTS' HOUSES. Illustrated by Lillian Hoban. Boston: Little, Brown; 1985.
Gr. 2-5. An anthology of 15 poems about grandparents.

Graphic Arts

145. Abramovitz, Anita. PEOPLE AND SPACES: A VIEW OF HISTORY THROUGH ARCHITECTURE. Illustrated. New York: Viking; 1979.
Gr. 6-up. History and society as reflected in architecture.

146. Ames, Lee J. DRAW 50 BUILDINGS AND OTHER STRUCTURES. New York: Doubleday; 1980.
Gr. 2-up. Step by step instructions for drawing various structures.

147. Cornelius, Chase and Sue Cornelius. THE CITY IN ART. Minneapolis: Lerner; 1966.
Gr. 5-up. Pictures and text about some works of art inspired by various aspects of the city.

148. THE ENCYCLOPEDIA OF VISUAL ART. Danbury, CT: Grolier Educational Corp; 1983.
Gr. 5-up. A ten volume set which provides a comprehensive source of information about artists and the many forms of art, from prehistoric to modern times.

149. Fisher, Leonard Everett. THE ARCHITECTS. Illustrated. New York: Watts; 1970.
Gr. 4-6. Traces the history of architecture in the American colonies, describing the influence of existing styles and the needs of environment.

150. Florian, Douglas. THE CITY. Illustrated. New York: Crowell; 1982.
Gr. Preschool-2. A woman's walk home takes her past many of the landmarks of a big city.

151. Gladstone, M. J. A CARROT FOR A NOSE: THE FORM OF FOLK SCULPTURE ON AMERICA'S CITY STREETS AND COUNTRY ROADS. New York: Scribner; 1974.
Gr. 4-8. Describes eight kinds of folk art including street utility lids, street and trade signs and snowmen.

152. NATIONAL GALLERY OF ART CATALOG. Washington, D.C: National Gallery of Art.
A complete listing of slides, postcards, color reproductions, and portfolios is available to schools and libraries. In addition, the Extension Service has many slide programs, films, and videocassettes which are available for free loan to educational institutions.

153. WHAT'S A MUSEUM FOR ANYWAY [Video Recording]. Washington, D.C.: National Gallery of Art; 1 videocassette.
Gr. 1-6. Gabe Kaplan conducts elementary students on a tour of the museum; he comments on some works of art, takes the children behind the scenes to workrooms, and elicits their reactions to art and museums. (free loan).

154. THE WHITE HOUSE: AN HISTORIC GUIDE. Washington, D.C: White House Historical Association; 1962.
Gr. 5-up. The changing appearance of the White House, documented by prints and photographs of floor plans, furniture and rooms.

155. Zaidenberg, Arthur. HOW TO DRAW LANDSCAPES, SEASCAPES, AND CITYSCAPES. New York: Crowell; 1963.
Gr. 4-up. Clear, step by step instructions for drawing.

THE PHYSICAL WORLD

The Natural World: Nature in the City

156. Anderson, Margaret J. EXPLORING CITY TREES AND THE NEED FOR URBAN FORESTS. New York: McGraw Hill; 1976.
Gr. 4-6. Presents activities city children can do to learn more about trees and discusses the role of trees in urban areas.

157. Aylesworth, Thomas G. THIS VITAL AIR, THIS VITAL WATER: MAN'S ENVIRONMENTAL CRISIS. Chicago: Rand McNally; 1973.
Gr. 6-up. Presents the facts about air, water, and noise pollution, focusing on causes and effects, methods of control, the role of science and research, and hope for the future.

158. Bova, Benjamin. MAN CHANGES THE WEATHER. Reading, MA: Addison-Wesley; 1973.
Gr. 6-up. Discusses the harmful and beneficial ways, intentional and unintentional, in which man has changed weather and climate throughout history, including a discussion of the effect of air pollution.

159. Cooper, Elizabeth. SCIENCE IN YOUR OWN BACK YARD. New York: Harcourt Brace; 1958.
Gr. 4-7. Contains ideas for exploring and experimenting with the nature children find in their close surroundings.

160. Dowden, Anne O. WILD GREEN THINGS IN THE CITY: A BOOK OF WEEDS. New York: Crowell; 1972.
Gr. 4-6. Shows development and survival of weeds in the city.

161. Elliott, Sara, M. OUR DIRTY AIR. Illustrated. New York: Messner; 1971.
Gr. 3-6. Discusses the problems of air pollution and describes the causes and methods of prevention.

162. Gallob, Edward. CITY ROCKS, CITY BLOCKS AND THE MOON. New York: Scribner; 1973.
Gr. 3-7. Looks at various types of rocks and where you are likely to find them in a city. Asks probing questions to aid in further discovery.

163. Lampman, Evelyn Sibley. THE CITY UNDER THE BACK STEPS. Illustrated by Honore Valincourt. New York: Doubleday; 1960.
Gr. 4-6. Two children observe the insect community under the back steps.

164. Lubell, Winifred and Cecil Lubell. BIRDS IN THE STREET: THE CITY PIGEON BOOK. Hillside, NJ: Enslow; 1971.
Gr. 1-4. Discusses pigeons in the city; their history, problems they create and how they survive.

165. May, Julian. WILDLIFE IN THE CITY. Edited by Bill Barss. Mankato, MN: Creative Education Society; 1970.
Gr. 2-4. Discusses both useful and harmful wildlife which live in cities, including insects, squirrels, rabbits, rats and toads.

166. Pringle, Laurence. CITY AND SUBURB: EXPLORING AN ECOSYSTEM. New York: Macmillan; 1975.
Gr. 5-up. Discusses the ecology of animals, plants and people living together in a city.

167. Rights, Mollie. BEASTLY NEIGHBORS: ALL ABOUT WILD THINGS IN THE CITY, OR WHY EARWIGS MAKE GOOD MOTHERS. Illustrated by Kim Solga. Boston: Little, Brown; 1981.
Gr. 3-up. Describes some of the animals that live in the soil, under leaves, bricks, or boards, and around the roots of plants and suggests ways the reader may study their characteristics and behavior more closely.

168. Simon, Seymour. SCIENCE IN A VACANT LOT. Illustrated by Kujo Koimoda, New York: Viking; 1970.
Gr. 2-5. Ideas for collecting and experimenting with natural materials to be found in vacant lots during various seasons.

The Natural World: Animal Communities

169. Alston, Eugenia. COME VISIT A PRAIRIE DOG TOWN. Illustrated by Sr. Tamara. New York: Harcourt Brace; 1976.
Gr. 1-4. A simple description of prairie dog society as well as growth, habits and behavior of these animals.

170. ECOLAB: A STUDY OF THE RURAL AND URBAN ENVIRONMENT [Card]. Written by J. Leonard Johnson and John H. Mann. San Diego, CA: Learning Concepts; 1971; 208 activity cards.
Gr. 4-6. Provides an organized approach to field studies of various aspects of urban and rural living. Developing appreciation of each environment provides a basis for comparison and contrast, and a deeper appreciation of both.

171. Hauser, Hillary. LIVING WORLD OF THE REEF. Illustrated by Bob Evans and Nancy Low. New York: Walker; 1978.
Gr. 5-8. Describes the coral reef and the various plants and animals that live there.

172. Hess, Lilo. SMALL HABITATS. New York: Scribner; 1976.
Gr. 2-7. A guide to setting up and maintaining terrariums. Discusses plants and animals that can be used in woodland, jungle, coastline, desert, or marshland terrariums.

173. Hussey, Lois Jackson, and Catherine Pessino. COLLECTING FOR THE CITY NATURALIST. Illustrated by Barbara Neill. New York: Crowell; 1975.
Gr. 5-up. Observing and recording data about rocks, trees, birds, and other aspects of nature in the city.

174. Hutchins, Ross E. A LOOK AT ANTS. New York: Dodd, Mead; 1978.
Gr. 3-5. Describes the life cyle of ants and life within various ant communities.

175. Lane, Margaret. BEAVER. Illustrated by David Nockels. New York: Dial; 1982.
Gr. 3-5. Describes behavior of beavers and creation of beaver dams.

176. Oxford Scientific Films. BEES AND HONEY. Illustrated by David Thompson. New York: Putnam; 1977.
Gr. 3-6. Brief text and full-page color photographs of the life of the beehive.

177. PLANTS AND ANIMALS IN THE CITY [Filmstrip]. Washington, D.C.: National Geographic; 1981; 2 filmstrips; 2 cassettes; teacher's guide.
Gr. K-4. Ways plants and animals find food, water, and places to live in the city. Contents: Plants in the City; Animals in the City.

178. Sarnoff, Jane and Reynold Ruffins. A GREAT AQUARIUM BOOK. New York: Scribner; 1977.
Gr. 1-up. Covers all aspects of aquarium life including fish care and how to create a proper environment.

179. Tanner, Ogden. URBAN WILDS. New York: Time-Life; 1975.
Gr. 6-up. Wilderness areas found in the New York City metropolitan area, with photographs of scenery and animal life.

180. Tresselt, Alvin. THE BEAVER POND. Illustrated by Roger Duvoisin. New York: Lothrop; 1970.
Gr. K-3. Shows the changes in a pond as beavers settle there and build a dam.

The Constructed World: City Systems

181. Adkins, Jan. HEAVY EQUIPMENT. New York: Scribner; 1980.
Gr. 1-4. Describes through detailed drawings various pieces of heavy machinery.

182. Barton, Byron. AIRPORT. New York: Crowell; 1982.
Gr. Preschool-2. A very simple summary of what happens at an airport.

183. Barton, Byron. WHEELS. New York: Crowell; 1979.
Gr. Preschool-1. A simple history in vivid color pictures the wheel and its uses.

184. Beame, Rona. WHAT HAPPENS TO GARBAGE. Illustrated. New York: Messner; 1975.
Gr. 3-5. Discusses the means used by New York City to dispose of its refuse.

185. Beekman, Dan. FOREST, VILLAGE, TOWN, CITY. Illustrated by Bernice Loewenstein. New York: Crowell; 1982.
Gr. 3-6. Chronicles the evolution of cities from the first simple Indian villages to today's large cities.

186. Corbett, Scott. BRIDGES. Illustrated by Richard Rosenblum. New York: Four Winds; 1978.
Gr. 5-6. A history of bridge-building with a discussion of some famous bridges.

187. Crews, Donald. HARBOR. Illustrated. New York: Morrow; 1982.
Gr. Preschool-2. Summary of boats and activities in a harbor.

188. Crews, Donald. TRUCK. Illustrated. New York: Greenwillow; 1980.
Gr. Preschool-2. Pictures show a truck taking a load of tricycles from one place to another. Signs are the only text.

189. Foote, Timothy. THE GREAT RINGTAIL GARBAGE CAPER. Illustrated by Normand Chartier. Boston: Houghton Mifflin; 1980.
Gr. 3-6. A group of desperate and daring raccoons organize a bold hijacking scheme when their food supply is threatened by a pair of efficient young garbage collectors.

190. Gibbons, Gail. NEW ROAD! Illustrated. New York: Crowell; 1983.
Gr. Preschool-2. Bright pictures show the steps in the creation of a highway.

191. Gibbons, Gail. TRUCKS. Illustrated. New York: Harper & Row; 1981.
Gr. Preschool-2. A variety of trucks with simple captions telling what they do.

192. Goor, Ron, and Nancy Goor. SIGNS. Illustrated. New York: Crowell; 1983.
Gr. Preschool-2. Shows over fifty familiar signs in contexts that help make their meanings clear.

193. Kempner, Carol. NICHOLAS. New York: Simon & Schuster; 1968.
Gr. Preschool-3. Young Nicholas wanders off on his own for a look at the unknown world of underground trains and a ride on the subway.

194. Lauber, Patricia. TOO MUCH GARBAGE. Illustrated by Victor Mays. Champaign, IL: Garrard; 1974.
Gr. 2-6. Discusses why we create so much garbage and ways we have found to deal with it.

195. Macaulay, David. UNDERGROUND. Illustrated. New York: Houghton Mifflin; 1976.
Gr. 5-7. Discusses the underground systems of a city such as water, sewage, drainage and building foundations.

196. Maestro, Betsy and Ellen Del Vecchio. BIG CITY PORT. New York: Scholastic/Four Winds; 1983.
Gr. Preschool-2. Everyday activity in a busy city port.

197. Olney, Ross. KEEPING OUR CITIES CLEAN. New York: Messner; 1979.
Gr. 2-4. Describes garbage collection, street cleaning, snow removal and removal of various other problems on city streets.

198. Oppenheim, Joanne. HAVE YOU SEEN ROADS? Reading, MA: Addison-Wesley; 1969.
Gr. K-2. Free verse and photographs capture many aspects of roads and streets.

199. PLANNING THE CITY OF GREENVILLE: A SIMULATION ACTIVITY IN URBAN PLANNING [Game]. Sun Valley, CA: Edu-Game; 1972.
Gr. 6-up. Simualtion activity in which the students are presented with a city planning problem.

200. Pringle, Laurence P. RECYCLING RESOURCES. New York: Macmillan; 1974.
Gr. 6-up. Considers the problem of refuse disposal and the importance of salvaging minerals and other useful substances from waste products.

201. Quackenbush, Robert M. CITY TRUCKS. Illustrated. Chicago: Whitman; 1981.
Gr. 3-8. Features the various trucks which are part of a city's maintenance and transportation system.

202. RECYCLING RESOURCES [Kit]. New York: Continental Can; 1971; 2 filmstrips; 1 game (4 copies); 1 sound disc; 3 student guides.
Gr. 6-up. Designed to give students instruction in recycling and environment through filmstrips and a pollution simulation game.

203. RECYCLING [Kit]. Washington: Aluminum Association; 1972; 1 filmstrip; 1 cassette; 4 teacher's guides.
Gr. 6-up. Parallels nature's recycling of natural resources to man's increasing reuse of the products of his technology.

204. Shanks, Ann Zane. ABOUT GARBAGE AND STUFF. New York: Viking; 1973.
Gr. 1-3. A simple introduction to garbage disposal and recycling.

205. Showers, Paul. WHERE DOES THE GARBAGE GO? New York: Harper & Row; 1974.
Gr. 1-3. Discusses city sanitation, recycling and dumps in simple language.

206. SIMPOLIS: SIMULATION OF AN ENCOUNTER WITH SEVEN MAJOR URBAN PROBLEMS [Game]. Cambridge, MA: Abt; 1974; 1 simulation: 50 copies of map; rules; 50 role profile sheets; label name tags; teacher's manual.
Gr. 6-up. Familiarizes students with issues of civil rights, crime, education, housing, pollution, poverty, and transportation in urban settings.

207. St. George, Judith. BROOKLYN BRIDGE: THEY SAID IT COULDN'T BE BUILT. New York: Putnam; 1982.
Gr. 4-6. Gives the history, construction and work involved in building a bridge over the East River.

208. Steptoe, John. TRAIN RIDE. New York: Harper & Row; 1971.
Gr. 1-3. Four friends take a subway ride to Times Square without their parents' permission.

209. URBAN AMERICA [Filmstrip]. Chicago: Encyclopaedia Britannica Educational Corp.; 1980; 5 filmstrips; 5 cassettes; teacher's guide.
Gr. 4-8. Contents: American Cities: Demography and Characteristics; Urbanization in America: Our Changing Ways of Life; The Working City: The City as a Functioning Unit; Living in a City: The Quality of Life; Urban Planning: Keeping the City Viable.

210. Zim, Herbert S. PIPES AND PLUMBING SYSTEMS. Illustated by James R. Skelly. New York: Morrow; 1974.
Gr. 3-6. Explains water, gas, heat and sewage pipe systems and their physical parts.

211. Zion, Gene. DEAR GARBAGE MAN. Illustrated by Margaret Bloy Graham. New York: Harper & Row; 1957.
Gr. Preschool-2. Stan, the garbage man, would rather find a home for trash than simply throw it away.

The Constructed World: City Structures

212. Adkins, Jan. HOW A HOUSE HAPPENS. Illustrated. New York: Walker; 1972.
Gr. 3-6. The design and construction of a house is shown using a format of architectural drawings.

213. Billout, Guy. STONE AND STEEL: A LOOK AT ENGINEERING. Englewood Cliffs, NJ: Prentice Hall; 1980.
Gr. 5-up. Text and illustrations describe bridges and buildings of historic interest.

214. Cherry, Mike. STEEL BEAMS AND IRON MEN. New York: Four Winds; 1980.
Gr. 4-8. An ironworker describes his experiences working on skyscrapers and other large buildings.

215. THE CITY PARK. In: PLACES WHERE PLANTS AND ANIMALS LIVE [Filmstrip]. Washington, D.C: National Geographic; 1975; 5 filmstrips; 5 cassettes; teacher's guide.
Gr. K-4. Pictures of the wildlife that can be seen in city parks.

216. Colby, Jean. BUILDING WRECKING: THE HOW AND WHY OF A VITAL INDUSTRY. New York: Hastings House; 1972.
Gr. 4-7. Discusses the building wrecking industry including tools and techniques.

217. Giblin, James Cross. THE SKYSCRAPER BOOK. Illustrated by Anthony Kramer. New York: Crowell; 1981.
Gr. 3-7. Includes information on building, architects and decorative details.

218. Grosvenor, Donna K. ZOO BABIES. Washington, D.C: National Geographic; 1978.
Gr. K-3. Portrays a variety of young animals in a zoo and shows how zoo personnel take care of them.

219. Hanlon, Emily. WHAT IF A LION EATS ME AND I FALL INTO A HIPPOPOTAMUS' MUD HOLE. Pictures by Leigh Grant. New York: Delacorte; 1975.
Gr. Preschool-3. Imagining all the possibilities for disaster that could happen at the zoo almost dissuades two friends from going.

220. Hoban, Tana. DIG, DRILL, DUMP, FILL. Illustrated. New York: Greenwillow; 1975.
Gr. K-2. Photographs show big earthworking machines at work.

221. Horwitz, Elinor Lander. HOW TO WRECK A BUILDING. Illustrated by Joshua Horwitz. New York: Pantheon Books; 1982.
Gr. 2-4. Recounts the day-by-day progress in the demolition of an old elementary school.

222. Kehoe, Michael. ROAD CLOSED. Ilustrated. Minneapolis: Carolrhoda; 1982.
Gr. 2-4. Text and photos describe tbe process of replacing a section of street.

223. Kelly, James E., and William R. Park. THE TUNNEL BUILDERS. Drawings by Herbert E. Lake. Reading, MA: Addison-Wesley; 1976.
Gr. K-3. Explains the many techniques used at various stages of building tunnels under streets and rivers or through mountains.

224. Lewis, Alun. SUPER STRUCTURES. New York: Viking; 1980.
Gr. 3-6. Explains construction of large structures like tunnels, stadiums, skyscrapers, and dams.

225. Lewis, Stephen. ZOO CITY. New York: Greenwillow; 1976.
Gr. 1-3. Matches animals with city objects which resemble them.

226. Loeper, John J. THE HOUSE ON SPRUCE STREET. Illustrated. New York: Atheneum; 1982.
Gr. 5-7. The history of a fictional house in Philadelphia and the families who live in it.

227. Macaulay, David. UNBUILDING. Illustrated. New York: Houghton Mifflin; 1980.
Gr. 3-6. Speculates on and describes how the Empire State Building would be taken apart if it were to be moved to another place.

228. MacGregor, Anne, and Scott MacGregor. BRIDGES: A PROJECT BOOK. New York: Lothrop; 1980.
Gr. 4-up. Discusses the history, use, and construction of three types of bridges. Includes instruction for making models and variations of each type.

229. Murphy, Jim. TRACTORS. Philadelphia: Lippincott; 1984.
Gr. 3-6. Black and white photographs and drawings give a history of tractors.

230. MUSEUMS AND MAN [Filmstrip]. Chicago: Encyclopaedia Britannica Educational Corp.; 1974; 5 filmstrips; 5 cassettes; teacher's guide.
Gr. 4-up. Depicts the scenes and the work of a museum, using the Smithsonian as an example.

Contents: What Is a Museum; An Exhibit: Behind the Scenes; Museum Conservation: Preserving Our Heritage; The Zoo: A Living Collection; Museums: New Directions.

231. Olney, Ross. CONSTRUCTION GIANTS. New York: Atheneum; 1985.
Gr. K-4. Photographs and descriptions of some of the machines used to build city structures.

232. Olney, Ross. THEY SAID IT COULDN'T BE DONE. New York: Dutton; 1979.
Gr. 4-7. Describes 10 feats of engineering that were believed to be impossible.

233. Paige, David. BEHIND THE SCENES AT THE ZOO. Illustrated by Roger Ruhlin. Chicago: Whitman; 1978.
Gr. 3-6. Uses Lincoln Park Zoo in Chicago to show various activities needed to care for animals and to run the zoo.

234. Panek, Dennis. CATASTROPHE CAT AT THE ZOO. Illustrated. Scarsdale, NY: Bradbury; 1979.
Gr. Preschool-2. Catastrophe Cat gets off a city bus hoping to snooze under a tree, but starts a romp through the zoo instead.

235. Rockwell Anne, and Harlow Rockwell. SUPERMARKET. Illustrated. New York: Macmillan; 1979.
Gr. K-2. A walking tour for young children through a supermarket.

236. Schaaf, Peter. APARTMENT HOUSE CLOSE UP. Illustrated. New York: Four Winds; 1980.
Gr. K-3. A photographic study of details of an apartment house.

237. Sharmat, Marjorie Weinman. GLADYS TOLD ME TO MEET HER HERE. Pictures by Edward Frascino. New York Harper & Row; 1970.
Gr. Preschool-3. Irving waits for Gladys at the zoo but she is nowhere to be seen.

238. Shuttlesworth, Dorothy Edwards. ZOOS IN THE MAKING. New York: Dutton; 1977.
Gr. 4-6. A look at the operations, residents, and special problems of zoos.

239. Siberell, Ann. HOUSES: SHELTERS FROM PREHISTORIC TIMES TO TODAY. New York: Holt, Rinehart & Winston; 1979. Gr. 2-5. A pictorial review of houses from the cave to modern energy-efficient homes.

240. Sobol, Harriett L. PETE'S HOUSE. Illustrated by Patricia Agre, New York: Macmillan; 1978. Gr. 1-3. Shows stages of construction of Pete's new house through black and white photos and text.

241. Sullivan, George. HOW DO THEY BUILD IT. Philadelphia: Westminster; 1972. Gr. 5-up. Explains methods of building bridges, houses, highways, and skyscrapers.

242. Tongre, Sally. WHAT'S FOR LUNCH: ANIMAL FEEDING AT THE ZOO. Washington, D.C: GMG; 1981. Gr. 3-6. Explains nutritional needs of zoo animals at the National Zoo by describing many of their zoo diets as well as explaining how zoo animals are fed.

243. WHY A ZOO [Picture]. St. Louis: Milliken; 1973; 8 photographs; teacher's guide. Gr. K-8. Designed to promote understanding of the development and purposes of modern zoos. Contents: Puma; Buffalo; Seals; Wolf; Polar Bears; Impala; Golden Eagle; Giraffe.

244. Yonker, Richard. ON SITE: THE CONSTRUCTION OF A HIGH RISE. Illustrated. New York: Crowell; 1980. Gr. 5-up. Shows excavation, foundation, framimg, enclosure and finishing of a skyscraper.

245. Zoo Adventure [Filmstrip]. Chicago: Encyclopaedia Britannica Educational Corp.; 1962; 4 filmstrips; teacher's guide. Gr. K-3. Set of captioned filmstrips showing strange and familiar animals. Contents: Large Zoo Animals; Monkeys and Other Small Zoo Animals; Birds of the Zoo; Zoo Snakes and Their Relatives.

PEOPLE

People in the City: Government

246. Arnold, Caroline. WHO KEEPS US SAFE? Illustrated by Carole Bertol. New York: Watts; 1982. Gr. K-2. A simple introduction to police, firefighters and emergency personnel.

247. Baker, Donna. I WANT TO A LIBRARIAN. Illustrated by Richard Wahl. Chicago: Children's Press; 1978.
Gr. K-4. After a school and a public librarian help her with an assignment, Jana decides she would like to be a librarian herself.

248. Bartlett, Susan. LIBRARIES: A BOOK TO BEGIN ON. Illustrated by Gioia Fiammenghi. New York: Holt, Rinehart & Winston; 1964.
Gr. K-3. Story of how libraries began and what they do.

249. Beame, Rona. LADDER COMPANY 108. New York: Messner; 1973.
Gr. 3-5. Shows the activities of one fire company in New York City over several days.

250. Cook, Fred. CITY COP. New York: Doubleday; 1979.
Gr. 4-7. Shows the training and early years on the force of a New York city cop.

251. Crews, Donald. SCHOOL BUS. New York: Greenwillow; 1984.
Gr. Preschool-2. An empty yellow school bus makes a trip across the city, picking up children on the way, and later taking them home.

252. Dean, Anabel. FIRE! HOW DO THEY FIGHT IT. Philadelphia: Westminister; 1978.
Gr. 5-up. Discusses the chemistry of fire, techniques and equipment used to combat different types of fires, and various activities of fire departments.

253. Demuth, Jack and Patricia Demuth. CITY HORSE. New York: Dodd, Mead; 1979.
Gr. 3-6. Describes the life of the horses who work for the New York City Police Department.

254. Ditzel, Paul C. FIRE ENGINES, FIRE FIGHTERS: THE MEN, EQUIPMENT, AND MACHINES, FROM COLONIAL DAYS TO THE PRESENT, Photographs by John Garetti and Jeffrey Kurtzeman. New York: Rutledge/Crown; 1976.
Gr. 4-6.

255. Eichner, James A. THE FIRST BOOK OF LOCAL GOVERNMENT. Illustrated by Dan Nevins. New York: Watts; 1976.
Gr. 6-up. An introduction to the most common forms of local government.

256. Gibbons, Gail. THE POST OFFICE BOOK: MAIL AND HOW IT MOVES. Illustrated. New York: Crowell; 1982.
Gr. Preschool-2. Discusses kinds of mail, post office workers, and how mail is sent from one place to another.

257. GOVERNMENT AND YOU [Filmstrip]. Chicago: Encyclopaedia Britannica Educational Corp.; 1976; 5 filmstrips; 5 cassettes; guide.
Gr. 6-up. Contents: The Presidency; The Congress; The Federal Courts; State Governments; Local and Municipal Governments.

258. Hoban, Tana. I READ SIGNS. New York: Greenwillow; 1983.
Gr. Preschool-1. Introduces signs and symbols frequently seen along the street.

259. Howe, James. THE HOSPITAL BOOK. Illustrated by Mal Warshaw. New York: Crown; 1981.
Gr. 2-5. A guide for a stay in the hospital - what people do there and how it feels to be there; who works the equipment.

260. INTRODUCTION TO THE LIBRARY [Filmstrip]. Washington, D.C: National Geographic; 1981; 2 filmstrips; 2 cassettes; guides.
Gr. 3-8. Contents: What's in a Library; How to Find What You Need.

261. Linzer, Jeff. THE FIRE STATION BOOK. Illustrated by Nancy Bundt. Minneapolis, MN: Carolrhoda; 1981.
Gr. 2-5. Explains fire station activities through photos and text.

262. Loeper, John. BY HOOK AND LADDER. New York: Atheneum; 1981.
Gr. 3-6. A history of fire fighting in America including bucket brigades, volunteer fire departments, fire equipment.

263. LOW INCOME HOUSING PROJECT: A SIMULATION ACTIVITY [Game]. Sun Valley, CA: Edu-Game; 1972.
Gr. 6-up. Simulation in which a community locates a low income housing project which will be occupied by minority groups.

264. MY COMMUNITY: SONGS FOR THE FLANNELBOARD [Kit]. Elgin, IL: David C. Cook; 1966; 1 sound disc; 6 song sheets; 18 flannelboard pieces.

Gr. Preschool-3. Introduces children to places and helpers in their community: the park, the school, the stores, the doctor, the policeman, and the fireman.

265. OUR COMMUNITIES [Filmstrip]. New York: Scholastic; 1982; 2 sets: 4 filmstrips; 4 cassettes; teacher's guide in each set.
Gr. 3-4. Contents of Set 1: Where Is Your Community; Community Needs; Working Together; Community Workers. Contents of Set 2: Community Rules How Communities Started;; Why Communities Change; Communities Around the World.

266. PEOPLE SERVING YOUR COMMUNITY [Filmstrip]. Washington, D.C: National Geographic; 1978; 4 filmstrips; 4 cassettes; teacher's guides.
Gr. K-4. Contents: People in Government; Police and Fire Fighters; Sanitation, Highway, and Other Workers; Doctors, Dentists, Nurses, and their Helpers.

267. Rockwell, Anne. THE EMERGENCY ROOM. Illustrated by Harlow Rockwell. New York: Macmillan; 1985.
Gr. K-2. A little boy learns about what happens in the emergency room when he is treated for his sprained ankle.

268. Rockwell, Anne. I LIKE THE LIBRARY. Illustrated. New York: Dutton; 1977.
Gr. K-2. A simple introduction to library services for young children.

269. Rodowsky, Colby. THE GATHERING ROOM. New York: Farrar, Straus & Giroux; 1981.
Gr. 5-7. Mudge and his family live in the gate house of the cemetery.

270. Roth, Harold. FIRST CLASS! THE POSTAL SYSTEM IN ACTION. Illustrated. New York: Pantheon; 1983.
Gr. 3-7. A tour of a large metropolitan post office showing the jobs of various machines and human employees.

271. Stevens, Leonard A. HOW A LAW IS MADE: THE STORY OF A BILL AGAINST AIR POLLUTION. Illustrated by Robert Galster. New York: Crowell; 1970.
Gr. 5-8. Describes the processes by which citizens change the law and improve the environment.

272. UNDERSTANDING THE LAW [Filmstrip]. Englewood, CO: Learning Tree; 1980; 4 filmstrips; 4 cassettes; guide.
Gr. 4-8. Contents: A Safe Society: Where Laws Come From; Judges, Lawyers, and Police; You and the Law.

273. Witty, Margot. DAY IN THE LIFE OF AN EMERGENCY ROOM NURSE. Illustrated by Sarah Lewis. Mahwah, NJ: Troll; 1980.
Gr. 4-8. Describes a typical day's activities of an emergency room nurse.

274. Wolf, Bernard. FIREHOUSE. Illustrated. New York: Morrow; 1983.
Gr. 3-up. New York City Engine Company 33 and Ladder Company 9 are examined - what they do, expecially in their neighborhood, which is plagued with arson.

275. YOUR COMMUNITY IN ACTION [Filmstrip]. Bedford Hills, NY: Educational Enrichment Materials; 1981; 6 filmstrips; 6 cassettes; 1 poster; 1 teacher's guide.
Gr. 4-6. Uses on-site photography to introduce young children to the community and its services. Contents: Police Department; Fire Department; Post Office; Sanitation Department; Bus Company; Courts.

People in the City: Work

276. Ancona, George. AND WHAT DO YOU DO? A BOOK ABOUT PEOPLE AND THEIR WORK. Illustrated. New York: Dutton; 1976.
Gr. 5-6. Briefly describes 21 interesting occupations.

277. Anderson, David. THE PIANO MAKERS. Illustrated. 1982: New York; Pantheon Books.
Gr. 5-up. Shows the making of a concert grand piano from selection of cabinet wood to stringing and tuning.

278. ANTHROPOLOGISTS AT WORK [Filmstrip]. New York: Globe Book, distributed by Coronet; 1975; 4 filmstrips; 4 cassettes; 1 teacher's guide.
Gr. 6-up. Contents: The Paleontologist; The Archeologist; The Historian; The Ethnologist.

279. Arnold, Caroline. WHO WORKS HERE? Illustrated by Carol Bertol. New York: Watts; 1982.
Gr. K-2. Looks at the jobs of various community workers.

280. Baker, Donna. I WANT TO BE A POLICE OFFICER. Illustrated by Richard Wahl. Chicago: Children's Press; 1978.
Gr. K-4. Ramon's uncle explains the work of police officers to Ramon and his friends.

281. Ditzel, Paul C. RAILROAD YARD. New York: Messner; 1977.
Gr. 4-6. A look at the operations of a large railroad yard.

282. Florian, Douglas. PEOPLE WORKING. Illustrated. New York: Crowell; 1983.
Gr. Preschool-2. Pictures many occupations in a tour of people on the job.

283. Giblin, James Cross. CHIMNEY SWEEPS: YESTERDAY AND TODAY. Illustrated by Margot Tomes. New York: Crowell; 1982.
Gr. 3-6. Explains the history and lore of this city craft and also looks at modern chimney sweeps.

284. Goffstein, M.B. TWO PIANO TUNERS. New York: Farrar, Straus & Giroux; 1970.
Gr. K-3. Debbie and her grandfather work as piano tuners but her grandfather would like her to be a great pianist.

285. Goor, Ron and Nancy Goor. IN THE DRIVER'S SEAT. Illustrated. New York: Crowell; 1982.
Gr. 1-2. What it's like to be in the driver's seat of a blimp jet, a train, a tank, a race car and four other vehicles.

286. Horwitz, Joshua. DOLL HOSPITAL. Illustrated. New York: Pantheon Books; 1983.
Gr. 4-6. A look at the work of repairing old dolls at a New York City doll hospital.

287. Jenness, Aylette. THE BAKERY FACTORY: WHO PUTS BREAD ON YOUR TABLE. Illustrated. New York: Crowell; 1978.
Gr. 2-5. Explores the processes at a bakery factory including bread and cake baking, packaging, sanitation and working conditions.

288. Kraus, Robert. OWLIVER. Pictures by Joze Aruego and Ariane Dewey. New York: Windmill; 1974.
Gr. 3-7. Although each of his parents has a different expectation of what he will be when be grows up, a little boy makes up his own mind in the end.

Kuskin, Karla. THE PHILHARMONIC GETS DRESSED. Illustrated by Marc Simont. New York: Harper & Row; 1982.
Gr. K-3. See #124.

289. LEARNING ABOUT WORK WITH THE JETSONS [Filmstrip]. Riverside, CA: Hanna Barbera; 1982; 3 filmstrips; 3 cassettes.
Gr. K-3. Includes: Why We Work; Sharing the Work; Jobs for Everyone.

290. Lewis, Stephen. HOW'S IT MADE? A PHOTO TOUR OF SEVEN SMALL FACTORIES. Illustrated. New York: Greenwillow; 1977.
Gr. K-3. A wordless book of photographs of factory processes which produce bicycles, flashlights, umbrellas, jump ropes, candy mints, rocking chairs and footballs.

291. Liebers, Arthur. YOU CAN BE A PLUMBER. Illustrated with photographs. New York: Lothrop; 1974.
Gr. 6-up. Describes the qualifications and preparations for a variety of jobs available in the plumbing-heating-air conditioning industry. Other titles in this series deal with electricians, printers, drivers, photographers, etc.

292. LOLLIPOP DRAGON WORLD OF WORK LEARNING MODULE [Kit]. Chicago: SVE; 1976; 6 filmstrips; 3 cassettes; 1 teacher's guide; 1 mural, 1 poster; 1 game mat; 48 playing cards; 50 activity cards; 2 kit guides.
Gr. K-3. The adventures of Lollipop Dragon in work situations.

293. OUR WONDERFUL COUNTRY. SET 4: ITS WORKERS [Picture]. Chicago: Coronet; 1973; 8 study prints; teacher's guide.
Gr. 1-6. Contents: Computer Worker; Factory Worker; Cargo Worker; Track Farmer; Office Worker; Scientist; Sales Clerk; Fire Fighter.

294. Paige, David. A DAY IN THE LIFE OF A POLICE DETECTIVE. Photography by Roger Rublin. Mahwah, NJ: Troll; 1981.
Gr. 4-up. A police homicide detective carries out such daily duties as examining evidence, investigating a fire, appearing in court, and arresting a suspect. Other titles in this series deal with a basketball coach, a rock musician, a marine biologist, etc.

295. SESAME STREET CAREER AWARENESS [Game], Springfield, MA: Milton Bradley, in conjunction with the Children's Television Worksohp; 1975; 4 games; directions.
Gr. K-3. Contents: Masquerade Party; People and Places; When I Grow Up; People Working Together. Activity boards that deal with people and tools, vocational environments, child's play/adult's work and vocational interaction.

296. Wolverton, Ruth. TRUCKS AND TRUCKING. New York: Watts; 1982.
Gr. 4-6. Examines the trucking industry through focus on a family's move to San Antonio.

297. WOMEN AT WORK. (Set 1) [Kit]. Chicago: Coronet; 1978; 4 sound cassettes; 24 books; 8 worksheet masters; 1 guide.
Gr. 2-3. Contents: Clowning Around; Hammer and Tongs; Hand and Glove; Behind the Scenes.

298. WOMEN AT WORK. (Set 2) [Kit]. Chicago: Coronet; 1978; 4 sound cassettes; 24 books; 8 worksheet masters; 1 guide.
Gr. 3-4. Contents: Maryan Makes Shapes; Ellie Sells Fish; Myra Builds a House; Doctor Mary.s Animals.

299. WOMEN AT WORK. (Set 3) [Kit]. Chicago: Coronet; 1978; 4 sound cassettes; 24 books; 8 worksheet masters; 1 guide.
Gr. 4-5. Contents: Take One; Ready for Take-Off; Open Wide; Let's Take a Vote.

300. WORKSTYLES/LIFESTYLES [Filmstrip]. Chicago: Eye Gate House; 1976; 6 filmstrips; 3 cassettes; teacher's manual.
Gr. 6-up. Presents on-the-spot interviews with well known personalities and others regarding their workstyles/lifestyles. Contents: Public Contact and

Service Careers; People Who Are Self Employed or Own Businesses; Working at a Job; People Who Work in the Arts; People Who Work in Professions; People Who Chose Unusual Jobs.

301. YOUR WORKING FUTURE [Filmstrip]. Chicago: Encyclopaedia Britannica Educational Corp.; 1973; 6 filmstrips; 6 cassettes; teacher's guide.
Gr. 6-up. Contents: The Dental Hygienist; Computer Careers; The Child Care Worker; The Insurance Salesman; The Television Service Technician; The Telephone Operator.

People in the City: City Life

302. Binzen, Bill. MIGUEL's MOUNTAIN. New York: Coward, McCann & Geoghegan; 1968.
Gr. K-3. A large pile of dirt left in the park becomes the favorite playground of the neighborhood children, but one day there's a rumor "the mountain" will soon be removed.

303. Bograd, Larry. LOST IN THE STORE. Pictures by Victoria Chess. New York: Macmillan; 1981.
Gr. K-3. Bruno is worried when he becomes separated from his parents in a large department store, until he meets Molly, who shows him the fun of being lost.

304. Carter, Katherine Jones. HOUSES. Illustrated. Chicago: Children's Press; 1982.
Gr. K-4. Briefly describes dwellings adapted to distinct climatic and physical conditions such as the igloo, sampan, wigwam, and the apartment house.

305. CITY SONG. THE LONGEST JOURNEY IN THE WORLD [Sound Recording]. New York: Holt, Rinehart, and Winston; 1971; 6 cassettes; 10 books; teacher's guide.
Gr. Preschool-2. Contents: Old Devil Wind; I'm Going to Build a Supermarket One of These Days; King of the Mountain; The Little Disaster; A Spooky Story; Tatty Mae and Cathy Mae; Old Mother Middle Muddle; Whistle, Mary, Whistle; City Song: The Longest Journey in the World.

306. Clifton, Lucille. THE BOY WHO DIDN'T BELIEVE IN SPRING. Pictures by Brinton Turkle. New York: Dutton; 1973.
Gr. 3-4. Two skeptical city boys set out to find spring which they've heard is "just around the corner."

307. Clifton, Lucille. EVERETT ANDERSON'S FRIEND. New York: Holt, Rinehart & Winston; 1974.
Gr. K-3. Everett is disappointed when he discovers the family moving into the apartment next door has only daughters.

308. Deveaux, Alexis. NA-NI. Illustrated. New York: Harper & Row; 1973.
Gr. 3-5. A little girl living in a New York city ghetto imagines all the wonderful things she'll be able to do with the bicycle her mother promised to buy.

309. Freedman, Russell. IMMIGRANT KIDS. New York: Dutton; 1980.
Gr. 3-7. Text and contemporary photographs chronicle the life of immigrant children at home, school, work, and play during the late 1800's and early 1900's.

310. GHETTO [Game]. Indianapolis, IN: Bobbs-Merrill; 1969; 1 game: playing area; 10 profile folders; record sheets; 160 cards; spinner card; 4 markers; 120 chips; dice; coordinator's manual.
Gr. 6-up. Simulates a direct experience of the frustrations and wants of ghetto life designed to reveal the reasons for ghetto people's actions.

311. Goffstein, M.B. NEIGHBORS. Illustrated. New York: Harper & Row; 1979.
Gr. K-2. A new neighbor tries to make friends with a long-time resident.

312. Greenfield, Eloise. SHE COME BRINGING ME THAT LITTLE BABY GIRL. Illustrated by John Steptoe. New York: Lippincott; 1974.
Gr. K-3. Kevin wanted a baby brother but instead he got a girl.

313. Hamilton, Virginia. PLANET OF JUNIOR BROWN. New York: Macmillan; 1971.
Gr. 6-up. Two young boys and their school custodian form a special friendship to protect themselves from the hardships in their lives.

314. Harper, Anita. HOW WE LIVE. Pictures by Christine Roche. New York: Harper & Row; 1977.
Gr. Preschool-3. Simple text and illustrations explore different types of homes in which people live.

315. Haskins, James. STREET GANGS: YESTERDAY AND TODAY. New York: Hastings House; 1974.
Gr. 6-up. Discusses the reasons gangs seem to form and people who belong to them using examples from the American Colonies to the present.

316. Hawkinson, John and Lucy Hawkinson. LITTLE BOY WHO LIVES UP HIGH. Illustrated. Chicago: Whitman; 1967.
Gr. K-2. A little boy who lives in a highrise apartment building in the city tells how his neighborhood looks from the sky and from the ground.

317. Hest, Amy. THE CRACK-OF-DAWN WALKERS. Illustrated by Amy Schwartz. New York: Macmillan; 1984.
Gr. K-3. Sadie and her grandfather take an early morning walk to the bakery shop.

318. Hill, Elizabeth Starr. EVAN'S CORNER. Illustrated. New York: Holt, Rinehart & Winston; 1967.
Gr. K-3. Evan has no place of his own in his family's crowded apartment.

319. Huntington, Lee Pennock. SIMPLE SHELTERS. Illustrated by Stefen Bernath. New York: Coward, McCann & Geoghegan; 1979.
Gr. 3-6. Describes basic types of shelters found in different geographical regions of the world.

320. Isadora, Rachel. CITY SEEN FROM A TO Z. Illustrated. New York: Greenwillow; 1983.
Gr. K-3. Alpbabet of city scenes. Objects from city life to match letters of the alphabet.

321. Jonas, Ann. ROUND TRIP. Illustrated. New York: Greenwillow; 1983.
Gr. K-2. Black-and-white pictures show a trip to the city. Turn the book upside-down and the return trip is shown.

322. Kessler, Ethel and Leonard Kessler. THE SWEENEYS FROM 9D. New York: Macmillan; 1985.
Gr. 1-4. Kathy, Tommy, and Amy start a new school in a new city, and make new friends.

323. Krasilovsky, Phyllis. L.C. IS THE GREATEST. Nashville, TN: Nelson; 1975.
Gr. 6-up. Growing up in Brooklyn during the depression, Louise, a Jewish girl, finally comes to terms with herself and her quarrelsome parents.

324. Langstaff, John. HOT CROSS BUNS, AND OTHER OLD STREET CRIES. New York: Atheneum; 1978.
Gr. 3-5. Contains words and music to old street cries.

325. Langstaff, John and Carol Langstaff. SHIMMY SHIMMY COKE-CA-POP: A COLLECTION OF CITY CHILDREN'S STREET GAMES AND RHYMES. Illustrated by Don MacSorley. New York: Doubleday; 1973.
Gr. 2-5. Urban children's games, chants, and rhymes.

326. Moak, Allan. A BIG CITY ABC. Plattsburgh, NY: Tundra; 1984.
Gr. K-4. City scenes, with each painting related to a letter of the alphabet.

327. Mohr, Nicholasa. FELITA. Illustrated. New York: Dial Press; 1979.
Gr. 3-6. The everyday experiences of an eight-year-old Puerto Rican girl growing up in a close-knit, urban community.

328. Murphy, Shirley Rousseau, and Pat Murphy. MRS. TORTINO'S RETURN TO THE SUN. Pictures by Susan Russo. New York: Lothrop; 1980.
Gr. K-3. Mrs. Tortino finds a way to preserve her family's Victorian home amidst the city's tall new buildings.

329. MY HOME AND ME [Filmstrip]. Chicago: Encyclopaedia Britannica Educational Corp.; 1972; 6 filmstrips; 6 cassettes; 6 guides.
Gr. K-2. Contents; My Seacoast Home; My Ranch Home; My City Home; My Forest Home; My Navajo Desert Home; My Island Home.

330. Oppenheim, Joanne. HAVE YOU SEEN HOUSES? Reading, MA: Addison-Wesley; 1973.
Gr. K-3. Describes in verse the different kinds of houses people live in throughout the world.

331. Raskin, Ellen. NOTHING EVER HAPPENS ON MY BLOCK. Illustrated. New York: Atheneum; 1966.
Gr. K-2. A small boy sits on the curb complaining that nothing ever happens as a wild series of events goes on behind him.

332. Rosenblum, Richard. MY BAR MITZVAH. New York: Morrow; 1985.
Gr. 4-8. Thirty years later Richard remembers how the whole neighborhood helped celebrate his Bar Mitzvah with presents, food, and tales.

333. Schick, Eleanor. ONE SUMMER NIGHT. Illustrated. New York: Greenwillow; 1977.
Gr. K-3. Laura dances one summer night and her music sets people to singing and dancing all around the neighborhood.

334. Schlein, Miriam. MY HOUSE. Illustrated by Joe Lasker. Chicago: Whitman; 1971.
Gr. Preschool-2. A boy tells why his house is a very special place.

335. SHELTER, A BASIC NEED [Filmstrip]. Chicago: Encyclopaedia Britannica Educational Corp.; 1981; 4 filmstrips; 4 cassettes; 4 student activity sheet masters; teacher's guide.
Gr. 1-4. Contents: Why We Need Shelter; How Shelter Has Changed; How a Building Is Built; Shelter Around the World.

Siberell, Anne. HOUSES: SHELTERS FROM PREHISTORIC TIMES TO TODAY. Illustrated. New York: Holt, Rinebart & Winston; 1979.
Gr. 2-5. See #239.

336. Steptoe, Jonn. STEVIE. Illustrated. New York: Harper & Row; 1969.
Gr. Preschool-3. Robert doesn't want to have to share his mamma with Stevie (whom she babysits) but misses Stevie when he's gone.

337. Thayer, Jane. THE MOUSE ON THE FOURTEENTH FLOOR. Illustrated by Beatrice Darwin. New York: Morrow; 1977.
Gr. Preschool-3. A mouse goes from floor to floor in a luxury apartment building, looking for a way to get back to his farm.

338. Thomas, Lanthe. MY STREET'S A MORNING COOL STREET. Illustrated by Emily A. McCully. New York: Harper & Row; 1976.
Gr. K-3. Describes a city neighborhood street on a morning walk to school.

339. Tusa, Tricia. MIRANDA. New York: Macmillan; 1985.
Gr. 2-8. Miranda loves to play the piano but when she plays Boogie-Woogie, it's too loud.

340. Voight, Cynthia. DICEY'S SONG. New York: Atheneum; 1983.
Gr. 6-up. Now that the four abandoned Tillerman children are settled in with their grandmother, Dicey finds that their new beginnings require love, trust, humor, and courage.

341. Voight, Cynthia. HOMECOMING. New York: Atheneum; 1981.
Gr. 5-up. Abandoned by their mother, four children begin a search for a home and an identity.

342. Williams, Vera B. A CHAIR FOR MY MOTHER. New York: Greenwillow; 1982.
Gr. K-3. A child, her waitress mother, and her grandmother save dimes to buy a comfortable armchair after all their furniture is lost in a fire.

343. Williams, Vera B. A CHAIR FOR MY MOTHER [Filmstrip]. New York: Random House/Miller-Brody; 1983; 1 filmstrip; 1 cassette; 1 teacher's guide.
Gr. K-3. Based on the book of the same title.

344. Williams, Vera B. SOMETHING SPECIAL FOR ME. New York: Greenwillow; 1983.
Gr. K-3. Rosa has difficulty choosing a special birthday present to buy with the coins her mother and grandmother have saved, until she hears a man playing beautiful music on an accordion.

COMPARISONS AND CONTRASTS

345. Baylor, Byrd. BEFORE YOU CAME THIS WAY. Illustrated by Tom Bahti. New York: Dutton; 1969.
Gr. K-5. Describes the life of the cliff dwellers of the Southwest with illustrations and poetic text.

346. Baylor, Byrd. THE BEST TOWN IN THE WORLD. Illustrated by Ronald Himler. New York: Atheneum; 1983.
Gr. 1-up. Nostalgic look back at the "best town" in the world, where dogs were smarter, chickens laid prettier eggs, and chocolate cakes were more chocolate.

347. Bonavia, David. PEKING. New York: Time-Life; 1978.
Gr. 6-up. Photographs and text give images of life in Peking today and a report of its history and traditions. Other Time-Life books in the Great Cities Series include ATHENS, MOSCOW, PARIS, TOKYO, and VENICE.

348. Burland, Cottie. SEE INSIDE AN AZTEC TOWN. New York: Watts; 1980.
Gr. 5-up. Describes the history and culture of the Aztecs, once the most powerful civilization in Mexico.

349. CITY AND TOWN [Filmstrip]. Englewood, CO: Learning Tree; 1982; 4 filmstrips; 2 cassettes; guide.
Gr. 2-6. Contents: The Megalopolis; The Town; The City; The Small Town.

350. Costabel, Eva Deutsch. A NEW ENGLAND VILLAGE. New York: Atheneum; 1983.
Gr. 4-up. New England village of about 1830 - crafts and customs.

351. Currier, Richard L. CITY PLANNING IN ANCIENT TIMES. Illustrated. Minneapolis: Lerner; 1976.
Gr. 5-up. Arthur Segal's book retold for young readers. Examines the art of city planning as it was in ancient times and describes some of the oldest planned cities.

352. Goetz, Delia. STATE CAPITAL CITIES. New York: Morrow; 1971.
Gr. 5-8. A three-page description of the history, points of interest, and present-day industrial and cultural activities of the fifty state capitals.

353. Goodall, John. THE STORY OF AN ENGLISH VILLAGE. New York: Atheneum; 1979.
Gr. 3-6. A wordless book which traces the growth of an English village from the Middle Ages to the present.

354. Hamblin, Dora Jane. THE FIRST CITIES. New York: Time-Life; 1973.
Gr. 6-up. A discussion of the origins and organization of early cities.

355. Hughes-Stanton, Penelope. SEE INSIDE AN ANCIENT CHINESE TOWN. New York: Watts; 1979.
Gr. 4-6. Color photographs and drawings show scenes of daily life in an ancient Chinese town.

356. Jacobs, David. CONSTANTINOPLE: CITY OF THE GOLDEN HORN. New York: Harper & Row; 1969.
Gr. 6-7. A history of the city of of Constantinople from its founding to the twentieth century.

357. JAPAN: A CHANGING NATION [Filmstrip]. Bedford Hills, NY: Educational Enrichment Materials; 1972; 1 of a set of 6 filmstrips; 6 cassettes; teacher's guide.
Gr. 4-up. Photographs of Tokyo show work and daily life as well as urban change.

358. Leacroft, Helen. THE BUILDINGS OF ANCIENT MAN. Illustrated. Reading, MA: Addison-Wesley; 1973.
Gr. 4-up. Discusses ancient man as he first lived in cave dwellings and later in simple types of lean-to shelters.

359. Lewis, Elizabeth. YOUNG FU OF THE UPPER YANGTZE. Illustrated by Ed Young. New York: Holt, Rinehart & Winston; 1973.
Gr. 4-7. In the 1920's a Chinese youth from the country comes to Chungking with his mother where the bustling city offers adventure; his apprenticeship to a coppersmith brings good fortune.

360. Macaulay, David. CITY: A STORY OF ROMAN PLANNING AND CONSTRUCTION. Illustrated. New York: Houghton Mifflin; 1974.
Gr. 5-up. Details planning, construction and growth of a typical ancient Roman city through text and drawings.

361. Muller, Jorg. THE CHANGING CITY. New York: Atheneum; 1977.
Gr. 4-up. A fold-out book which shows the changes a city neighborhood goes through over the course of years.

362. OUR WONDERFUL COUNTRY. SET 3: ITS CITIES AND TOWNS [Study Print]. Chicago: Coronet; 1973; 8 study prints; teacher's guide.
Gr. 1-6. Contents: New York City; Juneau, Alaska; Minneapolis; Portland, Oregon; The Suburbs; Aspen, Colorado; Chicago; New England Town.

363. Quackenbush, Robert. THERE'LL BE A HOT TIME IN THE OLD TOWN TONIGHT: THE GREAT CHICAGO FIRE OF 1871 TOLD WITH SONG AND PICTURES. Illustrated. New York: Lippincott; 1974.
Gr. Preschool-2. A humorous pictorial version of the song, including music.

364. Rutland, Jonathan. SEE INSIDE A ROMAN TOWN. Illustrated by Angus McBride, Bernard Robinson, Bill Stallion. New York: Warwick; 1978.
Gr. 4-7. Color photographs and drawings show scenes of daily life in an ancient Roman town.

365. Rutland, Jonathan. SEE INSIDE AN ANCIENT GREEK TOWN. Illustrated by Adrian Sington. New York: Watts; 1979.
Gr. 4-7. Photographs of present-day sites in Greece illustrate a text which reconstructs life in an ancient Greek town.

366. Sancha, Sheila. THE LUTTRELL VILLAGE: COUNTRY LIFE IN THE MIDDLE AGES. New York: Crowell; 1982.
Gr. 6-up. Traces a year in the Lincolnshire village of Gerneham, from ploughing through sowing, harvesting, and threshing, with illustrations of village life inspired by the fourteenth-century Luttrell Psalter.

367. Sasek, Miraslav. THIS IS SAN FRANCISCO. New York: Macmillan; 1973.
Gr. 3-6. An artist's view of the sights of San Francisco.

368. Sasek, Miraslav. THIS IS WASHINGTON, D.C. New York: Macmillan; 1973.
Gr. 3-6. An illustrated tour of the best-known sights in Washington D.C.

369. Switzer, Ellen Bichenwald. OUR URBAN PLANET. Photos by Michael and Jeffrey Switzer. New York; Atheneum; 1980.
Gr. 6-up. Discusses the growth and development of various types of cities.

370. Time-Life Books. THE COMMUNITY. Illustrated. New York: Time-Life; 1976.
Gr. 5-up. An overview of the types of communities found throughout the world.

371. Unstead, R.J. HOW THEY LIVED IN CITIES LONG AGO. New York: Arco; 1981.
Gr. 4-6. Life in ancient cities of Mexico, Egypt, Greece, Babylon, China, and others.

372. Ventura, Piero. PIERO VENTURA'S BOOK OF CITIES. Illustrated. New York: Random House; 1975.
Gr. 3-5. Presents some of the outstanding features of the world's most famous cities, such as Venetian gondolas, the New York subway, and the cathedral of Notre Dame de Paris.

373. Webster, Norman. CITY PEOPLE, CITY LIFE. Illustrated. St. Paul, MN: EMC; 1973.
Gr. 3-8. Photos and brief text introduce the historical sights of Peking and the daily life and work of the Chinese city dwellers.

Chapter 5

Mountains

When we think about mountains what sort of images do we see? What questions arise about mountain worlds? We might wonder who or what lives in the mountains and how they live. Or what makes mountains? What do we use mountains for? We might even ask why mountains seem to fascinate us so.

The AMERICAN HERITAGE DICTIONARY, COLLEGE EDITION, defines "mountain" in this way:

> Moun-tain: 1. A natural elevation of the earth's surface having considerable mass, generally steep sides, and a height greater than that of a hill. 2.a. A large heap: "a mountain of ironing." b. A huge quantity: "a mountain of trouble." 3. Capital M: The extreme revolutionary party of the French Revolution so called because its members occupied the uppermost seats in the National Convention Hall in 1793.

The dictionary definition reveals that mountains play a "big" role in our lives. They stand for something which is high or numerous or huge. After the definition for the word "mountain" in the dictionary, we find a string of words which reveal more about the mountain regions, telling us about the life there (for example, "mountain ash," "mountain goat," "mountain sickness," and "mountain top").

These definitions, our thoughts and our questions about mountains can be arranged into three broad areas: the physical world of the mountains, the natural world of the mountains, and the figurative world of the mountains.

The physical world of the mountains includes questions about the geology of the mountains: How were they formed? Are they finished? What are they made of? Does this change from place to place? What are volcanoes? Why do they erupt? Can we predict when this will happen? It includes questions about the geography of these regions: Where are the major mountains and mountain ranges of the world? Which are the tallest? The longest? Why are some mountains so much larger than others? What are the most famous mountains and why are they famous? It includes questions about mapping: How do you map a mountain? What kind of maps show height and how do they do it? It includes questions about exploring the physical world of the mountains: Who climbs mountains? What kind of equipment and clothing do they need? Who are the famous mountaineers? What have they helped us to know about the mountains? Why do they climb them? What are some sports that people enjoy when they are in the mountains? Are there rules for safe hiking, backpacking, climbing, rock climbing and so on?

The natural world of the mountains includes all of the questions we might have about who or what lives in the mountains and how this life survives there: What plants can live at high altitudes? How are they different from plants which live at sea level or in the desert? What animals, birds, and fish live in high altitudes? What features do they have that have helped them to adapt to living there? What animals are unique to the mountains? What are llamas and alpacas like? Mountain goats? Bighorn sheep?

The natural world of the mountains also includes the world of natural resources. When we think of the mountains, we might think of the resources of the forests which grow there: What kinds of forest grow at higher altitudes? Why do there seem to be more trees in the mountains than in the valleys? How does a forester decide which trees to cut down? How does the lumber industry work? What other products come from forestry? How can we protect our forests so we don't lose them and yet still be able to use them as resources? Other natural resources which come to us from the mountains are coal and other mineral products. What are the techniques of coal mining? What is the life of the miner like? What other mineral resources are found in the mountains? How do we protect the mountains and the people who mine them from the hazards of this kind of mining?

The figurative mountains are the mountains in our minds. These are the mountains we picture or imagine because of movies, books, songs, and folklore which portray them and the life of people who live there. We might ask what our images of certain mountains are: What are the Alps like? The Rocky Mountains? Mount Everest? Where did we get our ideas about these mountains? Perhaps it was from books: Could we read HEIDI, DAUGHTER OF THE MOUNTAINS, SECRET OF THE ANDES, and MY SIDE OF THE MOUNTAIN and learn something about mountain life? What about songs we can think of that tell about the mountains? What do "She'll be comin' 'round the mountain," and "The bear went over the mountain" tell us about the mountains? Could we learn about mountains from reading folktales such as Richard Chase's tales set in the Appalachian mountains or from stories such as Arnold Lobel's MING LO MOVES THE MOUNTAIN?

Each of these three branches of questions could be explored as a unique study of one aspect of the world of the mountains. However, because mountains represent a unique ecological system, all of these strands are connected to one another. Someone who begins with an interest in mountain climbers might begin by exploring the physical world of the mountains from this point of view: Who are the climbers? Where do they go? What do they take with them? Do they map the areas they explore? How? These questions fall into the physical world strand. They lead the student to resources such as biographies of climbers, articles in periodicals such as NATIONAL GEOGRAPHIC and GEO, books on mountain terrain, films and filmstrips on expeditions such as Hilary's to Everest or the more recent women's climb on Annapurna. But this same student might want to move to the figurative area of study, reading novels about mountain climbers such as BANNER IN THE SKY or try to write poems or ramblings about how it must feel to be so high in the sky. Or he or she might become interested in the people of mountain regions who act as guides to mountaineers such as the Sherpas, or the Indians of the Andes mountains. Or become interested in the creatures and plants the mountaineers found on their explorations. All of these questions emerge from the first interest in mountaineers and take the student all across the thematic chart and into various areas of inquiry and types of materials.

Students might also want to work their way across the chart horizontally by exploring all of the aspects of one mountainous area, looking at the physical, natural and figurative aspects of this one mountain world. We could, for example, explore the world of the Appalachian mountains by asking questions about the three major areas.

What are the physical characteristics of the Appalachian Mountains? To explore this area, we rely on many of the tools of the standard social studies program including books on Appalachia such as the Time/Life book on the region, Rebecca Caudill's MY APPALACHIA, filmstrips and films about the mountain region such as that done by National Geographic, and maps and other geographic works which help us to locate the region and its major centers of activity. Trail guides provided by touring associations or the Sierra Club help us to follow the Appalachian trail. Books on the geography of the Eastern coast of the United States provide contour maps and explanations of the origin of the mountains.

What are the natural characteristics of these mountains? Many of the same tools may prove helpful in answering these questions. What kinds of animals and birds and fish are native to the region or survive there? What kinds of vegetation do well in this region? Coal mining is a major natural resource of the area. Books and films on the processes of mining and refining ore and natural gas and on the lives of the miners would all help to reveal more about life in this area. Novels which are set in mining communities in these mountains would provide added insight.

Is forestry a major industry there? What kinds of woods are grown and forested? Are there books about lumberjacks and their life in these mountains?

An unusual kind of resource used by the people of the southern Appalachians is wildcrafting, the art of finding and collecting herbs for sale to medicinal companies. Are there books or filmstrips on wildcrafting? Novels such as the Cleavers' WHERE THE LILIES BLOOM help us to imagine this kind of small industry.

In addition, these southern mountain regions are the home of cottage industries such as quiltmaking, basketry, whittling and carving, dulcimer-making and so on. The Foxfire books and films provide an entry into our understanding of these crafts, as do books which discuss each of these individually.

To create a picture of the figurative landscape of the Appalachians in our mind, we can draw from a number of children's novels set in this region including Lenski's BLUE RIDGE BILLY, the Cleavers' WHERE THE LILIES BLOOM and TRIAL VALLEY, James Still's

SPORTY CREEK, and Virginia Hamilton's M. C. HIGGINS THE GREAT among others. Volumes of folktales and lore which come directly from this region include James Still's JACK AND THE WONDER BEANS and Richard Chase's GRANDFATHER TALES AND JACK TALES.

Recordings by The Folktellers, Richard Chase, and Ray Hicks capture the language and accents of these tales. The videotapes put out by Appalshop show tellers telling these tales. Collections of American folk songs for children reveal the origins of many songs known to them to be in these mountain regions. Children could begin to collect and sing songs from this region and to discuss what those songs reveal about the mountain life.

In conclusion, we see that it is possible to use the chart of mountains in several different ways. We can study the world of mountains as a whole, looking at physical, natural and figurative aspects of mountains which interest us. We can select individual questions we have about mountains and discover materials about those questions realizing that this may well lead us to consider other materials and questions beyond what we originally wanted to know. We can also take one particular mountain area and study that area in all its physical natural and figurative characteristics. Mountains offer a rich environment for discovery of a place and its possibilities for learners of all ages.

The lists which follow are not intended to be comprehensive. They represent an attempt to share materials for several grade levels, in a number of formats and genres, and in a variety of areas which might be used to help discover mountains. The materials on the Appalachian region are treated in somewhat fuller detail. Any mountain area could be expanded upon this way through literature, folklore and song as well as through informational sources.

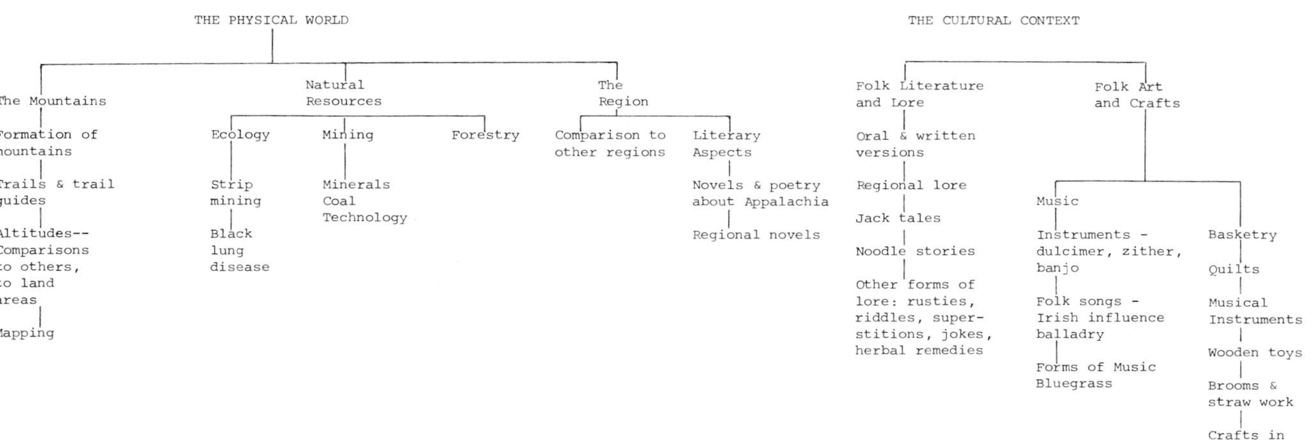
MOUNTAINS
THE PHYSICAL WORLD
The Mountains
Formation of mountains
Trails & trail guides
Altitudes--Comparisons to others, to land areas
Mapping
Natural Resources
Ecology
Strip mining
Black lung disease
Mining
Minerals
Coal
Technology
Forestry
The Region
Comparison to other regions
Literary Aspects
Novels & poetry about Appalachia
Regional novels
THE CULTURAL CONTEXT
Folk Literature and Lore
Oral & written versions
Regional lore
Jack tales
Noodle stories
Other forms of lore: rusties, riddles, super-stitions, jokes, herbal remedies
Folk Art and Crafts
Music
Instruments - dulcimer, zither, banjo
Folk songs - Irish influence balladry
Forms of Music Bluegrass
Basketry
Quilts
Musical Instruments
Wooden toys
Brooms & straw work
Crafts in Foxfire books

THE PHYSICAL WORLD

Geology

374. Aylesworth, Thomas G. GEOLOGICAL DISASTERS: EARTHQUAKES & VOLCANOES. New York: Watts; 1979.
Gr. 6-9. Explanation of plate tectonic theory with explanation of connections between volcanoes and earthquakes.

375. Baylor, Byrd. IF YOU ARE A HUNTER OF FOSSILS. Illustrated by Peter Parnell. New York: Scribner; 1980.
Gr. 2-6. A fossil hunter in the mountains of West Texas describes how the area might have looked in the distant past.

376. Berger, Melvin. DISASTROUS VOLCANOES. New York: Watts; 1981.
Gr. 4-up. Discusses formation and location of volcanoes along with descriptions of some of the best-known eruptions.

377. Brown, Billye, and Walter R. Brown. HISTORICAL CATASTROPHIES: VOLCANOES. Illustrated. Reading, MA: Addison-Wesley; 1970.
Gr. 5-8. Describes the eruptions of selected ancient and modern volcanoes around the world and the reactions of the people who lived near them. Includes an explanation of geysers, hot springs, paint pots, and fumaroles.

378. Creative Educational Society. FORCES OF NATURE. (Our Changing Environment Series). Mankato, MN: Creative Educational Society; 1971.
Gr. 4-8. Brief text and color photographs introduce some of nature's phenomena such as volcanoes, glaciers, wind and water erosion, rainbows, and fog.

379. Creative Educational Society. HISTORY OF THE EARTH. Mankato, MN: Creative Educational Society; 1971.
Gr. 4-8. Traces the history of the Earth from its birth through various stages of life to man's development.

380. Daily News and Journal America. VOLCANO, THE ERUPTION OF MOUNT ST. HELENS. Longview, Washington: Longview Publications; 1980.
Gr. 4-up. A compilation of contemporary news stories about Mount St. Helens.

381. Doolittle, Jerome. CANYONS AND MESAS. Illustrated by Wolf von dem Bussche. Morristown, NJ: Silver Burdett; 1974.
Gr. 6-up. A natural history of the canyons of the Southwest.

382. Drury, Roger W. THE FINCHES' FABULOUS FURNACE. Illustrated by Erik Blegvad. New York: Little, Brown; 1971.
Gr. 3-5. The Finches' house is perched on top of a volcano, which heats it and remains docile until the week of the Ashfield Bicentennial.

383. Fodor, R.V. EARTH AFIRE! VOLCANOES AND THEIR ACTIVITY. New York: Morrow; 1981.
Gr. 4-6. This lively book discusses the formation of volcanoes, some famous ones, types of eruptions, and the possible benefits of these spectacular phenomena of nature.

384. Fodor, R. WHAT DOES A GEOLOGIST DO? New York: Dodd, Mead; 1977.
Gr. 5. Describes a variety of jobs in the field of geology and highlights the necessary education and training.

385. FOSSILS SERIES [Filmstrip]. Chicago: Encyclopaedia Britannica Educational Corps; 1965-1966; 5 sound-filmstrips; 5 cassettes; 5 guides.
Gr. 4-8. Shows how fossils are used in the study of the earth's history.

386. FOSSILS: CLUES TO EARTH HISTORY [Study Prints]. Chicago: Encyclopaedia Britannica Educational Corp.; 1978; 8 study prints; teacher's guide.
Gr. 6-12. Demonstrates how fossils are formed and their relationship to geologic time.

387. Gans, Roma. CAVES. Illustrated by Giulio Maestro. New York: Crowell; 1976.
Gr. 1-3. Describes formation, sizes, geologic aspects, functions and uses of caves.

388. GEYSERS AND HOT SPRINGS [Study Print]. Chicago: Encyclopaedia Britannica Educational Corp.; 1976; 8 study prints.
Gr. 1-6. Pictures and explains various geothermal features in Yellowstone National Park. Contents: A

Geothermal Valley; A Hot Spring and Runoff Channel; A Geyser Erupts; A Terrace Forms; A Geyser Builds; A Landscape Changes; Yellowstone's Ecosystem, Parts I and II.

389. GLACIERS AND THE ICE AGE [Filmstrip]. Chicago: Encyclopaedia Britannica Educational Corp,; 1965; 4 filmstrips; 4 cassettes; guide.
Gr. 4-8. Shows how glaciers are formed, their movement, and how they affect the landscape.

390. Goetz, Delia. MOUNTAINS. Illustrated by Louis Darling. New York: Morrow; 1962.
Gr. 4-6. This introduction to mountains discusses their formation, climate, use to man, and other related topics.

391. Goldreich, Gloria and Esther Goldreich. WHAT CAN SHE BE? A GEOLOGIST. Photographs by Robert Ipcar. New York: Lothrop; 1976.
Gr. K-5. Introduces the possibilities of a career in geology using descriptions of a female geologist's many activities.

392. Harris, Susan. VOLCANOES. New York: Watts; 1979.
Gr. 1-4. Simple details on formation and eruptions of several volcanoes.

393. IGNEOUS ROCKS [Kit]. Rochester, NY: Wards; 1975; 12 rock specimens; teacher guide; 4 spirit masters.
Gr. 5-up. Specimens illustrate common compositional and textural varieties of igneous rocks. Activities emphasize identification, formation, distribution, and geologic history.

394. INVESTIGATING ROCKS [Filmstrip]. Chicago: Encyclopaedia Britannica Educational Corp.; 1969; 9 filmstrips; 9 cassettes,; 9 guides.
Gr. 5-8. Contents: Shale, Sandstone and Conglomerate; Coal; Limestone and Evaporites; Volcanic Rocks; Plutonic Rocks; Metamorphic rocks; Recognizing Rock-Making Minerals; Comparing Rocks; Rocks and the Landscape.

395. Laycock, George. CAVES. Illustrated by DeVere E. Burt. New York: Four Winds; 1976.
Gr. 5 up. Describes cave life and formation and the uses to which humans have put caves.

396. LOOKING AT MINERALS. [Study Print]. Chicago: Encyclopaedia Britannica Educational Corp.; 1977; 8 study prints.
Gr. 4-up. Introduces mineralogy and gemology with 25 large colored photographs.

397. Milne, Lorus, and Margery Milne. MOUNTAINS. Morristown, NJ: Silver Burdett; 1962.
Gr. 5-up. Text and photographs show formation, structure and changes of mountains and the life which lives there.

398. MOUNT ST. HELEN'S: A VOLCANO ERUPTS [Filmstrip]. Chicago: SVE; 1980; 1 filmstrip; 1 cassette; 1 teacher information booklet.
Gr. 4-9. Describes the physical force of the volcano and the ecological destruction to the rivers, forests, and nearby homes.

399. MOUNTAINS. In: EXPLORING THE EARTH AROUND US [Filmstrip]. Washington, D.C.: National Geographic; 1983; 1 in a set of 5 filmstrips; 5 cassettes.
Gr. 2-6. Examines mountains and their formation. Other filmstrips in set: Plains; Deserts; Rivers; Oceans.

400. NATURAL WONDERS OF NORTH AMERICA [Filmstrip]. Washington, D.C.: National Geographic; 1983; 2 filmstrips; 2 cassettes; 2 guides.
Gr. 3-8. Explores the geologic wonders of North America, including canyons, mountains, mesas and volcanoes.

401. Place, Marion T. MOUNT ST. HELENS: A SLEEPING VOLCANO AWAKES. New York: Dodd, Mead; 1981.
Gr. 5-up. Photographs and text describe the eruption of Mount St. Helens.

402. POWERS OF NATURE. Washington, D.C.: National Geographic Society; 1978.
Gr. 5-12. Discusses natural phenomena such as earthquakes, volcanoes, drought, floods and storms.

403. Poynter, Margaret. VOLCANOES, THE FIERY MOUNTAINS. Illustrated by Igor E. Sedor. New York: Messner; 1980.
Gr. 4-6. Discusses formation of volcanoes, gives famous examples and discusses volcanic action in the U.S.

404. PREHISTORIC WORLD. Illustrated. New York: Warwick; 1975.
Gr. 6-9. Describes the evolution of the earth from its formation to the development of the human.

405. Updegraff, Imelda, and Robert Updegraff. EARTHQUAKES AND VOLCANOES. New York: Puffin Books; 1982.
Gr. 2-4. Part of a series which uses the half flap page device to demonstrate how earthquakes and volcanoes evolve.

406. Updegraff, Imelda, and Robert Updegraff. MOUNTAINS AND VALLEYS. New York: Puffin Books; 1982.
Gr. 2-4. Uses full page spreads interspersed with half page flaps to demonstrate how mountains and valleys are formed in a before and after effect which would appeal to children.

407. A VISIT TO BRYCE CANYON NATIONAL PARK [Kit]. Big Springs, TX: Creative Visuals; 1974; 1 filmstrip; 1 sound cassette; 1 map; 4 rock samples; 1 teacher's manual.
Gr. 6-up. Explains and illustrates wind and water erosion. Discusses the uses of topographic maps.

408. VOLCANOES [Study Print]. Chicago: Encyclopaedia Britannica Educational Corp.; 1972; 10 pictures.
Gr. 4-8. Contents: A Giant Pit Crater; Molten Rock; A Gentle Volcano; The Eruptive Force; After the Eruption; Life and Death in One Flow; The Edge of a Lava Flow; The Pumice Forest; Volcanic Forms; The Earth's Volcanoes.

409. Wyckoff, Jerome. THE STORY OF GEOLOGY: OUR CHANGING EARTH THROUGH THE AGES. Illustrated with photos, and with paintings by William Sayles, Harry McNaught, and Raymond Perlman. New York: Golden Press; 1976.
Gr. 5-8. A study of the Earth's physical make-up, discussing the forces that affect this make-up, how they change the Earth and how scientists study various features of the Earth's surface and interior.

Geography

410. THE ALPS. Washington, D.C: National Geographic Society; 1973.
Gr. 6-up. Photographs, maps, and text describe many aspects of Alpine life.

411. Botting, Douglas. WILDERNESS EUROPE (The World's Wild Places). Illustrated. New York: Time-Life; 1976.
Gr. 6-up. Photographs and text describe the geography and natural history of Europe's wilderness areas.

412. Bowen, Ezra. THE HIGH SIERRA. New York: Time-Life; 1972.
Gr. 6-up. Photographs and text describe the physical and natural worlds of California's Sierra Nevada range.

413. Lobeck, Armin. THINGS MAPS DON'T TELL US: AN ADVENTURE INTO MAP INTERPRETATION. New York: Macmillan; 1956.
Gr. 4-6.

414. MAP BASICS [Filmstrip]. Created and produced by Michael Hardy Productions. Chicago: Denoyer-Geppert; 1980; 6 filmstrips; 6 sound cassettes; 25 duplicating masters; teacher's guide.
Gr. 4-6. Provides experiences in both mapping and map and globe interpretation. Contents: It Depends on Your Point of View; One Thing Stands for Another; Measures of the Land; Which Way from Here; Finding the Exact Spot; Flat Maps of a Round Earth.

415. Morrison, Tony. THE ANDES (The World's Wild Places). Illustrated. New York: Time-Life; 1975.
Gr. 6-up. An exploration of the geograpic and natural history of the Andes.

416. Nicolson, Nigel. THE HIMALAYAS (The World's Wild Places) Illustrated. New York: Time-Life; 1975.
Gr. 6-up. An exploration of the geography and natural history of the Himalaya Mountains.

417. PEOPLE AND PLACES WHERE THEY LIVE [Filmstrip]. Washington, D.C.: National Geographic; 1981; 3 filmstrips; 3 cassettes; 3 guides.
Gr. 2-6. Discusses the ways in which environment shapes peoples' lives. Contents: People in Mountains; People in Deserts; People Near Water.

418. Radlauer, Ruth Shaw. GLACIER NATIONAL PARK. Design and photography by Rolf Zillmer. Chicago: Children's Press; 1977.
Gr. 3-up. Introduces Glacier National Park, which has nearly fifty small glaciers. Includes discussions of the bighorn sheep and baking and camping in the Park.

419. Rhodes, Richard. THE OZARKS. Illustrated. New York: Time-Life; 1974.
Gr. 6-up. An exploration of the geography and natural history of the Ozark Mountains.

420. Walker, Bryce S. THE GREAT DIVIDE. Illustrated. New York: Time-Life; 1973.
Gr. 6-up. The world of mountains goats and aspen, of grizzly bears and sunflowers as they exist in the Rocky Mountain vastness.

421. WILDERNESS U.S.A. Washington, D.C: National Geographic Society; 1975.
Gr. 5-up. Explores wilderness areas of the U.S.

422. Williams, Richard L. THE CASCADES. New York: Time-Life; 1974.
Gr. 6-up. Photographs and text describe the physical and natural worlds of the Cascades.

Trails and Guides

423. Chase, Myron C. FIELD GUIDE TO EDIBLE & USEFUL PLANTS OF NORTH AMERICA. Irving, TX: Boy Scouts of America; 1965.
Gr. 4-6. Describes plants and their habitats and which wild plants can be used as food or for other purposes.

424. Fenner, Phyllis ed. PERILOUS ASCENT: STORIES OF MOUNTAIN CLIMBING. Illustrated by Charles Greer. New York: Morrow; 1970.
Gr. 4-8. Ten short stories about the drama and excitement of mountaineering.

425. George, Jean Craighead. MY SIDE OF THE MOUNTAIN. Illustrated. New York: Dutton; 1975.
Gr. 4-9. Sam Gribley, a New York boy, does what many boys dream of doing--spends a winter alone on the mountain in the Catskills.

426. Grant, Matthew G. JIM BRIDGER: THE MOUNTAIN MAN. Illustrated by Nancy Inderieden. Mankato, MN: Creative Education Society; 1974.
Gr. 1-3. A biography of mountain man and pioneer explorer of the West, Jim Bridger.

427. Gray, William R. CAMPING ADVENTURE. Illustrated by Steve Raymer. Washington, D.C: National Geographic; 1976.
Gr. 1-3. Text and photos show a family's camping trip to a mountain wilderness area.

428. Hawkinson, John. LET ME TAKE YOU ON A TRAIL. Chicago: Whitman; 1972.
Gr. Preschool-3. A walk along a trail in spring with a description of how to prepare for a field trip there.

429. Hildreth, Brian. HOW TO SURVIVE. Illustrated by Conrad Bailey. New York: Penguin; 1982.
Gr. 6-up. Discusses wilderness survival and safety measures.

430. Larson, Randy. BACKPACKING: FOR FUN AND GLORY. Illustrated by John R. Henshaw. Chippewa Falls, WI: Harvey House; 1979.
Gr. 4-6. Discusses history, selection of equipment and campsites.

431. Lyttle, Richard B. THE COMPLETE BEGINNER'S GUIDE TO BACKPACKING. New York: Doubleday; 1975.
Gr. 5-up. Includes ideas for planning trips, equipment to use and further reading.

432. Mohn, Peter B. HIKING. Mankato, MN: Crestwood; 1975.
Gr. 2-4. Photographs and a brief text explain what to take and how to enjoy the experience.

433. Poynter, Margaret. SEARCH AND RESCUE: THE TEAM AND THE MISSIONS. Photos by Jerry Newcomb, New York: Atheneum; 1980.
Gr. 5-7. Describes the work done by teams in Southern California conducting search and rescue operations in the mountains.

434. Pringle, Laurence. WILD FOODS: A BEGINNER'S GUIDE TO IDENTIFYING, HARVESTING AND COOKING SAFE AND TASTY PLANTS FROM THE OUTDOORS. New York: Four Winds; 1978.
Gr. 6-up. Twenty plants, with pictures, names, and how to recognize, harvest and cook them.

435. Thomas, Art. BACKPACKING IS FOR ME. Minneapolis: Lerner; 1980.
Gr. 2-4. A boy describes his backpacking trip, including planning, equipment and camping.

436. WEATHER IN THE WILDERNESS [Filmstrip]. Sacramento: The Great American Film Factory; 1 filmstrip; 1 cassette. Gr. 6-up. Describes weather related problems in the wilderness, hyperthermia, sunstroke, sunburn, dehydration, and frostbite and how to protect from the change of weather.

Natural Resources

437. Abrams, Kathleen; Abrams, Lawrence. LOGGING AND LUMBERING. New York: Messner; 1980.
Gr. 3-6. An overview of the industry including harvest, replanting and conservation techniques.

438. Chaffin, Lillie D. COAL, ENERGY AND CRISIS. Illustrated by Roy Abels, Chippewa Falls, WI: Harvey House; 1974. Gr. 4-6. Describes mining, past and present and explores problems of mining, manufacturing and use.

439. Crawford, Teri. THE FIRST FOREST RANGERS, PROTECTORS OF THE WILDERNESS. Illustrated by Connie Maltese, Morristown, NJ: Silver Burdett; 1978.
Gr. 4-6. Relates how the American forest came to be "watched over" and how the idea of conservation was born.

440. Graham, Ada; Graham, Frank. CAREERS IN CONSERVATION: PROFILES OF PEOPLE WORKING FOR THE ENVIRONMENT. Scribner; 1980.
Gr. 5-up. Describes careers in forestry, geology and other conservation careers.

441. Harter, Walter L. COAL: THE ROCK THAT BURNS. New York: Elsevier Nelson; 1979.
Gr. 5-8. History of coal, unions and manufacturing in the U.S.

442. Hirsch, S. Carl. GUARDIANS OF TOMORROW: PIONEERS IN ECOLOGY. Illustrated by William Steinel. New York: Viking Press; 1971.
Gr. 6-up. Brief biographies of eight American pioneers in conservation and ecology:
Henry David Thoreau, George Perkins Marsh, Frederick Law Olmsted, John Muir, Gifford Pinchot, George Norris, Aldo Leopold, and Rachel Carson.

443. Kerrod, Robin. ROCKS AND MINERALS. Illustrated by Ross Wardle and John Mariott. New York: Warwick; 1978.
Gr. 5-up. Discusses the formation and mining of different kinds of rocks and the many minerals found within.

444. Kraft, Betsy Harvey. COAL. New York: Watts; 1976.
Gr. 2-4. Basic information on coal geology, history of mining, and uses of coal.

445. Kurelek, William. LUMBERJACK. Illustrated. Boston: Houghton Mifflin; 1974.
Gr. 4-6. Memoirs with paintings of a man who worked as a lumberjack in Canada.

446. Parnall, Peter. THE MOUNTAIN. Illustrated. New York: Doubleday; 1971.
Gr. 5. Drawings and brief text reveal how an effort to preserve a wilderness area brought about its destruction.

447. Quackenbush, Robert M. CLEMENTINE. Philadelphia, PA: Lippincott; 1974.
Gr. K-3. An illustrated version of the song about the miner's daughter whose accidental fall into a river brings good fortune to her and her family. Includes the music and information on gold prospecting.

448. Skurzynski, Gloria. SAFEGUARDING THE LAND: WOMEN WORK IN PARKS, FORESTS AND RANGELANDS. New York: Harcourt Brace; 1981.
Gr. 6-12. Shows the careers of three women in conservation work.

449. Wallace, Robert. THE MINERS. New York: Time-Life; 1976.
Gr. 5-up. A history of gold and silver mining in the western U.S.

450. Williams, Richard L. THE LOGGERS. New York: Time-Life; 1976.
Gr. 5-up. Photos, pictures and text describe logging in the old Northwest.

451. Wiseman, David. JEREMY VISICK. Boston: Houghton Mifflin; 1981.
Gr. 5-up. Twelve-year-old Matthew is drawn almost against his will to help a boy his own age who was lost in a mining disaster a century before.

452. Witt, Matt. IN OUR BLOOD: FOUR MINING FAMILIES. Photos by Earl Dotter. New Market, TN: Highlander; 1979. Gr. 6-up.

The Natural World

453. Adrian, Mary. NORTH AMERICAN BIGHORN SHEEP. New York: Hastings House; 1966.
Gr. 3-6. Describes the life of a bighorn sheep and discusses conservation of these animals.

454. Berger, Gilda. MOUNTAIN WORLDS: WHAT LIVES THERE. Illustrated by Stefen Bernath. New York: Coward, McCann & Geoghegan; 1978.
Gr. 3-5. Discusses the plants and animals of mountain worlds and how they live.

455. Caudill, Rebecca. MY APPALACHIA. Illustrated by Edward Wallawich. New York: Holt, Rinehart & Winston; 1916.
Gr. 5-up. Caudill explores Harlan County, Kentucky, where she grew up.

Chase, Myron C. FIELD GUIDE TO EDIBLE & USEFUL PLANTS OF NORTH AMERICA. Irving, TX: Boy Scouts of Africa; 1965.
Gr. 4-6. See #423.

456. Conklin, Gladys. LLAMAS OF SOUTH AMERICA. Illustrated by Lorence F. Bjorklund. New York: Holiday House; 1974.
Gr. 3-7. Describes llamas, alpacas and vicunas and how they are utilized by human beings.

457. DISCOVERING OUR ENVIRONMENT [Study Print]. Chicago: Coronet Films; 1971; 40 pictures; game; guide.
Gr. 6-up. A study of the interrelationships in our physical environment.

458. Dowden, Anne Ophelia Todd. THE BLOSSOM ON THE BOUGH: A BOOK OF TREES. Illustrated. New York: Harper & Row; 1975.
Gr. 5-up. Discusses the importance of forests, the parts and cycles of trees, the functions of flowers and fruits, the distinctive features of conifers, and the forest regions in the United States.

459. Farb, Peter. ECOLOGY. Morristown, NJ: Silver Burdett; 1967.
Gr. 5-up. Explains ecology, the web of nature and the rhythms and patterns of life.

460. Ford, Barbara. ALLIGATORS, RACCOONS, AND OTHER SURVIVORS. New York: Morrow; 1981.
Gr. 5-up. Reports on endangered wildlife including the mountain goat.

461. George, Jean Craighead. ONE DAY IN THE ALPINE TUNDRA. Illustrated by Walter Gaffney-Kessell. New York: Crowell; 1984.
Gr. 6-up. A massive rock on the Alpine Tundra slipped and George chronicles the impact of this event on the Tundra.

462. Heady, Eleanor B. HIGH MEADOW: THE ECOLOGY OF A MOUNTAIN MEADOW. Illustrated by Harold F. Heady. New York: Grosset & Dunlap; 1970.
Gr. 4-6. Explains how the plants and animals of a mountain meadow interact with each other and the land and how they are affected by the weather.

463. Hoffman, Edwin. FIGHTING MOUNTAINEERS: THE STRUGGLE FOR JUSTICE IN THE APPALACHIANS. Boston: Houghton Mifflin; 1979.
Gr. 5-8. A history of struggles in the mountains of Appalachia.

464. Jaspersohn, William. HOW THE FOREST GREW. Illustrated by Chuck Eckart. New York: Greenwillow; 1980.
Gr. 2-4. A Massachusetts hardwood forest is examined from its birth through various stages of growth.

465. Jenkins, Marie M. GOATS, SHEEP AND HOW THEY LIVE. Illustrated by Matthew Kalmenoff. New York: Holiday House; 1978.
Gr. 5-up. Discusses goats and sheep including the ibex, chamois, and bighorn.

466. Johnson, Sylvia A. ANIMALS OF THE MOUNTAINS. Illustrated by Alcuin C. Dornisch. Minneapolis: Lerner; 1976.
Gr. 4-up. Describes the behavior and lifestyle of ten mountain animals.

467. Lavine, Sigmund. WONDERS OF THE EAGLE WORLD. New York: Dodd, Mead; 1974.
Gr. 4-up. Describes the life of eagles as well as myths about them and their relationships with humans.

468. Lerner, Carol. FLOWERS OF A WOODLAND SPRING. Illustrated. New York: Morrow; 1979.
Gr. 4-6. Gives life cycle of short blooming wild flowers of the woodlands.

469. Lucas, Joseph, Susan Hayes, and Bernard Stonehouse. FRONTIERS OF LIFE: ANIMALS OF MOUNTANS AND POLES. Illustrated. New York: Doubleday; 1976.
Gr. 6-up. Depicts animals which live in mountainous and polar regions; examines man's effect on the ecology in those regions.

470. McDearmon, Kay. COUGAR. New York: Dodd, Mead; 1977.
Gr. 4-6. Shows lifestyle and growth of cougars through photos and discussion of a mother and her cubs.

471. McDearmon, Kay. ROCKY MOUNTAIN BIGHORNS. Illustrated by Valerius Geust. New York: Dodd, Mead; 1980.
Gr. 4-6. Explains habitat, diet, enemies and mating, fighting and jumping skills of bighorn sheep.

Parnall, Peter. THE MOUNTAIN. Illustrated. New York: Doubleday; 1971.
Gr. 5. See #446.

Pringle, Laurence. WILD FOODS: A BEGINNER'S GUIDE TO IDENTIFYING, HARVESTING AND COOKING SAFE AND TASTY PLANTS FROM THE OUTOOORS. New York: Four Winds; 1978.
Gr. 3-6. See #434.

472. Roberts, Bruce, and Nancy Roberts. WHERE TIME STOOD STILL. New York: Crowell; 1970.
Gr. 5-up. A look at the people and problems of Appalachia, focusing on Madison County, North Carolina.

Regions: The Appalachians

473. Caudill, Rebecca. DID YOU CARRY THE FLAG TODAY, CHARLEY. Illustrated by Nancy Grossman. New York: Holt, Rinehart & Winston; 1966.
Gr. Preschool-3. Charlie wants to carry the flag at his school in the Hollow, but he keeps misunderstanding the rules.

Caudill, Rebecca. MY APPALACHIA. Illustrated by Edward Wallawich. New York: Holt, Rinehart & Winston; 1966.
Gr. 5-up. See #455.

474. Caudill, Rebecca. A POCKETFUL OF CRICKET. Illustrated. New York: Holt, Rinehart & Winston; 1964.
Gr. K-4. A six year old Kentucky boy finds a cricket and brings it with him on his first day of school.

475. Chaffin, Lillie D. WE BE WARM TIL SPRINGTIME COMES. New York: Macmillan; 1980.
Gr. K-3. A poor family works together to find fuel for their winter fire.

476. Chase, Richard, ed. GRANDFATHER TALES. Illustrated by Berkeley Williams, Jr. Boston: Houghton Mifflin; 1948.
Gr. 4-6. 24 humorous tales from Alabama, Kentucky, North Carolina and Virginia.

477. Chase, Richard, ed. THE JACK TALES. Illustrated by Berkeley Williams, Jr. Boston: Houghton Mifflin; 1943.
Gr. 4-6. Eighteen folk tales told in North Carolina dialect.

478. Cleaver, Vera, and Bill Cleaver. TRAIL VALLEY. Philadelphia, PA: Lippincott; 1977.
Gr. 5-8. Sequel to "Where the Lilies Blooms." Mary Call, now 16, tries to take care of the two younger children and an abandoned child and live her own life.

479. Cleaver, Vera, and Bill Cleaver. WHERE THE LILIES BLOOM. New York: Harper & Row; 1969.
Gr. 4-9. When their sharecropper father dies, 14 year old Mary Call Luther takes charge of her siblings and tries to keep the family together.

480. Doolittle, Jerome. THE SOUTHERN APPALACHIANS. Illustrated with photographs. Morristown, NJ: Silver Burdett; 1976.
Gr. 6-up. This book explores the life, geology and geography of this mountain region.

481. Draper, Cena. WORST HOUND AROUND. Philadelphia: Westminster Press; 1979.
Gr. 3-6. Jorie and his dog are joined by Cousin Sally and his three daughters in their mountain cabin.

482. Hamilton, Virginia. M.C. HIGGINS THE GREAT. New York: Macmillan; 1974.
Gr. 6-up. M.C., oldest son of a poor Black family, worries about the family's future on a coal-mined mountain.

Hoffman, Edwin. FIGHTING MOUNTAINEERS: THE STRUGGLE FOR JUSTICE IN THE APPALACHIANS. Boston: Houghton Mifflin; 1979.
Gr. 5-8. See #463.

483. Horwitz, Elinor L. MOUNTAIN PEOPLE, MOUNTAIN CRAFTS. Illustrated by Joshua and Anthony Horwitz. New York: Harper & Row; 1974.
Gr. 5-9. Photographs and folk artists' discussions of traditional Appalachian crafts.

484. Langstaff, John. SWAPPING BOY. Illustrated by Beth and Joe Krush. New York: Harcourt Brace; 1960.
Gr. Preschool-3. Song tells of the boy who keeps on making poorer and poorer trades.

485. Lee, Mildred. THE PEOPLE THEREIN. New York: Houghton Mifflin; 1980.
Gr. 6-up. Love blossoms and grows between a crippled girl and a troubled botanist who has abandoned turn-of-the-century Boston for a life in the southern Appalachians.

486. Miles, Mishka. HOAGIE'S RIFLE-GUN. Illustrated by John Schoenherr. Boston: Little, Brown; 1970.
Gr. 1-4. Hoagie and his brother go hunting, but in their hunger they shoot wild.

487. PORTRAITS AND DREAMS [Filmstrip]. Whitesbury, KY: Appalshop; 1984; 1 filmstrip; 1 cassette and accompanying materials.
Gr. 6-up. "A sensitive portrayal of Appalachia captured by black and white photographs taken by mountain children.".

488. Radlauer, Ruth. SHENANDOAH NATIONAL PARK. Illustrated by Ed and Ruth Radlauer. Chicago: Childrens Press; 1982.

Gr. 3-5. Includes geologic history, flora and fauna, trails and map of this part of the Appalachian Mountains.

489. Roberts, Bruce, and Nancy Roberts. WHERE TIME STOOD STILL. New York: Crowell; 1970.
Gr. 5-up. A look at the people and problems of Appalachia by focusing on Madison County, North Carolina.

490. Roberts, Nancy. APPALACHIAN GHOSTS. Illustrated. New York: Doubleday; 1978.
Gr. 5-7. Twelve tales of ghosts in the Appalachian Mountains.

491. Rylant, Cynthia. MISS MAGGIE. Illustrated by Thomas DiGrazia. New York: Dutton; 1983.
Gr. 1-3. Nat Crawford was afraid of old Miss Maggie until one winter day wben she needed him.

492. Rylant, Cynthia. WHEN I WAS YOUNG IN THE MOUNTAINS. Illustrated by Diane Goode. New York: Dutton; 1982.
Gr. 2-5. A reminiscence of life in the mountains of Kentucky.

493. Showell, Ellen. GHOST OF TILLIE JEAN CASSAWAY. Illustrated by Stephen Gammel. New York: Four Winds; 1978.
Gr. 4-6. Willie and his sister see a ghost girl who roams the Appalachian hills near their house.

494. Shull, Peg. CHILDREN OF APPALACHIA. New York: Messner; 1969.
Gr. 4-6. Tells about three families in Kentucky - one in the hills, one on a farm and one in town.

495. SOME MOUNTAIN TALES ABOUT JACK, [Sound Recording]. Told and sung by Billy Edd Wheeler. New Rochelle, NY: Spoken Arts; 2 cassettes: Vol, 1 and 2.
Gr. 3-6. Based on traditional mountaintales.

496. Still, James. JACK AND THE WONDER BEANS. Illustrated by Margot Tomes. New York: Putnam; 1977.
Gr. 1-4. "Jack and the Beanstalk" is retold with an Appalachian setting using dialect of the region.

497. Still, James. SPORTY CREEK: A NOVEL ABOUT AN APPALACHIAN BOYHOOD. Illustrated by Janet McCaffery. New York: Putnam; 1977.
Gr. 6-8. When work ceases in the Kentucky coal mines during the Depression, a young boy and his family move to the mountains to live off of their land.

498. THREE MOUNTAIN TALES [Filmstrip]. Whitesbury, KY: Appalshop; 1982; 1 filmstrip; 1 cassette.
Gr. 4-up. Three old stories ("Little Fish Story", "Big Toe", and "Fat or Lean") retold in the authentic Appalachian dialect with fiddle, banjo, and/or harmonica accompaniment.

499. Turkle, Brinton. THE FIDDLER OF HIGH LONESOME. Illustrated. New York: Viking; 1968.
Gr. 2-6. A young boy comes to live with his violent relatives but never quite meets their standards of behavior.

500. Wigginton, Eliot, ed. FOXFIRE BOOKS. New York: Doubleday; 1972.
Gr. 4-up. Series of eight books containing interviews with Appalachian folk craftsmen and material on their crafts.

THE CULTURAL CONTEXT

Folklore and Crafts

501. Chase, Richard. OLD SONGS AND SINGING GAMES. New York: Dover; 1972.
Gr. 2-5. Includes 21 songs from all over the United States.

502. D'AULAIRE'S TROLLS [Filmstrip]. New Rochelle, NY: Spoken Arts; 1982; 1 filmstrip; 1 cassette; 1 guide.
Gr. 3-6. A reproduction of the d'Aulaire's legendary mountain denizens.

503. De Paola, Tomie. PRINCE OF THE DOLOMITES: AN OLD ITALIAN TALE. Illustrated. New York: Harcourt Brace; 1980.
Gr. K-3. A retelling of the tale of how the love of Prince Pazzo for Princess Lucia of the moon, changed the black peaks of the Dolomite mountains to glimmering white, blue, pink, and yellow.

504. Fiarotta, Phyllis, and Noel Fiarotta. THE YOU AND ME HERITAGE TREE: CHILDREN'S CRAFTS FROM 21 AMERICAN TRADITIONS. New York: Workman; 1976.
Gr. 1-5. Step-by-step instructions for craft projects drawn from different ethnic traditions.

505. Kinney, Jean Brown. HOW TO MAKE NINETEEN KINDS OF AMERICAN FOLK ART FROM MASKS TO TV COMMERCIALS. New York: Atheneum; 1974.
Gr. 5-up. Examines new and traditional folk arts with directions for how to make them.

506. Kinney, Jean Brown. TWENTY-THREE VARIETIES OF ETHNIC ART AND HOW TO MAKE EACH ONE. Illustrated by Cle Kinney. New York: Atheneum; 1976.
Gr. 4-7. Explains the contributions to American culture of many different ethnic groups and provides instructions for making folk art for each group.

507. McDermott, Gerald. THE STONECUTTER: A JAPANESE FOLK TALE. Illustrated. New York: Viking; 1975.
Gr. K-3. A stonecutter takes pieces of a mountain.

508. MOUNTAIN SONGS AND STORIES FOR CHILDREN. Told and sung by Lee Knight [Sound Recording]. New Rochelle, NY: Spoken Arts; 1974; 1 sound cassette.
Gr. 1-8. Collection of nine folk stories and songs from American mountain regions.

Quackenbush, Robert M. CLEMENTINE. Philadelphia, PA: Lippincott; 1974.
Gr. K-3. See #447.

509. Quackenbush, Robert. SHE'LL BE COMING AROUND THE MOUNTAIN. Illustrated. Philadelphia, PA: Lippincott; 1973.
Gr. K-3. Uses the verses of the old railroad song to tell the story of a wild west train ride. Words and music included.

510. Rounds, Glen. OL' PAUL, THE MIGHTY LOGGER: BEING A TRUE ACCOUNT OF THE SEEMINGLY INCREDIBLE EXPLOITS AND INVENTIONS OF THE GREAT PAUL BUNYAN. Illustrated. New York: Holiday House; 1976.
Gr. 4-6. Ten tales of Paul Bunyan including how he built the Rockies, how the rain fell up one spring and how Paul stopped a river from whistling.

511. Seeger, Ruth. AMERICAN FOLK SONGS FOR CHILDREN. Illustrated by Barbara Cooney. New York: Doubleday; 1948.
Gr. 1-up. 90 folk songs from all parts of the country.

512. THE THREE BOLLY GOATS GRUFF. Illustrated by Paul Galdone. Boston: Houghton Mifflin; 1981.
Gr. Preschool-3. Three clever billy goats outwit a big ugly troll that lives under the bridge they must cross on their way up the mountain.

513. Zemach, Margot. HUSH, LITTLE BABY. Illustrated. New York: Dutton; 1976.
Gr. K-1. A pictorial representation of the folk song.

514. Zemach, Margot. MOMMY BUY ME A CHINA DOLL. Adapted From an Ozark Children's Song. Illustrated. New York: Farrar, Straus & Giroux; 1975.
Gr. Preschool-3. A picture book version of a cumulative song.

Literature

515. Babbitt, Natalie. KNEEKNOCK RISE. New York: Farrar, Straus & Giroux; 1970.
Gr. 3-6. Young Egan Climbs Kneeknock Rise to see the Monstrous Megrimum.

516. Branscum, Robbie. JOHNNY MAY. Illustrated by Charles Robinson. New York: Avon; 1975.
Gr. 5-up. A lonely girl in Arkansas hill country works on the farm and befriends a neighbor boy.

517. Branscum, Robbie. THREE BUCKETS OF DAYLIGHT. Illustrated by Allen Davis. New York: Lothrop; 1978.
Gr. 4-up. Two Arkansas mountain boys try to save themselves from a curse cast by a neighbor who catches them stealing.

518. Branscum, Robbie. TOBY ALONE. New York: Doubleday; 1979.
Gr. 5-up. Having driven Johnny Joe off in her grief at Granny's death, Toby, now 14, resolves to win him back. Sequel to "Toby, Granny, and George."

519. Burch, Robert. IDA EARLY COMES OVER THE MOUNTAIN. New York: Viking; 1980.

Gr. 4-6. Ida Early comes to care for the four Sutton children in the hills of Georgia after their mother dies.

520. Clark, Ann Nolan. SECRET OF THE ANDES. Illustrated by Jean Charlot. New York: Viking; 1952.
Gr. 4-8. A young Peruvian boy trains to be a llama herder and learns about his Inca ancestors.

521. Cleaver, Vera, and Bill Cleaver. THE WHYS AND WHEREFORES OF LITTABELLE LEE. New York: New American Library; 1976.
Gr. 6-up. Sixteen-year-old Littabelle lives alone with her grandparents in a barn and has to manage a great deal on her own.

522. Credle, Ellis. DOWN, DOWN THE MOUNTAIN. Nashville, TN: Thomas Nelson; 1961.
Gr. Preschool-2. Two children in the Blue Ridge Mountains earn money to buy new shoes.

523. Crook, Beverly. FAIR ANNIE OF OLD MULE HOLLOW. New York: McGraw Hill; 1978.
Gr. 6-up. When fair Annie, a sheltered mountain girl, inadvertently strays into forbidden McFarr territory, her life opens up to tragedy and to love.

524. Epstein, Anne Merrick. GOOD STONES. Illustrated by Susan Meddaugh. Boston: Houghton Mifflin; 1977.
Gr. 5-9. An ex-con who lives as a hermit joins with a 12-year-old orphan, and together they make a life for themselves.

525. Fisher, Alieen. I STOOD UPON A MOUNTAIN. Illustrated by Blair Lent. New York: Crowell; 1979.
Gr. K-3. Four stories explain the creation of the world using illustrations of the seasons of the year.

526. Hunter, Mollie. THE HAUNTED MOUNTAIN: A STORY OF SUSPENSE. Illustrated by Laszlo Kubinyi. New York: Harper & Row; 1979.
Gr. 5-8. McCallister and his son must fight the Great Gray Man, the spirit who haunts the mountain above their home.

527. Irving, Washington. RIP VAN WINKLE. With drawings by Arthur Rackham. Philadelphia, PA: Lippincott; 1967.

Gr. 4-6. Rip Van Winkle wakes up from a night's sleep to find that twenty years have passed.

528. Judson, William. COLD RIVER. New York: New American Library; 1976.
Gr. 4-6. Two children battle to survive a terrible snowstorm in the Adirondacks.

529. Lobel, Arnold. MING LO MOVES THE MOUNTAIN. New York: Greenwillow; 1982.
Gr. K-3. Ming Lo and his wife consult a wise man about moving a mountain which blocks their home from the sunlight.

530. MacDonald, George. THE PRINCESS AND THE GOBLIN. Illustrated by Arthur Hughes. New York: Penguin; 1964.
Gr. 3. Princess Irene and Curdie, a miner's boy, have unusual adventures with goblins who live in caverns in the mountain.

531. Rankin, Louise. DAUGHTER OF THE MOUNTAINS. Illustrated by Kurt Wiese. New York: Viking; 1948.
Gr. 4-7. A Tibetan girl travels to Calcutta to claim a dog, guided by the love of Buddha.

532. Spyri, Johanna. HEIDI. Milwaukee, WI: Raintree; 1978.
Gr. 4-6. Heidi lives with her Grandfather and her pet goats high in the Swiss Alps.

533. Ullman, James Ramsey. BANNER IN THE SKY: THE STORY OF A BOY AND A MOUNTAIN. Philadelphia, PA: Lippincott; 1954.
Gr. 6-8. A young boy joins a party of mountaineers attempting to climb the Citadel in the Swiss Alps, the mountain upon which his father lost his life.

534. Van Allsburg, Chris. BEN'S DREAM. Illustrated. Boston: Houghton Mifflin; 1982.
Gr. 3-up. On a terrifically rainy day, Ben has a dream in which he and his house float by the monuments of the world, half submerged in flood water.

Wiseman, David. JEREMY VISICK. Boston: Houghton Mifflin; 1981.
Gr. 5-up. See #451.

535. Yates, Elizabeth. MOUNTAIN BORN. Illustrated by Nora S. Urwin, New York: Coward, McCann & Geoghegan; 1943.
Gr. 4-1. The story of a mountain shepherd boy and his pet lamb.

536. Yates, Elizabeth. MOUNTAIN BORN [Sound Recording]. New York: Miller-Brody; 1977; 1 cassette.
Gr. 4-7. Based on the book of the same title.

Chapter 6

Oceans: Investigations In Depth

Humankind's fascination with the ocean is as old as humanity itself. The very word, ō shun, is onomatopoetic and evokes images of surging waves and endless undulating expanse. Tales of the sea and distant islands, pirates and sunken treasures, wondrous monsters and miraculous voyages abound in the literature and tradition of all cultures. Life came from the ocean and is dependent upon it. Without the millions of gallons of water vapor which evaporate from its surface daily, and return to the earth as rain, our world would be a vast desert. Without the teeming plankton at the bottom of the food chain, life could not exist. Without the steadying influence of the ocean's temperatures, our planet would be subject to extremes of heat and cold which would make life impossible.

The ocean is many things to us. It has for centuries provided us with food and transportation. We have harvested from its depths seafood, oils, livestock feeds, fertilizers, seaweed, pearls, and many other usable products. We have sailed ships upon it to exploit one another in acts of warfare and piracy. We have enjoyed it for boating and swimming. We have recorded it in painting, literature and music. We have dumped our refuse into it. We are now, finally, taking steps to study and understand the marine community upon which we have depended for so long. Although humanity has been using the ocean and exploring its surface since before recorded history, the science of oceanography was not truly initiated until 1872, with the voyage of the CHALLENGER, the first vessel equipped for ocean exploration. Since that historic expedition, this "new" science has expanded dramatically and our information about the sea and its marvels has also expanded dramatically. It is a science which will be increasingly important to future generations as the earth's land resources become more and more depleted.

Here, then, is another broad range of vital topics which lend themselves to exploration and discovery in all areas of the curriculum and across all grade levels. As with all our topics, we will probably begin with a brainstorming session, asking our students to list all the subjects they can think of that are related to the ocean. Younger children, unless they live in a seacoast community, will have limited knowledge of the ocean and will, therefore, be more dependent, initially, on teacher input. This age group might start off by experiencing the ocean vicariously through picture books, filmstrips, sound recordings, filmloops, pictures, study prints, puzzles, and games. Try things like ocean sounds from the CBS SOUND EFFECTS LIBRARY, the sound disc, SONGS OF THE HUMPBACKED WHALE, THE BEACH BEFORE BREAKFAST by Maxine Kumin, TIME OF WONDER by Robert McCloskey, the BFA filmstrip, THE BEACH, from the LISTENING, LOOKING, AND FEELING series, THE

LITTLE ISLAND by Golden MacDonald, ABEL'S ISLAND by William Steig, the filmstrip series LIFE IN THE SEA from National Geographic, ONE-EYED JAKE by Pat Hutchins, TIM TO THE LIGHTHOUSE by Edward Ardizzone. These and many others can evoke in younger students a sense of the vastness, wonder and drama of the ocean and the shore.

Our brainstorming session should result in an extensive list which we can then divide into a number of categories, encouraging our students all the while to contribute their suggestions and ideas. We could end up with a chart similar in organization to the chart in figure 7, or quite a different one. In any case, we will have, in effect, an outline which will provide focus for our explorations.

With kindergarten and first grade students, these explorations might be confined to such topics as the sights and sounds of the beach and ocean, beginning studies of marine animals and plants, recreation in, on, and near the ocean, perhaps a look at ships, and of course, fairy and folk tales of the sea. Picture books, both in print and audiovisual format, plus many fine informational books and kits for this level, provide a wealth of materials for enjoyment and examination. Field trips to zoos, aquariums, oceanariums and to the beach, if possible, will reinforce and expand these concepts. Second and third graders could: begin to explore the interrelationships in the ocean community in order to acquire a beginning understanding of marine ecology; look at the ways in which we have used the ocean to provide food and a means of transporting goods and people; begin to study oceanography to gain an understanding of the importance of this science for the future; begin to examine the geological forces related to the oceans; and, last but not least, explore the lore of sailors and pirates over the centuries. Some students or groups of students may wish to focus on sea animals of particular interest or appeal, such as sharks or whales, while others might focus on the many kinds of ships and their particular uses. Middle grade students could explore any of the above-mentioned topics in more depth and detail or might want to study the science of navigation or shipbuilding. The history of warfare on the oceans offers another field of study, as does an in-depth examination of the food chain or the water cycle.

The longer we work with our chart and extend its branches, the more possibilities there are, and it becomes apparent that we can encompass any area of the curriculum in one or another of these topics. The curriculum areas can be treated as discrete parts of the whole, so that each one, although focusing on oceans, is dealt with separately. A more cohesive approach would dictate that we examine the central concept of "Oceans" in all its variety and diversity, concentrating on the topics involved but taking care to implicitly include learnings in all curriculum areas and to discuss their interrelationships. Such an interdisciplinary approach seems more attuned to the real world as our students must learn to understand and deal with it. A study of plants and animals of the ocean, for example, can lead us to examine: their life cycles and ecology (science); their relationship to us and how and why we must learn to understand and protect as well as harvest them (social studies); the differences between them in form, size, and weight and the varying depths at which they exist (mathematics); their representation in folklore and literature (language arts), the graphic arts (art), the performing arts (music, dance, and drama); and the ways in which our students can represent them in any of these art forms (creative writing, art, music, drama, dance). Thus, we can chart a course which avoids a static, sterile approach to curriculum. We can, instead, allow our students latitude to pursue ideas and concepts in all their dimensions, encouraging them to perceive the relationship between the disciplines and the importance of these relationships.

To examine this approach in more detail, let's concentrate on the oceanography strand of our chart. As with all of our topics, this investigation can move vertically, through all aspects of oceanography, or horizontally to include subjects which are impacted on by oceanography, such as marine biology or the engineering of new vessels and diving apparatus. Moving vertically, then, materials to support our studies include: filmstrips such as the National Academy of Science series OCEANOGRAPHY: UNDERSTANDING OUR DEEP FRONTIER and United Learning's JUNIOR OCEANOGRAPHER, BFA's LISTENING, LOOKING, FEELING; models such as Hubbard's HYDROGRAPHIC RELIEF GLOBE; and study prints like EBE's OCEANOGRAPHY: VIEW FROM SPACE. Numerous books are available at differing levels: Issac Asimov's ABC'S OF THE OCEAN and Thomas Wright's THE UNDERSEA WORLD for younger children; Elizabeth's Clemons' WAVES, TIDES, AND CURRENTS, Robert Boyer's THE STORY OF OCEANOGRAPHY, Gilbert Voss's OCEANOGRAPHY, and Norman Carlisle's RICHES OF THE SEA for older students. If a student or group of students decides to concentrate on a more specific aspect of oceanography, for example underwater exploration, there are resources such as the filmstrip EXPLORING THE SEA from MultiDimensional Corporation's TODAY'S EXPLORER series, Genie Iverson's excellent biography, JACQUES COUSTEAU, James Parks' A DAY AT THE BOTTOM OF THE SEA, the National Geographic close-up of the diver's world, UNDERSEA TREASURES, and Walter Olesky's TREASURES OF THE DEEP. The last two books might lead students horizontally to explore the world of pirates and buccaneers with books such as Peter Briggs' BUCCANEER HARBOR, Howard Pyle's BOOK OF PIRATES, Frank Stockton's BUCCANEERS AND PIRATES OF OUR COAST, and one or more of the many versions of TREASURE ISLAND, including at least one audiovisual version, such as the learning kit from Films Incorporated or the sound recording from Spoken Arts. In addition, Encyclopaedia Britannica has a filmstrip series entitled UNDER THE JOLLY ROGER which relates a number of pirate stories. Another group of students might want to study ships and vessels of all kinds. The Elementary Science Study Kit, CLAY BOATS, helps children understand what kinds and shapes of objects float and provides an introduction to the principles of boat building. Books which expand on this topic include informational books such as TRUE BOOK OF TRAVEL BY WATER, Peter Lippman's BUSY BOATS, Christine Bernard's THE BOOK OF FANTASTIC BOATS, and picture books such as Chris Van Allsburg's THE WRECK OF THE ZEPHYR, and Ann Rockwell's OUT TO SEA. Older students might explore THE VIKING SHIPS by Ian Atkinson, TANKERS, GIANTS OF THE SEA by Charles Coombs, SUBMERGE: THE STORY OF DIVERS AND THEIR CRAFT by Anabel Dean, OARS, SAILS, AND STEAM by Edwin Tunis or TUGBOAT by David Plowden. Thus students will be embarked on their own treasure hunt to see how many different kinds of vessels they can discover.

The following materials for ocean exploration provide only a starting point for the continuing treasure hunt. Using the chart in figure 7 and the subject heading lists in the Appendix as guidelines, you and your students can expand the search in many dimensions of time and space.

OCEANS

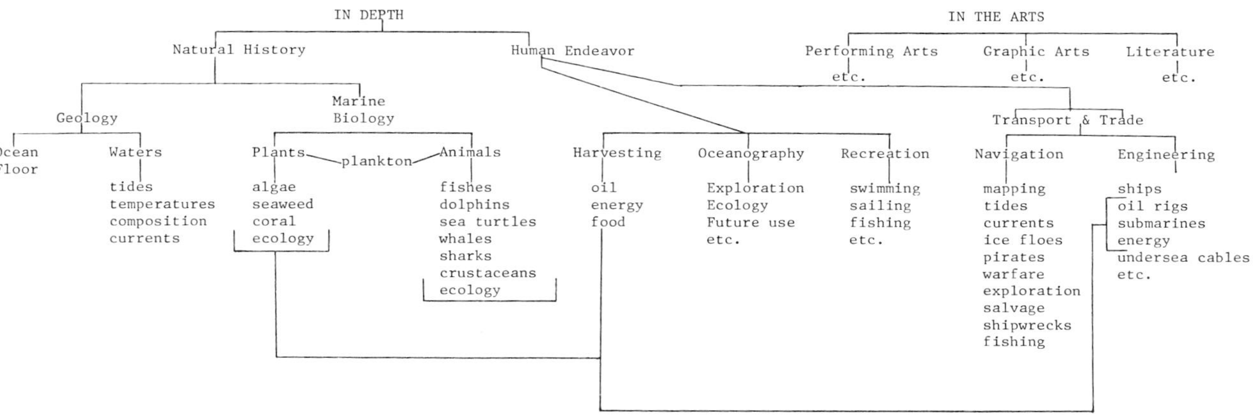
IN DEPTH
IN THE ARTS
Natural History
Human Endeavor
Performing Arts
Graphic Arts
Literature
etc.
etc.
etc.
Geology
Marine Biology
Transport & Trade
Ocean Floor
Waters
tides
temperatures
composition
currents
Plants
plankton
Animals
algae
seaweed
coral
ecology
fishes
dolphins
sea turtles
whales
sharks
crustaceans
ecology
Harvesting
oil
energy
food
Oceanography
Exploration
Ecology
Future use
etc.
Recreation
swimming
sailing
fishing
etc.
Navigation
mapping
tides
currents
ice floes
pirates
warfare
exploration
salvage
shipwrecks
fishing
Engineering
ships
oil rigs
submarines
energy
undersea cables
etc.

OCEANS IN DEPTH

Natural History: Geology and Geography

537. Allen, Hazel. UP FROM THE SEA CAME AN ISLAND. Illustrated by Marilyn Miller. New York: Scribner; 1962.
Gr. 2-6. Describes the long-ago formation of the island which becomes home for Keoki and his people.

538. Alth, Max and Charlotte Alth. DISASTROUS HURRICANES AND TORNADOES. New York: Watts; 1981.
Gr. 6-up. Discusses types of winds, the characteristics of hurricanes and tornadoes, specific devastating storms and safety precautions.

539. Anderson, Madelyn Klein. ICEBERG ALLEY. Illustrated. New York: Messner; 1976.
Gr. 4-6. Discusses the formation, characteristics, and movements of icebergs, their danger to ships, and the work of the ice patrol who cover "Iceberg Alley" in the North Atlantic.

540. Babbitt, Natalie. THE EYES OF THE AMARYLLIS. New York: Farrar, Straus & Giroux; 1977.
Gr. 5-7. Jenny's grandmother still searches the beaches each day for a sign of her husband, drowned in a hurricane years ago.

541. Bell, Neill. BOOK OF WHERE, OR HOW TO BE NATURALLY GEOGRAPHIC. Boston: Little, Brown; 1982.
Gr. 5-7. An introduction to geography with ideas for projects and activities.

542. Blackburn, Joyce. SUKI AND THE MAGIC SAND DOLLAR. Illustrated by Stephanie Clayton. Waco, TX: Word Books; 1969.
Gr. Preschool-3. The summer that Suki visited St. Simons had many firsts in it - first airplane flight, first visit to the ocean, and introductions to many scientific facts about the sea.

543. Bowden, Joan Chase. WHY THE TIDES EBB AND FLOW. Illustrated by Marc Brown. New York: Houghton Mifflin; 1979.

Gr. K-2. In this traditional explanation of the tides an old woman borrows a rock that plugs up the sea.

544. Branley, Franklin. NORTH, SOUTH, EAST AND WEST. Illustrated by Robert Galster. New York: Crowell; 1966.
Gr. Preschool-2. Lessons in directions and the compass for young children.

545. Brindze, Ruth. HURRICANES: MONSTER STORMS FROM THE SEA. New York: Atheneum; 1973.
Gr. 5-7. Discusses famous hurricanes and their impact on history and geography as well as explaing how storms form and are studied.

546. Brindze, Ruth. THE SEA: THE STORY OF THE RICH UNDERWATER WORLD. Illustrated. New York: Harcourt Brace Jovanovich; 1971.
Gr. 5-9. An exploration of the potential resources the sea offers for the future.

547. Buck, Pearl S. THE BIG WAVE. New York: Scholastic; 1948.
Gr. 3-6. A Japanese boy must face life after his village is destroyed by a tidal wave.

548. Carson, Rachel Louise. THE SEA AROUND US. New York: Watts; 1966.
Gr. 4-up. Revised edition, large type, A history of the oceans, including geologic history, natural history and natural resources.

549. Cartwright, Sally. WHAT'S IN A MAP? Illustrated by Dick Gackenbach. New York: Coward, McCann & Geoghegan; 1976.
Gr. K-3. An introduction to maps and mapmaking that discusses a feeling map, a pretend map, and a block map.

550. Devlin, Harry. HARRY DEVLIN'S TALES OF THUNDER AND LIGHTNING. Illustrated. New York: Parents. Magazine Press; 1975.
Gr. 1-4. Fifteen tales from many lands explaining nature's phenomena: thunder, lightning, and rain.

551. Fradin, Dennis B. HURRICANES, DISASTER! Illustrated. Chicago: Children's Press; 1982.
Gr. 4-6. A discussion of the impact of major hurricanes on the United States.

552. Gans, Roma. ICEBERGS. Illustrated by Bobri. New York: Crowell; 1964.
Gr. K-2. A simple explanation of the life of an iceberg.

553. Goetz, Delia. ISLANDS OF THE OCEAN. Illustrated. New York: Morrow; 1964.
Gr. 4-6. Explores the formation of various kinds of islands and how plant and animal life develops on them.

554. Hodges, Margaret. THE WAVE. Illustrated by Blair Lent, New York: Houghton Mifflin; 1964.
Gr. K-3. A tidal wave threatens a small Japanese village until an old man sets fire to his rice fields to warn the others.

555. HYDROGRAPHIC RELIEF GLOBE [Globe], Northbrook, IL: Hubbard Scientific; 1971; 1 relief globe; cradle base; guide.
Gr. 2-6. Ocean surface represented by clear plastic. Major land masses and oceans are identified. Markable surface. Shows earth's surface above and below ocean level.

MAP BASICS [Filmstrip]. Chicago: Michael Hardy Productions distributed by Denoyer-Geppert; 1980; 6 filmstrips; 6 cassettes; 25 duplicating masters; teacher's guide.
Gr. 4-6. See #414.

556. MAP READING, THE WORLD, PARTS I & II. [Transparency]. St. Louis, MO: Milliken; 1967; 12 transparencies, 28 duplicating masters, 1 guide in each part.
Gr. 4-6. Includes transparencies of continents and oceans, ocean currents and drifts.

557. MAPS SHOW THE EARTH [Kit]. Chicago: Nystrom; 1971; 1 kit: 3 filmstrips; 3 cassettes; 12 study prints; 20 flash cards; 1 floor map; 30 workbooks; 1 teacher's guide.
Gr. 1-3. A beginning map skills program which introduces map reading and map symbols.

558. McNulty, Faith. HURRICANE. Illustrated by Gail Owens. New York: Harper & Row; 1983.
Gr. 3-5. A family prepares for and lives through a coastal hurricane.

559. Rumsey, Marian. CAROLINA HURRICANE. Illustrated by Ted Lewin. New York: Scholastic; 1977.
Gr. 3-7. Lost in a crab boat in the middle of a South Carolina salt marsh, twelve-year-old Morgan endures the full brunt of a hurricane.

560. Schultz, Gwen M. ICEBERGS AND THEIR VOYAGES. Illustrated. New York: Morrow; 1975.
Gr. 5-9. Discusses the formation, history, and location of icebergs and the possiblities for their use.

561. Stephens, William M. ISLANDS. Illustrated by Lydia Rozier. New York: Holiday House; 1974.
Gr. 1-3. Describes the island building process and some of the animals and plants that inhabit them.

562. Wade, Harlan. SAND. Illustrated by Dennis Wrigley, Milwaukee, WI: Raintree; 1979.
Gr. Preschool-2. An explanation for young children of the creation of sand.

563. Yolen, Jane H. THE WIZARD ISLANDS. Illustrated by Robert Quackenbush. New York: Crowell; 1973.
Gr. 5-up. Includes tales, true and legendary, of various new and ancient islands throughout the world.

564. Zim, Herbert S. WAVES. Illustated by Rene Martin. New York: Morrow; 1967.
Gr. 3-5. A simple explanation of ocean waves.

Natural History: Marine Biology

565. Arkin, Alan. THE LEMMING CONDITION. Illustrated by Joan Sandin. New York: Harper & Row; 1976.
Gr. 4-up. A young lemming questions his family's headlong rush into the sea.

566. Asimov, Isaac. ABC'S OF THE OCEAN. Illustrated. New York: Walker; 1970.
Gr. 1-6.

Babbitt, Natalie. THE EYES OF THE AMARYLLIS. New York: Farrar, Straus & Giroux; 1977.
Gr. 4-up. See #540.

567. Blumberg, Rhoda. SHARKS. Illustrated. New York: Watts; 1976.

Gr. 4-up. Introduces the physical characteristics, habits, and natural environment of different varieties of sharks.

568. Bogner, Dorothy Childs. WATER PLANTS. Illustrated. New York: Holiday House; 1977.
Gr. 4-6. Describes the characteristics of a variety of water plants, both fresh and salt water.

569. Brady, Irene. ELEPHANTS ON THE BEACH. New York: Scribner; 1979.
Gr. 3-5. Sketches and text record the activities of elephant seals.

570. Brown, Anne Ensign. WONDER SEA HORSES. New York: Dodd, Mead; 1979.
Gr. 3-5. Explains physical appearance, habits and behavior of different species of sea horses and how to keep them as pets.

571. Brown, Joseph E. WONDERS OF SEALS AND SEA LIONS. New York: Dodd, Mead; 1976.
Gr. 4-up. Discusses the characteristics and habits of seals and sea lions.

572. Brown, Margaret Wise. THE LITTLE ISLAND [Filmstrip]. Illustrated by Leonard Weisgard. Weston, CT: Weston Woods; [1971]; 1 filmstrip; 1 cassette; 1 text booklet.
Gr. 1-3. The passing of the seasons is beautifully illustrated in this story of plant and animal life on a small island.

573. BUFFY: THE SEA OTTER [Sound Recording]. Chicago: SVE; 1978; 1 cassette; 10 books.
Gr. K-6. Explores the life, behavior and natural environment of the sea otter. Also available in filmstrip format.

574. Buxton, Ralph. NATURE'S WATER CLOWNS: THE SEA OTTERS. Pictures by Angus M. Babcock. Chicago: Children's Press; 1974.
Gr. 3-6. Describes the life cycle of the smallest mammal that lives in the sea.

575. Carrick, Carol. BLUE LOBSTER. Illustrated by Donald Carrick. New York: Dial Press; 1975.
Gr. 2-4. Lovely watercolors portray the life cycle of the American lobster.

576. Carrick, Carol. OCTOPUS. Illustated by Donald Carrick. New York: Seabury; 1978.
Gr. 2-4. Lovely drawings illustrate a simple explanation of the life of the octopus.

577. Carrick, Carol. SAND TIGER SHARK. Illustrated by Donald Carrick. New York: Seabury; 1977.
Gr. 1-5. Water colors present the underwater world of the sand tiger shark.

578. Carrick, Carol, and Donald Carrick. BEACH BIRD. Illustruated. New York: Dial Press; 1973.
Gr. K-3. Describes a day in the life of a gull, including feeding, territory and other habits.

579. Conklin, Gladys. THE OCTOPUS AND OTHER CEPHALOPODS. New York: Holiday House; 1977.
Gr. 3-6. Explains cephalopods, the mollusks which have mantle, tentacles and the ability to change color, such as octopus, squid, argonaut, cuttlefish and others.

580. Cook, Jan Leslie. MYSTERIOUS UNDERSEA WORLD. Washington, D.C.: National Geographic; 1980.
Gr. 3-6. A general exploration of life under the sea, including plant and animal life, exploration, and sunken treasure.

581. Copps, Dale. SAVAGE SURVIVOR: 300 MILLION YEARS OF THE SHARK.
Chicago: Westwind Press, distributed by Follett; 1976.
Gr. 6-up. Describes the evolution and biology of sharks, the legends about them, and their relationship with humans.

582. COUSTEAU OCEANOGRAPHY SERIES: THE WATER PLANET, SETS I & II [Filmstrip]. Burbank, CA: Walt Disney Educational Media; 1979; 2 sets of 5 filmstrips; 5 cassettes; 1 teacher's guide each.
Gr. 5-Up. More than 1,000 photographs tell the story of the ocean and its creatures.

583. DANGEROUS SEA CREATURES. Morristown, NJ: Silver Burdett; 1977.
Gr. 4-up. Includes selections from literature as well as discussion and photos of sharks, rats, eels, octopi, squids, sea snakes and other "monsters" of the ocean.

584. Davidson, Mickie. NINE TRUE DOLPHIN STORIES. Illustrated by Roger Wilson. New York: Hastings House; 1974.
Gr. 2-6. A collection of stories about the feats of dolphins.

585. ECOLOGY OF A BAY [Filmstrip]. Falls Church, VA: Enjoy Communicating; 1982; 1 filmstrip; 1 cassette; 1 guide.
Gr. 4-8. Explores the Chesapeake Bay - a valley into which many river tributaries flow. Shows effects of pollution. Discusses how a mix of saline and fresh water affects distribution of plants and animals.

586. Engel, Leonard. THE SEA. Morristown, NJ: Silver Burdett; 1977.
Gr. 3-8. Discusses origins, underwater landscape, currents, waves and tides, undersea life and potential uses of the oceans.

587. Ferrell, Nancy Werren. THE FISHING INDUSTRY. New York: Watts; 1984.
Gr. 6-8. An introduction to fishing as an industry, describing how fish are caught, problems of fishermen, and the future of the fishing industry.

588. Fletcher, Alan Mark. FISHES DANGEROUS TO MAN. Illustrated by Jane Teiko Oka and Willi Baum. Reading, MA: Addison-Wesley; 1969.
Gr. 4-7. Brief descriptions of the physical characteristics and habits of various species of fish dangerous to man.

589. Ford, Barbara. THE ISLAND PONIES: AN ENVIRONMENTAL STUDY OF THEIR LIFE ON ASSATEAGUE. Pbotos by Ronald Kelper. New York: Morrow; 1979.
Gr. 4-6. Describes the scientific study being undertaken on the wild ponies of Assateague Island which explores their role in the ecology of the barrier island.

590. Friedman, Judi. THE EELS' STRANGE JOURNEY. New York: Harper & Row; 1976.
Gr. 1-3. Describes the fascinating life cycle of eels and their migratory habits.

591. George, Jean Craighead. SPRING COMES TO THE OCEAN. Illustrated by John Wilson. New York: Crowell; 1966.

Gr. 6-up. Describes the changes that occur in the lives of sea animals as spring grows towards summer.

592. Goldin, Augusta. THE SUNLIT SEA. Illustrated by Paul Galdone. New York: Crowell; 1968.
Gr. 1-3. Describes plant and animal life that inhabits the top 200 feet of the sea where the sun provides some light.

593. Graham, Ada, and Frank Graham. WHALE WATCH. Illustrated by D. Tyler. New York: Delacorte; 1978.
Gr. 5-7. Describes whales and problems of whale conservation.

594. Graham, Ada, and Frank Graham. PUFFIN ISLAND. Photographs by Lew Line. New York: Cowles; 1971.
Gr. 6-10. Twin brothers and their biology teacher study the habits and characteristics of the wildlife found on Machias Seal Island in the Bay of Fundy.

595. Grosvenor, Donna K. THE BLUE WHALE. Illustrated. Washington, D.C.: National Geographic; 1977.
Gr. K-3. Describes the life and habits of the largest whale.

596. Hess, Lilo. A SNAIL'S PACE. New York: Scribner; 1974.
Gr. 2-6. Describes habits and behavior of land and sea snails including information on their shells.

597. Hogner, Dorothy Childs. SEA MAMMALS. Illustrated by Patricia Collins. New York: Crowell; 1979.
Gr. 2-4. An introduction to such sea mammals as whales, dolphins, porpoises, seals, sea lions and walruses.

598. Holling, Holling Clancy. PAGOO. Illustrated by Lucille Holling. New York: Houghton Mifflin; 1957.
Gr. 4-7. Life of a hermit crab and other tidepool creatures portrayed in text and watercolor illustrations.

599. Holling, Holling Clancy. SEABIRD. Illustrated. New York: Houghton Mifflin; 1948.
Gr. 3-6. An ivory gull carved by a boy on a whaling ship in 1832 goes with him and his descendants on many sea voyages.

600. Hurd, Edith Thatcher. THE MOTHER WHALE. Illustrated by Clement Hurd. Boston: Little, Brown; 1973.

Gr. K-3. A whale calf is born and cared for by its mother until it is independent. It then finds its way in the world of adult whales, mates, and fathers another calf.

601. Hurd, Edith Thatcher. STARFISH. Illustrated by Lucienne Bloch. New York: Crowell; 1962.
Gr. K-3. Describes starfish and their habits, using simple prose.

602. Jacobs, Francine. CORAL. Illustrated by D. Tyler. New York: Putnam; 1980.
Gr. 1-4. Describes the life cycle of a coral polyp, the formation of a coral reef, and the function of this structure in the sea.

603. Jacobson, Morris K. WONDERS OF STARFISH. Illustrated. New York: Dodd, Mead; 1977.
Gr. 5-up. Describes the physical characteristics and habits of different species of starfish and discusses their relationship to other sea creatures and human beings.

604. Jaspersohn, William. DAY IN THE LIFE OF A MARINE BIOLOGIST. Boston: Little, Brown; 1982.
Gr. 5-7. Follows the day of a marine biologist at Woods Hole Oceanographic Institute, focusing on activities and education needed for this career.

605. JELLYFISH AND OTHER SEA CREATURES. New York: Oxford Science Films; 1982.
Gr. 4-6. Color photographs with captions form the bulk of this book on jellyfish and others of the medusa group.

606. Lambert, David. SEASHORE. Illustrated by Graham Allen. Phil Weare, and Brian Pearce. New York: Warwick; 1978.
Gr. 5-up. Discusses those plants and animals that have adapted to the rugged life at the edge of the ocean.

607. Laycock, George. THE FLYING SEA OTTERS. Photos. New York: Grosset & Dunlap; 1971.
Gr. 4-6. The story of a sea otter and her pup who are moved to a new location along with many others in order to help ensure the survival of the species.

608. LIFE IN THE SEA [Filmstrip]. Washington, D.C.: National Geographic; 1978; 2 filmstrips; 2 cassettes; 2 guides.
Gr. 1-5. Discusses familar and unusual animals living in the ocean and their adaptations to their habitats.

609. LIFE IN A POND. (Wonders of Learning Kit) [Kit]. Washington, D.C: National Geographic; 1979; 1 cassette; 30 booklets; 6 duplicating masters; 1 teachers guide.
Gr. 3-6. Teaches specific concepts; helps improve reading skills. Discusses living things in different pond zones. Also available in the same format: LIFE IN THE SEA, 1982; LIFE AT THE SEASHORE, 1981; LIFE ON A CORAL REEF, 1982.

610. THE LIFE OF FISHES [Filmstrip]. Burbank, CA: Walt Disney Edcational Media; 1979; 6 filmstrips; 6 cassettes; teacher's guide.
Gr. 5-12. The Cousteaus survey the 400 million year evolution of fishes and discuss how the morphology and behavior of fish have adapted in response to environmental demands.

611. List, Ilka Katherine. GRANDMA'S BEACH SURPRISE. Illustrated by Ruth Sanderson. New York: Putnam; 1975.
Gr. K-3. On the way to her grandmother's birthday party, Jessie learns many things about the beach.

612. Martin, Dick. THE FISH BOOK. Illustrated, New York: Golden Press; 1964.
Gr. K-1. A picture story of fish in which the whale, the starfish, the sea horse, and others are presented with a few introductory words about each.

613. McClung, Robert M. SEA STAR. New York: Morrow; 1975.
Gr. 2-4. A simple explanation of the life of the starfish.

614. McGovern, Ann. SHARK LADY: TRUE ADVENTURES OF EUGENIE CLARK. Illustrated by Ruth Chew. New York: Four Winds; 1978.
Gr. 1-5. A biography of the ichthyologist whose interest in fish began at the age of nine during weekly trips to the Aquarium in New York City.

615. McGovern, Ann. SHARKS. Pictures by Murray Tinkelman. New York: Four Winds; 1976.
Gr. K-3. Easy-to read text and pictures answer basic questions about sharks.

616. McGovern, Ann. THE UNDERWATER WORLD OF THE CORAL REEF. New York: Four Winds; 1976.
Gr. K-3. Color photos and brief text describe the exotic underwater world of the coral reef.

617. McGowen, Tom. ALBUM OF SHARKS. Illustrated by Rod Ruth. Chicago: Rand McNally; 1977.
Gr. 5-7. A general introduction to sharks with specific descriptions of twelve different kinds.

618. McGregor, Craig. THE GREAT BARRIER REEF. Illustrated. New York: Time-Life; 1974.
Gr. 6-up. Photographs, maps and text describe the geography and natural history of the Great Barrier Reef.

619. McIntyre, Joan. MIND IN THE WATERS: A BOOK TO CELEBRATE THE CONSCIOUSNESS OF WHALES AND DOLPHINS. New York: Scribner; 1974.
Gr. 5-9.

620. McNulty, Faith. WHALES: THEIR LIFE IN THE SEA. Illustrated by John Schoenherr. New York: Harper & Row; 1975.
Gr. 5-7. Discusses the life cycle and habits of whales.

621. Morris, Robert A. DOLPHIN. Illustrated by Funai Mamoru. New York: Harper & Row; 1975.
Gr. 1-3. An introduction to the life of dolphins for very young children.

622. Morris, Robert A. SEA HORSE. Illustrated by Arnold Lobel. New York: Harper & Row; 1972.
Gr. K-2. A simple discussion about the strange habits and behavior of the seahorse.

623. Most, Bernard. MY VERY OWN OCTOPUS. New York: Harcourt Brace; 1980.
Gr. K-3. A boy imagines what fun he would have with a pet octopus.

624. Murray, Sonia Bennett. SHELL LIFE AND SHELL COLLECTING. Photographs by Gilbert Murray, Jr. New York: Sterling; 1969.

Gr. 6-up. An introduction to shell collecting and display.

625. Newton, James. THE MARCH OF THE LEMMINGS. New York: Harper & Row; 1976.
Gr. 2-4. A brief look at the strange rodents who periodically march into the sea, with some possible explanations for why they do it.

626. Overbeck, Cynthia. SPLASH, THE DOLPHIN. Illustrated. Minneapolis: Carolrhoda; 1976.
Gr. K-4. Two youngsters visit Marine Land where they learn that dolphins are intelligent and friendly creatures.

627. Parks, James. A DAY AT THE BOTTOM OF THE SEA. Illustrated. New York: Crane Russak; 1977.
Gr. 6-up. Describes a day's work in a research vessel at the bottom of the ocean.

628. Patent, Dorothy Hinshaw. FISH AND HOW THEY REPRODUCE. Drawings by Matthew Kalmenoff. New York: Holiday House; 1976.
Gr. 3-7. Describes the general characteristics of different kinds of fish with emphasis on their various reproductive processes.

629. Paterson, Katherine. JACOB HAVE I LOVED. New York: Crowell; 1980.
Gr. 6-up. Growing up in the Chesapeake Bay area and feeling deprived all her life of schooling, friends, mother, and even her name, Louise finally begins to find her identity.

630. Pluckrose, Henry. WHALES. Illustrated by Norman Weaver. New York: Gloucester; 1979.
Gr. K-8. Offers basic facts and pictures of whales.

631. Pringle, Laurence. WATER PLANTS. Illustrated by Kazue Mizumura. New York: Crowell; 1975.
Gr. 1-4. A simple discussion of plants which live in and around water.

632. Rehder, Harald A. AUDUBON SOCIETY FIELD GUIDE TO NORTH AMERICAN SEASHELLS. Illustrated by James Carmichael, Jr. New York: Knopf; 1981.
Gr. 4-up. Filled with photographs and written descriptions of North American seashells.

633. Riedman, Sarah Regal. SHARKS. Illustrated by Robert McGlynn. New York: Watts; 1977.
Gr. 2-4. Describes the physical characteristics and habits of sharks and their relatives and discusses myths about sharks.

634. Roever, J.M. WHALES IN DANGER. Illustrated. Austin, TX: Steck-Vaughn; 1975.
Gr. 2-5. Describes the life cycle and environmental needs of various species of whale and stresses man's threat to their survival.

635. Ronai, Lili. CORALS. Illustrated by Arabelle Wheatley. New York: Crowell; 1976.
Gr. K-3. A brief introduction to the physical characteristics and life cycle of different varieties of coral.

636. Russell, Solveig Paulson. THE CRUSTY ONES: A FIRST LOOK AT CRUSTACEANS. Drawings by Lawrence Di Fiori. New York: Walck; 1974.
Gr. 2-6. Surveys the class of animals called crustaceans, describing their characteristics, habitats, structure, development and their importance in the food cycle.

637. Scott, Jack Denton. LOGGERHEAD TURTLE: SURVIVOR FROM THE SEA. Illustrated by Ozzie Sweet. New York: Putnam; 1974.
Gr. 4-6. Explains the long life history of turtles and describes their habits and behavior along with scientists' efforts to understand them.

638. Scott, Jack Denton. THAT WONDERFUL PELICAN. Illustrated by Ozzie Sweet. New York: Putnam; 1978.
Gr. 5-up. Describes pelican lifestyle and discusses their endangerment.

639. Scott, Jack Denton, and Ozzie Sweet. THE GULLS OF SMUTTYNOSE. Illustrated. New York: Putnam; 1977.
Gr. 6-8. Describes the lives of gulls that live on large island gull rookerys off the Maine coast.

640. SEA LIFE [Filmstrip]. Washington, D.C.: National Geographic; 1973; 5 filmstrips; 5 cassettes; 5 guides.

Gr. 5-Up. Describes the adaptations of marine life. Contents: The Salt Water World; The Shell Builders; Curiosities of the Sea; Surface Breathers: The Mammals; The Octopus.

641. SEASHELL POSTERS [Study Prints]. Photography by James H. Carmichael. Palo Alto, CA: Creative Publications; 1984; 12 posters.
Gr. 1-up. Striking photographs and brief descriptions of eleven exquisitely beautiful homes of mollusks. Introductory poster describes the way in which shells are formed and the different types of shells.

642. Selsam, Millicent. A FIRST LOOK AT ANIMALS WITHOUT BACKBONES. New York: Walker; 1976.
Gr. 1-4. An overview of the invertebrates which shows how to distinguish between the major groups.

643. Selsam, Millicent. A FIRST LOOK AT SHARKS. Illustrated by Harriett Springer. New York: Walker; 1979.
Gr. K-3. Introduces the physical characteristics, habits, and natural environment of sharks.

644. Shaw, Evelyn. ELEPHANT SEAL ISLAND. Illustrated by Cherryl Pape. New York: Harper & Row; 1978.
Gr. 1-3.

645. Shaw, Evelyn. SEA OTTERS. Illustrated Cherryl Pape, New York: Harper & Row; 1980.
Gr. K-3. An introduction to sea otters through a glimpse at a mother otter and her pup.

646. SHELLS AND MARINE LIFE [Realia]. Fort Collins, CO: Earth Science Materials; 1975; 15 shell samples; container; guide.
Gr. 3-up. Shell samples and a study guide provide an introduction to the study of mollusks.

647. Shepherd, Elizabeth. TRACKS BETWEEN THE TIDES: BEING THE STORIES OF SOME SEA WORMS AND OTHER BURROWING ANIMALS. Illustrated by Arabelle Wheatley. New York: Lothrop; 1972.
Gr. 3-7. Describes the characteristics of such seashore-dwellers as razor clams, blood worms, sea nymphs, mud snails and sea cucumbers.

648. Silverstein, Alvin, and Virginia Silverstein. A STAR IN THE SEA. Illustrated by Symeon Shimin. New York: Warne; 1969.

Gr. 1-5. Describes the physical characteristics and life cycle of the starfish.

649. Simon, Hilda. SNAILS OF LAND AND SEA. Illustrated. New York: Vanguard; 1977.
Gr. 5-8. Explains the evolution and growth of freshwater and marine snails including vegetarians and carnivores. Also includes a chapter on sea slugs, sea hares and bubbles.

650. SNOOPY'S FACTS AND FUN BOOK ABOUT SEASHORES: BASED ON THE CHARLES M. SCHULZ CHARACTERS. New York: Random House; 1980.
Gr. Preschool-1. Snoopy and his friends explore the many different things one can observe and do at the seashore.

651. Stephens, William M. COME WITH ME TO THE EDGE OF THE SEA. Illustrated. New York: Messner; 1972.
Gr. 3-6. Discusses the plants, animals, waves, tides, sand, and shells to be found at the seashore.

652. Stix, Hugh, Marguerite Stix, and Tucker Abbott. THE SHELL. New York: Abrams; 1978.
Gr. 6-up. A magnificently photographed, aesthetically pleasing book with accompanying text which reveals an array of shells in all their beauty.

653. STORY OF THE SEA. Chicago: World Book-Childcraft International; 1979.
Gr. 1-4. An introduction to oceanography and marine biology for young children. An annual supplement to Childcraft.

654. Todd, Frank B. THE SEA WORLD BOOK OF PENGUINS. Illustrated. New York: Sea World Press, distributed by Harcourt Brace; 1981.
Gr. 3-6. Describes several species of penguins, including habits and behavior and chapter on zoos' work with them.

655. Vevers, Gwynne. OCTOPUS, CUTTLEFISH AND SQUID. Illustrated by Joyce Bee. New York: McGraw-Hill; 1978.
Gr. 4-6. Basic information on these three types of mollusks.

656. Victor, Joan Berg. SHELLS ARE SKELETONS. Illustrated. New York: Crowell; 1977.
Gr. K-3. A beginner's book about various kinds of shells with large colored illustrations.

657. THE WATER CYCLE: A LOOK AT THE SOURCE OF ALL WATER [Kit]. Boulder, CO: Biological Sciences Curriculum Study. Distributed by Hubbard; 1976; 1 model; 10 study cards; 1 poster; 1 teacher's guide.
Gr. 3-7. Uses three modes of presentation to illustrate the movement of water molecules from bodies of water, from the land, and from living things on the land into the air and back again .

658. Waters, John. HUNGRY SHARKS. Illustrated by Ann Dalton. New York: Crowell; 1973.
Gr. 1-3. Explains what sharks eat and how they find it.

659. Waters, John F. JELLYFISH IS NOT A FISH. Illustrated by Kazue Mizumura. New York: Crowell; 1979.
Gr. 2-4. An easy-to-read introduction to the habits, lives and varieties of jellyfish.

660. Waters, John F. THE MYSTERIOUS EEL. Illustrated by Peter Zallinger. New York: Hastings House; 1973.
Gr. 4-6. Discusses anatomy, migration and habits of eels and eel-like creatures as well as their economic importance.

661. WHALES [Filmstrip]. Washington, D.C.: National Geographic; 1979; 1 filmstrip; 1 cassette; teacher's guide.
Gr. K-4. An introduction to the behavior of whales and their adaptations to the marine environment. The diversity of whales, and their classification into two main groups: toothed and baleen. The study and protection of whales.

662. White, William. EDGE OF THE OCEAN. Illustrated with photographs. New York: Sterling; 1977.
Gr. 6-up. Explains the interrelationships and contributions of life forms at the edge of the ocean.

663. Wolcott, Patty. TUNAFISH SANDWICHES. Illustrated by Hans Zanders Reading, MA: Addison-Wesley; 1975.
Gr. Preschool-1. Introduces the concept of a food chain, from the tiny photo plankton in the sea to the tunafish we eat in sandwiches.

664. Young, Jim. WHEN THE WHALE CAME TO MY TOWN. Illustrated with photographs. New York: Knopf, distributed by Random House; 1974.
Gr. 3-up. The true story of a whale washed ashore on Cape Cod, as experienced by a little boy.

665. Zim, Herbert S. SEASHORES: A GUIDE TO ANIMALS AND PLANTS ALONG THE BEACHES. Illustrated by Dorothea and Sy Barlowe. New York: Golden Press; 1955.
Gr. 5-up. An aid to classifying marine animals and plants. Also contains information on evolution, adaptation and biological variation.

666. Zim, Herbert S., and Lucretia Krantz. SEA STARS AND THEIR KIN. Illustrated by Rene Martin. New York: Morrow; 1976.
Gr. 3-6. Discusses star fish, sea lilies, sea urchins, sea cucumbers and brittle stars, all echinoderms.

Human Endeavor: Harvest

667. Carlisle, Norman. RICHES OF THE SEA: THE NEW SCIENCE OF OCEANOLOGY. New York: Sterling; 1970.
Gr. 6-up. Describes the scientific methods and instruments used to explore and harvest the wealth of the oceans.

668. Dixon, Sarah, and Peter Dixon. CHILDREN, FAMILIES, AND THE SEA [Kit]. Photography by John Running and others. Columbus, OH: Carl E. Calgani; 1985; 5 multimedia kits: Each with 5 filmstrips; 5 filmstrip cassettes; 25 books (5 each of 5 titles); 5 book read-along cassettes; 30 worksheets; 5 teacher's guides.
Gr. 4-8. Describes the relationship of children to their families and their culture and each family's dependence on the sea.

669. ELLIE SELLS FISH, In: WOMEN AT WORK, SET 2 [Kit]. Chicago: Coronet; 1978; 1 of a kit: 4 sound cassettes; 24 booklets (6 each title); 8 worksheets; 1 teacher's guide.
Reading Level 3. A read-a-long cassette program to encourage students to read non-fiction. Describes the process of getting fish from lakes and oceans to the market and to the table.

Ferrell, Nancy Werren. THE FISHING INDUSTRY. New York: Watts; 1982.
Gr. 6-8. See #587.

670. Floethe, Louise. FISHING AROUND THE WORLD. Illustrated by Richard Floethe. New York: Scribner; 1972.
Gr. 2-5. Describes various methods of fishing as they are performed in various countries.

671. Goffstein, M. B. FISH FOR SUPPER. Illustrated. New York: Dial Press; 1976.
Gr. K-2. Grandmother gets up early every morning so she can fish all day for supper.

672. Hazelton, Elizabeth Baldwin. THE DAY THE FISH WENT WILD. Illustrated by Joe Servello. New York: Scribner; 1969.
Gr. 1-5. Two boys stowaway on a fishing cruiser and are discovered just in time to witness a bizarre happening among the fish in the Sea of Cortez.

673. Kipling, Rudyard. CAPTAINS COURAGEOUS. New York: New American Library; 1981.
Gr. 6-up. A pampered youth is transformed into a rugged and courageous sailor by his experiences aboard a fishing vessel.

674. Matteson, George. DRAGGERMEN: FISHING ON GEORGES BANK. New York: Four Winds; 1979.
Gr. 5-up. A portrait of commercial fishing. Describes the life of the fisherman and the lure of the sea.

675. McClung, Robert M. HUNTED MAMMALS OF THE SEA. Illustrated by William Downey. New York: Morrow; 1978.
Gr. 6-up. A description of the 8 sea-mammals which are endangered due to the exploitation of humans. Outlines the steps to be taken if they are to survive.

676. McMillan, Bruce. FINEST KIND OF DAY: LOBSTERING IN MAINE. New York: Lippincott; 1977.
Gr. 4-6. Black and white photos and text explain lobstermen's work through an account of a boy's day aboard a lobster boat.

677. Ross, Frank Xavier. JOBS IN MARINE SCIENCE: COMMERCIAL FISHING, MARINE CONSTRUCTION, AND SALVAGE. New York: Lothrop; 1974.
Gr. 5-up. Introduces career possibilities in the field of marine science.

Human Endeavor: Oceanography

678. Asimov, Isaac. HOW DID WE FIND OUT ABOUT LIFE IN THE DEEP SEA? Illustrated by David Wool. New York: Walker; 1982.
Gr. 5-8. Discusses the ocean surface and its floor, including undersea exploration techniques and undersea life.

679. Berger, Melvin. OCEANOGRAPHY LAB. New York: John Day; 1973.
Gr. 4-6. Describes the activities of scientists at Woods Hole Oceanographic Institution.

680. Blumberg, Rhoda. FIRST TRAVEL GUIDE TO THE BOTTOM OF THE SEA. Illustrated by Gen Shimada. New York: Lothrop, Lee & Shepard; 1983.
Gr. 4-6. A travelogue guide to all the sights one might see under the Atlantic Ocean.

681. Boyer, Robert E. THE STORY OF OCEANOGRAPHY. New York: Harvey House; 1975.
Gr. 5-7. Discusses the harvesting of the ocean and undersea mining.

Brindze, Ruth. THE SEA: THE STORY OF THE RICH UNDERWATER WORLD. Illustrated. New York: Harcourt Brace Jovanovich; 1971.
Gr. 5-9. See #546.

682. Davies, Eryl. OCEAN FRONTIERS. New York: Viking; 1980.
Gr. 5-6. Describes various types of equipment and ships used for undersea exploration.

683. Dean, Anabel. SUBMERCE! THE STORY OF DIVERS AND THEIR CRAFTS. Illustrated. Philadelphia: Westminster Press; 1976.
Gr. 6-9. Traces the history of the various crafts and shelters used by divers.

684. EXPLORING UNDER THE SEA: TODAY'S EXPLORERS [Filmstrip]. Chester, NY: Multi Dimensional Communications; 1977; 6 filmstrips; 6 cassettes; teacher's guide.

Gr. 4-6. A bilingual (Spanish/English) discussion of undersea exploration and possibilities for the future.

685. Heyerdahl, Thor. KON-TIKI: A SPECIAL RAND MCNALLY COLOR EDITION FOR YOUNG PEOPLE. Chicago: Rand McNally; 1960.
Gr. 4-up. An edition for young people of Heyerdahl's expedition across the Pacific on a raft.

686. INTRODUCING OCEANOGRAPHY [Filmstrip]. Chicago: SVE; 1983; 6 filmstrips; 6 cassettes; 36 skill sheets; guide.
Gr. 4-8. An exploration of the geography, physics, chemistry, meteorology, and biology of oceans.

687. Iverson, Genie. JACQUES COUSTEAU. Illustrated by Hal Ashmead. New York: Putnam; 1976.
Gr. K-4. A biography of the famous undersea explorer for young readers.

688. JUNIOR OCEANOGRAPHER [Filmstrip]. Niles, IL: United Learning; 1973; 4 filmstrips; 4 cassettes; 1 guide.
Gr. 4-6. Peter spends the day with his friend Sam, an oceanographer, and learns many things about the sea, its inhabitants, its currents and tides and man's relationships to it.

689. THE LAST FRONTIERS (The Encyclopedia of Discovery and Exploration). Illustrated. New York: Doubleday; 1971.
Gr. 6-up. Describes humanity's continuing efforts to explore the earth's frontier, including the polar regions, the highest mountains and the depths of the oceans.

690. Linder, Elisha, and Avner Raban. INTRODUCING UNDERWATER ARCHEOLOGY. Retold by Richard L. Currier. Minneapolis, MN: Lerner; 1976.
Gr. 4-8. Describes tools and techniques used in underwater archeology and some major discoveries found around the world.

691. McClung, Robert M. TREASURES IN THE SEA. Washington, D.C.: National Geographic; 1972.
Gr. 2-6. Describes undersea treasures including shipwrecks, treasure and underwater life.

692. Pick, Christopher C. UNDERSEA MACHINES. Milwaukee, WI: Raintree; 1979.
Gr. 3-5. Describes machines and ships used for various kinds of undersea study and exploration.

693. Russell, Solveig P. WHAT'S UNDER THE SEA? Illustrated by Nancy Gugelman Johnstone. Nashville, TN: Abingdon; 1982.
Gr. 3-5. A discussion of exploration, mapping and life on the ocean floor.

694. Rutland, Jonathan. THE SEA. (Silver Burdett Color Library), Morristown, NJ: Silver Burdett; 1984.
Gr. 5-7. Describes ocean formation and exploration, including recently developed research vehicles.

695. THE SCIENCE OF OCEANOGRAPHY [Filmstrip]. Washington, D.C.: National Geographic; 1981; 1 filmstrip; 1 cassette; 1 guide.
Gr. 5-12. Discusses oceanographic research in the open sea and near the shoreline.

696. UNDERSEA EXPLORATION [Filmstrip]. Burbank, CA: Walt Disney Educational Media; 1979; 4 filmstrips; 4 cassettes; teacher's guide.
Gr. 5-12. The Cousteaus explore 2,000 years of diving history to show how ancient people extracted treasures from the sea; how 19th century inventions contributed to modern man's ability to move with the freedom of fish underwater; how ocean scientists live in underwater communities to study man's capacity for survival there.

697. Updegraff, Imelda, and Robert Updegraff. SEAS AND OCEANS. New York: Puffin; 1982.
Gr. 2-4. Introduction to the subject using the half flap page device to demonstrate aspects such as erosion in a 'before and after' effect.

698. Voss, Gilbert L. OCEANOGRAPHY. Illustrated by Sy Barlowe. New York: Golden Press; 1972.
Gr. 5-up. A study of the marine environment surveying the evolution of the seas as well as their geological, chemical, physical, meteorlogical, and biological interactions.

699. Weiss, Malcom E. ONE SEA ONE LAW: THE FIGHT FOR A LAW OF THE SEA. New York: Harcourt Brace; 1982.

Gr. 6-up. Describes the need for international maritime law to insure that food and energy resources are not misused.

700. Westman, Paul. JACQUES COUSTEAU, FREE FLIGHT UNDERSEA. Illustrated by Reg Sandland. Minneapolis: Dillon; 1980.
Gr. 2-5. A biography of the French oceanographer using simple vocabulary.

701. Wright, Thomas. THE UNDERSEA WORLD. Illustrated. Morristown, NJ: Silver Burdett; 1979.
Gr. 3-5. Discusses various means and reasons for undersea exploration, including economic, military, and recreational use of the seas and warns against the dangers of over-exploitation.

Human Endeavor: Recreation

702. Burningham, John. COME AWAY FROM THE WATER, SHIRLEY. New York: Harper & Row; 1977.
Gr. 1-2. Shirley's adventures at the beach are interspersed with parental warnings.

703. Burton, Jane. AQUARIUM FISHES. New York: Crescent Books; 1978.
Gr. 5-up. Photographs of tropical fish and a guide to fish behavior which can be observed in the home aquarium.

704. Byars, Betsy Cromer. THE ANIMAL, THE VEGETABLE AND JOHN D. JONES. Illustrated by Ruth Sanderson. New York: Delacorte; 1982.
Gr. 5-8. Two sisters look upon a beach vacation with their father, his woman friend and her two sons, as two weeks in the wrong place with the wrong people.

705. Campbell, Gail. SALT-WATER TROPICAL FISH IN YOUR HOME. New York: Sterling; 1976.
Gr. 5-8. An introduction to the salt water aquarium and its inhabitants, discussing equipment, marine diseases, and fish compatability.

706. Goodall, John S. AN EDWARDIAN HOLIDAY. New York: Atheneum; 1979.
Gr. 3-up. Illustrations without a text depict a seashore vacation in England just before World War I.

707. Iwasaki, Chihiro. WHAT'S FUN WITHOUT A FRIEND. New York: McGraw Hill; 1975.
Gr. 1-3. Allison yearns to share her experiences at the seashore with her dog.

708. Jones, Claire. SAILBOAT RACING. Minneapolis: Lerner; 1981.
Gr. 5-7. Describes various sailboats used in racing, with color photographs.

709. Klein, H. Arthur. SURF-RIDING. Illustrated by Donald H. James. New York: Lippincott; 1972.
Gr. 2-5. A history and pictorial survey of surfing around the world.

710. PLAYING IT SAFE - IN THE WATER [Filmstrip]. Wilton, CT: Current Affairs; 1977; 2 filmstrips; 2 sound cassettes; 1 discussion guide.
Gr. 3-6. Provides guidance, backed with graphic examples, of how to play safely in, over, and under the water.

711. Radlauer, E. ON THE WATER. Illustrated with photographs. New York: Watts; 1973.
Gr. 4-7. Briefly describes such diversified water sports as surfing, drag boat racing, diving, and rafting.

712. Rockwell, Anne and Harlow Rockwell. OUT TO SEA. Illustrated. New York: Macmillan; 1980.
Gr. 1-4. A brother and sister are inadvertently swept out to sea while playing in an old row boat they have found on the beach.

713. Ryder, Joanne. A WET AND SANDY DAY. Illustrated by Donald Carrick. New York: Harper & Row; 1977.
Gr. 1-2. Tells about a "get-your-feet-wet" day on the beach.

Sarnoff, Jane, and Reynold Ruffins. A GREAT AQUARIUM BOOK. New York: Scribner; 1977.
Gr. 1-up. See #178.

714. Simon, Seymour. TROPICAL SALTWATER AQUARIUMS: HOW TO SET THEM UP AND KEEP THEM GOING. Illustrated by Karl Stuecklen. New York: Viking; 1976.
Gr. 4-7. Explains how to capture the world of the coral reef in an aquarium.

715. Tobias, Tobi. AT THE BEACH. Pictures by Gloria Singer. New York: McKay; 1978.
Gr. Preschool-4. A little girl describes a happy day at her family's beach house.

716. Waters, Barbara, and John Waters. SALT-WATER AQUARIUMS. Ilustrated by Robert Candy. New York: Holiday House; 1967.
Gr. 5-up. Outlines the necessary steps for setting up a salt-water aquarium and discusses ways of acquiring and caring for its inhabitants.

717. Wegen, Ronald. SAND CASTLE. Illustrated. New York: Greenwillow; 1977.
Gr. K-3. The sea creatures build a sand castle.

Human Endeavor: Trade and Transport: Navigation

718. Almgren, Bertil, et. al. THE VIKING. Illustrated. New York: Crescent; 1975.
Gr. 6-up. Describes the lives, homes and ships of the Vikings.

Anderson, Madelyn Klein. ICEBERG ALLEY. New York: Messner; 1976.
Gr. 4-6. See #539.

719. Ardizzone, Edward. LITTLE TIM AND THE BRAVE SEA CAPTAIN [Filmstrip]. Weston, CT: Weston Woods; 1975; 1 filmstrip; 1 cassette; 1 book.
Gr. Preschool-3. There's adventure on the high seas for Little Tim when he stows away on a steamer.

720. Bailey, Maurice. STAYING ALIVE: 117 DAYS ADRIFT. Drawings by Peter Milne. Maps by Alan Irving. New York: McKay; 1974.
Gr. 6-up. The incredible saga of a courageous couple who outwitted death at sea for a longer period than any humans before.

721. Botting, Douglas. THE PIRATES. Illustrated. New York: Time-Life; 1978.
Gr. 6-up. Chapters and essays describe the lives of some of the better known pirates.

722. Brown, Walter R., and Norman D. Anderson. SEA DISASTERS. Reading, MA: Addison-Wesley; 1981.
Gr. 4-6. Describes eight of the best-known sea disasters of the past two centuries.

723. Clifford, Eth. THE CURSE OF THE MOONRAKER. Boston: Houghton Mifflin; 1977.
Gr. 5-9. The survivors of a strange shipwreck in the Auckland Islands fight for survival under seemingly hopeless conditions.

724. Cumberlege, Vera G. SHIPWRECK. Illustrated by Charles Mikolaycak. Chicago: Follett; 1974.
Gr. 1-3. Anxious for the day when he can row out with the lifeboat crew, Jim is unhappy that the old boat is to be replaced with a powered one until he witnesses a shipwreck during a storm.

725. Day, Arthur Grove. THEY PEOPLED THE PACIFIC. Illustrated by George Wilson. New York: Duell, Sloan, and Pearce; 1964.
Gr. 5-9. How man conquered the largest ocean.

726. Donovan, Frank Robert. THE VIKINGS. New York: American Heritage, distributed by Harper & Row.
Gr. 6-up. A history of the Vikings and their travels.

727. Edey, Maitland Armstrong. THE SEA TRADERS. Illustrated. New York: Time-Life; 1974.
Gr. 6-up. The lives, ships and times of men who sailed the seas for commerce and trade.

728. EXPLORATION AND COLONIZATION [Transparency]. St. Louis: Milliken; 1967; 12 transparencies; 28 duplicating pages; teacher's guide/answer sheet.
Gr. 2-8. Outlines the early explorations of North America, including the Vikings, Balboa, Cortez and Columbus.

729. Ford, Barbara. UNDERWATER DIG. New York: Morrow; 1982.
Gr. 5-9. Story of the "Defense," a revolutionary war privateer, its mission and sinking and recent efforts to excavate it.

730. Freeman, Don. THE CHALK BOX STORY. Philadelphia: Lippincott; 1976.
Gr. Preschool-2. Pieces of colored chalk draw a story about a boy stranded on an island and the turtle who rescues him.

731. Fritz, Jean. BRENDAN THE NAVIGATOR: A HISTORY MYSTERY ABOUT THE DISCOVERY OF AMERICA. Illustrated by Enrico Arno. New York: Coward, McCann & Geoghegan; 1979.

Gr. 2-5. Tells of the Irish legend that St. Brendan discovered America well before the Vikings.

732. Graham, Robin Lee. THE BOY WHO SAILED AROUND THE WORLD ALONE. Illustrated. New York: Golden Press; 1973.
Gr. 6.up. The story of a young man's 5 year sailing trip around the world.

733. Gramatky, Hardie. LITTLE TOOT [Filmstrip]. Weston, CT: Weston Woods; [1971]; 1 filmstrip; 1 cassette; 1 booklet.
Gr. K-3. Based on book of same title.

734. GREAT EXPLORERS [Filmstrip]. Washington, D.C.: National Geographic; 1978; 4 filmstrips; 4 cassettes; 4 guides.
Gr. 5-12. Describes the voyages of these famous explorers through uncharted water to find new lands.
Contents: Columbus; Magellan; Drake; Cook.

735. Hall, Daniel Weston. ARCTIC ROVINGS OR THE ADVENTURES OF A NEW BEDFORD BOY ON SEA AND LAND. Edited by Jerome Beatty, Jr. Illustrated by William Hogarth. New York: William R. Scott; 1968.
Gr. 6-up. The story of a young boy's 4 year odyssey aboard whaling vessels and in Siberia.

736. Howarth, David Armine. THE MEN-OF-WAR. (The Seafarers) Illustrated. New York: Time-Life; 1978.
Gr. 6-up. In the form of chapters and essays, the men and their war ships are surveyed.

737. Humble, Richard. THE EXPLORERS. Illustrated. New York: Time-Life Books; 1978.
Gr. 6-up. Describes explorers and explorations through the centuries.

738. Hutchins, Pat. ONE-EYED JAKE. Illustrated. New York: Greenwillow; 1979.
Gr. Preschool-2. One-eyed Jake robs one ship too many and meets a deserving end.

739. Irwin, Constance. STRANGE FOOTPRINTS ON THE LAND: VIKINGS IN AMERICA. New York: Harper & Row; 1980.
Gr. 5-7. Speculates on evidence that the Vikings landed and settled in North America but leaves readers to reach their own conclusions.

740. Jacobs, Francine. THE RED SEA. Illustrated by Elsie Wrigley. New York: Morrow; 1978.
Gr. 4-6. A history of the political, economic and ecological impacts of the Red Sea on the lands around it.

741. Kellogg, Steven. THE ISLAND OF THE SKOG. New York: Dial Press; 1973.
Gr. Preschool-3. To escape the dangers of urban life, Jenny and her friends sail away to an island only to be faced with a new problem - The Skog.

742. Kellogg, Steven. THE ISLAND OF THE SKOG [Filmstrip]. Weston, CT: Weston Woods; 1976; 1 filmstrip; 1 cassette; 1 booklet.
Gr. Preschool-3. Based on the book of the same title.

743. Laing, Alexander Kinnan. THE AMERICAN HERITAGE HISTORY OF SEAFARING AMERICA. Illustrated. New York: American Heritage, distributed by McGraw-Hill; 1974.
Gr. 6-up. Tells of the growth of American shipping from the wooden ships of colonial days to diesel power.

744. Latham, Jean Lee. CARRY ON, MR. BOWDITCH. Illustrated by John O'Hara. New York: Houghton Mifflin; 1955.
Gr. 5-7. Biography of one of the greatest navigational geniuses in U.S. history. Also available from Random House with recording.

745. Lederer, Chloe. DOWN THE HILL OF THE SEA. Illustrated by Ati Forberg. New York: Lothrop; 1971.
Gr. 4-6. The peaceful tribe of a South Seas island is forced to abandon its ancestral home because an unknown chief in a big land across the sea plans to use the island to test a powerful new weapon.

746. Lyttle, Richard B. WAVES ACROSS THE PAST: ADVENTURES IN UNDERWATER ARCHEOLOGY. Illustrated. New York: Atheneum; 1981.
Gr. 5-8. Discusses underwater exploration in various locations around the world.

747. Manschot, William. THE GULF OF MEXICO [Filmstrip]. Edited by Ruth Young. New Orleans: Gateway; 1977; 6 filmstrips; 3 cassettes; teacher guide.
Gr. 5-10. Concentrates on cultural history and analysis of the coast rather than the body of water.

Contents: The Natural Setting; The Living Coast; Coastal Cities; Life on the Land; Life on the Water; The Historic Coast.

748. Marrin, Albert. THE SEA ROVERS: PIRATES, PRIVATEERS, AND BUCCANEERS. New York: Atheneum; 1984.
Gr. 6-8. Discusses Drake, Morgan, Blackbeard, and other pirates and privateers, both men and women, who have roamed the sea since 1500.

749. Monjo, F.N. PRISONERS OF THE SCRAMBLING DRAGON. Illustrated by Arthur Geisert. New York: Holt, Rinehart & Winston; 1980.
Gr. 3-6. Sam experiences the 19th century China trade firsthand when he sails on his uncle's Yankee Clipper to Canton.

750. NEPTUNE'S GOLD [Filmstrip]. Chicago: Encyclopaedia Britannica Educational Corp.; 1982-83; 4 filmstrips; 4 cassettes; 1 guide.
Gr. 4-up. Stories of sunken treasure and adventure. Also available in a captioned version without cassette.

751. OLD IRONSIDES [Microcomputer Program]. Middletown, CT: Optimum Resources, distributed by Xerox; 1983; 1 disk (Apple II).
Gr. 5-up. A simulation featuring masted sailing ships of the 19th century combating their opponents, the fog and the winds.

752. Olesky, Walter. TREASURES OF THE DEEP. New York: Messner; 1984.
Gr. 5-8. Discusses an array of famous quests for underwater treasures.

753. PACIFIC VOYAGES. (The Encyclopedia of Discovery and Exploration). Illustrated. New York: Doubleday; 1973.
Gr. 6-up. The story of the East Indies and the Pacific and of the first European voyages to China and Japan.

754. Pascall, Jeremy. PIRATES AND PRIVATEERS. Morristown, NJ: Silver Burdett; 1981.
Gr. 5-7. Text and many illustrations tell the stories of the most famous pirates.

755. Quin-Harkin, Janet. PETER PENNY'S DANCE. Illustrated by Anita Lobel. New York: Dial Press; 1976.
Gr. Preschool-3. Sailor Peter Penny dances his way around the ship and around the world.

756. Quin-Harkin, Janet. PETER PENNY'S DANCE [Filmstrip]. Illustrated by Anita Lobel. Weston, CT: Weston Woods; 1978; 1 filmstrip; 1 cassette,
Gr. Preschool-3. Based on the book of the same title.

757. Sayers, Ken W., and Norman Polmar. ANCHORS AND ATOMS: THE UNITED STATES NAVY TODAY. Illustrated. New York: McKay; 1974.
Gr. 5-up. The story of the United States Navy, its ships and its people.

758. Schoder, Judith. BROTHERHOOD OF PIRATES. Illustrated by Paul Frame. New York: Messner; 1979.
Gr. 3-6. Describes a crew of infamous pirates, including Captain Kidd, Jean Laeitte, Henry Morgan and two women who terrorized the Caribbean in the 17th and 18th centuries.

759. Smith, Arthur. LIGHTHOUSES. Boston: Houghton Mifflin; 1971.
Gr. 6-8. A history of lighthouses is traced with accompanying drawings by the writer.

760. Steig, William. ABEL'S ISLAND. Illustrated. New York: Farrar, Straus and Giroux; 1976.
Gr. 4-up. Castaway on an uninhabited island, Abel, a very civilized mouse, finds his resourcefulness and endurance tested to the limit.

761. Steig, Willlam. ABEL'S ISLAND [Sound Recording]. New York: Newbery Award Records; 1979; 3 cassettes; 1 teacher's guide.
Gr. 4-up. Based on the book of the same title.

762. Stockton, Frank Richard. BUCCANEERS AND PIRATES OF OUR COASTS. New York: Macmillan; 1963.
Gr. 5-up. A history of piracy along our Atlantic Coast including Morgan the pirate, Blackbeard, Captain Kidd, their adventures and deeds, plus stories of other less famous pirates.

763. Swahn, Sven Christer. THE ISLAND THROUGH THE GATE. Translated by Patricia Crampton. New York: Macmillan; 1974.

Gr. 5-9. Accidentally carried out to sea on an air mattress off the coast of Brittany, a young boy drifts to an isolated island where nothing seems normal.

764. Taylor, Theodore. TEETONCEY. Illustrated by Richard Cuffari, New York: Doubleday; 1974.
Gr. 5-7. A young girl is washed ashore on the Outer Banks and discovered by a young boy and his mother, who name her Teetoncey.

765. Thiele, Colin. THE FIGHT AGAINST ALBATROSS TWO. New York: Harper & Row; 1976.
Gr. 4-6. The residents of an Australian fishing village protest the placement of a huge oil rig in their fishing ground.

766. Tunis, Edwin. OARS, SAILS AND STEAM. Illustrated. New York: Crowell; 1952.
Gr. 4-6. A history of ships using many sketches as well as narrative.

767. UNDER THE JOLLY ROGER [Filmstrip]. Chicago: Encyclopaedia Britannica Educational Corp.; 1982-83; 4 filmstrips; 4 cassettes; 1 teacher's manual.
Gr. 4-up. Explores the legends of the men and women who sailed under the skull and crossbones. Also available in a captioned version without cassettes.

768. Van Allsburg, Chris. THE WRECK OF THE ZEPHYR. Illustrated. Boston: Houghton Mifflin; 1983.
Gr. 3-up. A boy's ambition to be the greatest sailor in the world brings him to ruin when he misuses his new ability to sail his boat in the air.

769. Verne, Jules. AROUND THE WORLD IN EIGHTY DAYS. Translated by George Towle. Illustrated. New York: Dodd, Mead; 1979.
Gr. 5-up. In 1872 Phineas Fogg wins a bet by traveling around the world in seventy-nine days.

Weiss, Malcom E. ONE SEA, ONE LAW? THE FIGHT FOR A LAW OF THE SEA. New York: Harcourt Brace; 1982.
Gr. 6-Up. See #699.

770. Whipple, Addison Beecher Colvin. FIGHTING SAIL. New York: Time-Life; 1978.
Gr. 6-up. In the form of chapters and essays the men of the navy are discussed.

771. Zim, Herbert S., and James R. Skelly. CARGO SHIPS. New York: Morrow; 1970.
Gr. 3-6. Describes how large ships are constructed, what they carry and how they are operated.

Human Endeavor: Trade and Transport: Engineering

772. Aaron, Chester. SPILL. New York: Atheneum; 1977.
Gr. 5-7. A family struggles to save wildlife caught in an oil spill off the coast of northern California.

773. Adkins, Jan. THE CRAFT OF SAIL. New York: Walker; 1973.
Gr. 5-7. Pen and ink drawings show the rigging, sailing and mooring of a sailboat.

774. Adkins, Jan. WOODEN SHIP. Illustrated. New York: Houghton Mfiflin; 1978.
Gr. 5-7. The story of the voyage of a fictional 19th century whaling ship, filled with detailed pen and ink drawings.

775. Ardizzone, Edward. TIM TO THE LIGHTHOUSE. Illustrated. New York: Oxford Unversity Press; 1979.
Gr. K-3. One stormy night the Lighthouse is dark, so Tim awakens Captain McFee and they row out to see what has happened to the keeper and the light.

776. Atkinson, Ian. VIKING SHIPS. Minneapolis: Lerner; 1980.
Gr. 4-6. Describes what we know about the design and construction of Viking ships.

777. Bernard, Christine. THE BOOK OF FANTASIC BOATS. Illustrated by Roy Coombs. New York: Golden Press; 1974.
Gr. 4-8. Gives brief descriptions of unusual boats from primitive outrigger canoes to modern hydrofoils.

778. Branley, Franklin M. FLOATING AND SINKING. Illustrated by Robert Galster. New York: Harper & Row; 1967.
Gr. 1-3. Experiments help young readers to understand flotation.

779. CLAY BOATS [Kit]. by Elementary Science Study, Nashua, NH: Delta Education; 1969; 1 kit: 15 plastic containers; 15 work trays; 15 medicine cups; plasticene clay; ceramic weights; balance; 3 plastic pails; foil; waxed paper; plastic bags; teacher's guide.

Gr. 4-6. Designed to help children understand what kinds and shapes of objects float, and to teach the basic principles of boat building .

780. Coombs, Charles Ira. TANKERS, GIANTS OF THE SEA. New York: Morrow; 1979.
Gr. 4-6. Discusses the use of tankers as oil carrying vehicles, their construction, and life aboard them.

781. Corbett, Scott. WHAT MAKES A BOAT FLOAT? Illustrated by Victor Mays. Boston: Little, Brown; 1970.
Gr. 3-5. Explains gravity, flotation and buoyancy as well as how to build boats which best travel on and under the water.

Crews, Donald. HARBOR. New York: Greenwillow; 1982.
Gr. Preschool-2. See #187.

Dean, Anabel. SUBMERGE: THE STORY OF DIVERS AND THEIR CRAFTS. Illustrated. Philadelphia: Westminster Press; 1976.
Gr. 6-9. See #683.

782. Dodge, Mary Mapes. HANS BRINKER. Illustrated by Cyrus L. Baldrige. New York: Grosset & Dunlap; 1945.
Gr. 5-8. This classic story underlines the role the dikes play in keeping the Netherlands safe from the sea. Sound versions available from Caedmon.

783. Domanzka, Janina. I SAW A SHIP A-SAILING. New York: Macmillan; 1972.
Gr. K-3. Geometric figures of ships elaborate on the simple text of this nursery rhyme.

784. Gibson, Walter B. FELL'S OFFICIAL GUIDE TO KNOTS AND HOW TO TIE THEM. New York: Frederick Fell; 1961.
Gr. 4-6. A guide to all kinds of knot-tying.

785. Gramatky, Hardie. LITTLE TOOT. Illustrated. New York: Putnam; 1981.
Gr. K-2. The classic story of a little tugboat which proves itself.

786. Green, Norma. HOLE IN THE DIKE. Illustrated by Eric Carle. New York: Harper & Row; 1975.
Gr. Preschool-3. Adapted from the best-known chapter

of "Hans Brinker," this tells the tale of the brave young boy who saved Holland by putting his finger in a hole in the dike.

787. Judson, Clara Ingram. BOAT BUILDER: THE STORY OF ROBERT FULTON. Illustrated by Armstrong Sperry. New York: Scribner; 1940.
Gr. 4-9. Robert Fulton inventor of the steamboat, a torpedo, and the first successful submarine.

788. Lippman, Peter J. BUSY BOATS. Illustrated. New York: Random House; 1977.
Gr. 2-3. Identifies and discusses the uses of different types of boats.

789. Loeper, John J. THE GOLDEN DRAGON: BY CLIPPER SHIP AROUND THE HORN. New York: Atheneum; 1978.
Gr. 4-6. A ten year old boy travels from New York to San Francisco by clipper ship in 1850.

790. Navarra, John Gabriel. SUPERBOATS. New York: Doubleday; 1977.
Gr. 3-5. An introduction to various types of ships of the world including hydrofoils, ocean liners, supertankers, container ships, ice breakers, and drill ships.

791. Oppenheim, Joanne. HAVE YOU SEEN BOATS? Reading, MA: Addison-Wesley; 1971.
Gr. 1-3. Describes boats and ships with a rhymed text.

792. Petersen, David. SUBMARINES (New True Book). Chicago: Children's Press; 1984.
Gr. 1-3. Discusses the history of submersible craft and their utilization in warfare and ocean exploration.

793. Plowden, David. TUGBOAT. Illustrated. New York: Macmillan; 1976.
Gr. 3-6. The story of a day's work for the Julia C. Moran, a tugboat in New York Harbor.

794. Rockwell, Anne. BOATS. Illustrated. New York: Dutton; 1982.
Gr. Preschool-2. A simple introduction to types of boats with bright illustrations.

795. Rutland, Johathan. SEE INSIDE A SUBMARINE. New York: Watts; 1980.
Gr. 3-6. A history and examination of current submarines using cut-aways and diagrams as well as text.

796. Rutland, Jonathan. SEE INSIDE AN OIL RIG AND TANKER. New York: Watts; 1979.
Gr. 4-6. Large picture spreads show the workings of rigs, drilling platforms, refineries and tankers.

797. Sullivan, George. SUPERTANKER: THE STORY OF THE WORLD'S BIGGEST SHIPS. New York: Dodd, Mead; 1978.
Gr. 6-up. Describes the development of the huge oil supertankers, supportive services such as superports and problems with accidents.

OCEANS IN THE ARTS

798. Alger, Leclaire. SEA-SPELL AND MOOR-MAGIC: TALES OF THE WESTERN ISLES. Illustrated by Vera Bock. New York: Holt, Rinehart and Winston; 1968.

799. Anderson, Lonzo. ARION AND THE DOLPHINS: BASED ON AN ANCIENT GREEK LEGEND. New York: Scribner; 1978.
Gr. K-3. Retells the Greek legend of Arion who plays his lute to entertain the dolphins.

800. Boston, Lucy. SEA EGG. Illustrated by Peter Boston. New York: Harcourt Brace; 1967.
Gr. 3-6. Two boys buy what is thought to be an egg-shaped stone, which hatches in a tidepool and takes them on some adventures.

801. Carroll, Ruth Robinson. THE DOLPHIN AND THE MERMAID. New York: Walck; 1974.
Gr. Preschool-2. The dolphin, the mermaid, and their friends lead a peaceful underwater existence until they are threatened by thoughtless humans.

802. Cole, William. THE SEA, SHIPS AND SAILORS: POEMS, SONGS AND SHANTIES. Drawings by Robin Jacques. New York: Viking Press; 1967.
Gr. 5-up.

803. Craig, M. Jean. THE SAND, THE SEA, AND ME. Painted by Audrey Newell. New York: Walker; 1972.

Gr. K-3. Poems by Elizabeth Coatsworth, Walter de le. Mare, and Rachel Field depict activities, creatures and feelings at the seashore.

804. Frame, Paul. DRAWING SHARKS, WHALES, DOLPHINS AND SEALS. New York: Watts; 1983.
Gr. 4-6. A brief study of the anatomy of these sea creatures along with tools, materials and techniques for drawing them effectively.

805. Glubok, Shirley. ART OF THE VIKING. New York: Macmillan; 1978.
Gr. 4-7. A description, with pictures, of the art and customs of the Vikings.

806. Gracza, Margaret. THE SHIP AND THE SEA IN ART. Illustrated. Minneapolis: Lerner; 1965.
Gr. 5-11.

807. Hunter, Mollie. A STRANGER CAME ASHORE. New York: Harper & Row; 1975.
Gr. 5-up. On a stormy night in the Shetland Islands a mysterious shipwreck victim comes ashore whom Robbie and his grandfather realize is actually the great Selchie.

808. THE ICE CREAM OCEAN, AND OTHER DELECTABLE POEMS OF THE SEA. Selected and illustrated by Susan Russo. New York: Lothrop; 1984.
Gr. 3-6. Humorous poems about the ocean from poets such as Ogden Nash, John Ciardi, and X.J. Kennedy.

809. Kumin, Maxine W. THE BEACH BEFORE BREAKFAST. Illustrated by Leonard Weisgard. New York: Putnam; 1961.
Gr. 2-4. Exploration of a beach during early morning.

810. Lear, Edward. THE FOUR LITTLE CHILDREN WHO WENT AROUND THE WORLD. Pictures by Arnold Lobel. New York: MacMillan; 1968.
Gr. K-3. One of Lear's nonsense stories, this concerns four children who make a fantastic voyage.

811. Lent, Blair. JOHN TABOR'S RIDE. Illustrated. Boston: Little, Brown; 1966.
Gr. 1-up. When John Tabor is shipwrecked on a desert isle, he is rescued by a strange old man who takes him for a real "Nantucket sleigh-ride" on the back of a whale.

812. LISTENING, LOOKING, AND FEELING [Filmstrip]. Santa Monica, CA: BFA Educational Media; 1970; 4 filmstrips; 4 cassettes; 1 teaching guide.
Gr. K-3. Provides students with the mood, sights and sounds of 4 different situations: the beach; the city; wind and rain; and flying.

813. Mendoza, George. AND I MUST HURRY FOR THE SEA IS COMING IN. Photographs by DeWayne Dalrymple. Design by Herb Lubalin. Englewood Cliffs, NJ: Prentice Hall; 1969.
Gr. 3-12. Photographs and verse describe a young boy's daydream of the sea.

814. PERCEPTION: THE SEA [Filmstrip]. Stamford, CT: Educational Dimensions; 1972; 2 filmstrips; 2 cassettes.
Gr. 1-up. Visual images that touch on every aspect of life on, around, and under the seas of the world.

815. Ransome, Arthur. THE FOOL OF THE WORLD AND THE FLYING SHIP: A RUSSIAN TALE. Illustrated by Uri Shulevitz. New York: Farrar, Straus & Giroux; 1968.
Gr. 1-4. A fool finds a flying ship and using it he is able to outwit the Czar.

816. Raynes, John. PAINTING SEASCAPES: A CREATIVE APPROACH. New York: Watson-Guptill; 1972.
A guide that encourages the reader's creativity in painting the sea, sky and shore.

817. Revius, Jacob. NOAH'S ARK. Illustrated by Peter Spier. New York: Doubleday; 1977.
Gr. 1-3. A brief one-page text of the Old Testament story followed by a wordless pictorial version.

818. Rockwell, Anne. TUHURAHURA AND THE WHALE. Illustrated. New York: Parents; 1971.
Gr. 2-5. Left to drown in the sea, a Maori boy is saved by a whale who returns him to shore.

819. THE SEA MONSTER AND THE FISHERMAN: AN ESKIMO FOLKTALE [Kit], Chicago: SVE; 1973; 3 puppets; 4 study prints; 1 cassette; 1 cardboard Eskimo; teacher's manual.
Gr. 1-3. The sea monster finds a friend to swim with and the fishermen get more fish than ever before.

820. THE SEA, IN FACT AND FANTASY [Filmstrip]. New York: Learning Corporation of America; 1970; 6 sound-filmstrips; 6 cassettes; script; teacher's guide.
Gr. 3-6. Using the sea as an example, children are shown how nature inspires story-telling.

821. Stevenson, Robert Louis. TREASURE ISLAND. Illustrated by N.C. Wyeth. New York: Scribner; 1981.
Gr. 6-up. The classic tale of pirates and buried treasure.

822. Stevenson, Robert Louis. TREASURE ISLAND [Kit]. Wilmette, IL: Films Inc; 1976; 1 Kit: 3 filmstrips; 3 sound cassettes; 15 activity cards; 1 book; 1 teacher's guide.
Gr. 5-8. Based on the book of the same title.

823. Turkle, Brinton. DO NOT OPEN. Illustrated. New York: Dutton; 1981.
Gr. 1-3. Miss Moody and her cat, Captain Kidd, find a mysterious bottle as they search the beach for "treasures."

824. Van Woerkom, Dorothy. SEA FROG, CITY FROG. Adapted from a Japanese folk tale. Pictures by Jose Aruego and Ariane Dewey. New York: MacMillan; 1975.
Gr. 1-4. Sea Frog sets out to visit the city and meets City Frog who is on his way to the sea.

825. Vaughn-Williams, Ralph. SEA SONG [Sound Recording]. Hollywood, CA: Chalfonte Records; 1975; 1 cassette.
Gr. 3-up. Orchestral variations of sea songs.

826. Yashima, Taro. SEASHORE STORY. New York: Viking Press; 1967.
Gr. K-3. Urashima, the ancient fisherman, returns to the world above the waves after experiencing the domain of the sea.

Zaidenberg, Arthur. HOW TO DRAW LANDSCAPES, SEASCAPES AND CITYSCAPES. New York: Crowell; 1963.
Gr. 4-up. See #155.

Chapter 7

Sound

For the great number of people who are able to hear, sound is an ever present part of existence. We are so accustomed to certain levels of sound, "background noise," that we become uncomfortable when that "noise" is absent.

Many of us wake to the sound of an alarm clock. We hear water running in the shower; bacon may sizzle in the pan; a thump outside the front door means the morning paper has arrived. We open the door and hear street noises, the swish of tires, the rumble of a truck. We step out to a world of sound, sound we hardly notice until it stops.

One of the purposes of this book is to suggest that a very general idea can be made more specific and at the same time can go in many different directions. Some of these directions come from an analysis of the idea, and some may come from encouraging your imagination to play with the idea. "Sound" is one of the concepts we might work with, looking for divisions of the idea which lead to further divisions and more specific topics.

Let us begin by consulting a dictionary. The several meanings we find may suggest some strands to explore.

Sound: our dictionary definition only hints at the levels of meaning contained in this word! "the sensation perceived by the sense of hearing; a particular auditory impression; mechanical radiant energy that is transmitted by longitudinal pressure waves in a material medium ... and is the objective cause of hearing; a speech sound; value in terms of speech sounds; meaningless noise; recorded auditory material" etc. (THE RANDOM HOUSE DICTIONARY OF THE ENGLISH LANGUAGE, UNABRIDGED EDITION)

Several of the dictionairies we consulted began the definition by explaining that sound was a sensation caused by the transmission of vibrations--an explanation relying on concepts of the science of physics. The sensation, or auditory impression, is able to be received because of the structure and function of the ear -- an explanation relying on concepts of physiology. Here is a beginning -- "The Physics and Physiology of Sound." These terms might be reworded for the young child, using such phrases as How We Hear or How Noise Travels.

Another part of the definition refers to speech sound, vocal utterance, and musical tone.

Many of the sounds we hear have meaning to us -- meaning which we have learned from experience, or meaning coded into the arrangements of sound. When we hear birds singing loudly at twilight we may say to ourselves that we'll soon have rain. When we hear a dog growl, we have learned that this sound is a warning. One kind of crying sound tells us the baby is hungry, while another kind of cry signals discomfort. The blast of a horn as we step into the street tells us to watch out, to step back, to look for a car approaching. Through our life experience we have come to associate specific meaning to unspoken, physical sound.

The human voice also produces sounds intended to communicate. Meanings coded into the sounds of human speech have developed into human languages. Arbitrary, auditory symbols used in conventional ways, with conventional meanings, enable us to use voice to communicate with each other. Very young children learn the meaning of these speech sounds, and also learn how to produce and arrange these sounds to communicate their feelings and their needs.

Here, then, is our other major division -- "Sound and Meaning." Humans communicate through spoken and written language; they *intend* to convey an idea when they speak. Animals, too, communicate through patterns of sound, although their use of sounds may depend more on instinct.

Another kind of sound which communicates meaning and emotion is music. This opens a whole new avenue of exploration -- singing, instrumental music, rhythm, tone. When we hear music do we feel happy, sad, exhilarated? What can music tell us? How is it made?

How would you explain music to a child who could not hear? You might place the child's hand on a string as you played a guitar, or on your throat as you sang. The hearing impaired child would feel vibrations -- and perhaps would notice that these vibrations -- these sounds -- were evoking a response from others in the room, the response of rhythmical body movement.

Now we have moved from physics to meaning, from meaning, to music, and from music back to the physics of sound.

In so doing, we see that the concept of sound can be carried across the curriculum.

In the science classroom we might be concerned with how sound is generated, or how it travels. A simple but dramatic demonstration of sound waves can be made by placing a bowl of colored water on an overhead projector, tapping a tuning fork, and gently placing the fork in the water. What are those widening circles? Does anything happen if we tap the tuning form and hold it in the air? Does sound exist if there is no one to hear it? How do we hear sound? How does the structure of the ear enable us to hear? A study of the anatomy of the ear may be followed in a physical education class with a discussion of the care of the ear -- cleaning it or protecting it when playing body contact games.

In the language arts class sound can be linked with language. The development of language as human communication, the meanings of words, some of which may "sound" alike, the development of writing, which enables us to communicate with others when we cannot see or hear them -- these ideas can become a part of vocabulary, pantomine, and listening skills. Often the early training in listening skills will start with games based on sound discrimination and the identification of sounds. A group of children could make an audiotape and tell a story by recording sounds. For instance, the tape might start with an alarm clock, then some shuffling feet, a door closing, water running --or calliope music, animal sounds, and we can imagine we are at the circus.

Music, of course, _is_ sound. Learning about musical instruments, how the vibration of a violin string or air blown through the flute's reed can generate the sounds we call music would fit nicely with the study of the physics of sound.

Let us consider sound in terms of grade level. Kindergarten children might move rhythmically to music, playing "follow me" games or simply dancing to express their feelings. First and second graders could use the simple instruments of a rhythm band, learning to use the instruments to produce a composite sound, music. These young students might also be introduced to the idea of their senses, especially the sense of hearing. Older students could examine the ideas of sound as noise, or language, or music. They, too, would learn about hearing, but they might also begin to think about the inability to hear. Through literature they could learn how deaf people manage to communicate and they might gain some insight into how those others feel. Ada Litchfield's WORDS IN OUR HANDS, and A BUTTON IN HER EAR, and Emily Hanlon's THE SWING give us a glimpse of the world of the deaf, while Patricia Curtis' CINDY, A HEARING EYE DOG and Lotte Rickehof's THE JOY OF SIGNING show some ways that deaf people cope with their environment.

Now we might look at the strands of our chart. One of the major divisions, "The Physics and Physiology of Sound," can be considered from the viewpoints of generating sound or hearing sound. In both cases the study might be introduced with National Geographic's filmstrip set, INTRODUCING SOUND, LIGHT, AND COLOR, or with Focus Media's filmstrip set, SCIENCE, THE WORLD OF SOUND ENERGY. BFA's filmstrip set, SOUND could be used in grades 3-6, and Encyclopaedia Britannica's LEARNING ABOUT SOUND would be useful for younger students.

Following down the chart to Direct Sound, we find the sounds of the human voice, of animals, and of natural phenomena such as thunder and wind. Harry Devlin's TALES OF THUNDER AND LIGHTNING relates some of the ways people in many cultures have explained to themselves what thunder or the sound of the rain means. One of the classic nature stories is Robert McCloskey's TIME OF WONDER made into a filmstrip by Weston Woods. Kenneth Heuer explains some of these natural phenomena in THUNDER, SINGING SANDS, AND OTHER WONDERS: SOUNDS IN THE ATMOSPHERE, while Susan Sussman's HIPPO THUNDER and Charlotte Zolotow's HOLD MY HAND are both stories guaranteed to reassure a youngster frightened by the loud claps of a thunderstorm.

The sounds of animals is a topic students will enjoy. The filmstrip LIONS DON'T ALWAYS ROAR might be used with a sound recording ANIMALS AND CIRCUS. Francine Jacobs' book SOUNDS IN THE

SEA is a good introduction to marine bioacoustics and might be followed with Capitol Records' FAREWELL TO TARWATHIE.

Man made sounds can be pleasant, but they might just be noise. Jerry Grey talks about noise pollution in NOISE, NOISE, NOISE, while SIREN IN THE NIGHT by Jim Aylesworth is a story about a little boy's reaction to the noise of a fire siren.

Going across the chart we come to mediated sound -- sound heard or amplified mechanically or electronically. THE WONDERS OF THE AGE: MR. EDISON'S NEW TALKING PHONOGRAPH by Kevin Daley gives historical perspective to this subject, as does Sally Berke's WHEN TV BEGAN: THE FIRST TV SHOWS. Betsy Byars' book THE TV KID is also available as a sound recording. Instead of watching a play, or reading one, students might listen to the recording of Maurice Sendak's REALLY ROSIE, with Carole King as vocalist. After that, they could read the libretto.

MUSIC ALL AROUND US, a set of sound filmstrips, explores this idea with images and sound. Children might begin with this and then move to listening to music, with some of the Bowmar Orchestral Library recordings. The instruments in an orchestra are pictured in a set of study prints and a filmstrip, KNOW THE ORCHESTRA; for further explorations one might use the game MUSIC MAESTRO, about musical instruments and music sounds. As a culminating activity, students could follow the instructions in Hawkinson's MUSIC AND INSTRUMENTS FOR CHILDREN to make and form their own band with their own instruments.

Language itself is our principal means of communication, but how did humans develop language? We might begin to examine the historical development of language, using the Time-Life book, LANGUAGE, by David Thomson and Guidance Associates' filmstrip set SPEAKING OF LANGUAGE. Language is a way of communicating, and Hap Palmer's record FEELIN' FREE has young children expressing themselves through movement. ON STAGE: WALLY, BERTHA AND YOU is a wonderful kit which has activity cards and two hand puppets, Wally Walrus and Bertha Bird. Using the puppets to communicate their thoughts, children become less self conscious in their use of oral language.

In these examples we have followed strands from general subjects to more specific topics. The direction might as easily be reversed. Especially with young children, one starts with a concrete experience, and then broadens the scope of inquiry.

Words make up our language, and vocabulary development can be painlessly assisted with word games such as BACKPACK, WORDSWORTH, or THE ELECTRIC COMPANY WORD BUILDERS. Herbert Kohl's A BOOK OF PUZZLEMENTS: PLAY AND INVENTION WITH LANGUAGE encourages creative approaches to language, while Isaac Asimov's books WORDS ON THE MAP, WORDS FROM HISTORY, and WORDS OF SCIENCE remain fresh and useful.

We haven't even begun to list the possibilities open to us as we look at -- or listen to -- our language. Written language is based on symbols -- letters -- which might lead to the study of the development of alphabets or to the fun of alphabet books. Students might draw their own alphabet books -- or they might make a picture book of sounds. The free play of the imagination can enliven learning. How we encourage students to play with words, to relate ideas, and to follow up on their questions, will have a profound influence on their development of intellectual curiosity and their mental growth.

The chart presented here suggests some branches one could take. It is just a beginning. Add your own topics. The process of relating one idea and one instructional material to another in all subjects -- this is what makes learning fun! The list of materials that follows has been divided into a number of subtopics, which may provide a basis for developing "sound" relationships across the curriculum.

SOUND

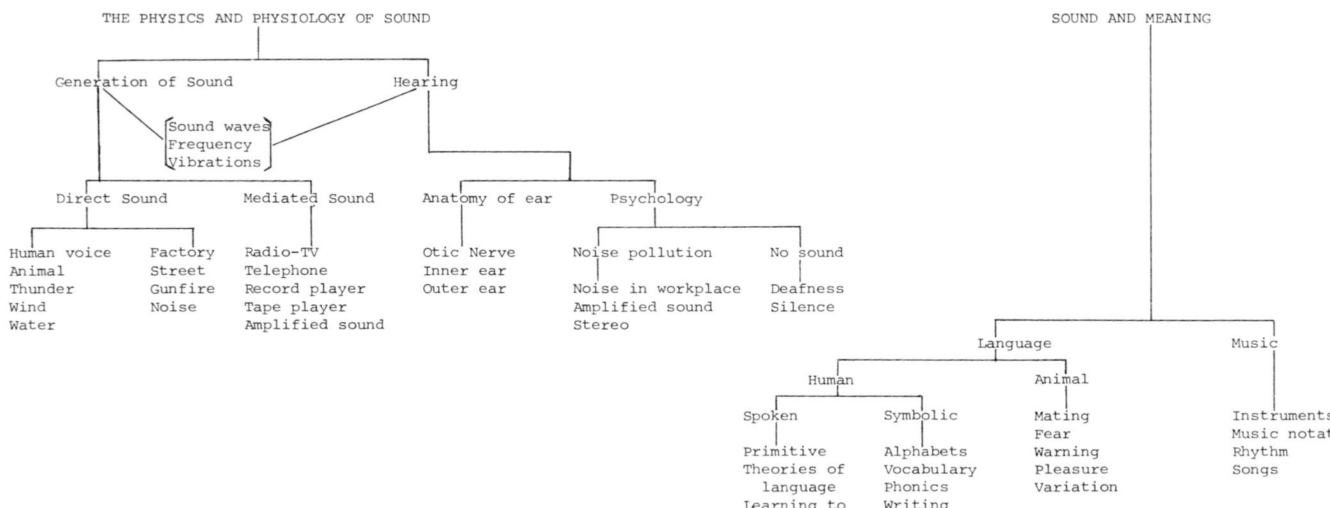
THE PHYSICS AND PHYSIOLOGY OF SOUND
Generation of Sound
Hearing
Sound waves
Frequency
Vibrations
Direct Sound
Mediated Sound
Anatomy of ear
Psychology
Human voice
Animal
Thunder
Wind
Water
Factory
Street
Gunfire
Noise
Radio-TV
Telephone
Record player
Tape player
Amplified sound
Otic Nerve
Inner ear
Outer ear
Noise pollution
Noise in workplace
Amplified sound
Stereo
No sound
Deafness
Silence
SOUND AND MEANING
Language
Music
Human
Animal
Spoken
Primitive
Theories of language
Learning to talk
Symbolic
Alphabets
Vocabulary
Phonics
Writing
Mating
Fear
Warning
Pleasure
Variation
Instruments
Music notation
Rhythm
Songs

PHYSICS AND PHYSIOLOGY OF SOUND

What Is Sound

827. Branley, Franklyn M. HIGH SOUNDS, LOW SOUNDS. New York: Harper & Row; 1967.
Gr. 1-3. Explains how sounds are produced and heard and suggests simple experiments using sound.

828. INTRODUCING SOUND, LIGHT, AND COLOR [Filmstrip]. Washington, D.C.: National Geographic; 1981; 3 filmstrips; 3 cassettes; 1 teacher's guide.
Gr. 4-8. Describes sound production in terms of vibration, pitch, intensity and resonance.

829. Kettelkamp, Larry. MAGIC OF SOUND. Illustrated by Anthony Kramer. New York: Morrow; 1982.
Gr. 4-7. Simple experiments to help children understand various aspects of sound.

830. Kohn, Bernices. ECHOES. Illustrated by Dan Connor. New York: Dandelion; 1979.
Gr. 2-5. A simple explanation of echoes, with some of the uses to which people have put them.

831. LEARNING ABOUT SOUNDS [Filmstrip]. Chicago: Encyclopaedia Britannica Educational Corp.; 1970; 5 filmstrips; 5 cassettes.
Gr. 4-8. Contents: Listen! What Do You Hear; How Sounds Are Made; How Sound Travels; How We Hear; Musical Instruments Make Special Sounds.

832. Podendorf, Illa. SOUNDS ALL ABOUT. Illustrated by Darrell Wiskur. Chicago: Children's Press; 1970.
Gr. K-2. Many different sounds - from the bark of a dog to the thump a marble makes when it is dropped on a rug.

833. SCIENCE, THE WORLD OF SOUND ENERGY [Filmstrip]. Plainview, NY: Focus Media; 1980; 5 filmstrips; 5 cassettes; 1 teacher's guide.
Gr. 6-up. Contents: Making Sound: A Vibration Creation; Pitch and Loudness: The Ups and Downs of Sound; The Speed of Sound: How Fast; Echoes: The Reflection of Sound; Music: The Refining of Sound.

834. Sootin, Harry. SCIENCE EXPERIMENTS WITH SOUND. New York: Norton; 1964.

Gr. 5-8. Simple experiments clearly explained and illustrated, such as Sounding Board, Different Kinds of Waves, and others.

835. SOUND [Filmstrip]. Santa Monica, CA: BFA; 1971; 4 filmstrips; 4 cassettes.
Gr. 3-6. Discusses the generation, transmission, reception, and interpretation of sound.

Direct Sound

836. Aylesworth, Jim. SIREN IN THE NIGHT. Chicago: Whitman; 1983.
Gr. K-2. A mother reassures her little boy when the noise of a firetruck and siren disturb their quiet walk.

837. Barrett, Judith. THE WIND THIEF. Illustrated by Diane Dawson. New York: Atheneum; 1977.
The Wind wants his own bat.

838. Behrens, June. WHAT I HEAR IN MY SCHOOL. Photos by Michele and Tom Grimm. Chicago: Children's Press; 1976.
Gr. K-3. Illustrates with text and photography some of the sounds that you might hear if you stop and listen.

839. Branley, Franklyn M. FLASH, CRASH, RUMBLE AND ROLL. New York: Harper & Row; 1964.
Gr. K-3. Explains the courses of thunder and lightning and the reason for the noise.

840. Brewer, Mary. WIND IS AIR. Elgin, IL: Child's World; 1975.
Gr. Preschool-3. Describes wind as the movement of air; its importance to us.

841. Brown, Margaret Wise. THE CITY NOISY BOOK. Illustrated by Leonard Weisgard. New York: Harper & Row; 1976.
Gr. Preschool-2. A little dog, Muffin, hears all of the sounds of the city. A reprint of the 1939 edition, THE NOISY BOOK.

842. Brown, Margaret Wise. COUNTRY NOISY BOOK. Illustrated by Leonard Weisgard. New York: Harper & Row; 1976.
Gr. K-2. A book of country sounds.

843. Brown, Margarget Wise. INDOOR NOISY BOOK. Illustrated by Leonard Weisgard. New York: Harper & Row; 1976.
Gr. K-2. A reprint of the 1942 story of Muffin, a little black dog who hears noises in the house.

844. Brown, Margaret Wise. MUFFIN IN THE CITY [Sound Recording]. Told by Norman Rose: Young Peoples Records; 1964; 1 disc.
Gr. K-2. Based on THE NOISY BOOK.

845. Campbell, Ethel M. THE WIND, NATURE'S GREAT VOICE. Minneapolis: Dennison; 1959.
Gr. K-6. Discusses air pressure, wind movement, trade winds, prevailing westerlies, etc.

846. Crowe, Robert L. TYLER TOAD AND THE THUNDER. New York: Dutton; 1980.
Gr. Preschool-2. T. Tyler Toad isn't comforted by the animals' explanations of where thunder comes from.

Devlin, Harry. HARRY DEVLIN'S TALES OF THUNDER AND LIGHTNING. New York: Parents Magazine Press; 1975.
Gr. 1-4. See #550.

847. Heuer, Kenneth. THUNDER, SINGING SANDS, AND OTHER WONDERS: SOUNDS IN THE ATMOSPHERE. New York: Dodd, Mead; 1981.
Gr. 5-8. Discusses reasons for some acoustical phenomena in nature.

848. Keats, Ezra Jack. APT. 3. New York: Macmillan; 1971.
Gr. Preschool-2. On a rainy day two brothers try to discover who is playing the harmonica they hear in their apartment building.

849. Lemieux, Michele. WHAT'S THAT NOISE? Illustrated. New York: Morrow; 1985.
Gr. K-1. When Brown Bear wakes up from his winter sleep, he hears strange noises. He searches and finds a wonderful surprise.

850. McCloskey, Robert. TIME OF WONDER [Filmstrip]. Weston, CT: Weston Woods; 1971; 1 filmstrip; 1 cassette.
Gr. K-4. Based on the Caldecott Medal book of the same title, published in 1957. The wonders of nature on a Maine island are described so that the reader vividly experiences the smells and sounds of the ocean.

851. McGovern, Ann. TOO MUCH NOISEE. Illustrated by Simms Taback. Boston: Houghton Mifflin; 1967.
Gr. K-2. The house is too noisy for Peter so he goes to the wise man for help.

852. Spier, Peter. CRASH! BANG! BOOM. New York: Doubleday; 1972.
Gr. Preschool-1. Detailed pictures show all kinds of sounds from household noises to those in the country, school, at play, and so on.

853. Sussman, Susan. HIPPO THUNDER. Chicago: Whitman; 1982.
Gr. Preschool-2. Father finds a way to banish the fear that comes with claps of thunder.

854. WEATHER, SEASONS AND CLIMATE [Filmstrip]. Santa Monica, CA: BFA; 1977; 4 filmstrips; 4 cassettes; 1 teacher's guide.
Gr. 4-8. Contents: What Causes Weather; Our Sun and Time and Seasons; The Earth's Climate; Storms and Clouds.

855. Zemach, Margo. IT COULD ALWAYS BE WORSE. Illustrated. New York: Farrar, Straus & Giroux; 1977.
Gr. 1-3. The Yiddish tale of a villager who consults the Rabbi because his house is so crowded and noisy.

856. Zolotow, Charlotte. HOLD MY HAND. New York: Harper & Row; 1972.
Gr. K-3. Taking a walk on a winter's day, two little girls hear the sounds of winter.

Mediated Sound

857. Allen, Jeffrey. MARY ALICE, OPERATOR NUMBER 9. Boston: Little, Brown; 1975.
Gr. K-3. When an efficient duck who gives the time over the telephone gets sick, other animals think the job is easy and try to take her place.

858. AMERICA: THE MECCA OF ELECTRONIC MUSIC [Filmstrip]. New Haven, CT: Keyboard Publications; 1970; 2 filmstrips; 1 cassette; 20 booklets; 1 guide.
Gr. 6-up. Presents the origin and development of electronics, the synthesizer, and the contributions of Benjamin Franklin and Thomas Edison.

859. Berke, Sally. WHEN TV BEGAN: THE FIRST TV SHOWS. New York: CPI; 1978.
Gr. 4-6. A brief survey of the early days of television and some of the popular shows of the fifties and sixties.

860. Byars, Betsy Cromer. THE TV KID. Illustrated by Richard Cuffari, New York: Viking Press; 1976.
Gr. 6-up. To escape failure, boredom and loneliness, a young boy immerses himself in television - until an encounter with a rattlesnake forces him to re-evaluate his life.

861. Byars, Betsy. THE TV KID [Sound Recording]. New York: Viking; 1977; 1 cassette; guide.
Gr. 6-up. A recorded dramatization based on the book of the same title.

862. Collier, James Lincoln. CB. Illustrated. New York: Watts; 1977.
Gr. 6-up. Introduces the equipment, mechanics, and terminology of citizens band radios.

863. Dignazio, Fred. CREATIVE KID'S GUIDE TO HOME COMPUTERS: SUPER GAMES AND PROJECTS TO DO WITH YOUR HOME COMPUTER. New York: Doubleday; 1981.
Gr. 4-6. Discusses a number of various projects children can do with a home computer.

864. Dolan, Edward F. Jr. IT SOUNDS LIKE FUN: HOW TO USE AND ENJOY YOUR TAPE RECORDER AND STEREO. New York: Messner; 1981.
Gr. 5-up. An introduction to the use of various kinds of sound equipment.

865. Hawkins, Robert. ON THE AIR: RADIO BROADCASTING. New York: Messner; 1984.
Gr. 5-9. History of radio, kinds of jobs available, uses of computers and telecommunications in radio.

866. Hunt, Bernice Kohn. COMMUNCATIONS SATELLITES: MESSAGE CENTERS IN SPACE. Illustrated by Jerome Kohl. New York: Four Winds; 1975.
Traces the development of the satellites which provide instant global communication via television and telephone.

867. Lieberman, Jethro K., and Neil S. Rhodes. THE COMPLETE CB HANDBOOK. Illustrated: McKay; 1976.
Gr. 6-up.

868. Lipson, Shelly. IT'S BASIC: THE ABC's OF COMPUTER PROGRAMMING. Illustrated by Janice Stapleton. New York: Holt, Rinehart & Winston; 1982.
Gr. 2-4.

869. Math, Irwin. MORSE, MARCONI, AND YOU. New York: Scribner; 1979.
Gr. 6-up. Describes how the telephone, telegraph, and radio work.

870. THE NEW CBS AUDIO-FILE SOUND EFFECTS LIBRARY [Sound Recording]. Produced by Ed Hoppe and Joel Dulberg. New York: CBS; 1977; 3 sound discs.
Gr. 3-up. Contents: Planes; Trains; Fire Engines; Baseball; and other sounds.

871. NIGHTLY NEWS [Filmstrip]. New York: Scribner; 1977; 2 filmstrips; 2 cassettes.
Gr. 5-up. A behind-the-scenes look at television news.

872. ON THE AIR: A COLLECTION OF RADIO AND TV PLAYS. New York: Scribner; 1977.
Gr. 5-up. Contents: Return to Dust; The Final Hour; The Lady or the Tiger; The Speckled Band; Twelve Angry Men; The Foundling; Back There; The Trouble with Tribbles.

873. Quackenbush, Robert. AHOY. AHOY. ARE YOU THERE? A STORY OF ALEXANDER GRAHAM BELL. Englewood Clifts, NJ: Prentice Hall; 1981.
Gr. 2-4. A biography of the inventor.

874. Taylor, Paula. WALTER CRONKITE: THIS IS WALTER CRONKITE. Chicago: Children's Press; 1975.
Gr. 4-6. A biography of the CBS anchorman who starred in television's longest running news program.

875. THE WONDERS OF THE AGE: MR. EDISON'S NEW TALKING PHONOGRAPH [Sound Recording]. Compiled by Kevin Daly. England: Argo Record; 1970; 2 discs; 1 pamphlet.
Gr. 6-up. The story of sound recording 1877-1925 compiled from contemporary writings and illustrated by archive recordings.

Hearing, Deafness, and the Ear

Aylesworth, Thomas G. THIS VITAL AIR, THIS VITAL WATER: MAN'S ENVIRONMENTAL CRISIS. Chicago: Rand McNally; 1973.
Gr. 6-up. See #157.

876. BODY IMAGERY [Activity Cards]. Springfield, MA: Milton Bradley; 1976; 8 activity cards.
Gr. K-2. Teaches parts of the body and their functions.

877. Brenner, Barbara. FACES. New York: Dutton; 1970.
Gr. Preschool-1. Photographs show the reactions of the eye, ear, nose, and tastebuds to pleasant and unpleasant stimuli. Also available in Spanish version: Caras.

878. Cobb, Vicki. HOW TO REALLY FOOL YOURSELF: ILLUSIONS FOR ALL YOUR SENSES. New York: Lippincott; 1981.
Gr. 5-up. Demonstrates and explains how the senses can be fooled.

879. Cowley, Joy. THE SILENT ONE. New York: Knopf; 1981.
Gr. 4-6. A deaf-mute boy tames a huge white turtle and becomes a target for the superstitious villagers.

880. Curtis, Patricia. CINDY, A HEARING EAR DOG. New York: Dutton; 1981.
Gr. 3-5. Describes how young dogs are selected and trained to help their deaf owners by alerting them to sounds, guiding them, and providing companionship.

881. Davidson, Margaret. HELEN KELLER. Illustrated by Wendy Watson. New York: Scholastic; 1973.
Gr. K-3. The childhood of Helen Keller, who overcame the handicaps of blindness and deafness.

882. EXPERIENCES IN PERCEPTUAL GROWTH [Filmstrip]. Chicago: Encyclopaedia Britannica Educational Corp.; 1976; 3 filmstrips; 3 cassettes;; 1 guide.
Gr. K-3. Contents: Texture: Squish and Prickles; Sounds: Lions Don't Always Roar; Numbers: Peep Counts Sheep.

883. Greenberg, Joanne. IN THIS SIGN. New York: Avon; 1972.
Gr. 6-up. Three generations of a family have to cope with deafness.

884. Grey, Jerry. NOISE, NOISE, NOISE. Philadelphia: Westminster; 1975.
Gr. 6-up. Discusses the principles of sound and hearing, noise in everyday life, and noise pollution.

885. Hanlon, Emily. THE SWING. Scarsdale, NY: Bradbury; 1979.
Gr. 5-7. An eleven year old deaf girl and a thirteen year old boy with family problems have a special swing where they meet and share their thoughts.

886. HELLO, EVERYBODY [Filmstrip]. Santa Monica, CA: James Stanfield Films; 1977; 6 filmstrips; teacher's guide.
Gr. 4.-up. Children with various disabilities talk about themselves and their interactions with other children.

887. Hyman, June. DEAFNESS. New York: Watts; 1980.
Gr. 4-up. Discusses types of hearing loss, the effect on the individual, how deaf people learn language, and the ways they communicate.

888. INVISIBLE HANDICAP [Videorecording], Washington, D.C: Gallaudet College; 1979; 1 video cassette.
Gr. 6 up. Gives the hearing world some basic information about deaf people - who they are, where they work, and how they communicate.

LEARNING ABOUT SOUNDS [Filmstrip]. Chicago: Encyclopaedia Britannica Educational Corp.; 1970; 5 filmstrips; 5 cassettes; 1 guide.
Gr. 4-8. See #831.

889. Levine, Edna S. LISA AND HER SOUNDLESS WORLD. Illustrated by Gloria Kamen. New York: Human Sciences; 1974.
Gr. K-2. Lisa's story is told: how she has received help for her deafness and her special education.

890. Litchfield, Ada Bassett. BUTTON IN HER EAR. Illustrated by Eleanor Mill. Niles, IL: Whitman; 1976.
Gr. 2-4. A simple story of a young girl with hearing problems, describing her visits to the doctor, her hearing aid and relationship to her friends. Filmstrip available from Random House.

891. Litchfield, Ada B. WORDS IN OUR HANDS. Pictures by Helen Cogancherry. Chicago: Whitman; 1980.
Gr. 2-6. Michael, who is nine, talks about living with deaf parents.

892. NOISE: HOW MUCH CAN WE TAKE [Filmstrip]. Stamford, CT: Educational Dimensions; 1983; 2 filmstrips; 2 cassettes; 1 guide.
Gr. 6-up. Discusses physics of sound and hearing, and noise pollution.

893. Peter, Diana. CLAIRE AND EMMA. New York: John Day; 1977.
Gr. K-4. Photographs and text show two deaf sisters who are learning to lip-read and to speak.

894. Peterson, Jeanne. I HAVE A SISTER - MY SISTER IS DEAF. Illustrated by Deborah Ray. New York: Harper & Row; 1977.
Gr. K-3. A little girl talks about her deaf sister, who can do so many things, even when she can't hear.

895. Rickehof, Lotte L. THE JOY OF SIGNING: THE NEW ILLUSTRATED GUIDE FOR MASTERING SIGN LANGUAGE. Springfield, MO: Gospel Publishing; 1978.
Gr. 2-up. A guide to signing and the manual alphabet.

896. SESAME STREET FIVE SENSES [Game]. Springfield, MA: Milton Bradley; 1975; 4 games.
Gr. K-3. How the Senses Protect Us; Discovering the Environment through the Senses; Using the Senses; How the Senses Work Together.

897. Silverstein, Alvin. THE STORY OF YOUR EAR. Illustrated by Susan Gaber. New York: Coward McCann & Geoghegan; 1981.
Gr. 5-up. Describes the structure of the ear, how the ear receives sound, how the ear affects balance.

898. Simon, Seymour. FINDING OUT WITH YOUR SENSES. New York: McGraw Hill; 1971.
Gr. K-3. Text and activities focus on different aspects of the senses.

899. SPECIAL PEOPLE [Filmstrip]. Westport, CT: Aspect IV Project; 1978; 4 filmstrips; 4 cassettes; 1 guide.
Gr. 6-up. Four people talk about their work, their families, their education, and their relationships.

900. Tresselt, Alvin R. WHAT DID YOU LEAVE BEHIND? Illustrated by Roger Duvoisin. New York: Lothrop; 1978.
Gr. K-3. The memories of images, smells, and sounds are the intangible souvenirs of a visit to the beach, the woods, or a country fair.

901. Wilkie, Katherine E. HELEN KELLER: FROM TRAGEDY TO TRIUMPH. New edition. New York: Bobbs-Merrill; 1983.
Gr. 2-up. The story of how Helen Keller lost both hearing and vision as a young child and how she overcame this tragedy.

902. Wolf, Bernard. ANNA'S SILENT WORLD. New York: Lippincott; 1977.
Gr. 2-4. A photographic essay which follows 6 year old Anna's activities including talking, reading, writing, and dance class.

903. YOUR SENSES AND HOW THEY HELP YOU [Filmstrip]. Washington, D.C: National Geographic; 1977; 2 filmstrips; 2 cassettes; teacher's guide.
Gr. K-3. Contents: Seeing and Hearing; Tasting, Touching, Smelling, and Other Senses.

SOUND AND MEANING

Human Language: Spoken and Symbolic

904. Adkins, Jan. SYMBOLS: A SILENT LANGUAGE. New York: Walker; 1978.
Gr. 4-6. Shows hundreds of symbols we see around us every day, including musical, religious, and weather symbols.

905. Adler, Irving. LANGUAGE AND MAN. Illustrated by Laurie Jo Lambie. New York: John Day; 1970.
Gr. 3-6. Explains why language is important, how it differs from the communication or sounds of animals, and how it is used to retain the knowledge of the past.

906. Albert, Burton. MORE CODES FOR KIDS. Illustrated by Jerry Warshaw. Chicago: Whitman; 1979.
Gr. 3-6. More codes for cryptanalysts to crack, many with jokes or riddles for answers. Includes, among others, a Code-a-Nut Tree and Back-Flip Triple Decker codes.

907. ALL PURPOSE PHOTO LIBRARY [Study Prints]. Niles, IL: Developmental Learning Materials; 1980; 300 photo cards in case; 1 teacher's manual.
Gr. K-4. Reinforcement of language skills through identification of common objects.

908. Amon, Aline. TALKING HANDS: INDIAN SIGN LANGUAGE. Illustrated. Garden City, NY: Doubleday; 1968.
Gr. 4-6. Describes how the Indians communicated with a sign language.

909. Babson, Walt. ALL KINDS OF CODES. New York: Four Winds; 1976.
Gr. 4-6. Directions for creating codes, making inks, breaking codes and some code games.

910. Baker, Eugene H. SECRET WRITING -CODES AND MESSAGES. Illustrated by Lois Axeman. Chicago: Children's Press; 1980.
Gr. 2-4. An introduction to various kinds of codes as well as a recipe for invisible ink.

911. Baron, Nancy. GETTING STARTED IN CALLIGRAPHY. New York: Sterling Publishing; 1979.
Gr. 5-up. Clear lessons in calligraphy as well as materials needed.

912. Bennett, Merily B., and Sylvia Sanders. HOW WE TALK: THE STORY OF SPEECH. Illustrated by William R. Johnson. Minneapolis, MN: Lerner; 1966.
Gr. 4-6. Describes how babies learn to talk, and how humans produce sound and speech.

913. Bielewicz, Julian A. SECRET LANGUAGES. Illustrated. New York: Elsevier-Nelson; 1976.
Gr. 6-up. Describes the history, methods and types of codes, ciphers and other ways of communicating privately.

914. Bolian, Polly. SYMBOLS: THE LANGUAGE OF COMMUNICATION. Illustrated. New York: Watts; 1975.
Gr. 5-up. Defines symbols, describes their evolution and meaning, and discusses their importance in the communication of ideas.

915. Castle, Sue. FACE TALK, HAND TALK, BODY TALK. Photographs by Frances McLaughlin-Gill. New York: Doubleday, 1977.
Gr. 2-4. People say things to each other in many ways, often without words.

916. Charlip, Remy. HANDTALK: AN ABC OF FINGER SPELLING; AND SIGN LANGUAGE. Illustrated. New York: Four Winds; 1974.

Gr. 1-up. An introduction to two kinds of sign language: finger spelling, or forming words letter by letter with the fingers, and signing, or making signs with one or two hands for each word or idea.

917. Claiborne, Robert. THE BIRTH OF WRITING. New York: Time-Life; 1974.
Gr. 5-up. A history and exploration of man's written language.

918. Fronval, George, and Daniel DuBois. INDIAN SIGNS AND SIGNALS. Illustrated by Jean Marcellin. New York: Sterling Publishing; 1978.
Gr. 4-7. Photographs and text describe more than 800 signs used by the nomadic tribes of the Great Plains to communicate with each other.

919. Hanson, Joan. SOUND WORDS: JINGLE, BUZZ, SIZZLE, AND OTHER WORDS THAT IMITATE THE SOUNDS AROUND US. Minneapolis, MN: Lerner; 1976.
Gr. K-3. Lists 28 words that echo and imitate the natural sounds of objects and actions.

920. Helfman, Elizabeth S. SIGNS AND SYMBOLS AROUND THE WORLD. New York: Lothrop; 1967.
Gr. 5-up. A history of the development of signs and symbols from ancient, even primitive times, until today. Illustrations of signs fron ampersand and branding to Yang-yin and zero.

921. HIDDEN ALPHA-PIX [Card]. Columbus, OH: Zaner-Bloser; 1973; 26 activity cards; 6 finger-fitting marking pencils; teacher's guide.
Gr. K-2. Illustrations based on nursery rhymes contain small objects with the same initial letter sound hidden within the larger picture for students to locate and circle. Lines on back allow students to practice writing capitals.

922. Hoban, Tana. I READ SYMBOLS. New York: Greenwillow; 1983.
Gr. Preschool-2. 27 photographs of symbolic street signs in bright primary colors.

923. Hofsinde, Robert. INDIAN PICTURE WRITING. Illustrated. New York: Morrow; 1959.
Gr. 4-up. Lists 248 symbols used in Indian picture writing; includes five letters in picture writing with their translations, page of exploit markings, and Cree alphabet.

924. James, Elizabeth; Barkin, Carol. HOW TO KEEP A SECRET: WRITING AND TALKING IN CODE. New York: Lothrop; 1978.
Gr. 4-6. Discusses encoding and various kinds of coding devices.

925. Janeczko, Paul B. LOADS OF CODES AND SECRET CYPHERS. New York: Macmillan; 1984.
Gr. 4-8. Discusses making and breaking codes, and transmitting secret messages.

926. Katan, Norma Jean. HIEROGLYPHS, THE WRITING OF ANCIENT EGYPT. Illustrated. New York: Atheneum; 1981.
Gr. 4-7. Explains the origins of hieroglyphs and what they mean, tells how this ancient form of writing was decoded, and describes the training and importance of scribes.

927. Kettelkamp, Larry. SONG, SPEECH AND VENTRILOQUISM. Illustrated. New York: Morrow; 1967.
Gr. 5-7. Explains how humans speak and sing as well as throw their voices.

928. KIN-TAC CURSIVE ALPHABET CARDS [Card]. Columbus, OH: Zanner-Bloser; 1974; 26 activity cards; teacher guide.
Gr. K-2. Cards with impressed letters to introduce cursive letters, reinforce learning letters, and to correct difficulties in letter formation.

929. Mann, Peggy. TELLTALE LINES: THE SECRETS OF HANDWRITING ANALYSIS. New York: Macmillan; 1976.
Gr. 4-6. An introduction to handwriting analysis.

930. Martin, Bill, and Peggy Brogan. SOUNDS OF LANGUAGE READERS. New York: Holt; 1972.
Gr. K-2. Contents: Sounds of Home (Preprimer); Sounds of Numbers (Primer); Sounds in the Wind (Grade 1); Sounds of a Powwow (Grade 2).

931. Meadow, Charles T. SOUNDS AND SIGNALS: HOW WE COMMUNICATE. Illustrated. Philadelphia: Westminster Press; 1975.
Gr. 3-6. Discusses the purposes and methods of communication, the way codes are used, and future trends.

932. Myller, Rolf. SYMBOLS AND THEIR MEANING. Illustrated. New York: Atheneum; 1978.
Gr. 4-6. Shows a variety of symbols including signs, flags, body language, numbers, zodiac and so on.

933. ON STAGE: WALLY, BERTHA, AND YOU [Kit]. Chicago: Encyclopaedia Britannica Educational Corp.; 1971; 2 felt hand puppets; 206 activity cards; 1 program guide; 1 teacher's handbook.
Gr. Preschool-2. Activity cards include ice breaker activities, suggestions for the construction of props and more.

934. PICTOGRAPHIC-CUNEIFORM UNIT [Model]. Long Island City, NY: Educational Division of Alva Museum Replicas; 1968; 5 replicas; 1 student activity program.
Gr. 4-up. 3 copies of a Mesopotamian pictographic tablet and 2 copies of a Sumerian cuneiform tablet with activities exploring early written languages.

935. Porter, David Lord. HELP! LET ME OUT. Illustrated by David Macaulay. Boston: Houghton Mifflin; 1982.
Gr. K-3. Hugo learns to be a ventriloquist, but when he throws his voice it doesn't come back for a long time.

936. ROSETTA STONE [Model]. New York: Alva Museum Replicas; 1965; 1 model; 16 students activity sheets.
Gr. 6-up. An investigation of ancient Egyptian pictographic writing.

937. Sarnoff, Jane, and Reynold Ruffin. THE CODE AND CIPHER BOOK. New York: Scribner; 1975.
Gr. 4-6. Describes codes and ciphers and presents a number of types of codes.

938. Sassoon, Rose. THE PRACTICAL GUIDE TO CALLIGRAPHY. New York: Thames and Hudson; 1982.
Gr. 6-up. Detailed instructions and alphabets.

939. Schwartz, Alvin. CAT'S ELBOW: AND OTHER SECRET LANGUAGES. Illustrated by Margot Zemach. New York: Farrar, Straus and Giroux; 1982.
Gr. 3-6. Thirteen language codes actually used in the past are presented in a humorous manner.

940. Scott, Henry Joseph, and Lenore Scott. HIEROGLYPHS FOR FUN: YOUR OWN SECRET CODE LANGUAGE. Illustrated. New York: Van Nostrand Reinhold; 1974.

Gr. 3-7. Presents the basic "alphabet" or twenty-four hieroglyphic letters with the approximate English sound they represent and briefly discusses various other aspects of Egyptian culture.

941. SESAME STREET SIGN LANGUAGE FUN. New York: Random House; 1980.
Gr. K-3. Presents sign language words grouped in such categories as the family, school, color, and seasons; featuring Jim Henson's Sesame Street Muppets; prepared in cooperation with the National Theatre of the Deaf.

942. Showers, Paul. HOW YOU TALK. New York: Harper & Row; 1967.
Gr. K-3. Explains how we produce sounds and learn language.

943. SPEAKING OF LANGUAGE [Filmstrip]. Pleasantville, NY: Guidance Associates; 1971; 2 filmstrips; 2 cassettes; guide.
Gr. 6-up. "Tongue-in-cheek" approach, free from specialized terminology, helps students grasp key ideas about the origins of modern languages including English; their relationships to thought, essential similarities among all languages and how languages grow out of each other.

944. Steckler, Arthur. 101 WORDS AND HOW THEY BEGAN. Illustrated by James Flora. New York: Doubleday; 1979.
Gr. 5-6. Presents the origin and use of 101 words, Sequel: 101 MORE WORDS AND HOW THEY BEGAN (1980).

945. TRACE-A-BET: DIFFICULT JOININGS [Chart]. Columbus, OH: Zaner-Bloser; 1979; 13 activity cards; 4 pencils with extra leads; instructions.
Gr. K-2. Supplemental learning aids to provide practice in tracing and writing cursive letter forms, with emphasis on joining letters together.

946. Wolff, Diane. CHINESE WRITING: AN INTRODUCTION. Illustrated by C. Wang. New York: Holt; 1975.
Gr. 4-6. Explains the formation and meaning of Chinese writing. Includes characters to practice on.

Human Language: Alphabet Books

947. ALPHABET STEW. In LET'S LEARN THE BASICS [Filmstrip]. Chicago: Encyclopaedia Britannica Educational Corp.; 1977; 5 filmstrips; 5 cassettes; 1 teacher's guide.
Gr. K-2. Introduces the letters of the alphabet as visual symbols for a "stew" of sounds.

948. Baskin, Leonard. HOSIE'S ALPHABET. New York: Viking; 1972.
Gr. K-3. Creatures for every letter of the alphabet from a bumptious baboon to a quintessential quail.

949. Beller, Janet. A-B-C-ING: AN ACTION ALPHABET. New York: Crown; 1984.
Gr. K-2. Black and white photographs of Climbing, Dancing, Eating, etc.

950. Black, Floyd. ALPHABET CAT. New York: Gingerbread House; 1979.
Gr. K-3. Private detective Alphabet Cat searches from A to Z for the Pack Rat Gang who kidnapped the countess.

951. Burningham, John. JOHN BURNINGHAM'S ABC. New York: Random House; 1985.
Gr. K-3. Lower case letters show a boy interacting with animals and objects from A to Z, alligator, ice cream, etc.

Charlip, Remy. HANDTALK: AN ABC OF FINGER SPELLING AND SIGN LANGUAGE. New York: Four Winds; 1974.
Gr. 1-up. See #916.

952. Chess, Victoria. ALFRED'S ALPHABET WALK. New York: Greenwillow; 1979.
Gr. K-3. On his walk Alfred meets animals from A to Z.

953. Fisher, Leonard Everett. ALPHABET ART: THIRTEEN ABCS FROM AROUND THE WORLD. New York: Four Winds; 1978.
Gr. 6-up. Includes: Arabic, Cherokee, Chinese, Eskimo, Gaelic, German, Greek, Hebrew, Japanese, Thai, and Tibetan alphabets.

954. Hall, Nancy C. MACMILLAN FAIRY TALE ALPHABET BOOK. New York: Macmillan; 1983.
Gr. K-5. Illustrated by John O'Brien. Words for every letter of the alphabet against a background of pictures from children's lore.

955. Hyman, Trina S. A LITTLE ALPHABET. Boston: Little, Brown; 1980.
Gr. K-3. Each letter of the alphabet is illustrated by a picture of a child playing with an object beginning with the letter.

956. Kitchen, Bert. ANIMAL ALPHABET. New York: Dial; 1984.
Gr. Preschool-up. Large scale illustrations of unusual animals -armadillo, quetzal, or yak, as well as lion and frog make up this wonderfully original alphabet book. A game, "Spot the Creatures/Give Each its Name," can be played with this book.

957. Lobel, Arnold. ON MARKET STREET. New York: Greenwillow; 1980.
Gr. K-3. A child buys presents from A to Z in the shops on Market Street.

958. Lobel, Arnold. ON MARKET STREET [Filmstrip]. New York: Random House; 1982; 1 filmstrip; 1 cassette.
Gr. K-3. Based on the Caldecott award book of the same title.

959. MODALITY ALPHABET CARDS WITH MODALITYSPECIFIC STIMULUS WORDS [Flash Cards]. Columbus, OH: Zaner-Bloser; 1981.
Gr. K-2. Modality alphabet cards with modality-specific stimulus words.

960. Moncure, Jane Belk. MY SOUND BOX. Chicago: Children's Press; 1979.
Gr. K-2. A little girl fills her sound box with many words beginning with the letters "a, b, and c". Each book in the series centers on different letters of the alphabet.

961. Niland, Deborah. ABC OF MONSTERS. New York: McGraw Hill; 1978.
Gr. K-3. A monster party where guests include annoying apes, drawing dragons, and ogly ogres.

962. A PEACEABLE KINGDOM: THE SHAKER ABECEDARIUS. Illustrated by Alice and Martin Provensen. New York: Viking; 1978.
Gr. K-3. An alphabet rhyme which first appeared in the Shaker Manifesto of 1882.

963. Rey, H.A. CURIOUS GEORGE LEARNS THE ALPHABET. Boston: Houghton Mifflin; 1963.

Gr. K-3. The man with the yellow hat illustrates the alphabet for his curious monkey friend.

964. CURIOUS GEORGE LEARNS THE ALPHABET [Kit]: Educational Enrichment Materials; 1977.
Gr. K-3. Based on the book of the same title.

965. Rockwell, Anne F. ALBERT B. CUB AND ZEBRA: AN ALPHABET STORYBOOK. New York: Crowell; 1977.
Gr. K-3. Albert tries to find who stole his zebra.

Human Language: Words and Word Games

966. Asimov, Isaac. WORDS FROM HISTORY. Boston: Houghton Mifflin; 1968.
Gr. 6-up. From Admiral to Zionism, Asimov gives a brief account of the historical origins of words.

967. Asimov, Isaac. WORDS OF SCIENCE, AND THE HISTORY BEHIND THEM. Illustrated by William Barss. Boston: Houghton Mifflin; 1959.
Gr. 6-up. The Asimov WORDS books are probably difficult for 6th graders but they offer fascinating insights into language and many of the words are already in the student's vocabulary.

968. Asimov, Isaac. WORDS ON THE MAP. Boston: Houghton Mifflin; 1962.
Gr. 6-up. The meaning behind places names from A to Z.

969. BACKPACK: A LANGUAGE DEVELOPMENT GAME [Game]. Niles, IL: Developmental Learning Materiasl; 1978; 1 game board; spinner; tokens; markers; cards.
Gr. 4-6. Offers practice in using modifiers, forming sentences, and expressing concepts in various ways.

970. Carroll, Lewis. JABBERWOCKY. Illustrated by Jane Breskin Zalben. New York: Warne; 1977.
Gr. 1-3. An illustrated version of Caroll's nonsense poem.

971. De Regnier, Beatrice Schenk. CATCH A LITTLE FOX. Illustrated. Boston: Houghton Mifflin; 1970.
Gr. Preschool-2. Simple verses expand on the nursery song of "A Hunting We Will Go."

972. THE ELECTRIC COMPANY WORD BUILDERS [Game]. Produced by Milton Bradley. Springfield, MA: Children's Television Workshop; 1975; 4 games in a bag; directions.
Gr. 1-2. Activity boards that deal with root words, compound words, comparative/superlatives and contractions.

973. Emberly, Barbara. DRUMMER HOFF. Illustrated by Ed Emberly. Englewood Cliffs, NJ: Prentice Hall; 1967.
Gr. K-2. Each member of the unit had a job in preparing the cannon, but Drummer Hoff fired it off. Also available as a filmstrip from Weston Woods.

974. FLAPDOODLE, PURE NONSENSE FROM AMERICAN FOLKLORE. Collected by Alvin Schwartz. Illustrated by John O'Brien. New York: Lippincott; 1980.
Gr. 5-up. A collection of spoonerisms, word plays, visual jokes and riddles, punctuation rhymes, nursery rhyme parodies, nonsense speech, verses, and folk stories.

975. FOIL [Game]. St. Paul, MN: 3M Company; 1971; 1 game: 4 word holders; 2 decks of letter cards; 1 card holder; 1 timer.
Gr. 4-up. A word game, with players forming and scrambling words.

976. Hanson, Joan. ANTONYMS: HOT AND COLD AND OTHER WORDS THAT ARE DIFFERENT AS NIGHT AND DAY. Minneapolis: Lerner; 1972.
Gr. K-4.

977. Hanson, Joan. HOMOGRAPHS: BOW AND BOW AND OTHER WORDS THAT LOOK THE SAME BUT SOUND AS DIFFERENT AS SOW AND SOW. Minneapolis, MN: Lerner; 1972.
Gr. K-4.

978. Hanson, Joan. HOMONYMS: HAIR AND HARE AND OTHER WORDS THAT SOUND THE SAME BUT LOOK AS DIFFERENT AS BEAR AND BARE. Minneapolis: Lerner; 1972.
Gr. K-4.

979. Horowitz, Edward. WORDS COME IN FAMILIES. New York: Hart; 1977.
Gr. 4. Root words are defined, placed in a historical context, and used in sentences. Cartoons illustrate some meanings.

980. Hunt, Bernice Kohn. THE WHATCHAMACALLIT BOOK. Pictures by Tomie de Paola. New York: Putnam; 1976.
Gr. 3-5. The reader is invited to name the elusive words for dozens of definitions.

981. Kohl, Herbert R. A BOOK OF PUZZLEMENTS: PLAY AND INVENTION WITH LANGUAGE. New York: Schocken; 1981.
Gr. 4-up. Puzzles and games and suggestions for creating new ones.

982. Pomerantz, Charlotte. IF I HAD A PAKA: POEMS IN ELEVEN LANGUAGES. Illustrated by Nancy Tafuri. New York: Greenwillow; 1982.
Gr. 3-6. Poems using words in other languages, the words for dozens of definitions.

983. THE READING GAME SIGHT VOCABULARY PROGRAM [Kit]. Chicago: American Learning Corp.; 1974; 3 Sets. Each set contains: 160 audio sound cards; 10 blank audio sound cards; 4 pads of 35 worksheets; 35 progress record sheets; 1 placement test; 1 teacher's guide.
Gr. 1-4. This is an auditory and visual program to teach and improve vocabulary skills. Set 1: Simple Sight Words. Set 2: Basic Sight Words. Set 3: Simple Sight Phrases.

984. Sarnoff, Jane. WORDS: A BOOK ABOUT THE ORIGINS OF EVERYDAY WORDS AND PHRASES. New York: Scribner; 1981.
Gr. 4-7.

985. Schwartz, Alvin. TOMFOOLERY: TRICKERY AND FOOLERY WITH WORDS. Illustrated by Glen Rounds. New York: Harper & Row; 1973.
Gr. 5-up. Folk games, songs and lore which use language play.

986. Tremain, Ruthven. FOOLING AROUND WITH WORDS. New York: Greenwillow; 1976.
Gr. 1-4. Riddles, knock, knock games, and other word games.

987. Tremain, Ruthven. TEAPOT, SWITCHEROO, AND OTHER SILLY WORD GAMES. New York: Greenwillow; 1979.
Gr. 1-4. Games involving homonyms, spoonerisms, pig latin, and root words.

988. WORDS IN CONTEXT. SETS 1, 2, and 3 [Filmstrip]. Old Greenwich, CT: Listening Library; 1979; 4 filmstrips; 4 cassettes; 1 teacher's guide in each set.

Gr. 6-9. Each set presents dramatized episodes featuring words selected from the Dale-O'Rourke word list, and introduces 5 to 15 new vocabulary words in each episode.

989. WORDSWORTH [Game]. New York: Invicta; 1975; 1 game: playing board; pegs; word marker; eraser.
Gr. 4-up. A word game for two involving the use of logic and thought to guess the mystery word.

Animal Sounds and Language

990. ANIMALS AND CIRCUS [Sound Recording]. Los Angeles, CA: Bowmar/Noble; 1962; 1 disk.
Gr. K-up. Part of Bowmar Orchestral Library, Series 1. Contents: Carnival of the Animals/Camille Saint-Saens; Circus Polka/Igor Stravinsky; Under the Big Top/Herbert Donaldson.

991. Dean, Anabel. HOW ANIMALS COMMUNICATE. Illustrated by Harris Petie. New York: Messner; 1977.
Gr. 4-6. Discusses animal communication along with various reasons why they communicate.

992. Friedman, Judi. NOISES IN THE WOODS. Pictures by John Hamberger. New York: Dutton; 1979.
Gr. 1-4. Explains how to follow sounds to find forest animals during the day and at night and identifies the makers of some familiar sounds.

993. Gans, Roma. BIRD TALK. Illustrated by Jo Polseno. New York: Harper & Row; 1971.
Gr. K-3. A simple introduction to the various voices and songs of birds and what they mean.

994. Gross, Ruth. WHAT IS THE ALLIGATOR SAYING? A BEGINNING BOOK ON ANIMAL COMMUNICATION. Illustrated by John Hawkinson. New York: Hastings House; 1972.
Gr. 2-4. Describes why and how animals communicate. Includes several results of experiments about communication.

995. Jacobs, Francine. THE SECRET LANGUAGE OF ANIMALS: COMMUNICATION BY PHEROMONES. New York: Morrow; 1976.
Gr. 4-6. The discovery and use of pheromones, chemical substances used for communication by animals and humans.

996. Jacobs, Francine. SOUNDS IN THE SEA. Illustrated by Jean Zallinger. New York: Morrow; 1977.
Gr. 3-7. An introduction to marine bioacoustics, the study of underwater sounds and the hearing abilities of marine animals.

997. Kuskin, Karla. ROAR AND MORE. New York: Harper & Row; 1956.
Gr. Preschool-3. Tells the habits of animals in rhyme, with a description of the sounds they make.

998. LIONS DON'T ALWAYS ROAR [Filmstrip]. From Experiences in Perceptual Growth. Chicago: Encyclopaedia Britannica Educational Corp.; 1 in a set of 3 filmstrips; 3 cassettes.
Gr. K-3. A mouse and a lion imitate sounds as they try to describe the sound of a roar.

999. Patent, Dorothy Hinshaw. HOW INSECTS COMMUNICATE. New York: Holiday House; 1975.
Gr. 4-6. Shows many forms of insect communication.

1000. Raskin, Ellen. WHO, SAID SUE, SAID WHO?. New York: Atheneum; 1973.
Gr. K-3. The sounds of various animals put into verse.

1001. Ricciuti, Edward R. SOUNDS OF ANIMALS AT NIGHT. New York: Harper & Row; 1977.
Gr. 4-6. A survey of animal night noises including the reasons that frogs, birds, insects and mammals make the noises they do.

1002. SONGS OF THE HUMPBACK WHALE [Sound Recording]. Hollywood, CA: Capitol Records; 1970; 1 sound disk.
Gr. 2-up. Recordings of the many and varied songs of the humpback whale.

1003. SOUNDS OF ANIMALS [Sound Recording]. New York: Folkway Records; 1955. 1 sound disc.
Gr. Preschool-2. Farm Animals: Fowl, Sheep, Goats, and Pigs; Zoo Animals: Tigers, Lions, Monkeys, Rhinoceros, Hippopotamus, Elephants, and others.

1004. Spier, Peter. GOBBLE, GROWL, GRUNT. New York: Doubleday; 1971.
Gr. K-1. Illustrations of over six hundred animals and the sounds they make.

1005. Van Woerkom, Dorothy. HIDDEN MESSAGES. New York: Crown; 1979.
Gr. 1-4. Describes Ben Franklin's experiments with ant communication. Fabre's with moths, and the discovery of pheromones, by which animals communicate.

Making Music

1006. Bethancourt, T. Ernesto. T.H.U.M.B.B. New York: Holiday House; 1983.
Gr. 6-up. A high school student tells in his own language how he and his friend "arranged" for "The Hippiest Underground Marching Band in Brooklyn" to march in New York's Saint Patrick's Day parade.

1007. Bierhorst, John. A CRY FROM THE EARTH: MUSIC OF THE NORTH AMERICAN INDIANS. New York: Scholastic; 1979.
Gr. 4-7. Discusses musical instruments, songs and dances of Native Americans.

1008. Bodecker, H.M. THE LOST STRING QUARTET. New York: Atheneum; 1981.
Gr. 1-up. A quartet get a bit lost on their way to a concert.

1009. BOWMAR/NOBLE ORCHESTRAL LIBRARY [Sound Recording]. Los Angeles, CA: Bowmar/Noble; 36 sound discs. Series I: 11 discs; lesson guide; 150 themes on overhead transparencies. Series 2: 7 discs; lesson guides; 100 themes on overbead transparencies. Series 3: 18 discs; lesson guides; 245 themes on overhead transparencies.
Gr. K-up. These offer an introduction to classical music. The selections move from melodious to complex compositions.

1010. BRITANNICA BOOK OF MUSIC. Edited by Benjamin Hadley. New York: Doubleday; 1980.
Gr. 6-up. A complete dictionary of information about music and musicians.

1011. Britten, Benjamin. BRITTEN: THE YOUNG PERSON'S GUIDE TO THE ORCHESTRA [Sound Recording]. Conducted by Neville Marriner. Minnesota Orchestra. Hollywood, CA: Angel; 1984; 1 sound disc.
Gr. 4-up. Purcell's Theme is used to demonstrate the sound of brasses, woodwinds, percussion, and string instruments; the quality of the sound, from birdlike flute to sad oboe, is shown.

1012. Diagram Group. MUSICAL INSTRUMENTS OF THE WORLD: AN ILLUSTRATED ENCLYCLOPEDIA. New York: Diagram Group; 1976.
Gr. 6-up. A comprehensive reference to all of the musical instruments of the world.

Diagram Group. THE SCRIBNER GUIDE TO ORCHESTRAL INSTRUMENTS. New York: Atheneum; 1983.
Gr. 6-up. See #116.

1013. DISNEY'S MUSIC EDUCATION [Filmstrip]. Burbank, CA: Walt Disney Educational Media; 1981; 6 filmstrips; 6 cassettes; 6 spirit masters; teacher's guide.
Gr. 4-8. Contents: Music All Around Us; Rhythm and Notation; Meter and Tempo; Melody and Harmony; Composition and Form; The Many Moods of Music.

English, Betty Lou. YOU CAN'T BE TIMID WITH A TRUMPET: NOTES FROM THE ORCHESTRA. Illustrated by Stan K. Skardinski. New York: Lothrop; 1980.
Gr. 5-up. See #118.

1014. THE FEEL OF MUSIC: BY HAP PALMER [Sound Recording]. Freeport, NY: Educational Activities; 1974; 1 sound disc or cassette.
Gr. K-3. Characteristics of music are related to movement (tempo, volume, pitch, etc,).

1015. Gilson, Jamie. DIAL LEROI RUPERT, DJ. Illustrated by John Wallner. New York: Lothrop; 1979.
Gr. 4-up. An unusual jazz combo "hits the Chicago subway" to earn money, but the players get stage fright.

1016. Glass, Henry, and Rosemary Hallum. RHYTHM STICK ACTIVITIES [Sound Recording]. Freeport, NY: Educational Activities; 1974; 1 sound disc; teacher's guide.
Gr. K-3.

1017. Goldreich, Gloria, and Esther Goldreich. WHAT CAN SHE BE? A MUSICIAN. Photographs by Robert Ipcar. New York: Lothrop; 1975.
Gr. K-5. A day in the life of Leslie Pearl, who plays piano and guitar, teaches, and sometimes conducts.

1018. Haseley, Dennis. THE OLD BANJO. Illustrated by Stephen Gammell. New York: Macmillan; 1983.
Gr. 1-4. A depression-era father and son live on a farm filled with musical instruments which one day come alive and play.

1019. Hawkinson, John, and Martha Faulhaber. MUSIC AND INSTRUMENTS FOR CHILDREN TO MAKE. Illustrated by John Hawkinson. Chicago: Whitman; 1969.
Gr. 3-up. Instructions for making a drum, box harp, and pan pipes as well as suggestions for ways of creating music.

1020. Hawkinson, John; Faulhaber, Martha. RHYTHMS, MUSIC, AND INSTRUMENTS TO MAKE. Illustrated. Chicago: Whitman; 1970.
Gr. 3-up. Instructions for making simple musical instruments and inventing and writing down melody.

1021. HOMEMADE BAND: BY HAP PALMER [Sound Recording]. Freeport, NY: Educational Activities; 1973; 1 sound disc or cassette.
Gr. K-3. Rhythm activities for the young child. A materials kit can be ordered which contains 20 pre-cut pieces for students to assemble rhythm instruments.

1022. Hughes, Langston. JAZZ. New York: Watts; 1982.
Gr. 5-up. An introduction to and highlights of the history of jazz.

1023. Hurd, Michael. THE OXFORD JUNIOR COMPANION TO MUSIC. 2nd edition. New York: Oxford University; 1979.
Gr. 6-up. Based on the original publication by Percy Scholes, this reference includes over 3,000 alphabetically arranged definitions of musical terms, examples of music, and biographical sketches of famous composers and musicians.

1024. Isadora, Rachel. BEN'S TRUMPET. Illustrated. New York: Greenwillow; 1979.
Gr. 1-5. Ben imagines be's a trumpeter like the nightclub musicians, but is discouraged by teasing of neighborhood boys.

Kuskin, Karla. THE PHILHARMONIC GETS DRESSED. New York: Harper & Row; 1982.
Gr. K-3. See #124.

MUSIC MAESTRO [Game]. Ann Arbor, MI: Aristoplay; 5 gameboards; playing pieces; cards; 1 audio cassette.
Gr. 3-up. See #128.

1025. THE MUSIC MAKERS [Sound Recording]. Columbus, OH: Carl E. Caligani; 1972; 10 sound discs.
Gr. 4-up. Fifty musicians play and talk about their instruments.

1026. MUSICAL VISIONS OF AMERICA [Filmstrip]. Columbus, OH: Carl E. Caligani; 1976; 4 filmstrips; 4 cassettes; teacher's guide.
Gr. 5-up. The story of America through its music, from marches to jazz to country western.

1027. Polk, Elizabeth. ORCHESTRATED MUSIC FOR SPECIAL CHILDREN [Sound Recording]. Waldick, NJ: Hoctor Records; 1975; 1 sound disc.
Gr. K-6. Musical pieces of distinct rhythmic characteristics. Contents: Yellow Rose of Texas; Beautiful Ohio; Alley Cat; Teddy Bear's Picnic; Waltzing in a Flat; Born Free.

1028. Price, Christine. TALKING DRUMS OF AFRICA. New York: Scribner; 1973.
Gr. 2-5. Discusses the role of drums as storytellers and communicators in Ghana and Nigeria.

1029. Prokofiev, Sergel. PETER AND THE WOLF. Illustrated by Charles Mikolaycak. New York: Viking; 1982.
Gr. 1-up. Story originally written in 1936 to accompany the score Prokofiev used to teach children the instruments of the orchestra.

1030. Prokofiev, Sergei. PETER AND THE WOLF [Sound Recording]. Conducted by Zubin Mehta. Israel Philharmonic; Narrated by Itzhak Perlman. Hollywood, CA: Angel; 1984; 1 sound disc.
Gr. 1-up. In this story, written to teach the instruments of the orchestra, Peter is represented by a string quartet and the wolf by three horns. (Many other recordings of this classic are available).

1031. RHYTHM STICK KIT [Realia]. Byron, CA: Front Row Experience; 1975; 24 rhythm sticks; 1 pamphlet.
Gr. K-3. The rhythm sticks provide students with a wide range of perceptual-motor tasks.

1032. Stecher, Miriam B., and Alice S. Kandell. MAX, THE MUSIC-MAKER. Illustrated. New York: Lothrop; 1980.
Gr. K-2. Max finds music everywhere: in the roar of a train, in the purr of a pussycat, and in the instruments he makes himself.

1033. THERE'S MUSIC ALL AROUND US [Filmstrip]. Englewood, CO: Learning Tree; 1980; 4 filmstrips; 4 cassettes; guide.
Gr. K-6. Contents: It's Everywhere; It's a Language; How the Language Works; Around the World.

1034. THIS IS RHYTHM [Sound Recording]. Sung by Ella Jenkins. New York: Folkways; 1961; 1 sound disc.
Gr. K-3. Ella Jenkins helps children hear rhythm and everyday sounds; she uses wood and stone blocks, rhythm sticks, conga drums, and maracas.

1035. Vulliamy, Graham. JAZZ AND BLUES. Boston: Routledge & Kegan Paul; 1982.
Gr. 6-12. Overview of the development of jazz and the blues.

1036. Weik, Mary H. THE JAZZ MAN. Illustrated by Ann Grifalconi. New York: Atheneum; 1966.
Gr. 2-6. Woodcuts illustrate a story of a lonely young boy who is comforted by the music of the jazz trumpeter next door.

1037. Wiseman, Ann. MAKING MUSICAL THINGS: IMPROVISED INSTRUMENTS. New York: Scribner; 1979.
Gr. 3-6. Clear directions for making 50 simple musical instruments from easily obtainable materials such as milk cartons and embroidery hoops.

1038. Yolen, Jan. RING OUT! A BOOK OF BELLS. Boston: Houghton Mifflin; 1974.
Gr. 5-7. The history and folklore of bells explaining their uses since ancient times.

Songs, Games and Ballads

1039. AMERICAN HISTORY IN BALLAD AND SONG [Sound Recording]. New York: Folkways Records; 1962; 6 sound discs; teaching guide, including texts of the songs.
Gr. 5-up.

1040. THE AMERICAN REVOLUTION IN SONG AND BALLAD [Sound Recording]. New York: Folkways Records; 1975; 1 sound disc.
Gr. 5-up. Contents: Come, Come; To The Ladies; Revolutionary Tea; Banks of the Dee; and others.

1041. AMERICAN SONGS TO SING [Sound Recording]. Compiled by Judy Wathen. New York: Scholastic; 1976; 1 sound disc.
Gr. 3-up. Yankee Doodle; The Ballad of the Tea Party; Ten Green Apples; The Erie Canal; Goober Peas; I've Been Working on the Railroad; Whoopey Ti Yi Yo; and others.

1042. Berger, Melvin. THE STORY OF FOLK MUSIC. New York: Phillips; 1976.
Gr. 6-up. The origins and presentation of folk music, including photographs, brief biographies and some songs.

1043. Bierhorst, John. SONGS OF THE CHIPPEWA. Pictures by Joe Servello. New York: Farrar, Straus & Giroux; 1974.
Gr. 4-up. Adapted from the collections of Frances Densmore and Henry Rowe Schoolcraft, and arranged for piano and guitar.

1044. Bley, Edgar S. THE BEST SINGING GAMES FOR CHILDREN OF ALL AGES. Illustrated by Patt Willen. New York: Sterling; 1957.
Gr. 2-5. Over fifty singing games including rules and music.

1045. Brand, Oscar, ed. SONGS OF '76: A FOLKSINGER'S HISTORY OF THE REVOLUTION. Illustrated. New York: Evans, distributed by Lippincott; 1972.
Gr. 5-up. Melodies with chord symbols.

1046. Brumley, Albert E. SONGS OF THE PIONEERS. Camdenton, MO: Brumley & Sons; 1970.
Gr. 4-up. A collection of 60 old-time favorite songs, arranged or selected by a prominent folk song writer and publisher.

1047. Brumley, Albert E. SONGS OF THE PIONEERS: NO. 2. Camdenton, MO: Brumley & Sons; 1973.
Gr. 4-up. A further collection of old-time favorite songs, arranged or selected by a prominent folk song writer and publisher.

1048. Bryan, Ashley. I'M GOING TO SING; BLACK AMERICAN SPIRITUALS, VOLUME 2. Illustrated. New York: Atheneum; 1982.
Gr. 2-5. 25 spirituals illustrated with woodcuts and an introduction which emphasizes the spiritual's distinctive style.

1049. FOLK SONG CARNIVAL [Sound Recording]. Arranged and sung by Hap Palmer. New York: Educational Activiteis; 1971; 1 sound disc.
Gr. Preschool-3. Folk songs to use for sing-along, movement, and dance.

1050. Fowke, Edith. SALLY GO ROUND THEN: THREE HUNDRED CHILDREN'S SONGS, RHYMES AND GAMES. New York: Doubleday; 1969.
Gr. 2-4. Three hundred singing games and songs with music.

1051. FREE TO BE ... YOU AND ME. Illustrated. New York: McGraw Hill; 1974.
Gr. K-3. A number of stories, poems, and songs which demonstrate that people can choose to do or be whatever they desire. Conceived by Marlo Thomas. Edited by Carole Hart and others.

1052. Garson, Eugenia, ed. THE LAURA INGALLS WILDER SONGBOOK. Arranged for piano and guitar by Herbert Haufrecht. Illustrated by Garth Williams. New York: Harper & Row; 1968.
Gr. 4-up. Ballads, folk songs, hymns, gospel songs, and minstrel show tunes familiar to the Ingalls family.

1053. Hart, Jane, ed. SINGING BEE! A COLLECTION OF FAVORITE CHILDREN'S SONGS. Illustrated by Anita Lobel. New York: Lothrop; 1982.
Gr. Preschool-1. A collection of over one hundred songs, including lullabies, holiday and traditional songs, singing games, and finger plays.

1054. Houston, James A. SONGS OF THE DREAM PEOPLE. Illustrated by James Houston. New York: Atheneum; 1972.
Gr. 4-up. Chants and images from the Indians and Eskimos of North America.

1055. John, Timothy, ed. GREAT SONG BOOK. Illustrated by Tomi Ungerer. New York: Doubleday; 1978.
Gr. 1-up. Over 60 of the best loved and most familiar songs for children, with most words and music.

1056. Johnson, James, and J. Rosamond Johnson. LIFT EVERY VOICE AND SING. Illustrated by Mozelle Thompson. New York: Hawthorne Books; 1970.
Gr. 4-up. The song sometimes called the national anthem of black Americans with piano arrangement and guitar chords.

1057. Keats, Ezra Jack. THE LITTLE DRUMMER BOY. Words and music by Katherine Davis, Henry Onorati, and Harry Simeone. New York: Macmillan; 1968.

Gr. Preschool-2. Lyrics and music for a classic Christmas song, illustrated by Caldecott Medal winner Ezra Jack Keats.

1058. Langstaff, John, ed. THE SEASON OF SINGING. Music arranged by Seymour Barab. New York: Doubleday; 1974.
Gr. 1-up. American Christmas carols and songs, particularly those based on traditional folk melodies, Afro-American songs, and early hymn tunes.

1059. Langstaff, John M., ed. SWEETLY SINGS THE DONKEY: ANIMAL ROUNDS FOR CHILDREN TO SING OR PLAY ON RECORDERS. Pictures by Nancy Winslow Parker. New York: Atheneum; 1976.
Gr. 3-8. Rounds from all over the world, which can be sung or played.

1060. Leisy, James F., ed. THE GOOD TIMES SONGBOOK. Illustrated by David Dawson. Nashville, TN: Abingdon; 1974.
Gr. 4-up. 160 songs for informal singing with resources for song leaders, accompanists, and singers.

1061. MUSIC OF GOLDEN AFRICA [Sound Recording]. New York: CMS; 1975; 1 sound disc.
Gr. 4-up. Vocal and instrumental music; Egbe Omo Nago Folkloric Ensemble.

1062. Nelson, Esther L. THE FUNNY SONGBOOK. Illustrated by Joyce Behr. New York: Sterling; 1984.
Gr. K-up. Songs fun to sing, from Bible songs to camp songs to rounds to old favorites such as Do Your Ears Hang Low.

1063. PATRIOTIC AND MORNING TIME SONGS [Sound Recording]. New York: Educational Activities; 1969; 1 sound disc.
Gr. Preschool-2. Includes marches and songs.

1064. Peek, Merle. ROLL OVER!: A COUNTING SONG. Illustrated by Merle Peek. New York: Houghton Mifflin; 1981.
Gr. Preschool-2. Before going to sleep a little boy keeps rolling over and as he does, the ten imaginary animals that are crowded into the bed with him fall out one after the other.

Quackenbush, Robert. Clementine. Philadelphia: Lippincott; 1974.
Gr. K-3. See #447.

1065. Quackenbush, Robert. SHE'LL BE COMIN' 'ROUND THE MOUNTAIN [Filmstrip]. Weston, CT: Weston Woods; 1975; 1 filmstrip; 1 cassette; 1 book.
Gr. K-6. An illustrated version of this song done in the form of a Wild West Show.

1066. Rounds, Glen. CASEY JONES [Filmstrip]. Weston, CT: Weston Woods; 1970; 1 filmstrip; 1 cassette; 1 book.
Gr. K-up. Based on the book about a fearless railroad engineer who stays with his train as it crashes.

1067. Seeger, Ruth. AMERICAN FOLK SONGS FOR CHRISTMAS. Illustrated by Barbara Cooney. New York: Doubleday; 1953.
Gr. 1-up. Carols, hymns, response songs, and some songs only indirectly related to Christmas.

1068. Sendak, Maurice. MAURICE SENDAK'S REALLY ROSIE: STARRING THE NUTSHELL KIDS. Illustrated. New York: Harper & Row; 1975.
Gr. 1-5. 10 year old Rosie directs neighborhood children, the Nutshell Kids, in a dramatized version of life in Brooklyn.

1069. Sendak, Maurice. THE MAURICE SENDAK SOUNDBOOK [Sound Recording]. Performed by Tammy Grimes. Music by Wolfgang Amadeus Mozart and Carole King: New York; Caedmon; 4 sound discs.
Gr. K-4. Contents: Higglety Pigglety Pop!; Where the Wild Things Are; and others.

1070. Silber, Irwin. SONGS OF THE CIVIL WAR [Sound Recording]. Sung by Pete Seeger and others. New York: Folkways Records; 1960; 2 sound discs.
Gr. 5-up.

1071. SING A SONG OF PEOPLE [Kit]. Los Angeles: Bowmar/Noble; 1972; 3 filmstrips; 3 discs; 1 songbook; felt figures for the flannel board; 3 minibook sets (each of which includes 2 filmstrips, 2 cassettes, and 20 minibooks; teacher's guide.
Gr. K-4. Music from the many cultures that make up America. Contents: Holidays and Seasons; Home and Community; Neighors.

1072. SONGS AND BALLADS OF COLONIAL & REVOLUTIONARY AMERICA [Sound Recording]. New York: Folkways Recording; 1976; 1 sound disc.

Gr. 5-up. Billy Broke Locks; Trappan'd Maiden; Fare Thee Well Ye Sweethearts; Mad Anthony Wayne; One Morning in May; The Fate of John Burgoyne; and others.

1073. SONGS FOR CHILDREN WITH SPECIAL NEEDS [Sound Recording]. Los Angeles: Bowmar/Noble; 1967; 3 sound discs.
Gr. Preschool-3. Recordings and a songbook for 27 songs, some familiar and some orginal compositions.

1074. SONGSTORIES: I AM SPECIAL [Filmstrip]. Chicago: Encyclopaedia Britannica Educational Corp.; 1976; 4 filmstrips; 4 cassettes; teacher's guide.
Gr. K-3. Contents: Katy - Somethng Different; Murphy the Grump; Martin the Artist; Freda and her Flowers.

1075. SONGSTORIES: WHAT MAKES ME THE ONLY ME [Filmstrip]. Chicago: Encyclopaedia Britannica Educational Corp.; 1976; 4 filmstrips; 4 cassettes; teacher's guide.
Gr. K-3. Contents: What Makes Me the Only Me; People I Know; My Favorite Place; A Holiday Is a Special Day.

1076. Winn, Marie. WHAT SHALL WE DO AND ALLEE GALLOO! PLAY SONGS AND SINGING GAMES FOR CHILDREN. New York: Harper & Row; 1972.
Gr. K-2. Words to 47 play songs, including musical arrangements.

1077. Winn, Marie, ed. THE FIRESIDE BOOK OF FUN AND GAME SONGS. Illustrated by Whitney Darrow, Jr., New York: Simon & Schuster; 1974.
Gr. 1-up. Musical arrangements by Allan Miller.

1078. Yolen, Jane, ed. ROUNDS ABOUT ROUNDS. Illustrated by Gail Gibbons. Musical arrangements by Barbara Green. New York: Watts; 1977.
Words and music to 57 well known rounds, from Row, Row, Row your Boat to How Lovely Is the Evening.

1079. YOU CAN SING IT YOURSELF [Sound Recording]. New York: Folkways Records; 1960; 1 sound disc.
Gr. 3-6. Folksinger Robin Christenson sings with children, helping them learn as he goes along. Spontaneous, not rehearsed, performance.

1080. Yurchenco, Henrietta, ed. A FIESTA OF FOLK SONGS FROM SPAIN AND LATIN AMERICA. Illustrated by Jules Maidoff. New York: Putnam; 1967.
Gr. 2-up. Includes music and words for songs about animals, singing games and dances, songs about people, and songs for Christmas.

Chapter 8

Monsters

What is a monster? The fascination with monstrous beings exists for both children and adults. Monsters of various sorts have existed in folklore down through the ages. When we don't have monsters we tend to create them. They provide something strange and terrifying which may repulse us, or excite our love and pity, or against which we can courageously do battle. But for each society and for each individual the idea of what is monstrous may differ. Some monsters are supernatural, some are all too real. The AMERICAN HERITAGE DICTIONARY, COLLEGE EDITION defines monsters in these ways:

> Monster n. 1. A fabulous being compounded of elements from various human or animal forms. 2. An animal or plant having structural defects or deformities. 3. Pathology: A fetus or infant that is grotesquely abnormal. 4. Any large animal, plant or object. 5. One who inspires disgust. Often used in rhetorical overstatements: a monster of selfishness -adj. Gigantic; huge, enormous.

The definition includes forms composed of human and animal elements such as griffins and satyrs; human, animal, or plant forms which suffer from structural deformities; things which inspire disgust; and even things which are simply large. It is the notion of persons or creatures which inspire disgust which makes the concept of monsters so broad. What may inspire disgust in one person may be considered beautiful in another. For example, to some, spiders are terrifying and horrible monstrous creatures. For others, these web-spinners represent an ideal of beauty. E.B. White used this contrast between disgust with spiders and the idea of their beauty in CHARLOTTE'S WEB.

The study of monsters can help children begin to really look at the concept of monster and to examine which things may be truly monstrous and which may hide a beauty, such as beauty discovered in BEAUTY AND THE BEAST. It can help children make distinctions between monstrous forms and monstrous behavior. It can help them see that in certain contexts, monsters are natural.

Monsters can be categorized broadly into three major groups: "real" monsters, that is, animals of the past and present which have been regarded as frightening or which are simply huge, or humans or animals with deformities or handicaps; imaginary monsters, that is, the various ghosts and dragons and other creatures of folklore, some of which are believed in and others not; and lastly, "artistic" monsters, that is, monsters which have been created by writers, poets, artists and filmmakers.

The world of "real" monsters is very broad because each of us may have a different idea of a monster. One large group of these "real" monsters are the prehistoric reptiles and mammals, often called monstrous because of their size. Most of us are fascinated by the idea of these gigantic creatures inhabiting the earth so long ago, and then disappearing, leaving only their fossil remains.

Because children do find this subject so fascinating, there are a great number of books and pieces of media such as Cohen's WHAT REALLY HAPPENED TO THE DINOSAURS and Pringle's DINOSAURS AND THEIR WORLD which explore these topics. For children interested in the habits of dinosaurs, Mash's HOW TO KEEP DINOSAURS is a delightfully innovative approach to the subject.

Those prehistoric reptiles and mammals which are ancestors of life we know today are also fascinating "monsters" to study. Books and media on the La Brea Tar Pits, Cole's SABER-TOOTH TIGER AND OTHER ICE-AGE MAMMALS and Aliki's WILD AND WOOLY MAMMOTHS look at these subjects. The Carricks' THE CROCODILES STILL WAIT is a simple poetic explanation of the ties of present life to life of the past.

A number of contemporary animals have earned reputations as monsters. Some of these animals are monsters because their behavior is dangerous or revolting to humans.

Probably the best-known examples of these monstrous animals are sharks and grizzly bears. Other monsters may or may not be dangerous, but are seen to be physically unappealing or unpleasant. Alligators and crocodiles, buzzards, iguana, komodo dragons, and tarantulas are examples of these.

It is interesting to collect both stories and informational material on these creatures because we see so many different images of them. Some materials attempt to put monstrous nature in the context of natural history, evolution and protection. Others, notably folklore, portray these creatures as natural antagonists who help humans to learn important lessons about life and survival. Story books for young children often show characters such as crocodiles or bears as friendly and loving; LYLE, LYLE CROCODILE by Waber and Minarek's LITTLE BEAR books are examples.

There is not a great deal of informational material on genetic misfortunes, that is, people, plants, or animals who are born with severe deformities which cause them to be seen as monstrous. Older children might want to read Skurzynski's MANWOLF, a speculative novel about a boy with a disease which may have been the root of the werewolf legends, or Montagu's THE ELEPHANT MAN, about a severely deformed man treated as a sideshow freak in Victorian London.

People can seem to be monstrous because of monstrous behavior. Younger children can understand this better after reading Steptoe's MY DADDY IS A MONSTER SOMETIMES. Older students might want to study the lives of historic figures known for monstrous behavior such as Attila the Hun, or Adolph Hitler, or the lives of people who made monstrous behavior a lifestyle such as pirates or mercenaries.

The category of imaginary and mythical monsters is equally broad because each culture or society has stories of monstrous beings and each is different. Trolls, witches, dragons (and

Eastern and Western dragons are very different), devils, djinn, ghosts, werewolves, giants, ogres, vampires, and many other creatures inhabit this monstrous world. Books such as Hoyt's DEMONS, DEVILS AND DJINN and Epstein's MONSTERS: THEIR HISTORIES, HOMES AND HABITS discuss some of these. Collections of tales and myths from any culture will include a few monster tales. Some collections such as Fenner's GIANTS AND WITCHES AND A DRAGON OR TWO collect a number of monster stories into one volume. Because there are so many folk stories about various monsters only a selection of possibilities have been included here.

There is a second category of monster folklore and that is those monsters that people today believe may still exist. Modern scientific investigations are ongoing to discover the truth about such creatures as the Loch Ness Monster, the Abominable Snowman, Bigfoot and aliens from outer space. Children might want to study the evidence for and against the existence of such creatures and form their own conclusions.

As happens with "real" monsters, many of the monstrous creatures of folklore appear in the world of "artistic" monsters in various forms. Often, as with the "real" monsters, they can become benign. Thus, the troll in the classic tale of THE THREE BILLY GOATS GRUFF and D'Aulaire's TROLLS becomes a rather nice creature in DePaola's HELGA'S DOWRY: A TROLL LOVE STORY. And cruel dragons of folklore become the poor RELUCTANT DRAGON of

Kenneth Grahame or the cheerful dreamer of Pavey's ONE DRAGON'S DREAM.

The "artistic" monsters are those which are created by individuals for literature, film, painting, sculpture and drawing to represent human imaginings, fears and beliefs. Some are as fiercely terrifying as their folk ancestors. Mary Shelley's FRANKENSTEIN and Bram Stoker's DRACULA, re-created on film and used as characters in other books, cartoons and comics, are classic artistic monsters. The range of possible monsters is also very wide. They may be created to scare away demons of various types, such as the gargoyles in FACES ON PLACES and the figures in THE SCARECROW BOOK. Various monstrous ritual masks are shown in THEY PUT ON MASKS and DANCING MASKS OF AFRICA and in Marcia Brown's SHADOW.

Literary monsters may be benign and affectionate as are Sendak's "Wild Things" and Mayer's "Nightmare" in THERE'S A NIGHTMARE IN MY CLOSET. They may be ridiculous, as are the monsters of the knock-knock and riddle books.

Monsters affect our lives in many ways. We may revile and fear them, we may vanquish them or turn them into objects of ridicule, but they do not go away. Psychologists have long pointed out that if we are not given monsters in lore and literature we will create them ourselves. The study of monsters is endlessly fascinating. It reveals as much about human beings and our attitudes as it does about the monsters themselves.

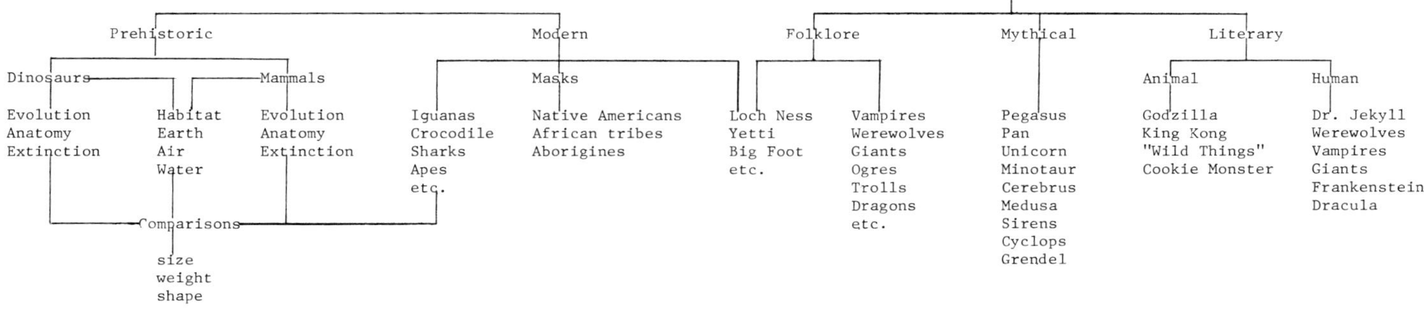
MONSTERS
REAL
IMAGINARY
Prehistoric
Modern
Folklore
Mythical
Literary
Dinosaurs
Mammals
Masks
Animal
Human
Evolution
Anatomy
Extinction
Habitat
Earth
Air
Water
Evolution
Anatomy
Extinction
Iguanas
Crocodile
Sharks
Apes
etc.
Native Americans
African tribes
Aborigines
Loch Ness
Yetti
Big Foot
etc.
Vampires
Werewolves
Giants
Ogres
Trolls
Dragons
etc.
Pegasus
Pan
Unicorn
Minotaur
Cerebrus
Medusa
Sirens
Cyclops
Grendel
Godzilla
King Kong
"Wild Things"
Cookie Monster
Dr. Jekyll
Werewolves
Vampires
Giants
Frankenstein
Dracula
Comparisons
size
weight
shape

REAL MONSTERS

Prehistoric Monsters

1081. Aliki. DIGGING UP DINOSAURS. New York: Crowell; 1981.
Gr. K-3. Briefly introduces various types of dinosaurs whose skeletons and reconstructions are seen in museums and explains how scientist uncover, preserve, and study fossilized dinosaur bones.

1082. Aliki. MY VISIT TO THE DINOSAURS. New York: Crowell; 1969.
Gr. 1-3. A young boy learns all about dinosaurs as he tours a museum.

1083. Aliki. WILD AND WOOLY MAMMOTHS. Illustrated. New York: Crowell; 1977.
Gr, 1-3. Describes in simple text the huge mammoths which roamed the earth in the distant past.

1084. AMAZING WORLD OF DINOSAURS [Kit]. Burbank, CA: Walt Disney Educational Media; 1977; 3 filmstrips; 3 cassettes; 30 spirit masters, 6 activity cards; 1 teacber's guide.
Gr. 2-5. A look at the evolution of these prehistoric monsters and their ultimate extinction. Contents: How Worlds Began; In Search of Dinosaurs, Parts I and II.

1085. ANIMALS: PREHISTORIC AND PRESENT [Filmstrip]. Chicago: Encyclopaedia Britannica Education Corp.; 1978; 4 filmstrips; 4 cassettes; 1 teacher's manual.
Gr. 1-6. Describes the development of life on earth. Contents: Life in the Sea: From Reptile to Bird; Dinosaurs - The Terrible Lizards; Came the Mammals. Also available in captioned version: Animals fron the Prehistoric Ages.

1086. ANIMALS FROM THE PREHISTORIC AGES [Filmstrip]. Produced by Pomfret House. Chicago: Encyclopaedia Britannica Education Corp.; 1979; 4 filmstrips; 4 cassettes; 1 guide.
Gr. 1-6. Captioned filmstrips describe prehistoric animals from their evolution from sea life to the emergence of man. Also available without sound accompaniment.

1087. Brown, Marc Tolon. DINOSAURS, BEWARE!: A SAFETY GUIDE. Illustrated. Boston: Little, Brown; 1982.

Gr. K-3. Approximately sixty safety tips are demonstrated by dinosaurs in situations at home, during meals, camping, in the car, and in other familiar places.

1088. Carrick, Carol. THE CROCODILES STILL WAIT. Illustrated by Donald Carrick. Boston: Houghton Mifflin; 1980.
Gr. 1-4. Talks about the life of the giant prehistoric crocodile, ancestor of the modern monster.

1089. Cohen, Daniel. WHAT REALLY HAPPENED TO THE DINOSAURS? Illustrated by Hara Wells. New York: Dutton; 1977.
Gr. 4-6. Discusses environmental factors which might have caused tbe extinction of the dinosaurs.

1090. Cole, Joanna. DINOSAUR STORY. Illustrated by Nore Kunstler. New York: Morrow; 1974.
Gr. K-3. Discusses ten different dinosaurs, their habits and time period.

1091. Cole, Joanna. SABER-TOOTHED TIGER AND OTHER ICE AGE MAMMALS. Illustrated by Lydia Rosier. New York: Morrow; 1977.
Gr. 3-6. Describes such ice-age mammals as the saber-toothed tiger, tbe mastodon and the cave bear.

1092. Cuisin, Michel. NATURE'S HIDDEN WORLD: PREHISTORIC LIFE. Illustrated by Jose Olivier. Morristown, NJ: Silver Burdett; 1980.
Gr. 3-6. Describes the prehistoric animals as they have been reconstructed from fossil evidence.

1093. THE DINOSAURS [Filmstrip]. Glendale, CA: Cypress; 1977; 4 filmstrips; 4 cassettes; 1 teacber's guide.
Gr. 1-3. Features cartoon characters that provide the focus for the development of language and logical thinking skills while exploring the age of dinosaurs. Contents: The Museum; The Great Marshland; The Changing Dinosaurs; When Reptiles Ruled the Earth.

1094. DINOSAURS [Filmstrip], Washington, D.C: National Geographic; 1978; 1 filmstrip; 1 cassette; 1 guide.
Gr. K-4. A survey of the reign of tbe dinosaurs, beginning with their ancestors and ending with their extinction.

1095. Freeman, Russell. THEY LIVED WITH THE DINOSAURS. New York: Holiday House; 1980.

Gr. 2-5. Describes animals which are the modern-day relations of creatures which lived in prehistoric times and shows fossil remains of their ancestors.

1096. Geis, Darlene. DINOSAURS AND OTHER PREHISTORIC ANIMALS. Pictures by R.F. Peterson. New York: Grosset & Dunlap; 1959.
Gr. 4-6.

1097. HOW TO SPEAK DINOSAUR: A LOOK AT PREHISTORIC CREATURES [Sound Recording]. North Hollywood, CA: Audiotronics; 1977; 54 audiocards; 4 experience sheets; 1 guide with answer sheet.
Gr. K-6. The audiocards introduce the scientific names, together with a brief description of 54 dinosaurs and other extinct prehistoric animals.

1098. Kaufmann, John. FLYING REPTILES IN THE AGE OF DINOSAURS. New York: Morrow; 1976.
Gr. 1-5. Discusses the pterosaurs, the prehistoric flying reptiles.

1099. Kaufmann, John. LITTLE DINOSAURS AND EARLY BIRDS. Illustrated. New York: Crowell; 1977.
Gr. K-3. An introduction to the prehistoric birds and a discussion of how they might have evolved.

1100. LEARNING ABOUT DINOSAURS [Study Print]. Chicago: Encyclopedia Britannica Educational Corp.; 1966; 7 pictures; 1 teacher's guide.
Gr. 4-6. Contents: Introduction; Fossils; Stegosaurus; Brontosaurus; Ankylosaurus; Tyrannosaurus Rex; Triceratops.

1101. Mash, Robert. HOW TO KEEP DINOSAURS: THE COMPLETE GUIDE TO BRINGING UP YOUR BEAST. Illustrated by Philip Hood and others. New York: Penguin; 1983.
Gr. 4-6. Arranged in categories such as dinosaurs as lap pets, as flying pets, for zoos, for the circus and so on, this book is filled with facts about dinosaur habits, living conditions and size.

1102. May, Julian. DODOS AND DINOSAURS ARE EXTINCT. Illustrated. Mankoto, MI: Creative Educational Society; 1970.
Gr. 6-9. Describes the various animals that have become extinct.

1103. May, Julian. THE WARM-BLOODED DINOSAURS. Drawings by Lorence Bjorklund. New York: Holiday House; 1978.
Gr. K-3. A simple discussion of new evidence that dinosaurs were warm-blooded animals and not reptiles as previously believed.

1104. McGowen, Tom. ALBUM OF DINOSAURS. Illustrated by Rod Ruth. Chicago: Rand McNally; 1972.
Gr. 3-12. A brief introduction to tbe history and characteristics of dinosaurs in general and specific descriptions of twelve different kinds.

1105. Moody, Richard. A NATURAL HISTORY OF DINOSAURS. Illustrated. Secaucus, NJ: Chartwell Books; 1977.
Gr. 4-8. A description of distribution, ecology, and evolution of dinosaurs from the early tiny forms to the later giants.

1106. Parish, Peggy. DINOSAUR TIME. Illustrated by Arnold Lobel, New York: Harper & Row; 1974.
Gr. K-3. An I-Can-Read Book introduces eleven dinosaurs.

1107. Pringle, Laurence. DINOSAURS AND THEIR WORLD. New York: Harcourt Brace; 1968.
Gr. 3-5. Discusses the life of the dinosaur of the distant past along with museums where dinosaur fossils can be seen.

1108. Pringle, Laurence. DINOSAURS AND PEOPLE: FOSSILS, FACTS AND FANTASIES. New York: Harcourt Brace; 1978.
Gr. 5-7. Presents some new theories about dinosaurs and their decline as well as a history of past discoveries.

1109. Ricciuti, Edward R. OLDER THAN THE DINOSAURS: THE ORGIN AND RISE OF THE MAMMALS. Illustrated by Edward Malsbery. New York: Crowell; 1980.
Gr. 3-6. Development of earliest mammals and their adaptation through the ages.

1110. Sattler, Helen Roney. THE ILLUSTRATED DINOSAUR DICTIONARY. Illustrated by Pamela Carroll. New York: Lothrop; 1983.
Gr. 4-up. A dictionary with entries for all known dinosaurs, about 300 at last count, and other animals of the Mesozoic Era, as well as general topics relating to dinosaurs, from Acanthopholis to Zigongosaurus.

1111. Selsam, Millicent. SEA MONSTERS OF LONG AGO. New York: Scholastic; 1977.
Gr. 1-3. Discusses the lives of the strange ocean reptiles who lived during the age of tbe dinosaurs.

1112. Sibley, Gretchen. LA BREA STORY. Illustrated. Los Angeles: Ward Ritchie; 1967.
Gr. 5-9. A history of life around the La Brea tar pits from 40,000 years ago to the present.

1113. Simon, Seymour. THE SMALLEST DINOSAURS. Illustrated by Anthony Rao. New York: Crown; 1982.
Gr. K-3. Discusses seven dinosaurs, all about the size of a dog or chicken, which are believed to be the bird's prehistoric cousin.

1114. Sullivan, Nora. DINOSAURS. Illustrated by Jim Robins, New York: Watts; 1076.
Gr. 2-4. Introduces different types of dinosaurs, their characteristics and habits, and the scientific studies of dinosaur fossils.

1115. Sundgaard, Arnold. JETHRO'S DIFFICULT DINOSAUR. New York: Pantheon; 1977.
Gr. Preschool-3. Once the egg Jethro found in Central Park hatches, it proves to be an unusual but difficult pet.

Modern Monsters

1116. AMERICAN REPTILES IN THEIR ENVIRONMENT [Filmstrip]. Pleasantville, NY: Imperial Educational Resources; 1969.
Gr. 4-6. Describes the fascinating world of reptiles. Contents: Place of Reptiles in Nature; Snakes Are Mighty Hunters.

1117. Ancona, George. MONSTERS ON WHEELS. Illustrated. New York: Dutton; 1974.
Gr. 3-up. Text and photographs introduce the physical characteristics and functions of a variety of machines designed for heavy labor.

Blumberg, Rhoda. SHARKS. New York: Watts; 1976.
Gr. 4-up. See #567.

1118. Carr, Archie. THE REPTILES. Amsterdam: Time-Life; 1968. Gr. 5-9. Looks at the origins of reptiles in prehistoric times, and the life cycles of reptiles now living on the earth.

Carrick, Carol. SAND TIGER SHARK. Illustrated by Donald Carrick. Burlington, MA: Clarion; 1977. Gr. 1-5. See #577.

1119. Chace, Earl. THE WORLD OF LIZARDS. Illustrated. New York: Dodd, Mead; 1982. Gr. 5-up. Contains a long chapter on iguanas.

1120. ENDANGERED SPECIES: REPTILES AND AMPHIBIANS [Study Print]. Chicago: Encyclopaedia Britannica Educational Corp.; 1976; 8 study prints; study guide. Gr. 4-8. Contents: American Crocodile; San Francisco Garter Snake; Giant Galapagos Tortoise; Hawks-bill Turtle; Gila Monster; Tuatara; Houston Toad; Santa Cruz Long-toed Salamander.

1121. FASCINATING SNAKES [Filmstrip]. Shawnee Mission, KS: Marshfilm; 1970; 1 filmstrip; 1 cassette; 1 guide. Gr. 1-8. Gives students a better understanding of snakes and their role in the balance of nature. Describes poisonous and non-poisonous snakes of North America.

Fletcher, Alan Mark. FISHES DANGEROUS TO MAN. Illustrated by Jane Teiko Oka and Willi Baum. Reading, MA: Addison Wesley; 1969. Gr. 4-7. See #588.

1122. Freschet, Berniece. BIOGRAPHY OF A BUZZARD. Illustrated by Bill Elliott. Lyndburst, NJ: Putnam; 1976. Gr. 2-5. Shows buzzards in a New Mexico environment; discusses feeding habits, life cycle and folklore about them.

1123. Freschet, Berniece. GRIZZLY BEAR. Illustrated by Donald Carrick. Totowa, NJ: Scribner; 1975. Gr. 2-4. Describes a year in the life of a Grizzly bear mother and her twin cubs.

1124. Graham, Ada, and Frank Graham. ALLIGATORS. Illustrated by D. Tyler. New York: Delacorte; 1979. Gr. 5-up. Discusses the habits and behavior of the alligator and the recent efforts of conservationists to protect this fierce-looking reptile from extinction.

1125. Harris, Margaret. SHARKS AND TROUBLED WATERS. Illustrated. Milwaukee, WI: Raintree; 1977.
Gr. 4-6. A study of this dangerous animal's habits as well as tales and superstitions.

1126. Hopf, Alice L. BIOGRAPHY OF A KOMODO DRAGON. Illustrated by Jean Zallinger. Lyndhurst, NJ: Putnam; 1981.
Gr. 2-4. Habits and behavior of this Indonesian lizard.

1127. Hornblow, Leonora. REPTILES DO THE STRANGEST THINGS. Illustrated by Michael Frith. Westminster, MD: Random House; 1970.
Gr. 2-4. A brief survey of some of the unusual habits of reptiles.

1128. Lauber, Patricia. WHO NEEDS ALLIGATORS? Illustrated. Champaign, IL: Garrard; 1974.
Gr. 2-4. Discusses the natural history and life habits of alligators and their importance to our ecology.

McGovern, Ann. SHARKS. Illustrated by Murry Tinkelman. New York: Four Winds; 1976.
Gr. K-3. See #615.

McGowen, Tom. ALBUM OF SHARKS. Illustrated by Rod Rutb. Chicago: Rand McNally; 1977.
Gr. 5-7. See #617.

1129. Montagu, Ashley. ELEPHANT MAN: A STUDY IN HUMAN DIGNITY. New York: Dutton; 1979.
Gr. 4-up. A study of the life of an unfortunate man who was rescued from a degrading existence by a caring physician.

1130. Patent, Dorothy Hinshaw. REPTILES AND HOW THEY REPRODUCE. Drawings by Matthew Kalmenoff. New York: Holiday House; 1977.
Gr. 5-7. Discusses the characteristics and habits of members of the reptile family with particular attention to their mating and reproductive behavior.

1131. Perkins, Laurence. ALL COLOR BOOK OF REPTILES. London: Octopus Books, distributed by Crescent; 1974.
Gr. 3-up. Striking photographs and brief text introduce many members of this family of small "monsters."

1132. Pringle, Laurence. COCKROACHES: HERE, THERE AND EVERYWHERE. New York: Harper & Row; 1971.
Gr. 1-3. A positive look at this insect which is generally reviled.

1133. Pruitt, Jim, and Nancy McGowan. THE NORTH AMERICAN ALLIGATOR. Illustrated. Austin, TX: Steck-Vaughn; 1974.
Gr. 3-up. Discusses the origin, characteristics, habits, and habitat of the North American alligator and what must be done to protect it from extinction.

1134. REPTILES AND AMPHIBIANS. New York: Time-Life; 1976.
Gr. 4-up. Discusses the habits and life cycles of these creatures using photographs, drawings and text.

Riedman, Sarah. SHARKS. Illustrated by Robert McClynn. New York: Watts; 1977.
Gr. 2-4. See #633.

Selsam, Millicent, and Joyce Hunt. A FIRST LOOK AT SHARKS. Illustrated by Harriett Springer. New York: Walker; 1979.
Gr. K-3. See #643.

1135. SHARKS AND THE UNDERWATER WORLD [Kit]. Bedford Hills, NY: Orange Cherry Media; 1979; 4 filmstrips; 4 cassettes; 2 books; 1 duplicating book; 1 guide.
Gr. 1-6. Explores the realm of sharks and rays, describes the unique way that sharks detect prey and attack, shows unusual species of sharks, and discusses whale, dolphins and seals. Contents: Underwater Killers and Devils; The Shark - Underwater Airplane; Creatures of the Sea; Whales and Other Mammals of the Sea.

1136. Shuttlesworth, Dorothy E. ANIMALS THAT FRIGHTEN PEOPLE: FACT VERSUS MYTH. New York: Dutton; 1973.
Gr. 3-6. Chapters on animals known as monsters to many: wolves, big cats, bears, bats, snakes, alligators and crocodiles, sharks, octopi, squids, predatory birds and poisonous spiders.

1137. Simon, Hilda. SNAKES: THE FACTS AND FOLKLORE. Illustrated. New York: Viking; 1973.
Gr. 2-4. Looks at types of snakes and legends and folklore that surround them.

1138. Singer, Marilyn. ARCHER ARMADILLO'S SECRET ROOM. Picures by Beth Lee Weiner, New York: Macmillan; 1985.

Gr. 3-6. Archer Armadillo refuses to leave his secret room when the rest of the family moves to a new burrow.

1139. Skurzynski, Gloria. MANWOLF. Boston: Houghton Mifflin; 1981.
Gr. 5-up. Adam's ravaged skin and reddened teeth lead the people around to suspect that he is a werewolf.

1140. Soule, Gardner. MYSTERY MONSTERS OF THE DEEP. New York: Watts; 1981.
Gr. 1-3. A collection of strange undersea creatures. Includes lists of further readings.

1141. SPIDERS [Filmstrip]. Washington, D.C: National Geographic; 1981; 1 filmstrip; 1 cassette; 1 guide.
Gr. K-6. Shows different kinds of spiders and describes how they live, how they grow and how they get food.

1142. Steptoe, John. DADDY IS A MONSTER...SOMETIMES. Illustrated. Philadelphia, PA: Lippincott; 1980.
Gr. 1-3.

1143. Stonehouse, Bernard. A CLOSER LOOK AT REPTILES. Illustrated by Gary Hinks. New York: Gloucester Press; 1979.
Gr. 5-8. Discusses the evolution of reptiles and describes today's lizards, snakes, turtles, tortoises, crocodiles, alligators, their relatives, and the unique tuatara.

1144. TODAY'S DRAGONS: THE LIZARDS [Slide]. Elmira, NY: Educational Images; 1973; 20 slides; text.
Gr. 1-up. A study of the largest group of reptiles.

1145. THE VERTEBRATES GAME [Game]. Chicago: Coronet; 1962; 1 game; playing board; 48 cards.
Gr. 4-8. 2-5 players, plus judge, Rules and answers on container envelope. Based on Coronet study print series, "Discovering Vertebrates". Object of game is to gain points by placing cards in correct categories on game board.

1146. Victor, Joan Berg. TARANTULAS. Illustrated. New York: Dodd, Mead; 1979.
Gr. 2-5. Explains life patterns of this primitive spider.

1147. Warner, Matt. REPTILES AND AMPHIBIANS. Illustrated. New York: Golden Press; 1974.
Gr. 4-7. A close look at amphibians (frogs, toads, and salamanders) and reptiles (turtles, lizards, snakes, alligators, and crocodiles).

1148. Wise, William. MONSTERS FROM OUTER SPACE? Illustrated by Richard Cuffari. New York: Putnam; 1978.
Gr. 2-5. Explains that most sightings of unidentified flying objects are actually understandable phenomena and discusses the possibility of intelligent life existing elsewhere in the universe.

IMAGINARY MONSTERS

In Literature

1149. A-HAUNTING WE WILL GO: GHOSTLY STORIES AND POEMS. Selected by Lee Bennett Hopkins. Illustrated by Vera Rosenberry. Chicago: Whitman; 1977.
Gr. 3-6. Tales to make you wonder whether or not there really are ghosts.

1150. ALFRED HITCHCOCK'S MONSTER MUSEUM. New York: Random House; 1982.
Gr. 5-up. A collection of short stories about monsters.

1151. Aruego, Jose, and Ariane Aruego. A CROCODILE'S TALE: A PHILIPPINE FOLK STORY, Illustrated, New York: Scribner; 1972.
Gr. K-3. A little boy saves a crocodile's life only to have the animal threaten to eat him.

1152. Babbitt, Natalie. THE SOMETHING. Illustrated. New York: Farrar, Straus & Giroux; 1970.
Gr. 1-3. An ugly little monster fears that "something" (a pretty little girl) will get him in the night.

1153. Bang, Molly. THE GREY LADY AND THE STRAWBERRY SNATCHER. New York: Four Winds; 1980.
In this story without words, an old woman is pursued by a strange man with a passion for strawberries.

1154. Bang, Molly. THE GREY LADY AND THE STRAWBERRY SNATCHER [Filmstrip]. Westminster, MD: Random House; 1981; 1 filmstrip; 1 cassette; 1 guide.
Gr. K-4. Based on the book of the same title.

1155. Bang, Molly. WILEY AND THE HAIRY MAN. Illustrated. New York: Macmillan; 1976.
Gr. 2-4. Wiley has to go into the swamp where the "hairy man" monster lives.

1156. Brewton, Sara, and John E. Brewton. SHRIEKS AT MIDNIGHT: MACABRE POEMS, EERIE AND HUMOROUS. Illustrated by Ellen Raskin. New York: Crowell; 1969.
Gr. 5-up. A collection of many kinds of poems about monsters, many by well-known poets.

1157. Bright, Robert. GEORGIE'S HALLOWEEN. Illustrated. New York: Doubleday; 1958.
Gr. K-3. Georgie the ghost almost wins the prize for the best costume at the Halloween party.

1158. Butterworth, Oliver. THE ENORMOUS EGG. Illustrated by Lois Darling. Boston: Little, Brown; 1956.
Gr. 4-6. Nate's hen lays a dinosaur egg. Also available in paperback edition: Dell, 1978.

1159. Cohen, Barbara. LOVELY VASSILISA. Illustrated by Anatoly Ivanov. New York: Atheneum; 1980.
Gr. K-3. When the terrible witch Baba Yaga vows to eat her supper, Vassilisa escapes with the help of a doll from her mother.

1160. Cole, William. MONSTER KNOCK-KNOCKS. Illustrated by Mike Thaler, New York: Pocket Books; 1982.
Gr. 3-5. A collection of knock-knock jokes based on monsters.

1161. Cole, William, ed. DINOSAURS AND BEASTS OF YORE. Illustrated by Susanna Natti. New York: Philomel; 1979.
Gr. 1-5. Line drawings and humorous poetry about dinosaurs performing modern activities.

1162. CREATURE CREATOR [Micro Computer Program]. San Francisco: Designware; 1983; 1 disk (Apple II+, IIe).
Gr. 4-8. Students are encouraged to create creatures by selecting heads, bodies, arms, and legs and then to program dances for them.

1163. Crowe, Robert. CLYDE MONSTER. Illustrated by Kay Chorao. New York: Dutton; 1976.
Gr. K-2. Clyde is a monster who is afraid of people but his parents help him to overcome his fears.

1164. D'Aulaire, Ingri. TERRIBLE TROLL-BIRD. Illustrated. New York: Doubleday; 1976.
Gr. 1-3. When villagers kill the huge rooster who is the trolls' pet, the trolls come to get revenge.

1165. De Groat, Diane. ALLIGATOR'S TOOTHACHE. Illustrated. New York: Crown; 1977.
Gr. Preschool-1. It is a serious problem when an alligator gets a toothache, especially when it is afraid of the dentist.

1166. De Paola, Tomie. HELGA'S DOWRY: A TROLL LOVE STORY. Illustrated. New York: Harcourt, Brace; 1977.
Gr. 1-3. Helga the troll goes in search of a dowry for herself.

1167. Dickens, Charles. A CHRISTMAS CAROL. Illustrated by Arthur Rackham. Philadelphia: Lippincott; 1964.
Gr. 5-up. The miser, Scrooge, has a series of dreams which change his way of celebrating Christmas.

1168. Domanska, Janina. KING KRAKUS AND THE DRAGON. Illustrated. New York: Greenwillow; 1979.
Gr. 1-3. Polish tale of a shoemaker's apprentice who found a way to slay a dragon.

1169. Drescher, Henrik. SIMON'S BOOK. New York: Lothrop; 1983.
Gr. K-3. A monster pursues Simon until he fights it with pen and ink.

1170. Fisk, Nicholas. MONSTER MAKER. New York: Macmillan; 1980.
Gr. 5-9. Matt works at a movie studio where the movie monsters one day come to life.

1171. Flora, James. GRANDMA'S GHOST STORIES. Illustrated. New York: Atheneum; 1978.
Gr. K-4. Grandpa tells ghost stories during a storm.

1172. Freedman, Sally. MONSTER BIRTHDAY PARTY. Pictures by Diane Dawson. Chicago: Whitman; 1983.
Gr. K-3. With deft waves of the hand, a rich boy's kindly butler enlivens Peter's birthday celebration with his sedate uncles and aunts by producing messy, but merry monsters.

1173. Gage, Wilson. MRS. GADDY AND THE GHOST. Illustrated by Marylin Hofner. New York: Greenwillow; 1979.
Gr. 1-3. Mrs. Gaddy finds a ghost in her kitchen.

1174. Galdone, Paul. THE MONKEY AND THE CROCODILE: A JATAKA TALE FROM INDIA. Illustrated. New York: Seabury Press; 1969.
Gr. Preschool-3. A retelling of one of the Indian fables relating to the former births of Buddha in which as a monkey he manages to outwit the crocodile who decides to capture him.

1175. Gardner, John C. DRAGON, DRAGON AND OTHER TALES. Illustrated by Charles Shields. New York: Knopf, distributed by Random House; 1975.
Gr. 4-up. Four tales about dragons with modern twists.

1176. Garfield, Leon. RESTLESS GHOST: THREE STORIES. Illustrated by Saul Lambert. New York: Pantheon; 1969.
Gr. 6-up. The specter of a drummer boy, a young apprentice, and a petty criminal figure in these three ghost stories.

1177. Grahame, Kenneth. THE RELUCTANT DRAGON. Illustrated by Michael Hague. New York: Holt, Rinehart & Winston; 1983.
Gr. 6-up. A mild-mannered dragon doesn't want to fight St. George.

1178. Green, Anne M. GOOD-BY, GRAY LADY. Drawings by Alton Raible. New York: Atheneum; 1964.
Gr. 4-6. The Gray Lady was the ghost who walked when the Gilbert's home was in danger.

1179. Haley, Gail. GO AWAY, STAY AWAY. Illustrated. New York: Scribner; 1977.
Gr. 1-3. A Swiss family's house is haunted by invisible creatures so they plot to get rid of them.

1180. Hogrogian, Nonny. THE DEVIL WITH THE THREE GOLDEN HAIRS: A TALE FROM THE BROTHERS GRIMM. Illustrated. New York: Knopf; 1983.
Gr. 2-4. A boy born to a poor couple receives the hand of the King's daughter in marriage, but in order to keep his bride, be must bring the King three golden hairs from the head of the devil.

1181. Hoke, Helen. A CHILLING COLLECTION: TALES OF WIT AND INTRIGUE. New York: Elsevier-Nelson; 1980.
Gr. 4-8. Nineteen scary stories about monstrous characters and ghosts.

1182. Hoke, Helen. UNCANNY TALES OF UNEARTHLY AND UNEXPECTED HORRORS: AN ANTHOLOGY. New York: Lodestar; 1983.
Gr. 6-up. Stories involving ghosts and monsters, both human and otherwise.

1183. Hopkins, Lee Bennett. MONSTERS, GHOULIES AND CREEPY CREATURES. Chicago: Whitman; 1977.
Gr. 4-6. A collection of stories and poems about various monstrous creatures.

1184. Howe, Deborah, and James Howe. BUNNICULA. Illustrated by Alan Daniel. New York: Atheneum; 1979.
Gr. 3-5. The Monroe family's new pet rabbit seems to be a werewolf.

1185. Irving, Washington. THE LEGEND OF SLEEPY HOLLOW [Sound Recording]. Read by Hurd Hatfield. New Rochelle, NY: Spoken Arts; 1968; 1 cassette.
Gr. 5-up. The tale of a greedy, superstitious schoolmaster who encounters a ghostly headless horseman.

1186. Irving, Washington. THE LEGEND OF SLEEPY HOLLOW. In: EPISODES FROM FAMOUS STORIES [Filmstrip]. Chicago: Encyclopaedia Britannica Educational Corp.; 1973; 1 of a set of 6 filmstrlps; 6 cassettes; 6 teacher's guides.
Gr. 4-up.

1187. Jacobs, Joseph. JACK THE GIANT-KILLER. Illustrated by Fritz Wegner. New York: Walck; 1970.
Gr. K-3. A farmer's son, living in King Arthur's time, fights the terrible giant Cormoran, menacing the people of Cornwall.

1188. Janosch. THE CROCODILE WHO WOULDN'T BE KING. Illustrated. New York: Putnam; 1971.
Gr. K-3. The little crocodile does not want to be king and goes to live in a zoo where all animals live together peacefully.

1189. Kellogg, Steven. THE MYSTERIOUS TADPOLE. Illustrated. New York: Dial Press; 1977.
Gr. 1-2. Louis thinks he's received a tadpole from his uncle until it continues to grow.

1190. Kennedy, Richard. INSIDE MY FEET: THE STORY OF A GIANT. Illustrated by Ronald Himler. New York: Harper & Row; 1979.

Gr. 2-6. When enchanted boots carry away his father and mother, a boy tries to find a way to fight the enchantment.

1191. Kent, Jack. THERE'S NO SUCH THING AS A DRAGON. Illustrated. New York: Western; 1975.
Gr. K-2. Billy's mother says there's no such thing a dragon, but the dragon keeps getting bigger until she has to admit that it's real.

1192. LAKE MURKWOOD MONSTER. (Tales of Winnie the Witch Cassette Books) [Kit]. Adapted by Judith Conaway. Chicago: SVE; 1978; 1 cassette; 10 booklets.
Gr. 3-6. A story in which Murky the monster almost gets punished for something he didn't do.

1193. Leach, Maria. WHISTLE IN THE GRAVEYARD: FOLKTALES TO CHILL YOUR BONES. Illustrated by Ken Rinciari. New York: Viking Press; 1974.
Gr. 4-6. A collection of folktales from around the world about ghosts, bogeys, witches, and other haunts.

1194. Levy, Elizabeth. FRANKENSTEIN MOVED IN ON THE FOURTH FLOOR. Illustrated by Mordicai Gerstein. New York: Harper and Row; 1979.
Gr. 3-5. Two boys become convinced that their new neighbor is Frankenstein.

1195. Lines, Kathleen, ed. THE HOUSE OF THE NIGHTMARE, AND OTHER EERIE TALES. New York: Farrar, Straus & Giroux; 1968.
Gr. 5-up. A collection of macabre and sinister tales.

1196. Lively, Penelope. THE GHOST OF THOMAS KEMPE. Illustrated by Anthony Maitland. New York: Dutton; 1973.
Gr. 3-6. A seventeenth-century ghost tries to make a young boy his apprentice.

1197. Low, Joseph. BEASTLY RIDDLES: FISHY, FLIGHTY, AND BUGGY, TOO. Illustrated. New York: Macmillan; 1983.
Gr. 1-3. A collection of riddles pertaining to animals.

1198. Manning-Sanders, Ruth. A BOOK OF MONSTERS. New York: Dutton; 1976.

Gr. 2-6. Tales about monsters, good-natured as well as horrible.

1199. Mayer, Mercer. LIZA LOU AND THE YELLER-BELLY SWAMP. Illustrated. New York: Four Winds; 1980.
Gr. 2-4. Liza Lou has to trick several terrible swamp monsters as she runs errands in the swamp.

1200. Mayer, Mercer. THERE'S A NIGHTMARE IN MY CLOSET. Illustrated. New York: Dial Press; 1968.
Gr. K-2. A small boy fears the monster in his closet until he confronts it.

1201. McGinnis, Lila Sprague. THE GHOST UPSTAIRS. Illustrated by Amy Rowen. New York: Hastings; 1982.
Gr. 4-7. An eleven-year-old ghost moves in with Albert.

1202. McPhail, David M. BUMPER TUBBS. Illustrated. Boston: Houghton Mifflin; 1980.
Gr. K-3. An alligator turns accident into success with the help of friends.

1203. MONSTERS AND OTHER FRIENDLY CREATURES [Filmstrip]. Chicago: Encyclopaedia Britannia Educational Corp.; 1974; 5 filmstrips; 5 cassettes; 1 teacher's guide.
Gr. K-6. Contents: Monsters in the Closet; Emil, the Tap Dancing Frog; Monster Seeds; Charlie and the Caterpillar; Andrew and the Strawberry Monsters.

1204. THE MONSTROUS GLISSON GLOG. In: THE SEA, IN FACT AND FANTASY [Filmstrip]. New York: Learning Corporation of America; 1970; 1 of a set of 6 filmstrips: 6 cassettes; 1 script; 1 teacher's guide.
Gr. 3-6. Using the sea as an example, children are shown how nature inspires story-telling.

1205. Nic Leodhas, Sorche. GAELIC GHOSTS. Illustrated by Nonny Hogogrian. New York: Holt, Rinehart and Winston; 1963.
Gr. 4-6. A collection of supernatural Scots.

Niland, Deborah. ABC OF MONSTERS. Illustrated. New York: McGraw Hill; 1978.
Gr. K-3. See #963.

1206. Nolan, Dennis. ALPHABRUTES. Illustrated. Englewood Cliffs, NJ: Prentice Hall; 1977.
Gr. Preschool-2. The letters of the alphabet are introduced by a collection of friendly monsters.

1207. Nolan, Dennis. MONSTER BUBBLES: A COUNTING BOOK. Illustrated. Englewood Cliffs, NJ: Prentice Hall; 1976.
Gr. K-2. Monsters blow numbers of bubbles in groups up to twenty.

1208. Norton, Andre, ed. SMALL SHADOWS CREEP. New York: Dutton; 1974.
Gr. 3-.7. A collection about all kinds of ghosts.

1209. Parish, Peggy. NO MORE MONSTERS FOR ME! Illustrated by Marc Simont. New York: Harper & Row; 1981.
Gr. K-2. Minneapolis Simpson is not allowed to have a pet, so she finds the most unusual replacement.

1210. Pavey, Peter. ONE DRAGON'S DREAM. Illustrated. Scarsdale, NY: Bradbury; 1979.
Gr. K-2. A dragon dreams several dreams, each with a number of items in it.

1211. Peterson, Esther Allen. FREDERICK'S ALLIGATOR. Illustrated by Susanna Natti. New York: Crown; 1979.
Gr. K-3. Frederick becomes the owner of a baby alligator.

1212. Prelutsky, Jack. THE HEADLESS HORSEMAN RIDES TONIGHT. Illustrated by Arnold Lobel. New York: Greenwillow; 1980.
Gr. 3-6. A collection of poems and portaits of terrifying creatures.

1213. Prelutsky, Jack. NIGHTMARES: POEMS TO TROUBLE YOUR SLEEP. New York: Greenwillow; 1976.
Gr. 2-5. Twelve cautionary poems about various monsters to watch out for.

1214. Prelutsky, Jack. NIGHTMARES: POEMS TO TROUBLE YOUR SLEEP [Sound Recording]. Music composed by Don Heckman. New York: Caedmon; 1983; 1 sound disc.
Gr. 2-5. Based on the book of the same title.

1215. Raskin, Ellen. FRANKLIN STEIN. Illustrated. New York: Atheneum; 1972.
Gr. 1-3. Franklin makes himself a friendly monster out of household objects.

1216. Rettich, Margret. THE TIGHTWAD'S CURSE AND OTHER PLEASANTLY CHILLING STORIES. Illustrated by Rolf Rettich. New York: Morrow; 1979.
Gr. 4-6. Twenty "ghost" stories whose eerie events are caused by human quirks rather than supernatural sources.

1217. Riley, James Whitcomb. THE GOBBLE-UNS'LL GIT YOU EF YOU DON'T WATCH OUT. New York: Lippincott; 1975.
Gr. 1-4. New illustrations of the classic poem about "Little Orphant Annie."

1218. Saint-Saens, Camille. DANSE MACABRE [Sound Recording]. The Orchestre de Paris conducted by Pierre Dervaux. Los Angeles, CA: Angel Records; 1980; 1 sound disk.
Gr. 3-up. Evokes images of the spirits that emerge from their graves on all Hallow's Eve.

1219. Sarnoff, Jane. THE MONSTER RIDDLE BOOK. Illustrated by Reynold Ruffins, New York: Scribner; 1978.
Gr. 4-6. All kinds of monsters are included in this riddle collection.

1220. Schwartz, Alvin. KICKLE SNIFTERS AND OTHER FEARSOME CRITTERS. Illustrated by Glen Rounds. New York: Lippincott; 1976.
Gr. 3-6. A humorous collection of monstrous "critters."

1221. Sechrist, Elizabeth Hough, ed. THIRTEEN GHOSTLY YARNS. Illustrated. Philadelphia: Macrae-Smith; 1942.
Gr. 3-up. A collection of ghost stories by authors such as Mark Twain, Edgar Allen Poe, Rudyard Kipling, and Shakespeare.

1222. Sendak, Maurice. ALLIGATORS ALL AROUND. Illustrated. New York: Harper and Row; 1962.
Gr. Preschool-2. An alliterative alphabet book, from Alligators to Zippity Zound!

1223. Sendak, Maurice. WHERE THE WILD THINGS ARE. New York: Harper & Row; 1963.
Gr. 1-3. After being a "monster" himself Max sails off to the island where the wild things are.

1224. Sharmat, Marjorie Weinman. GILA MONSTERS MEET YOU AT THE AIRPORT. Illustrated. East Rutherford, NJ: Penguin; 1983.

1225. Shelley, Mary. FRANKENSTEIN. West Haven, CT: Pendulum Press; 1973.
Gr. 5-up. Dr. Frankenstein creates a monster from human body parts.

1226. Slepian, Jan, and Ann Seidler. THE HUNGRY THING. Illustrated by Richard Martin. New York: Scholastic; 1967.
Gr. K-3. Hungry thing comes to town demanding food.

1227. Snyder, Zilpha Keatley. THE HEADLESS CUPID. Illustrated by Alton Raible. New York: Atheneum; 1971.
Gr. 5-8. Life is never quite the same again for eleven-year old David after the arrival of his new stepsister, a student of the occult.

1228. SPOOKS AND SPIRITS AND SHADOWY SHAPES. Illustrated by Robert Doremus. New York: Dutton; 1965.
Gr. 2-5.

1229. Stevenson, Robert Louis. DR. JEKYLL AND MR. HYDE. West Haven, CT: Pendulum Press; 1973.
Gr. 5-up. A classic tale of a man who turns himself into a monster.

1230. Stoker, Bram. DRACULA. West Haven, CT: Pendulum Press; 1973.
Gr. 5-up. The mysterious Count Dracula lures people to his castle and then kills them for their blood.

1231. Supraner, Robyn. HAPPY HALLOWEEN: THINGS TO MAKE AND DO. Illustrated by Renzo Brto. Mahwah, NJ: Troll Associates; 1981.
Gr. 3-6. Monster masks, skeletons and other scary things to make for Halloween.

Turkle, Brinton. DO NOT OPEN. Illustrated. New York: Dutton; 1981.
Gr. 1-3. See #823.

1232. Ungerer, Tomi. THE BEAST OF MONSIEUR RACINE. New York: Farrar, Straus & Giroux; 1971.
Gr. 3-5. A strange beast is stealing the pears off of Monsieur Racine's tree.

1233. Ungerer, Tomi. ZERALDA'S OGRE. Illustrated. New York: Harper and Row; 1967.
Gr. 1-2. An ogre eats children until young Zeralda finds a way to pacify him.

1234. Viorst, Judith. MY MAMA SAYS THERE AREN'T ANY ZOMBIES, GHOSTS, VAMPIRES, CREATURES, DEMONS, MONSTERS, FIENDS, GOBLINS OR THINGS. Illustrated. New York: Atheneum; 1973.
Gr. K-2. Nick is troubled by monsters but his mother says they don't exist.

1235. Waber, Bernard. LYLE, LYLE, CROCODILE. Illustrated. Boston: Hougthon Mifflin; 1965.
Gr. K-3. Lyle lives with the Primms in New York City.

1236. Wagner, Jenny. THE BUNYIP OF BERKELEY'S CREEK. Scarsdale, NY: Bradbury; 1977.
Gr. K-2. While the Bunyip is traditionally a fierce Australian monster this Bunyip only wants to be loved for himself.

1237. Wallace, Daisy, ed. GIANT POEMS. Illustrated by Margot Tomes. New York: Holiday House; 1978.
Gr. 2-4. Seventeen poems about giants illustrated with pen-and-ink drawings.

1238. Wallace, Daisy, ed. MONSTER POEMS. Illustrated by Kay Chorao. New York: Holiday House; 1976.
Gr. 2-4. A collection of both humorous and scary monsters in poetry.

1239. Wallner, Alexandra. GHOULISH GIGGLES AND MONSTER RIDDLES. Illustrated. Chicago: Whitman; 1982.
Gr. 1-5. Over ninety riddles about various kinds of monsters.

1240. Westall, Robert. THE WATCH HOUSE. New York: Greenwillow; 1977.
Gr. 5-9. While spending the summer with her old nurse on the north English coast, a teen-age girl discovers that her presence in the nearby Watch House, a museum containing relics of shipwrecks and rescues, releases a powerful and evil ghost.

1241. Williams, Jay. EVERYONE KNOWS WHAT A DRAGON LOOKS LIKE. Illustrated. New York: Mercer; 1976.
Gr. 2-5. Han discovers that everyone doesn't know what a dragon looks like when he befriends a mmall old man.

1242. Wrightson, Patricia. A LITTLE FEAR. New York: Atheneum; 1983.

Gr. 6-up. An elderly woman battles an ancient Australian Gnome, the Njimbin, which resents her efforts to settle on its land.

1243. Wrightson, Patricia. THE NARGUN AND THE STARS. New York: Atheneum; 1974.
Gr. 5-up. Simon and his older cousins fight the power of the great stone Nargun with the help of other supernatural creatures.

1244. Yolen, Jane. DRAGON'S BLOOD. New York: Delacorte; 1982.
Gr. 6-up. Jakkin, a bond boy who works as a keeper in a dragon nursery on the planet Austar IV, secretly trains a fighting pit dragon of his own in hopes of winning his freedom.

1245. Yolen, Jane H. THE WIZARD ISLANDS. Illustrated by Robert Quackenbush. New York: Crowell; 1973.
Gr. 5-up. Includes tales, true and legendary, of various new and ancient islands throughout the world.

1246. Young, Ed. THE TERRIBLE NUNG GWANA: A CHINESE FOLKTALE. Illustrated. New York: Collins World; 1978.
Gr. Preschool-3. A retelling of the Chinese tale in which a poor young woman outwits the terrible monster, Nung Gwama, before he eats her.

1247. Zemach, Harve. THE JUDGE, AN UNTRUE TALE. Illustrated by Margot Zemach. New York: Farrar, Straus & Giroux; 1969.
Gr. 1-3. Prisoners keep warning the judge that a monstrous thing is coming but he doesn't believe them.

In the Arts

1248. Aylesworth, Thomas G. MOVIE MONSTERS. New York: Harper & Row; 1975.
Gr. 4-7. Describes some of the best-known monster films with information about the monsters as well as guidelines for criticism.

1249. Cendrars, Blaise. SHADOW. Illustrated and translated by Marcia Brown. New York: Scribner; 1982.
Gr. 2-5. An eerie depiction of Shadow which haunts the story teller and the African people.

1250. Gates, Frieda. EASY-TO-MAKE MONSTER MASKS AND DISGUISES. New York: Harvey House; 1979.
Gr. 1-3. Patterns and instructions for making about 20 masks using a variety of materials.

1251. Gates, Frieda. MONSTERS AND GHOULS: COSTUMES AND LORE. New York: Walker; 1980.
Gr. 4-9. Includes patterns and directions for a variety of monster costumes, some easy and some harder.

1252. Giblin, James, and Dale Ferguson. THE SCARECROW BOOK. New York: Crown; 1980.
Gr. 2-4. Describes scarecrows used by farmers in many parts of the world and throughout history.

1253. Haldane, Suzanne. FACES ON PLACES: ABOUT GARGOYLES AND OTHER STONE CREATURES. New York: Viking; 1980.
Gr. 3-7. Photographs and text describe the work of sculptors, model makers, stone cutters, and stone carvers in creating gargoyles and other creatures.

1254. Horner, Deborah R. MASKS OF THE WORLD TO CUT AND WEAR. New York: Scribner; 1977.
Gr. 3-6. Masks from many cultures printed in color on heavy paper, suitable to cut out and wear.

1255. THE IGUANA WHO WAS ALWAYS RIGHT. In: FOLKTALES FROM MANY LANDS [Filmstrip]. Chicago: Encyclopaedia Britannica Educational Corp.; 1977; 1 of a set of 6 filmstrips; 6 cassettes; 1 teacher's guide.
Gr. 1-6. Tells the Central African tale of an iguana who thinks he's always right, even after being tricked by the rabbit.

1256. Kalina, Sigmund. HOW TO MAKE A DINOSAUR. Illustrated by Guilio Maestro. New York: Lothrop; 1976.
Gr. 1-6. Step-by-step directions for modeling three different dinosaurs from papermache and reinforced styrofoam.

1257. MASKS. In: DISCOVERING THE WORLD [Kit]. New Rochelle, NY: Spoken Arts; 1970; 1 of a set of 4 filmstrips; 4 cassettes; 1 guide; 1 poster.
Gr. 1-6. Shows examples of Navajo Indian masks and discusses their relationship to the Navajo's life and culture.

1258. Ormsby, Alan. MOVIE MONSTERS: MONSTERS, MAKEUP AND MONSTER SHOWS TO PUT ON. New York: Scholastic; 1975.
Gr. 4-7.

1259. OUR OTHER FACE - THE MASK [Filmstrip]. Stamford, CT: Educational Dimensions Group; 1979; 2 filmstrips; 2 cassettes; 1 teacher's guide.
Gr. 4-6. Discusses the use of masks as a form of human expression from the beginning of time to the present, and shows how changes in mask styles reflect changes in artistic styles.

1260. Price, Christine. DANCING MASKS OF AFRICA. New York: Scribner; 1975.
Gr. 2-6. Describes the function of masks in West African society, with block prints which portray their variety.

1261. Price, Christine. THE MYSTERY OF MASKS. New York: Scribner; 1978.
Gr. 3-up. An overview of masks from various cultures and their meanings.

1262. Quackenbush, Robert M. MOVIE MONSTERS AND THEIR MASTERS. Niles, IL: Whitman; 1980.
Gr. 3-up. A history of horror movies using text and photographs.

1263. Williams, Diane. DEMONS AND BEASTS IN ART. Minneapolis, MN: Lerner; 1970.
Gr. 4-6. Shows various forms of art through the ages and their depiction of fantastic creatures.

In Folklore and Mythology

1264. Anderson, Jean. THE HAUNTING OF AMERICA: GHOST STORIES FROM OUR PAST. Illustrated by Eric Von Schmidt. Boston: Houghton Mifflin; 1973.
Gr. 6-7. 24 stories of ghosts from all over the country and in various time periods.

Aruego, Jose, and Ariane Aruego. A CROCODILE'S TALE: A PHILIPPINE FOLK STORY. Illustrated. New York: Scholastic; 1976.
Gr. K-3. See #1151.

1265. Asbjornsen, P.C., and J.E. Moe. THE THREE BILLY GOATS GRUFF. Illustrated by Marcia Brown. New York: Harcourt Brace; 1957.
Gr. K-1. A troll is tricked by a family of goats.

1266. Aylesworth, Thomas G. SCIENCE LOOKS AT MYSTERIOUS MONSTERS. New York: Messner; 1982.
Gr. 5-up. An inquiry into the nature of the abominable snowman, Bigfoot, the Loch Ness monster, and other monstrous creatures, the existence of which has never been finally proven or disproven.

1267. Aylesworth, Thomas G. THE STORY OF VAMPIRES. New York: McGraw Hill; 1977.
Gr. 4-7. Includes the history, legends, books and films about vampires.

1268. Aylesworth Thomas G. THE STORY OF WEREWOLVES. New York: McGraw Hill; 1982.
Gr. 3-6. Discusses the historic lore of werewolves as well as contemporary movies about them.

1269. Baumann, Elwood D. MONSTERS OF NORTH AMERICA. Illustrated by Nicholas Krenitsky. New York: Watts; 1978.
Gr. 5-7. Relates information on monster sightings in the United States.

1270. BEAUTY AND THE BEAST. Illustrated by Diane Goode. Scarscale, NY: Bradbury; 1978.
Gr. K-up. Traditional tale of a young girl who comes to love a beast.

1271. Blythe, Richard. DRAGONS AND OTHER FABULOUS BEASTS. Illustrated by Fiona French and Joanna Troughton. New York: Grossett & Dunlap; 1980.
Gr. 3-7. Stories of mystical beasts throughout the ages.

1272. D'Aulaire, Ingri, and Parin D' Aulaire. TROLLS. New York: Doubleday; 1972.
Gr. 3-6. Relates lifestyle, appearance and some of the best known stories about Norwegian trolls.

1273. Dickinson, Peter. THE FLIGHT OF DRAGONS. Illustrated by Wayne Anderson. New York: Harper & Row; 1979.
Gr. 4-up. An exploration of Eastern and Western dragons with fabulous illustrations depicting various monsters.

1274. Epstein, Perle. MONSTOERS: THEIR HISTORIES, HOMES AND HABITS. New York: Doubleday; 1973.
Gr. 3-6. Presents material on a selection of monsters from various parts of the world.

1275. EXPLORING THE UNEXPLAINED. (Basic Research Skills Development Series) [Filmstrip]. Niles, IL: United Learning; 1974; 4 filmstrips; 4 cassettes; 1 teacher's guide with student activities.
Gr. 4-up. A program intended to foster research skills. Contents: The Tropical Mystery Creature; The Riddle of Capistrano; Bigfoot; The Treacherous Triangle; The Thousand Year Old Airplane.

1276. FAMOUS MYSTERIES [Filmstrip]. Produced by Pomfret House. Chicago: Encyclopaedia Britannica Educational Corp,; 1979; 6 filmstrips; 6 cassettes; 1 teacher's guide.
Gr. 4-up. Captioned filmstrips retell six classic thrillers in order to introduce students to an intriguing literary form - the mystery. Also available without sound accompaniment.

1277. Fenner, Phyllis L., ed. GIANTS AND WITCHES AND A DRAGON OR TWO. Illustrated by Henry Pitz. New York: Knopf; 1943.
Gr. 4-6. 17 stories from all over the world of various monstrous creatures.

1278. Galdone, Joanna. THE TAILYPO: A GHOST STORY. Illustrated by Paul Galdone, Burlington, MA: Clarion; 1977.
Gr. 2-5. An old man in a cabin in the woods is haunted by a strange creature.

Galdone Paul. THE MONKEY AND THE CROCODILE: A JATAKA TALE FROM INDIA. New York: Seabury; 1969.
Gr. K-3. See #1174.

1279. Haley, Gail. GO AWAY, STAY AWAY [Filmstrip]. Weston, CT: Weston Woods; 1978; 1 filmstrip; 1 cassette; 1 booklet.
Gr. 1-4. Based on the book of the same title, 1977. A father blames the misfortunes that befall the members of his family on various demons and spirits, which he and the rest of the village then drive away with a noisy procession.

1280. Harper, Wilhelmina. THE GUNNIWOLF. Illustrated by William Wiesner. New York: Dutton; 1967.

Gr. K-1. The author retells the story of a little girl wbo disobeys her mother and wanders into the jungle where she encounters the Gunniwolf.

1281. Harris, Rosemary. BEAUTY AND THE BEAST. Illustrated by Errol Le Cain. New York: Doubleday; 1980.
Gr. 1-3. A version of the traditional tale with elaborate illustrations.

1282. Hoyt, Olga. DEMONS, DEVILS, AND DJINN. New York: Harper & Row; 1974.
Gr. 6-up. Examines belief in demons and devils around the world.

Leach, Maria. WHISTLE IN THE GRAVEYARD: FOLKTALES TO CHILL YOUR BONES. Illustrated by Ken Rinciari. New York: Viking; 1974.
Gr. 4-6. See #1193.

1283. THE LOCH NESS MONSTER. In: STRANGE PHENOMENA [Filmstrip]. Chicago: Encyclopaedia Britannica Educational Corp; 1972; 1 of a set of 6 filmstrips; 6 cassettes; 1 teacher's guide.
Gr. 4-8. This captioned filmstrip describes the evidence concerning the Loch Ness Monster which has been scientifically examined but is without conclusion. Also available without sound accompaniment. Other titles in series: Unusual Science Facts; ESP; Mind Over Matter; ESP in Animals and Men; Precognition.

1284. THE LOCH NESS MONSTER AND THE ABOMINABLE SNOWMAN: ATLANTIS AND UFO'S (Mysteries Old and New) [Filmstrip]. Washington, D.C: National Geographic; 1984; 2 filmstrips; 2 cassettes.
Gr. 4-8. These well known legendary monsters and phenomena can serve as an introduction to the process of scientific inquiry.

1285. Mayer, Marianna. BEAUTY AND THE BEAST. Illustrated. New York: Four Winds; 1978.
Gr. K-4. A retelling of the traditional tale.

1286. Mayer, Marianna. THE UNICORN AND THE LAKE. New York: Dial Books; 1982.
Gr. 2-4. Beautiful, noble, and pure, the magical unicorn battles the venomous serpent, dispelling the poison the creature injected into the lake.

1287. McDermott, Beverly B. THE GOLEM: A JEWISH LEGEND. Illustrated. New York: Harper & Row; 1975.
Gr. 2-5. A clay man, the Golem, made by a Rabbi to protect his people, begins a path of destruction.

1288. McHargue, Georgess. MEET THE VAMPIRE. Illustrated by Stephen Gammell, Philadelphia: Lippincott; 1979.
Gr. 4-7. An exploration of the vampire through history and across cultures, with fact and legend.

1289. McHargue, Georgess. MEET THE WEREWOLF. Illustrated by Stephen Gammell. Philadelphia: Lippincott; 1976.
Gr. 4-7. Retelling of popular stories about werewolves.

1290. MONSTERS OF THE GREEK MYTHS [Filmstrlp]. Chicago: SVE; 1981; 1 filmstrlp; 1 cassette; 1 guide.
Gr. 4-9. A filmstrip revision of Nathaniel Hawthorne's retelling of the Greek myths which feature confrontations between great heroes and horrific monsters.

1291. Mosel, Arlene. THE FUNNY LITTLE WOMAN. Illustrated by Blair Lent. New York: Dutton; 1972.
Gr. K-2. A Japanese tale about an old woman who follows a rolling rice dumpling down into the earth and discovers the wicked oni.

1292. MYTHS? MONSTERS? MYSTERIES? [Filmstrip]. Chicago: SVE; 1975; 6 filmstrips; 6 cassettes; 1 teacher's manual.
Gr. 4-up. Captioned filmstrips reinforce reading and comprehension skills. Contents: Atlantis - Where Are You?; UFO's - Are We Being Watched?; The Abominable Snow Man - Myth or Monster?; Reincarnation - Have We Lived Before?; Sasquatch - Fact or Fiction?; Witchcraft - An Evil to Fear?.

1293. Newton, Michael. MONSTERS, MYSTERIES, AND MAN. Illustrated. Reading, MA: Addison Wesley; 1979.
Gr. 5-up. Examines such persistent mysteries as monsters, UFO's and experiences with the supernatural.

1294. Place, Marian T. BIGFOOT ALL OVER THE COUNTRY. New York: Dodd, Mead; 1978.
Gr. 5-7. Cites sightings of Bigfoot in 40 states and questions the accuracy of each one.

1295. Place, Marian T. ON THE TRACK OF BIGFOOT. New York: Dodd, Mead; 1974.
Gr. 5-7. A collection of stories people tell about the 8 foot Sasquatch of the Pacific Northwest.

1296. Rabonwich, Ellen. THE LOCH NESS MONSTER. Illustrated by Sally Law. New York: Watts; 1979.
Gr. 3-5. Discusses the facts and theories which surround the monster purported to live in Loch Ness.

1297. Singer, Isaac Bashevis. THE GOLEM. Illustrated by Uri Shulevitz. New York: Farrar, Straus, Giroux; 1982.
Gr. 3-8. A clay giant miraculously brought to life by a saintly rabbi saves a Jewish banker who has been falsely accused in the Prague of Emperor Rudolf II.

1298. Small, Ernest. BABA YAGA. Illustrated by Blair Lent. Boston: Houghton Mifflin; 1966.
Gr. K-3. The wicked witch, Baba Yaga takes Marusia captive but Marusia outsmarts her.

1299. Thorne, Ian. MONSTER TALES OF NATIVE AMERICANS. Illustrated by Barbara Howell Furan. Mankato, MN: Crestwood; 1978.
Gr. 3-6. Native American monster tales and legends which explain why things are the way they are.

1300. VAMPIRES AND DRACULA. In: FACT OR FICTION [Filmstrip]. Produced by Pomfret House. Chicago: Encyclopaedia Britannica Education Corp.; 1978; 1 of a set of 6 filmstrips; 6 cassettes; and 1 teacher's guide.
Gr. 4-up. This captioned filmstrip is open-ended and will stimulate critical thinking. Also available without sound accompaniment.

1301. Wise, William. MONSTERS OF NORTH AMERICA. Illustrated by Ben F. Stahl. New York: Putnam; 1976.
Gr. K-4. Discusses a number of monsters seen in North America over the years including the Indians' Wendigo and Big Foot.

Chapter 9

Bodies: Links To Learning

What is a body? What sort of images parade past the mind's eye when we hear or read this word? Context, of course, gives us clues, so that, in communicating with each other, we are able to understand what is being said and how to interpret it. We are not likely to confuse the term "body of warm air" with "human body" or "legislative body." These phrases, though related in the basic concept of "unit," are clear and distinct in our minds as totally separate ideas.

If we start with the word "body" where will it lead us? THE AMERICAN HERITAGE DICTIONARY, COLLEGE EDITION, gives eight broad definitions with a number of examples/extensions/explanations:

> bod.y (bode) n., pl., -ies. 1. a. The entire material structure and substance of an organism, especially of a human being or an animal. b. A corpse or carcass. 2. a. The trunk or torso of a human being or animal. b. The part of a garment covering the torso. 3. Law. a. A person. b. A group of individuals regarded as an entity; corporation. 4. A number of persons, concepts, or things regarded collectively; a group: We walked out in a body. 5. The main or central part of something, as: a. The nave of a church. b. The content of a book or document exclusive of prefatory matter, codicils, indexes, and the like. c. The passenger- and cargo-carrying part of an aircraft, ship, or vehicle. d. The sound box of a musical instrument. 6. Any bounded aggregate of matter: a body of water. 7. Consistency of substance, as in paint, textiles, wine, and the like: a sauce with body. 8. Printing. The part of a block of type underlying the impression surface.

We can begin by classifying these concepts broadly into three groups: biological bodies, physical bodies and figurative bodies. Each of these is important to us in ways which are interrelated. Biological bodies are, of course, ourselves and the living world around us. Physical bodies provide a congenial environment in which biological bodies exist. Figurative bodies include the social entities which humans and other animals have developed to aid in their survival, and the metaphorical use of the word "body" to enhance the expressiveness of language. In order for us to be healthy, productive persons we must achieve a basic understanding of these concepts, know how to appreciate and use them and how to improve upon them for ourselves and for future generations.

Exploring further in these broad areas, we can begin to see the wealth of subject matter available to us. "Biological bodies," as we have said, include plant, animal, and human bodies. We can examine all the systems which support growth, reproduction and general functioning in any one of these three broad categories; we can look at individual families or species; we can consider the factors which affect the health and well being of any of these "bodies;" we can consider dead bodies and how society deals with the concept of death; or we can focus on the evolution of a particular type of body. Another approach will send us into the field of the arts to examine how "bodies" are treated in the graphic arts, in the performing arts, and in literature. To further expand our understanding of the arts, we must, of course, consider these topics both from the point of view of participation and of appreciation.

"Physical bodies" include celestial bodies, as in the study of astronomy and astrology; geographic bodies such as bodies of water, islands and continents; and man made bodies such as automobile bodies, airplane bodies, truck bodies, and robots. "Physical bodies" have also been widely replicated in the arts, affording us yet another field for enrichment.

"Figurative bodies" can be divided into at least two major categories: social bodies, and the literary use of the word "body." A study of the former leads us to the sociology of herds, prides, flocks, tribes, associations and legislative bodies, to name just a few. An exploration of the word "body," as it is used in metaphors, similes and other figures of speech, offers us an opportunity to play with words, expand vocabulary, and increase our awareness of the richness of language.

Having suggested a few of the directions which can be pursued in developing topics and themes, let us briefly outline ways in which these themes can be expanded to encompass all areas of the curriculum. Essentially all aspects of science can be covered by giving attention to one or another of the bodies in the preceding discussion: the physics of the motion of bodies; the ecology of bodies; the anatomy and physiology of bodies; the growth and maturation of bodies; the evolution of bodies, the death of bodies. Bodies can also contribute broadly to our understandings of the social sciences. We can study humankind in all its variety; the geography of lakes, oceans, islands and continents; the ways in which individuals, both human and animal, form bodies or units of various types and function within them; the history of bodies, as in the family unit, the village, legislative bodies, etc; the history and impact on society of the development of mechanical bodies such as airplane bodies and robots. We can quickly see the wealth of possibilities available to us. Focusing on language arts, we find many forms of children's literature concerned with bodies; picture books, concept books, informational books, biographies, poetry, ghost stories, mystery stories. Any of these genre can provide rich experiences for reading and the exploration of language. This approach also encourages the use of inventive material for developing vocabulary, spelling and writing skills and for self expression through pantomine and creative dramatics. Children could, for example, list and share all the "body" words they can think of and then write a poem or story using as many of their words as possible. Mathematical concepts can be developed and reinforced through myriad sorting, counting, measuring and arithmetical activities; through comparisons of size, weight and shape; or through an examination of geometric patterns in our world and how they are related to the functioning of a given body. We might look at crustaceans and their shells and try to discover how the variations in patterns and shapes help them to survive in their particular environments. Other areas of the curriculum, such as art, music, physical education, and health, can also benefit from this thematic approach. An exploration of body movements in physical education can significantly enhance a student's understanding of anatomy. The study of anatomy will help children understand the renderings of bodies in art, both from the practitioner's viewpoint and from the observer's viewpoint. This use of an interrelated approach will make the curriculum more meaningful to students. They can begin to see that the various areas of the curriculum are simply different ways of describing and studying the world around us, not just isolated bodies of knowledge they are required to learn.

In terms of grade level, also, the study of bodies gives us considerable latitude in what will be covered. Kindergarten students might be concerned just with their own bodies: drawing body outlines; comparing their bodies to those of other students; beginning to have some basic understanding of what makes a body work. They might make an initial exploration of other types of bodies; zoo animals, farm animals, trees, flowers, etc. Primary level students could study their own bodies at increasing levels of depth and detail, examining what keeps a body well or makes it sick and how the various systems of the body contribute to its function. They could begin to acquire an understanding of how various animal or plant bodies are grouped, and how the groups relate to each other. Middle grade students could begin to look at the various systems of their bodies and other bodies in some detail to achieve an understanding of how each system functions and supports the whole. They might also begin to look at the evolution of various bodies, or examine the classifications of the biological and physical world.

Our seemingly simple topic, then, covers a wide range of subjects which can contribute to learnings in all areas of the curriculum and across all grade levels. We have looked at some of the possibilities in this discussion and in the chart that follows. We can now examine in detail one strand of the chart to serve as a road map for further exploration.

If we start with the animal strand, our chart and its extensions can lead us in any one of several directions. Our choice of which way to go, how much time to spend, and how thorough to make our explorations will depend on several factors. We must decide which curriculum areas we wish to incorporate into our schema, and grade level must certainly be considered; but, perhaps more important than either of these is student interest and enthusiasm. We should let the flow of the strand evolve gradually as new ideas surface and take root. A student or a group of students may start by studying the sounds that animals make, using books such as Edward R. Ricciuti's SOUNDS OF ANIMALS AT NIGHT, Peter Spier's whimsical GOBBLE, GROWL, GRUNT, or Judi Friedman's NOISES IN THE WOODS and sound recordings such as SOUNDS OF ANIMALS or SONGS OF THE HUMPBACK WHALE. From this they could be led into an investigation of animal communication. Materials which cover this topic include Dorothy Hinshaw Patent's HOW INSECTS COMMUNICATE, Dorothy Van Woerkom's HIDDEN MESSAGES, Bill Gilbert's HOW ANIMALS COMMUNICATE, the filmstrip ANIMAL COMMUNICATIONS from SVE's filmstrip series ANIMALS, ANIMALS. This investigation could, in turn, arouse curiosity about how animals care for their young. Any one of the kits from Encyclopaedia Britannica's series, ANIMAL LIFE STORIES, will provide insights into this aspect of animal life, as will Russell Freedman's two excellent books, HANGING ON: HOW ANIMALS CARRY THEIR YOUNG and HOW ANIMALS DEFEND THEIR YOUNG. This type of exploration is a dynamic process which should be encouraged and supported in every way possible.

Our animal strand may lead us vertically through the chart to study the anatomy of various animal groups or an individual group. The BONES kit from the Elementary Science Study project provides 6 skeletons of 3 different animals with foam padded trays on which to assemble them. There are good clear transparency masters from 3M which compare the different forms of animal life and structure plus many books such as Herbert Zim's WHAT'S INSIDE OF ANIMALS?, Gale Cooper's INSIDE ANIMALS or Joan Rahn's GROCERY STORE ZOOLOGY for more advanced students. If we have chosen an individual group such as birds, there, as well, we find many sources available to us. We can start with Maurice Burton's excellent overview of birds, THE LIFE OF BIRDS, Herbert Zim's BIRDS, the kit BIRDS AND HOW THEY GROW from National Geographic, the study print series from Coronet, DISCOVERING VERTEBRATES, the game associated with the study prints, THE VERTEBRATE GAME and then progress to the many materials available about individual species of birds. A few of these are: Ian Strange's PENGUIN WORLD: Jack Denton Scott's THE GULLS OF SMUTTY NOSE ISLAND: Ada Graham's PUFFIN ISLAND; the Centre Productions filmstrip series, HUNTERS OF THE WIND, HUNTERS OF THE NIGHT.

If we decided to branch horizontally, we can look at the many ways in which animal bodies are or can be represented in art, music, or literature. Books of animal poetry abound: Karla Kuskin's ROAR AND MORE; John Garner's A CHILD'S BESTIARY, Leslie Brook's JOHNNY CROW'S GARDEN (which is also available in a Weston Woods filmstrip version), or John Brewton's UNDER THE TENT OF THE SKY: A COLLECTION OF POEMS ABOUT ANIMALS LARGE AND SMALL, to name just a few. A recording of Saint-Saens' CARNIVAL OF THE ANIMALS gives children an opportunity to pantomime the movements of different animals as will Doris Jones' record, ACTIVITY RHYTHMIC MOVEMENTS OF ZOO ANIMALS. Animals in art can be approached with a view to participation (Ed Emberly's DRAWING BOOK OF ANIMALS, Alexander Calder's ANIMAL SKETCHING) or from the appreciation aspect (LITTLE ADVENTURES IN ART, a filmstrip from Warren Schloat Productions, and Kenneth Clarke's ANIMALS AND MEN.) Another horizontal branch which we might pursue would involve the study of animals which live in herds, prides, flocks, and other such groupings. Again, LIFE OF BIRDS by Maurice Burton has a chapter on BIRDS IN GROUPS which provides a brief introduction to the topic. An enchanting view of animal communities for younger children is Brian Wildsmith's WILD ANIMALS, also available in a filmstrip version. More depth can be provided by books such as Hallie Black's ANIMAL COOPERATION, Niko Tinbergen's ANIMAL BEHAVIOR and audiovisuals such as the filmstrip Animal Societies (another in the SVE ANIMALS, ANIMALS series) and SOCIAL PATTERNS AND COMMUNICATION from the Imperial Education Resources' filmstrip series ANIMAL BEHAVIOR.

We can continue branching in various directions, including any tangent directions that present themselves as we progress through the unit, all the while keeping our focus on the creative and explorative process. If we give free rein (within a structure) to the natural curiosity of children, we allow them to retain the excitement of discovery and learning that characterizes their preschool years, thus encouraging them to be lifelong learners. The list of materials which follows, while not comprehensive, will provide a sound foundation for creating the connections to foster this process.

Included is a section on a specific animal group, birds, to serve as an example of an in-depth examination of one category. The same process could be followed with any other group: reptiles; deciduous trees; or, perhaps, airplane bodies. Some strands have only a few entries to indicate possible directions to follow, while other have many entries to demonstrate the wealth of materials available. There are myriad possibilities to explore, and your student's and your own imaginations are the only limits.

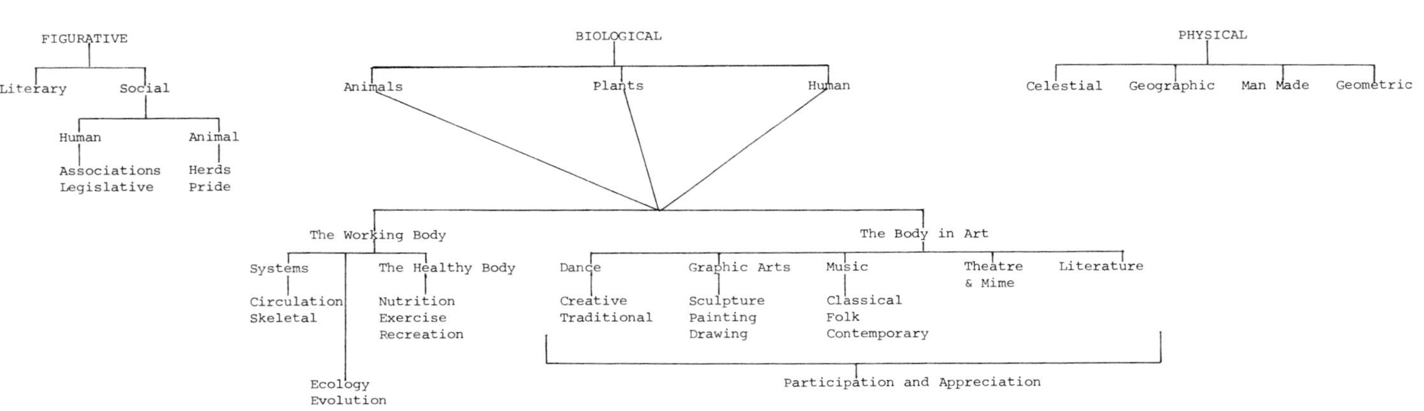
BODIES
FIGURATIVE
Literary
Social
Human
Animal
Associations
Legislative
Herds
Pride
BIOLOGICAL
Animals
Plants
Human
PHYSICAL
Celestial
Geographic
Man Made
Geometric
The Working Body
Systems
Circulation
Skeletal
The Healthy Body
Nutrition
Exercise
Recreation
Ecology
Evolution
The Body in Art
Dance
Creative
Traditional
Graphic Arts
Sculpture
Painting
Drawing
Music
Classical
Folk
Contemporary
Theatre
& Mime
Literature
Participation and Appreciation

FIGURATIVE BODIES

Literary

1302. Barrett, Judith. ANIMALS SHOULD DEFINITELY NOT WEAR CLOTHING. Illustrated by Ron Barrett. New York: Atheneum; 1970,
Gr. K-2, A collection of humorous pictures of animals in inappropriate clothes.

1303. Basil, Cynthia. NAILHEADS AND POTATO EYES. Illustrated by Janet McCaffery. New York: Morrow; 1976.
Gr. 1-3, Uses riddles which include parts of the body.

1304. Collodi, Carlo. ADVENTURES OF PINOCCHIO. New York: Macmillan; 1969.
Gr. 4-6. The classic story of the boy-puppet and his master, the carpenter Gepetto.

1305. Crompton, Anne Eliot. THE WINTER WIFE: AN ABENAKI FOLKTALE. Illustrated by Robert Andrew Parker. Boston: Little, Brown; 1975.
Gr. 2-5. An Indian hunter is cared for on his winter hunting trips by a young woman who is actually a moose.

1306. Goble, Paul. BUFFALO WOMAN, Illustrated. Scarsdale, NY: Bradbury; 1984.
Gr. 4-up. A buffalo cow is transformed into a beautiful woman as a gift from the Buffalo Nation.

1307. Grimm, Jacob, and Wilhelm Grimm. THE FISHERMAN AND HIS WIFE. Illustrated by Margot Zemach. New York: Farrar, Straus, Giroux; 1980.
Gr. K-3. This story, translated by Randall Jarrell, tells about the fisherman's greedy wife, who always wants to be granted another wish.

1308. Hutton, Warwick. NOSE TREE, New York: Atheneum; 1981.
Gr. K-3. Three soldiers outwit a witch with a magical gift that makes her nose grow.

1309. Lipton, James. AN EXALTATION OF LARKS. 2d ed. New York: Viking; 1968.
Gr. 6-up, Explains how collective terms such as "a gaggle of geese" came about and invents other collective terms.

1310. Mobley, Jane. THE STAR HUSBAND. Illustrated by Anna Vojtech. New York: Doubleday; 1979.
Gr. 1-3. A young Indian maiden marries a star husband but misses her life on earth.

1311. Wildsmith, Brian. WILD ANIMALS. New York: Oxford; 1979.
Gr. K-3. A set of pictures of animals and the collective terms which describe them.

1312. Yorinks, Arthur. LOUIS THE FISH. Illustrated by Richard Egielski. New York: Farrar, Straus & Giroux; 1980.
Gr. 2-5. "One day last Spring, Louis, a butcher, turned into a fish."

Social

Alston, Eugenia. COME VISIT A PRAIRIE DOG TOWN. Illustrated by St. Tamara. New York: Harcourt Brace; 1976.
Gr. 1-4. See #169.

1313. Coy, Harold. CONGRESS. New York: Watts; 1981.
Gr. 3-6. Discusses the U.S. Congress, elections, duties of congresspersons and organization of the body.

1314. Hartman, Jane E. ANIMALS THAT LIVE IN GROUPS. New York: Holiday House; 1979.
Gr. 4. Discusses social behavior patterns that cause animals to develop structured societies.

1315. Haskins, James. ANDREW YOUNG, MAN WITH A MISSION. New York: Lothrop; 1979.
Gr. 5-up. An account of the life of Andrew Young, including his activities as a clergyman, civil rights worker, legislator, and United States Ambassador to the United Nations.

Hauser, Hilary. LIVING WORLD OF THE REEF. Illustrated by Bob Evans and Nancy Low. New York: Walker, 1978.
Gr. 5-8. See #171.

Hess, Lilo. SMALL HABITATS. New York: Scribner; 1976.
Gr. 4-6. See #172.

1316. Hoopes, Roy. WHAT A UNITED STATES SENATOR DOES. New York: John Day; 1975.

Gr. 4-up. Text and more than 150 photographs describe the background, responsibilities, and daily routines of seven Senators.

Hutchins, Ross E. A LOOK AT ANTS. New York: Dodd, Mead; 1978.
Gr. 3-5. See #174.

1317. Lane, Margaret. BEAVER. Illustrated by David Nockels. New York: Dial Press; 1982.
Gr. 3-5. Describes behavior of beavers and creation of beaver dams with text and many colored drawings.

Oxford Scientific Films. BEES AND HONEY. Illustrated by David Thompson. New York: Putnam; 1977.
Gr. 3-6. See #176.

Sarnoff, Jane, and Reynold Ruffins. GREAT AQUARIUM BOOK. Illustrated by Reynold Ruffins. New York: Scribner; 1977.
Gr. 1-up. See #178.

Tresselt, Alvin. THE BEAVER POND. Illustrated by Roger Duvoisin. New York: Lothrop; 1970.
Gr. K-3. See #180.

BIOLOGICAL BODIES

Animals

1318. ANIMALS, ANIMALS. [Filmstrip]. Chicago: SVE; 1976; 6 filmstrips; 6 cassettes; teacher's guide.
Gr. 3-4, Contents: Animal Societies; How Animals Build; How Animals Protect Themselves; How Animals Migrate; How Animals Communicate; How Animals Feed Themselves.

1319. Anno, Mitsumasa. ANNO'S ANIMALS. New York: Collins; 1979.
Gr. K-up. The reader is invited to find a variety of animals hidden amidst woodland scenes.

1320. Arnold, Caroline. ANIMALS THAT MIGRATE. Pictures by Michele Zylman, Minneapolis: Carolrhoda; 1982.
Gr. 1-3. Describes the habits of animals that regularly change their home to find better weather, safer conditions, or more food.

1321. Arnosky, Jim. SECRETS OF A WILDLIFE WATCHER. Illustrated. New York: Lothrop; 1983.
Gr. 5-up. Explains the techniques used in finding wild animals such as owls, turtles, squirrels, foxes, beavers, and deer, and in getting close enough to study their behavior.

1322. Aruego, Jose, and Ariane Dewey. WE HIDE, YOU SEEK. Illustrated. New York: Greenwillow; 1979.
Gr. Preschool-2, A rhino plays hide and seek with his animal friends,

1323. Barker, Will. WINTER-SLEEPING WILDLIFE. Illustrated by Carl Burger. New York: Harper & Row; 1958.
Gr. 4-6. Discusses hibernation and diapause in animals.

Barrett, Judith. ANIMALS SHOULD SHOULD DEFINITELY NOT WEAR CLOTHING. Drawings by Ron Barrett. New York: Atheneum; 1970.
Gr. Prescbool-2. See #1302.

1324. Barrett, Judith. ANIMALS SHOULD DEFINITELY NOT ACT LIKE PEOPLE. Drawings by Ron Barrett, New York: Atheneum; 1980.
Gr. Preschool-2. Depicts the inconveniences animals would be burdened with if they behaved like people.

1325. Barrett, Judith. A SNAKE IS TOTALLY TAIL. Illustrated by Lonni Sue Johnson. New York: Atheneum; 1983.
Gr. Preschool-1. Describes 28 animals giving their essence using alliteration.

1326. Batherman, Muriel. ANIMALS LIVE HERE. New York: Greenwillow, 1979.
Gr. 1-3. Describes living quarters that animals build or borrow from others above, on, and beneath the ground.

1327. Baum, Thomas. HUGO THE HIPPO. New York: Harcourt Brace; 1976.
Gr. 1-5. A young hippopotamus explains why he trusts children but has a healthy distrust of all grownups.

1328. Bethell, Jean. BATHTIME. New York: Holt, Rinehart & Winston; 1979.
Gr. K-1. Describes the bathing and grooming practices of a variety of animals including ostriches, elephants, and beavers.

1329. Boorer, Michael. ANIMALS. Morristown, NJ: Silver Burdett; 1984.
Gr. 5-7. Looks at main groups discussing similarities and differences and discusses important subgroups. Excellent diagrams.

1330. Brady, Irene. BEAVER YEAR. Illustrated. Boston: Houghton Mifflin; 1976.
Gr. 1-5. Chronicles the lives of two beavers from the time they are born until they begin their own family.

1331. Brady, Irene. WILD BABIES: A CANYON SKETCHBOOK. Illustrated Boston: Houghton Mifflin; 1979.
Gr. 4-6. Uses sketches to show the young of six animal families from birth to adulthood.

1332. Chace, G. Earl. WONDERS OF PRAIRIE DOGS. Illustrated with photographs. New York: Dodd, Mead; 1976.
Gr. 5-up. Discusses the prairie dog and its distribution, classification, society, burrow behavior, and the controversy over its control.

Curtis, Patricia. CINDY, A HEARING EAR DOG. Photographs by David Cupp, New York: Dutton; 1981.
Gr. 3-5. See #880.

1333. Dalton, Stephen. CAUGHT IN MOTION. New York: Van Nostrand; 1982.
Gr. 1-up. High speed photographs of small animals, insects, birds.

1334. DEVELOPING LANGUAGE SKILLS: ANIMALS WE SEE AROUND US [Filmstrip]. Chicago: Encyclopaedia Britannica Educational Corp.; 1976; 5 filmstrips; 5 cassettes; 1 teacher's guide .
Gr. K-2. Encourages descriptive vocabulary development, Contents: All Kinds of Dogs; All Kinds of Cats; All Kinds of Birds; All Kinds of Fish; All Kinds of Small Furry Animals.

1335. Fichter, George S. INSECT PESTS. Illustrated by Nicholas Strekalovsky. Edited by Herbert Zim, New York: Golden; 1966.
Gr. 5-up. A guide to more than 350 pests of home, garden, field, and forest.

1336. FOSSILS: TRACES OF THE PAST [Filmstrip]. Washington, D.C: National Geographic; 1982; 1 filmstrip; 1 cassette; 1 teacher's guide.

Gr. 5-8. Discusses how fossils are formed and techniques for recovering them.

1337. Freschet, Berniece. POSSUM BABY. Illustrated by Jim Arnosky. New York: Longman; 1978.
Gr. K-3. The growth of a possum from birth to young adulthood.

Friedman, Judi. NOISES IN THE WOODS. Pictures by John Hamberger. New York: Dutton; 1979.
Gr. 1-4. See #992.

1338. Goudey, Alice E. HOUSES FROM THE SEA. Illustrated by Adrienne Adams. New York: Scribner; 1959.
Gr. K-4. A poetic introduction to shells, introducing a variety both in words and watercolor pictures.

Grosvenor, Donna K. THE BLUE WHALE. Washington, D.C: National Geographic; 1977.
Gr. K-3. See #595.

1339. Heller, Ruth. ANIMALS BORN ALIVE AND WELL. New York: Grosset & Dunlap; 1982.
Gr. 2-6. A simple rhymed text introduces the varieties of mammals.

Hess, Lilo. A SNAILS'S PACE. Illustrated. New York: Scribner; 1974.
Gr. 2-6. See #596.

1340. Hoban, Tana. BIG ONES, LITTLE ONES. Illustrated. New York: Greenwillow; 1976.
Gr. K-3. Photographs without text depict the mature and young of various animals, both domestic and wild.

1341. Hogan, Paula. THE BEAVER. Illustrated by Yoshi Miyake. Milwaukee, WI: Raintree; 1979.
Gr. K-3. Describes in simple terms the life cycle of the beaver.

1342. Hurd, Edith. THE MOTHER BEAVER. Illustrated by Clement Hurd. Boston: Little, Brown; 1971.
Gr. Preschool-3. Traces a year in the life cycle of a female beaver as she mates, gives birth, raises her kits, and helps strengthen the dam.

1343. Hutchins, Ross E. THE BUG CLAN. Illustrated with photographs. New York: Dodd, Mead; 1973.

Gr. 5-up. A general description of the characteristics and life cycles of a number of true bugs, insects with sucking mouthparts.

1344. Jourdan, Eveline. BUTTERFLIES AND MOTHS AROUND THE WORLD. Illustrated with color photographs. Minneapolis: Lerner; 1981.
Gr. 4-up. Outlines the life cycle of moths and butterflies and discusses the specific habits and characteristics of more than 50 of these abundant insects.

1345. LIFE CYCLES [Filmstrip]. Washington, D.C.: National Geographic; 1974; 5 filmstrips; 5 cassettes; 5 guides.
Gr. 5-12. Describes the life cycles of various species of animals.

1346. LIONS, TIGERS, AND OTHER BIG CATS [Filmstrip]. Washington, D.C: National Geographic; 1981; 1 filmstrip; 1 cassette; 1 teacher's guide.
Gr. K-4. Introduces a variety of big cats that live in grasslands, mountains, and forests.

1347. Mari, Lela, and Enzo Mari. THE APPLE AND THE MOTH. New York: Pantheon; 1970.
Gr. Preschool-3. The life cycle of the moth is represented in a brightly colored wordless book.

1348. McClung, Robert M. BEES, WASPS, AND HORNETS, AND HOW THEY LIVE. Illustrated. New York: Morrow; 1971.
Gr. 3-7. Describes the common characteristics of most membrane-winged insects and explores in further detail the specific characteristics of the different wasps, bees, and hornets belonging to this group.

1349. Milne, Lorus Johnson, and Margery Milne. GADABOUTS AND STICK-AT-HOMES. Illustrated by Sarah Landry. San Francisco: Sierra Club Books; 1980.
Gr. 4-up. Discusses the homes and habitations of a variety of animals.

1350. Olney, Ross Robert, and Pat Olney. KEEPING INSECTS AS PETS. Illustrated, New York: Watts; 1978.
Gr. 4-up. Discusses acquiring, caring for, and observing certain insects such as crickets, ants, and spiders that make suitable pets.

1351. Pettit, Theodore S. WILDLIFE AT NIGHT. Illustrated. New York: Putnam; 1976.

Gr. 6-8. Anecdotes about nocturnal animals explore their behavior and offer hints for making observations.

Pluckrose, Henry. WHALES. Illustrated by Norman Weaver. New York: Gloucester; 1979.
Gr. K-8. See #630.

1352. PREHISTORIC LIFE [Filmstrip]. Chicago: SVE; 1983; 6 filmstrips; 6 cassettes; guide.
Gr. 6-up. Introduces the concepts of evolution, natural selection and adaptation, focusing primarily on animals.

1353. Riedman, Sarab Regals. BIOLOGICAL CLOCKS. Illustrated by Leslie Morrill. New York: Harper & Row; 1982.
Gr. 6-8. Shows how the inner clock that regulates the behavior of all living creatures works.

1354. Rinard, Judith E. CREATURES OF THE NIGHT. Washington, D.C.: National Geographic; 1977.
Gr. 2-4. Describes the after-dark activities of many nocturnal animals.

1355. Rounds, Glen. THE BEAVER, HOW HE WORKS. Illustrated, New York: Holiday House; 1976.
Gr. K-3. Describes the life of a beaver and the methods he uses to dam streams and build himself a lodge.

1356. Ryder, Joanne. SNAIL IN THE WOODS. Pictures by Jo Polseno. New York: Harper & Row; 1979.
Gr. K-3. A snail's life from the time it is hatched to the time it lays its own eggs.

Sarnoff, Jane; Ruffins, Reynold. A GREAT AQUARIUM BOOK: THE PUTTING-IT-TOGETHER GUIDE FOR BEGINNERS. Illustrated. New York: Scribner; 1977.
Gr. 1-up. See #178.

1357. Selsam, Millicent. QUESTIONS AND ANSWERS ABOUT ANTS. Pictures by Arabelle Wheatley. New York: Four Winds; 1967.
Gr. 2-5. Answers questions such as: What do ants eat? How do ants find their way? Can ants learn? Explains the habits and behavior of ordinary ants and tells how to keep ants.

1358. Selsam, Millicent. WHERE DO THEY GO? INSECTS IN WINTER. New York: Four Winds; 1982.

Gr. 1-3. Describes ways in which twelve varieties of insects cope with winter.

1359. SHARKS [Filmstrip]. Washington, D.C: National Geographic; 1977; 1 filmstrip; 1 cassette; 1 teacher's guide.
Gr. 3-8. Introduces the life and habits of many varieties of these fishes and discusses the ways in which scientists study them.

SHELLS AND MARINE LIFE [Realia]. Fort Collins, CO: Earth Science Materials; 1975; 15 shell samples; 1 guide.
Gr. 3-up. See #646.

1360. Simon, Seymour. ANIMAL FACT/ANIMAL FABLE. Illustrated by Diane de Groat, New York: Crown; 1979.
Gr. K-3. Describes common beliefs about animals and explains which are fact and which are fable.

1361. Simon, Seymour. STRANGE CREATURES. New York: Four Winds; 1981.
Gr. 4-6. Describes a number of animals that look or behave oddly or have strange powers, including the hoatzin, tuatara, grunion, and gecko.

1362. Smith, Hobart Muir. REPTILES OF NORTH AMERICA: A GUIDE TO FIELD IDENTIFICATION. Illustrated by David M. Dennis and Sy Barlowe. New York: Golden Press; 1982.
Gr. 5-up. Discusses location and collecting of reptiles as well as identification. Includes a section on snakebite.

SPIDERS [Filmstrip]. Washington, D.C: National Geographic; 1981; 1 filmstrip; 1 cassette; 1 teacher's guide.
Gr. K-6. See #1141.

1363. Stone, Lynn M. ENDANGERED ANIMALS (NEW TRUE BOOKS). Chicago: Children's Press; 1984.
Gr. 1-3. Investigates the threats to the survival of certain animal species. Discusses efforts to save rare animals.

1364. Torgersen, Don Arthur. GIRAFFE HOOVES AND ANTELOPE HORNS. ELEPHANT HERDS AND RHINO HORNS. KILLER WHALES AND DOLPHIN PLAY. LION PRIDES AND TIGER TRACKS. Illustrated by Lee Trail and author. Chicago: Children's Press; 1982.

Gr. 4-6. Discussion of 4 animal groups in 4 volumes includes general characteristics, pbysical appearance, behavior, habitat, etc.

1365. Ungerer, Tomi. SNAIL, WHERE ARE YOU? Illustrated. New York: Harper & Row; 1962.
Gr. Preschool-3. Invites you to try to find the snail design which is hidden in the various pictures.

Van Woerkom, Dorothy. HIDDEN MESSAGES. Illustrated by Lynne Cherry. New York: Crown; 1979.
Gr. 1-4. See #1005.

1366. Verite, Marcelle. ANIMALS AROUND THE YEAR. Illustrated by Romain Simon. New York: Golden; 1972.
Gr. 4-8. Describes the habits of more than 60 animals at different seasons of the year.

WHALES [Filmstrip]. Washington, D.C.: National Geographic; 1979; 1 filmstrip; 1 cassette; 1 teacher's guide, including script.
Gr. K-4. See #661.

1367. WHAT IS AN AMPHIBIAN [Kit]. Washington, D.C: National Geographic; 1978; 1 filmstrip; 1 cassette; 2 tests and duplicating masters; 3 study prints; 1 teacher's guide.
Gr. 2-6. Helps improve reading skills, increase reading and listening comprehension, and build vocabulary while teaching specific concepts.

1368. Wildsmith, Brian. BRIAN WILDSMITH'S WILD ANIMALS. [With] THE RICH MAN AND THE SHOEMAKER: A FABLE BY LA FONTAINE [Filmstrip], Weston, CT: Weston Woods; 1972; 1 filmstrip; 1 cassette; 1 text booklet.
Gr. Preschool-2. Two stories by Wildsmith, one based on his book entitled WILD ANIMALS, shows groups of various wild animals to which man has given unusual names; the other story, an adaptation of La Fontaine's fable tells a story about a poor, but cheerful shoe-maker.

1369. WONDERS OF LEARNING KIT: LEARNING ABOUT ANIMALS: INSECTS [Kit], Washington, D.C: National Geographic; 1982; 1 cassette; 1 booklet (30 copies); 13 duplicating masters; activity folder and guide.
Gr. 3-6. Discusses types of insects, metamorphosis, and insects listening comprehension.

1370. WONDERS OF LEARNING KIT: LEARNING ABOUT ANIMALS: MAMMALS [Kit]. Washington, D.C: National Geographic; 1982; 1 cassette; 1 booklet (30 copies); 13 duplicating masters; activity folder and guide.
Gr. 3-6. A general introduction highlighting several groups.

1371. Yabuuchi, Masayuki. ANIMALS SLEEPING. Illustrated. New York: Philomel Books; 1983.
Gr. Preschool-1. Simple text and pictures show sleeping habits of the koala, leopard, sea otter, and albatross, and of flamingos, bats, and camels.

Young, Jim. WHEN THE WHALE CAME TO MY TOWN. Photographs by Dan Sernstein. New York: Knopf, distributed by Random House; 1974.
Gr. 3-up. See #664.

1372. Zim, Herbert S., and Clarence Cottam. INSECTS: A GUIDE TO FAMILIAR AMERICAN INSECTS. Illustrated by James Gordon Irving. New York: Golden; 1956.
Gr. 5-up. This book deals with 225 species of common and important insects. A key to insect groups is provided for quick identification and information. Insects are often shown on the plant that provides their food.

1373. Zim, Herbert S., and George S. Fichter, eds. ZOO ANIMALS. Illustrated by Arthur Singer. New York: Golden; 1967.
Gr. K-4. The most common mammals, birds, reptiles and amphibians exhibited in the world's zoos are surveyed in this volume. Includes information on the purposes of zoos and how zoo animals are obtained, displayed, cared for and fed.

1374. Zim, Herbert S., and Lucretia Krantz. SNAILS. Illustrated by Rene Martin. New York: Morrow; 1975.
Gr. 3-7. An introduction to gastropods, or snails, of which there are approximately 80,000 kinds.

Animals: The Working Body

1375. BONES [Realia]. Boston: American Science and Engineering; 6 skeletons; 6 foam-lined work trays.
Gr. 4-6. A study of bones which includes 2 skeletons each of minks, cats and rabbits.

1376. Branley, Franklyn Mansfield. SHIVERS AND GOOSE BUMPS: HOW WE KEEP WARM. Illustrated by True Kelley. New York: Crowell; 1984.
Gr. 4-up. Describes how certain animals keep warm, how the human body loses and retains its heat, and how various types of clothing and dwellings aid in heat retention.

1377. THE CELL: BASIC UNIT OF LIFE [Filmstrip]. Washington, D.C: National Geographic; 1981; 1 filmstrip; 1 cassette; guide.
Gr. 5-9. Shows how cells move, grow and reproduce and discusses current research.

1378. Cole, Joanna. A CAT'S BODY. Illustrated by Jerone Wexler. New York: Morrow; 1982.
Gr. K-3. Describes physical characteristics of cats and how their bodies work for them.

1379. Cole, Johanna. A HORSE'S BODY. Illustrated by Joane Wexler. New York: Morrow; 1981.
Gr. 2-6. Introduction to body, habits and behavior of horses.

1380. Cole, Joanna. AN INSECT'S BODY. New York: Morrow; 1984.
Gr. 4-5. Examines the common house cricket and shows why its body is ideally suited for survival.

1381. Cooper, Gale. INSIDE ANIMALS. Illustrated. Boston: Little, Brown; 1978.
Gr. 3-7. Introduces some rather unique aspects of many different animals such as: an earthworm has both male and female reproductive organs, a camel's hump stores fat, and a snake has one lung.

1382. Earle, Olive Lydia, and Michael Kantor. ANIMALS AND THEIR EARS. Illustrated. New York: Morrow; 1974.
Gr. 3-7. Describes the many varieties of ears, visible and invisible, found in the animal kingdom.

1383. Ford, Barbara. ANIMALS THAT USE TOOLS. Illustrated by Janet D'Amato. New York: Messner; 1978.
Gr. 4-6. Discusses the ability of many different animals including crabs, vultures, otters, elephants, and chimpanzees to use tools and the ability of a fewer number of species to make tools.

1384. Freedman, Russell. ANIMAL GAMES. Illustrated by St. Tamara, New York: Holiday House; 1976.

Gr. 1-4. Describes the games that different young animals play for fun and to help develop skills and strength needed for survival.

1385. Freedman, Russell. FARM BABIES. Illustrated. New York: Holiday House; 1981.
Gr. K-3. Describes the offspring of eleven familiar farm animals including a calf, piglet, and foal.

1386. Freedman, Russell. HANGING ON: HOW ANIMALS CARRY THEIR YOUNG. Illustrated. New York: Holiday House; 1977.
Gr. 1-4. A brief description of the various ways different animals transport their young.

1387. Freedman, Russell. HOW ANIMALS DEFEND THEIR YOUNG. New York: Dutton; 1978.
Gr. 5-9. Discusses shelters, signals, camouflage and bluffs used by parent animals to protect their young.

1388. Freedman, Russell. TOOTH AND CLAW: A LOOK AT ANIMAL WEAPONS. Illustrated. New York: Holiday House; 1980.
Gr. 1-4. Text and photographs describe animal weapons including sprays, quills, teeth claws, horns, poisons and stings.

1389. Goor, Ron; Goor, Nancy. ALL KINDS OF FEET. Illustrated with photographs. New York: Crowell; 1984.
Gr. Preschool-3. Text and photographs present the different types of feet found in the animal kingdom.

1390. Heller, Ruth. CHICKENS AREN'T THE ONLY ONES. Illustrated. New York: Grodset & Dunlap; 1981.
Gr. Preschool-2. Describes all the different creatures which hatch from eggs.

1391. Hewett, Joan. WATCHING THEM GROW: INSIDE A ZOO NURSERY. Photographs by Richard Hewett. Boston: Little, Brown; 1979.
Gr. 3-7. A behind-the-scenes peek into tbe baby animal nursery at the San Diego Zoo.

1392. Hirsch, S. Carl. HE AND SHE: HOW MALES AND FEMALES BEHAVE. Illustrated by William Steinel. Philadelphia: Lippincott; 1975.
Gr. 5-8. Examines and compares tbe differences and similarities in the behavior patterns of males and females in various species including human beings.

1393. Hutchins, Ross E. HOW ANIMALS SURVIVE. Illustrated with photographs. New York: Parents Magazine Press; 1974.
Gr. 3-7. Describes how animals survive by using their armor, camouflage, horns, stings and other natural protective devices.

1394. INTRODUCING INSECTS [Filmstrip]. Philadelphia, PA: Curtis Publishing; 1971; 6 filmstrips; teacher's guide.
Gr. 4-6. Contents: Insect Anatomy; Insect Growth; Insect Protection; Insect Locomotion; Useful Insects; Harmful Insects.

1395. Ipsen, D. WHAT DOES A BEE SEE. Reading, MA: Addison-Wesley; 1971.
Gr. 5-up. Traces the scientific experiments on the honeybees' capacity to see color.

1396. Isenbart, Hans-Heinrich. A FOAL IS BORN. Photographs by Hanns-Jorg Anders. Translated by Catherine Edwards. New York: Putnam; 1976.
Gr. K-5. Describes the birth and first few hours of a foal's life.

Jacobs, Francine. THE SECRET LANGUAGE OF ANIMALS: COMMUNICATION BY PHEROMONES. Illustrated by Jean Zallinger. New York: Morrow; 1976.
Gr. 4-6. See #995.

Jacobs, Francine. SOUNDS IN THE SEA. Illustrated by Jean Zallinger. New York: Morrow; 1977.
Gr. 3-7. See #996.

1397. Komori, Atsushi. ANIMAL MOTHERS. Illustrated by Masayuki Yabuuchi, New York: Philomel Books; 1983.
Gr. Preschool-1. Text and illustrations describe how baby animals are aided by their mothers in moving from place to place.

1398. Lauber, Patricia. WHAT'S HATCHING OUT OF THAT EGG?. Illustrated. New York: Crown; 1979.
Gr. 2-4. Text and illustrations introduce a variety of eggs and the animals that hatch out of them. Includes ostrich, python, bullfrog and monarch butterfly eggs among others.

1399. LIFE CYCLE OF THE FROG [Motion Picture]. Chicago: Encyclopedia Britannica Educational Corp.; 1968; 8mm filmloop.

Gr. 3-up. The frog is shown both in and out of water and from tadpole stage to maturity.

1400. LIFE FROM LIFE [Filmstrip], Santa Monica, CA: BFA; 6 filmstrips; 6 cassettes.
Gr, K-3. Introduces subjects of reproduction, growth and development.

1401. Livaudais, Madeleine, and Robert Dunne. THE SKELETON BOOK: AN INSIDE LOOK AT ANIMALS. Illustrated. New York: Walker; 1972.
Gr. 3-6, Compares the similarities and differences of the skeletons of a variety of vertebrates.

1402. Mason, George Frederick. ANIMAL WEAPONS. New York: Morrow; 1949.
Gr. 4-6. A wild animal must have a weapon with which to defend himself if he is to survive. Explains how horns, hoofs, claws, teeth, poison, odor, strings and quills are used as weapons in nature.

1403. Mason, George Frederick. ANIMAL TOOLS. New York: Morrow; 1951.
Gr. 4-6. Compares animal tools with man-made ones and explains how an animal, by specialized appendages or organs, is able to adapt himself to his environment.

1404. Patent, Dorothy Hinshaw. FROGS, TOADS, SALAMANDERS AND HOW THEY REPRODUCE. Illustrated by Matthew Kalmenoff. New York: Holiday House; 1975.
Gr. 4-7. Describes the general characteristics of various amphibians with emphasis on their reproductive processes.

Patent, Dorothy Hinshaw. HOW INSECTS COMMUNICATE. Illustrated. New York: Holiday House; 1975.
Gr. 4-6. See #999.

1405. Rahn, Joan Elma. GROCERY STORE ZOOLOOGY: BONES AND MUSCLES. Illustrated by Ginny Linville Winter. New York: Atheneum; 1977.
Gr. 5-9. Introduces the function of bones, joints and muscles using the chicken and other meat available at the grocery store.

1406. Schilling, Betty. TWO KITTENS ARE BORN: FROM BIRTH TO TWO MONTHS. New York: Holt, Rinebart, & Winston; 1980.
Gr. 1-3. Follows the growth of two kittens from birth to two months.

1407. Selsam, Millicent Ellis. HOW KITTENS GROW. Photographs by Esther Bubley. New York: Four Winds; 1973.
Gr. K-3. An account in pictures and words of four kittens, from birth to eight weeks. Shows how the mother cat cares for and teaches them.

1408. Silverstein, Alvin, and Virginia Silverstein. THE SKELETAL SYSTEM: FRAMEWORKS FOR LIFE. Illustrated by Lee J. Ames. Englewood Cliffs, NJ: Prentice Hall; 1972.
Gr. 3-7. Analyzes the structure and function of the human skeletal system and compares it with that of other animals.

1409. Simon, Hilda. SIGHT AND SEEING: A WORLD OF LIGHT AND COLOR. New York: Philomel Books 1983.
Gr. 5-up. Discusses the importance of tbe sense of sight, the difference between sensitivity to light and the actual formation of images, and the various sight organs found in animals.

SONGS OF THE HUMPBACK WHALE [Sound Recording]. Hollywood, CA: Capitol Records; 1970; 1 sound disc.
Gr. 2- up. See #1002.

SOUNDS OF ANIMALS [Sound Recording]. New York: Folkways Records; 1955; 1 sound disc; descriptive notes.
Gr. Preschool-up. See #1003.

Spier, Peter. GOBBLE, GROWL, GRUNT. New York: Doubleday; 1971.
Gr. K. See #1004.

1410. Van Gelder, Richard George. WHOSE NOSE IS THIS? Illustrated. New York: Walker; 1974.
Gr. 2-4. Introduces a variety of noses.

Van Woerkom, Dorothy. HIDDEN MESSAGES. Illustrated by Lynne Cherry. New York: Crown; 1979.
Gr. 1-4. See #1005.

1411. WAYS ANIMALS COMMUNICATE [Filmstrip]. Washington, D.C.: National Geographic; 1980; 1 filmstrip; 1 cassette; guide.
Gr. K-6. Bees perform intricate dances to give direction of food sources, male crickets attract mates by rubbing their wing coverings, baboons groom each other to reinforce social bonding.

1412. Winter, Ruth. SCENT TALK AMONG ANIMALS. Illustrated by Richard Cuffari. Philadelphia, PA: Lippincott; 1977.
Gr. 3-7. Discusses the scent language used by animals for communication and behavior control.

1413. WONDERS OF LEARNING KITS: WAYS ANIMALS COMMUNICATE [Kit]. Washington, D.C: National Geographic; 1982; 1 cassette; 30 booklets, guide.
Gr. 3-6. Discusses ways in which animals signal each other to avoid danger, establish territories and live together peacefully.

1414. Yount, Lisa. TOO HOT, TOO COLD, JUST RIGHT: HOW ANIMALS CONTROL THEIR TEMPERATURES. Illustrations by Harriett Springer. New York: Walker; 1981.
Gr. 4-7. Discusses the many ways that animals have of controlling their body temperature.

Birds

1415. THE 1983 CHILDCRAFT ANNUAL: FEATHERED FRIENDS. Chicago: World Book; 1983.
Gr. 4-up. Drawings and coloured photographs accompany concise text to detail birds ranging from those inhabiting woodlands and forests, to jungle, desert and sea shore.

1416. Arnold, Caroline. FIVE NESTS. Pictures by Ruth Sanderson, New York: Dutton; 1980.
Gr. 1-3. Describes the ways robins, redwing blackbirds, rheas, Mexican jays, and cowbirds care for their young.

1417. Austin, Oliver L. FAMILIES OF BIRDS. (A Golden Science Guide) Illustrated by Arthur Singer. New York: Western; 1971.
Gr. 6-up. An illustrated guide to the elements of bird classification giving information on 34 orders and 208 families of birds throughout the world.

1418. BIRDS AND HOW THEY GROW [Sound Recording]. Washington, D.C: National Geographic; 1982; 1 sound cassette; 1 booklet (30 copies); 3 guides.
Gr. K-2. Shows the physical appearance and anatomy of birds, bird nests, eggs and embryos.

1419. Borror, Donald Joyce. SONGS OF EASTERN BIRDS [Sound Recording]. New York: Dover; 1970; 1 sound disc; 1 booklet.
Gr. 2-up. Gives field recordings of the songs of 60 common birds of the eastern United States.

1420. Brenner, Barbara. HAVE YOU EVER HEARD OF A KANGAROO BIRD: FASCINATING FACTS ABOUT UNUSUAL BIRDS. Illustrated by Irene Brady. New York: Coward, McCann & Geoghegan; 1980.
Gr. 3-5. Presents facts about unusual birds.

1421. Brown, Margaret Wise. THE DEAD BIRD. Illustrated by Remy Charlip. New York: Scott; 1958.
Gr. K-2. A child finds a dead bird and other children join in giving it a suitable burial, placing spring flowers on the grave.

1422. COMMON LAND BIRDS OF NORTH AMERICA [Study Print]. Chicago: Encyclopaedia Britannica Educational Corp.; 1968; 10 pictures.
Gr. 1-6. Designed to help children recognize and identify birds commonly seen in fields, woods and backyards.

1423. Day, Jenifer W. WHAT IS A BIRD? Illustrated by Tony Chen. New York: Golden; 1975.
Gr. K-4. Pictures many different categories of birds: tropical birds; land birds; water-fowl; etc.

1424. ENDANGERED SPECIES: BIRDS. [Study Print]. Chicago: Encyclopaedia Britannica Educational Corp.; 1976; 8 study prints.
Gr. 4-8. Gives facts about the life cycles of 8 American birds and discusses how each has become endangered.

Graham, Ada, and Frank Graham. PUFFIN ISLAND. Photographed by Les Lane, New York: Cowles; 1971.
Gr. 6-10. See #594.

1425. Hopf, Alice L. CHICKENS AND THEIR WILD RELATIVES. Illustrated with photographs. New York: Dodd, Mead; 1982.
Gr. 5-up. Tells the story of the development of the wild chicken and some of its wild relatives.

1426. INVESTIGATING BIRDS [Filmstrip]. Chicago: Coronet; 1975; 6 filmstrips; 6 cassettes; guide.

Gr. 4-6. Stimulates interest in common and exotic birds, adaptations, characteristics and behaviors are stressed.

1427. Jacobs, Francine. AFRICA'S FLAMINGO LAKE. Photographs by Jerome Jacobs. New York: Morrow; 1979.
Gr. 4-6. An exploration of Lake Nakuru and the national park that surrounds it.

1428. Jacobs, Joseph. THE MAGPIE'S NEST: A PICTURE BOOK. Chicago: Follett; 1970.
Gr. 1-3. Each bird leaves the magpie's nest with a different idea on how to build a nest.

1429. Lionni, Leo. TICO AND THE GOLDEN WINGS. Illustrated. New York: Pantheon Books; 1964.
Gr. K-4. A wingless bird is granted his wish for a pair of golden wings.

1430. May, Julian. BIRDS WE KNOW. Illustrated. Chicago: Creative Educational Society, distributed by Children's Press; 1973.
Gr. 2-4. Describes the characteristics and life cycle of several familiar birds: the bluebird, mallard, meadowlark, swan, hummingbird, and roadrunner.

1431. Parnall, Peter. A DOG'S BOOK OF BIRDS. New York: Scribner; 1977.
Gr. K-5. Illustrates a dog's self-sought encounters with a variety of birds including a blue heron, albatross, loon, and eagle.

1432. PELICANS [Motion Picture]. Burbank: Walt Disney Productions. 1966; 1 film loop.
Gr. 4-up. Shows pelicans as fliers, diving for fish, nesting in groups, and feeding their young.

1433. Simon, Norma. BENJY'S BIRD. Pictures by Joe Lasker. Chicago: Whitman; 1965.
Gr. 1-3. Benjy finds a baby robin, nurses it, and makes it a pet. Fall comes and Benjy watches the bird leave.

1434. Velthuijs, Max. THE PAINTER AND THE BIRD. Translated by Ray Broekel. Reading, MA: Addison-Wesley; 1975.
Gr. Preschool-2. After an artist sells his favorite painting of a bird, the bird becomes so homesick he flies out of the picture and sets off to find his creator.

1435. Wetmore, Alexander. SONG AND GARDEN BIRDS OF NORTH AMERICA. Washington, D.C: National Geographic; 1964.
Gr. 6-up. Includes album of bird song recordings in back pocket of book.

1436. Wildsmith, Brian. BRIAN WILDSMITH'S BIRDS. New York: Watts; 1967.
Gr. K-3. Depicts various birds in striking paintings.

1437. Wildsmith, Brian. BRIAN WILDSMITH'S BIRDS. With: THE NORTH WIND AND THE SUN: A FABLE BY LA FONTAINE [Filmstrip]. Weston, CT: Weston; 1975; 1 filmstrip; 1 cassette; 1 booklet.
Gr. K-3.

Ecology

Hess, Lilo. SMALL HABITATS. Illustrated, New York: Scribner; 1976.
Gr. 2-7. See #172.

1438. Johnson, Sylvia A. ANIMALS OF THE GRASSLANDS. Illustrated by Alcuin C. Dornisch. Minneapolis: Lerner; 1976.
Gr. 4-up. Describes ten animals living on the savanna and in other grassland environments: the lion, red kangaroo, pronghorn, ostrich, mara, African elephant, blackbuck, zebra, bison, and giraffe.

Johnson, Sylvia A. ANIMALS OF THE MOUNTAINS. Illustrated by Alcuin C. Dornisch, Minneapolis: Lerner; 1976.
Gr. 4-up. See #466.

1439. Johnson, Sylvia A. ANIMALS OF THE TEMPERATE FORESTS. Illustrated by Alcuin C. Dornisch. Minneapolis: Lerner; 1976.
Gr. 4-up. Explores the physical characteristics and habits of ten animals living in the temperate forest,

1440. Johnson, Sylvia A. THE WILDLIFE ATLAS. Illustrated by Alcuin C. Dornesch. Minneapolis: Lerner; 1977.
Gr. 4-up. Describes sixty animals that inhabit deserts, grasslands, temperate and tropical forests, mountains, and polar regions.

1441. THE LIVING DESERT [Filmstrip]. Burbank, CA: Walt Disney Educational Media; 1971; 5 filmstrips; 5 cassettes; teacher's guide.
Gr. K-12. Describes how plants and animals survive in one of harshest environments on Earth.

1442. Pringle, Laurence P. FERAL: TAME ANIMALS GONE WILD. New York: Macmillan; 1983.
Gr. 5-up. Explores the controversial problem of domesticated animals gone wild, and its impact on people and on the environment.

1443. Schlein, Miriam. SNAKE FIGHTS, RABBIT FIGHTS, & MORE: A BOOK ABOUT ANIMAL FIGHTING. Illustrated by Sue Thompson. New York: Crown; 1979.
Gr. 2-4. Explores the reasons, including food, nesting places, mates, rank, and territory, why animals display aggressive behavior and fight with other animals like themselves.

1444. Silverstein, Alvin. ANIMAL INVADERS: THE STORY OF IMPORTED WILDLIFE. New York: Atheneum; 1974.
Gr. 4-6. Describes how animals introduced into a new geographic area, such as tbe rabbit in Australia and the mongoose in Jamaica, can destroy the ecological balance and become pests.

1445. SMALL WORLDS OF LIFE [Filmstrlp]. Washington, D.C: National Geographic; 1972; 7 filmstrips; 7 cassettes; 7 guides.
Gr. 5-12. Explores the interaction of organisms in several ecological communities. Contents: The Pond; The Coral Reef; The Apple Tree; The Desert; The Tundra; The Salt Marsh; The Everglades.

1446. WHITE WILDERNESS [Filmstrip]. Burbank, CA: Walt Disney Educational Media; 1974; 5 filmstrips; 5 cassettes; teacher's guide.
Gr. K-12. Explores one of the last habitats still virtually undisturbed by man and investigates how polar wildlife struggle to adapt to their barren environment.

1447. WILL THEY SURVIVE? [Filmstrip], Boulder, CO: Centre Productions; 1983; 2 filmstrips; 2 cassettes; guide.
Gr. 4-up. Describes the situations of several endangered species and possible steps to ensure their survival.

Evolution

Baylor, Byrd. IF YOU ARE A HUNTER OF FOSSILS. New York: Scribner; 1980.
Gr. 2-6. See #375.

1448. Branley, Franklyn Mansfield. DINOSAURS, ASTEROIDS, & SUPERSTARS: WHY THE DINOSAURS DISAPPEARED. Illustrated by Jean Zallinger. New York: Crowell; 1982.
Gr. 5-up. Discusses possible causes of the sudden extinction of dinosaurs at the close of the Cretaceous Period.

1449. Rice, Paul, and Peter Mayle. AS DEAD AS A DODO. Illustrated by Shawn Rice. Boston: Godine; 1981.
Gr. 5-up. Informal text and exaggerated pictures introduce a number of creatures which are now extinct.

1450. Smith, Howard E. LIVING FOSSILS. Drawings by Jennifer Dewey. New York: Dodd, Mead; 1982.
Gr. 4-8. Describes rare and unusual animals and plants with such ancient connections that they deserve to be called living fossils.

1451. Thompson, Ida. THE AUDUBON SOCIETY FIELD GUIDE TO NORTH AMERICAN FOSSILS. Illustrated with photographs by Townsend P. Dickinson. Visual key by Carol Nehring. New York: Knopf; 1982.
Gr. 5-up.

Plants

1452. Alexander, Taylor, Will Burnett, and Herbert Zim. BOTANY. New York: Golden; 1971.
Gr. 5-up. An introduction to botany, ranging from simple to complex plants, and explaining such aspects as nutrition, sensitivity and reactions, reproduction, inheritance evolution and relation to the environment.

1453. Buller, Dave. LAWN GUIDE: A GUIDE FOR IDENTIFYING ORGANISMS FOUND IN AND AROUND THE LAWN. Illustrated by Lonnie Kennedy. Berkeley, CA: Outdoor Biology Instructional Strategies: Lawrence Hall of Science, University of California; 1978.
Gr. 4-6.

1454. Cosgrove, Margaret. PLANTS IN TIME: THEIR HISTORY AND MYSTERY. Illustrated. New York: Dodd, Mead; 1967.
Gr. 4-6. Discusses the first plant life on our planet and how this life disappeared or adapted itself to a changing environment.

1455. Fisher, Aileen. NOW THAT SPRING IS HERE [Filmstrip]. Illustrated by Symeon Shimin. Los Angeles, CA: Bowmar/Noble; 1977; 1 filmstrip; 1 sound cassette.
Gr. K-3. Combines artwork and narration with live photographs to show how the spring season stimulates growth in plants.

1456. Fisher, Aileen. PRIZE PERFORMANCE. Illustrated by Margot Tomes. Los Angeles, CA: Bowmar/Noble; 1977.
Gr. K-3. Relates in verse how a variety of common plants are related to each other.

1457. Hunken, Jorie, John Madama, and Pamela Pacelli. LADYBUGS AND LETTUCE LEAVES. Washington, D.C: Center for Science in the Public Interest; 1982.
Gr. 4-6. Two volumes (student guide and teacher's manual) prepared by project Inside/Outside; Somerville Public Schools students explore the wonders of nature through a gardening project. The emphasis is on understanding life cycles, and increasing awareness of the importance of working with nature.

1458. Johnson, Sylvia. MUSHROOMS. Illustrated by M. Isawa. New York: Lerner; 1982.
Gr. 4-6. Discusses anatomy of mushrooms, and how they get their food and reproduce.

1459. KINGDOM OF PLANTS [Filmstrip]. Washington, D.C: National Geographic; 1974; 5 filmstrips; 5 cassettes; 5 guides.
Gr. 5-12. Discusses the many varieties of plants and the roles they play in the environment.

1460. Lavine, Sigmund A. WONDERS OF TERRARIUMS. Illustrated by Jane O. Regan. New York: Dodd, Mead; 1977.
Gr. 5-up. Describes the methods for setting up and maintaining a terrarium, including plant selection.

1461. LEARNING ABOUT PLANTS SERIES [Filmstrip]. Chicago: Encyclopaedia Britannica Educational Corp.; 1966; 6 filmstrips.

Gr. 1-3. Presents principles of plant development and reproduction through study of familiar flowers.

1462. Martin, Alexander C. WEEDS. Illustrated by Jean Zallinger. New York: Golden; 1972.
Gr. 6-up. An identification guide to the varieties of weeds common in the United States, containing illustrations and descriptions of these plants and indicating their distribution across the country.

1463. Milne, Lorus Johnson, and Margery Milne. BECAUSE OF A FLOWER. Drawings by Kenneth Gosner. New York: Atheneum; 1975.
Gr. 4-6. Discusses various plants that provide centers for small communities of animal life attracted by their flowers, fruits and seeds.

1464. Morton, Julia F. EXOTIC PLANTS. Illustrated by Richard E. Younger. New York: Golden Press; 1971.
Gr. 5-up. A guide to the ornamental plants, trees, and vines found in gardens in tropical and subtropical regions or in greenhouses in cooler areas.

1465. Norris, Louanne, and Howard Smith. AN OAK TREE DIES AND A JOURNEY BEGINS. Illustrated by Allen Davis. New York: Crown; 1979.
Gr. K-3. A big, old oak tree on the bank of a river is felled by weather and age and, after experiencing life on the ground, in the river, and at sea, is claimed from the beach.

1466. Overbeck, Cynthia. CARNIVOROUS PLANTS. Illustrated by Kiyoshi Shimizo. New York: Lerner; 1982.
Gr. 4-6. A discussion of the world of carnivorous plants including types, adaptations and locations around the world.

1467. Overbeck, Cynthia. HOW SEEDS TRAVEL. Photographs by Shabo Hana, Minneapolis: Lerner; 1982.
Gr. 4-6. Describes how seeds are moved from place to place by wind, water, and animals, and how they function in plant reproduction.

1468. Paterson, Allen. THE WONDER WHY BOOK OF GROWING PLANTS. Illustrated by Elsle Wrigley. New York: Grosset & Dunlap; 1977.

Gr. 2-4. Provides a brief explanation of the life of plants, with some practical projects to do to learn about plant growth.

1469. PLANTS: WHAT HAPPENS IN WINTER [Filmstrip]. Washington, D.C: National Geographic; 1983; 1 filmstrip; 1 cassette; 1 guide.
Gr. 1-4. Shows the effects of weather changes on plantlife.

1470. Pringle, Laurence. WILD FOODS: A BEGINNER'S GUIDE TO IDENTIFYING, HARVESTING, AND COOKING SAFE AND TASTY PLANTS FROM THE OUTDOORS. New York: Four Winds; 1978.
Gr. 6-up. An introduction to the world of edible wild foods. It is a beginner's guide to identifying, harvesting, and preparing safe and tasty plants from the outdoors.

1471. Quackenbush, Robert. HERE A PLANT, THERE A PLANT. Englewood Cliffs, NJ: Prentice Hall; 1982.
Gr. 3-4. Life of Luther Burbank includes the idea that his experiments were highly controversial, though they would be taken for granted now.

1472. Rahn, Joan Elma. PLANTS UP CLOSE. Illustrated with photographs, Boston: Houghton Mifflin; 1981.
Gr. 2-5. Examines five different plants in order to show how the parts of a plant function and how they contribute to the plant's life.

1473. Rahn, Joan Elma. WATCH IT GROW, WATCH IT CHANGE. Illustrated. New York: Atheneum; 1978.
Gr. 4-6. A diary with sketches of various plants showing their growth and change.

1474. Selsam, Millicent E. TREE FLOWERS. New York: Morrow; 1984.
Gr. 4-6. Text and drawings follow the growth cycle of twelve common flowering plants like the pussy willow and sugar maple.

1475. Selsam, Millicent Ellis. THE PLANTS WE EAT. New York: Morrow; 1981.
Gr. 5-8. This newly revised edition discusses the development of the most common food plants, and their changing uses. Includes simple directions for growing some of the plants at home.

1476. Selsam, Millicent Ellis, and Joyce Hunt. A FIRST LOOK AT FLOWERS. Illustrated by Harriett Springer, New York: Walker; 1976.
Gr. K-3. An introduction to the distinguishing characteristics of flowers.

1477. Selsam, Millicent Ellis, and Joyce Hunt. A FIRST LOOK AT THE WORLD OF PLANTS. Illustrated by Harriett Springer. New York: Walker; 1978.
Gr. K-3. Defines plants, examines their distinguishing characteristics, and introduces scientific classification.

1478. Shuttleworth, Floyd S, and Herbert S. Zim. NON-FLOWERING PLANTS. Illustrated by Dorothea Barlowe and others. New York: Golden; 1967.
Gr. 5-up. A guide to non-flowering plants - algae, fungi, lichens, mosses, liverworts and hornworts, ferns and fern allies, and gymnosperms.

1479. STUDY OF PLANT GROWTH [Chart]. Paoli, PA: Instructo; 1 flannel board set: 43 pieces; teaching guide.
Gr. K-6. Contains illustrations to show growth of bean and corn plants, parts of a plant, and plants that grow from parts other than seeds.

1480. TERRARIUMS AND HOW TO MAKE THEM [Filmstrip]. San Luis Obispo, CA: Vocational Education Productions: California Polytechnic State University; 1976; 1 filmstrip; 1 cassette; 1 filmstrip script
Gr. 5-up. Background and methods for planting terrariums.

1481. Tribe, Ian. THE PLANT KINGDOM. Illustrated by Henry Barnet. New York: Grosset & Dunlap; 1970.
Gr. 5-up. Presents distinctive specimens of the plant family describing outstanding characteristics of the major groups.

1482. Venning, Frank D. A GUIDE TO FIELD IDENTIFICATION: WILDFLOWERS OF NORTH AMERICA. Illustrated. New York: Golden; 1984.
Gr. 6-up. Includes criteria for selection as garden plants: range, abundance, attractiveness, and distinction.

1483. Welch, Martha McKeen. CLOSE LOOKS IN A SPRING WOODS. Illustrated with photographs, New York: Dodd, Mead; 1981.

Gr. 1-6. Describes the changes in plants and animals that takes place in the forest as spring replaces winter.

1484. Wilson, Ron. HOW PLANTS GROW. Illustrated. New York: Larousse; 1980.
Gr. 4-6. Explains the development and structure of plants and how they live and grow. Also discusses food chains, ecology, and conservation.

1485. Wong, Herbert H. PLANT COMMUNITIES: WHERE CAN CATTAILS GROW? Illustrated by Michael Eagle. Reading, MA: Addison-Wesley; 1970.
Gr. 1-3. Describes many different kinds of plant habitats, only one of which is just right for growing cattails.

1486. THE WORLD OF PLANTS [Filmstrip]. Washington, D.C.: National Geographic; 1976; 5 filmstrips; 5 cassettes; 5 teacher's guides with scripts.
Gr. K-4. Variety, habitats, and importance of plants, as well as the structure and function of the parts. Contents: The Parts of a Plant; How Plants Grow; Kinds of Plants; Where Plants Grow; Plants and People.

Humans: The Working Body: Systems

1487. Aliki. MY FIVE SENSES. New York: Crowell; 1962.
Gr. K-3. Describes the senses with pictures and brief text.

1488. Allison, Linda. BLOOD AND GUTS: A WORKING GUIDE TO YOUR OWN LITTLE INSIDES. Boston: Little, Brown; 1976.
Gr. 4-8. Body is described and experiments and projects you can do to discover how parts function.

1489. Baker, Gayle Cunningham. SPECIAL DELIVERY: A BOOK FOR KIDS ABOUT CESAREAN AND VAGINAL BIRTH. Illustrated. Edmonds, WA: Franklin Press; 1981.
Gr. Preschool-5. "Split text", larger type and simpler text for younger children, more detailed, small type text for older children.

1490. Berger, Gilda. THE WHOLE WORLD OF HANDS. Illustrated by True Kelley. Boston: Houghton Mifflin; 1982.
Gr. 4-6. All around treatment of hands, including anatomy, hand languages, injuries, etc.

1491. Berry, James R. WHY YOU FEEL HOT; WHY YOU FEEL COLD; YOUR BODY'S TEMPERATURE. Illustrated by William Ogden. Boston: Little, Brown; 1973.
Gr. 2-4. Explains body temperature and why it fluctuates as well as experiments you can do to understand body temperature.

1492. BIOLOGY OF THE HUMAN BODY [Filmstrip]. Chicago: Encyclopaedia Britannica Educational Corp,; 1979; 8 filmstrips; 8 cassettes; instructor's guide.
Gr. 4-up. Examines the various systems of the human body and bow they interrelate to carry on life functions.

BODY IMAGERY [Card]. Springfield, MA: Milton Bradley; 1976; 8 activity cards.
Gr. K-2. See #876.

1493. BODY MOVEMENT FLOOR GAME [Game]. Springfield, MA: Milton Bradley; 1 game; directions.
Gr. K-3. Floor game designed to develop gross motor skills.

1494. BODY PARTS: THE DOLL OF TALL THINGS. In: LET'S LEARN THE BASICS [Filmstrip]. Chicago: Encyclopaedia Britannica Educational Corp.; 1977; 1 of a set of 5 filmstrips; 5 cassettes; teacher's guide.
Gr. K-3. Helps familiarize students with naming and classifying body parts.

1495. THE BRAIN: ITS WONDERS AND THE MYSTERIES [Filmstrip], Washington, D.C: National Geographic; 1982; 2 filmstrips; 2 cassettes.
Gr. 5-12. Excellent introductory overview to the workings of the brain using non-technical terms. Contents: Introducing the Wonders of the Brain; Mysteries of the Brain.

1496. Brenner, Barbara. BODIES. Photographs by George Ancona. New York: Dutton; 1973.
Gr. Preschool-3. Photographs and text explore what a body is made of, how it differs from other things, and how it works.

Brenner, Barbara. FACES. Photographs by George Ancona. New York: Dutton; 1970.
Gr. Preschool-1. See #877.

1497. Burstein, Jobn. SLIM GOODBODY, THE INSIDE STORY. Photography by J. Paul Kirouac. Illustrated by Craigwood Phillips. New York: McGraw Hill; 1977.
Gr. K-6. Demonstrates how various body parts work.

Castle, Sue. FACE TALK, HAND TALK, BODY TALK. Illustrated by Frances McLaughlin-Gill. New York: Doubleday; 1977.
Gr. K-2. See #915.

1498. Caveney, Sylvia. INSIDE MOM: AN ILLUSTRATED ACCOUNT OF CONCEPTION, PREGNANCY, AND CHILDBIRTH. Pictures by Simon Stern. New York: St. Martin's Press; 1977.
Gr. 5-up. Explains the birth cycle from conception to birth.

1499. CIRCULATION: AN INCREDIBLE JOURNEY [Game]. New York: Teaching Concepts; 1973; 1 game: board; 4 plasma trays; 4 players' boards; 1 spinner; cards; playing Pieces; 1 manual.
Gr. 5-up. "...simulates the workings of the human circulatory system." Designed for up to 4 players.

1500. Doss, Helen. YOUR SKIN HOLDS YOU IN. New York: Messner; 1978.
Gr. 3-5. Explains functions of skin as well as pigmentation, protective devices, first aid and care.

1501. Elgin, Kathleen. THE HUMAN BODY: THE FEMALE REPRODUCTIVE SYSTEM. Illustrated. New York: Watts; 1969.
Gr. 5-up. Describes the female reproductive organs and their function in housing the fetus before birth.

1502. Elgin, Kathleen. HUMAN BODY: THE MALE REPRODUCTIVE SYSTEM. Illustrated. New York: Watts; 1969.
Gr. 5up. Describes the male reproductive system.

1503. Epstein, Sam, and Beryl Epstein. DR. BEAUMONT AND THE MAN WITH THE HOLE IN HIS STOMACH. Illustrated by Joseph Scrofani. New York: Coward, McCann & Geoghean; 1978.
Gr. 3-5. A biography of a physician who carried out experiments concerning digestion.

1504. Fryer, Judith. HOW WE HEAR: THEORY OF HEARING. Illustrated by George Overlie. Minneapolis: Medical Books for Children; 1961.
Gr. 3-9.

1505. Gay, Kathlyn. BODY TALK. Photographs by David Sassman. New York: Scribner; 1974.
Gr. 3-8. Introduces the concept of body language and discusses how to interpret the body's silent messages.

1506. Goldin, Augusta. STRAIGHT HAIR, CURLY HAIR. New York: Harper & Row; 1966.
Gr. K-2. Explains why hair is the color and texture it is on different people and provides experiments to try to understand more about the hair.

1507. Harris, Robie H. BEFORE YOU WERE THREE: HOW YOU BEGAN TO WALK, TALK, EXPLORE, AND HAVE FEELINGS. Photographs by Henry E. F. Gordillo. New York: Delacorte; 1977.
Gr. 2-5.

1508. Holzenthaler, Jean. MY HANDS CAN. New York: Dutton; 1978.
Gr. Preschool-K. Describes in simple text and bright pictures a number of things hands can do.

1509. HOW WE HEAR. In: LEARNING ABOUT SOUNDS [Filmstrip]. Chicago: Encyclopaedia Britannica Educational Corp.; 1970; 1 of a set of 5 filmstrips; 5 cassettes; guide.
Gr. 1-6. Describes the parts of the ear and their functions.

1510. THE HUMAN BODY-SYSTEMS FOR SENSING AND MOVING [Study Print]. Chicago: Encyclopaedia Britannica Educational Corp.; 10 study prints; study guide.
Gr. 4-8. Full color outline drawings detail various systems of the body.

1511. THE HUMAN BODY SERIES [Filmstrip]. Washington, D.C: National Geographic; 1980; 3 sets of 2 filmstrips; 2 cassettes; 2 guides each.
Gr. 5-8. Describes the incredible human body using special optics which provide remarkable detail.

1512. THE HUMAN BODY [Microcomputer Program]. New York: Brain Bank; 1981; 1 disk (Apple II).
Gr. 6-up. An examination of the systems of the human body and their function. Other computer versions available.

1513. THE HUMAN BODY-SYSTEMS FOR MAINTAINING LIFE [Study Print]. Chicago: Encyclopaedia Britannica Educational Corp.; 10 study prints.
Gr. 4-8. Detailed, color drawings of body systems.

1514. HUMAN TORSO MODEL [Model]. Northbrook, IL: Hubbard; 1967; 1 model; 1 lesson plan book.
Gr. 4-6. An "exact scale anatomical model of a young boy," with 3 removable organ sections and a complete lesson plan book, including 10 reproducible observation sheets.

1515. INSIDE ME [Kit]. Niles, IL: Developmental Learning Materials; 1980; 6 picture cards; 6 blackline masters; 1 teacher's manual.
Gr. 3-6. Activities to help students understand the functions of the basic systems of the human body.

1516. INSIDE YOUR BODY [Filmstrip], Washington, D.C: National Geographic; 1984; 4 filmstrips; 4 cassettes; 4 guides.
Gr. K-8. Fosters a sense of wonder about the human body and it's physiology.

1517. INSTANT ZOO. [Microcomputer Program]. Cupertino, CA: Apple Computer for Children's Television Workshop; 1982; 1 disk (Apple II & IIe 64K, color monitor).
Gr. 1-4. Games in perception, hand eye coordination and word recognition to help students who are having perception problems.

1518. Kalina, Sigmund. YOUR BLOOD AND ITS CARGO. Illustrated by Arabelle Wheatley. New York: Lothrop; 1974.
Gr. 2-6. Describes the composition of blood, how it circulates, and its function in sustaining life in the human body.

1519. Knight, Bernard. DISCOVERING THE HUMAN BODY: HOW PIONEERS OF MEDICINE SOLVED THE MYSTERIES OF THE BODY'S STRUCTURE AND FUNCTION. New York: Crowell; 1980.
Gr. 6-up. History of medicine that focuses on the body's individual organs and systems.

1520. Limburg, Peter R. THE STORY OF YOUR HEART. Illustrated by Ellen Going Jacobs. New York: Coward, McCann & Geoghegan; 1979.

Gr. 3-7. Discusses the structure, function, and malfunctions of the heart and techniques used to repair this vital organ. Includes a discussion of ways to prevent heart damage.

1521. Lindsay, Rae. THE LEFT-HANDED BOOK. New York: Watts; 1980.
Gr. 4-up. A general discussion of causes of left-handedness, folklore about it, and famous people who have been lefties.

1522. THE MAGIC OF SIGHT: FOR GRADES 5 AND 6 [Kit]. New York: National Society to Prevent Blindness; 1980; 1 filmstrip; 1 cassette; 1 poster; first aid sticker; 3 tests; 1 crossword puzzle; and instructor's folder.
Gr. 5-6. Discusses vision, eye health and safety.

1523. McGough, Elizabeth. YOUR SILENT LANGUAGE. Illustrated by Tom Huffman, New York: Morrow; 1974.
Gr. 6-up. Discusses how people talk to each other with body movements and facial expressions.

1524. Miller, Jonathan. THE HUMAN BODY. Illustrated by Harry Willock. New York: Viking; 1983.
Gr. 6-up. Full color pop-up illustrations show the body from the skeleton out.

1525. MY SENSES AND ME [Filmstrip]. Chicago: Encyclopedia Britannica Educational Corp.; 1971; 4 filmstrips; 4 cassettes; 1 guide.
Gr. K-3. Photos of youngsters enjoying familiar activities encourage investigation of the senses.

1526. Nourse, Alan E. YOUR IMMUNE SYSTEM. New York: Watts; 1982.
Gr. 3-6. A good basic introduction to the body's immune system.

1527. Portal, Colette. THE BEAUTY OF BIRTH. New York: Knopf; 1971.
Gr. 6-up. Adapted from the French by Guy Daniels, this book follows the process of human reproduction from the production of ovum and sperm to the birth of the baby.

1528. Rahn, Joan Elma. KEEPING WARM, KEEPING COOL. Illustrated. New York: Atheneum; 1983.

Gr. 5-9. Discusses mechanics of warm and cold-blooded creatures. Describes how humans keep warm and cool in various climates and circumstances.

1529. Riedman, Sarah R. HEART. Illustrated by Harry McNaught and Enid Kotsching. New York: Golden; 1974.
Gr. 5-up. A concise examination of the cardiovascular system, concentrating on the anatomy, physiology, chemistry and pathology of the heart, with information on the latest medical advances in this area.

1530. Rudolph, Marguerita. LOOK AT ME. Pictures by Karla Kuskin. New York: McGraw Hill; 1967.
A boy describes himself and the things he can do.

SESAME STREET FIVE SENSES [Game]. Springfield, MA: Milton Bradley; 1975; 4 games; directions.
Gr. K-3. See #896.

1531. Showers, Paul. WHAT HAPPENS TO A HAMBURGER? Illustrated by Anne Rockwell. New York: Harper & Row; 1970.
Gr. 1-3. A simple introduction, with experiments, to human digestion.

1532. Showers, Paul. YOU CAN'T MAKE A MOVE WITHOUT YOUR MUSCLE. Illustrated by Harriet Barton. New York: Crowell; 1982.
Gr. 1-3. An elementary book to explain the workings of the muscles in the human body.

Silverstein, Alvin, and Virginia Silverstein. THE SKELETAL SYSTEM: FRAMEWORKS FOR LIFE. Illustrated by Lee J. Ames. Englewood Cliffs, NJ: Prentice Hall; 1972.
Gr. 3-7. See #1408.

Silverstein, Alvin, and Virginia Silverstein. THE STORY OF YOUR EAR. Illustrated by Susan Gaber. New York: Coward, McCann & Geoghean; 1981.
Gr. 5-9. See #897.

Simon, Seymour. FINDING OUT WITH YOUR SENSES. Illustrated by Emily McCully, New York: McGraw Hill; 1971.
Gr. K-3. See #898.

1533. UNDERSTANDING YOUR BODY, SERIES I [Filmstrip], Chicago: Encyclopedia Britannica Educational Corp.; 1967; 8 filmstrips.
Gr. 4-8. Captioned filmstrips describe the parts of the human body and their function.

1534. UNDERSTANDING YOUR BODY, SERIES II [Filmstrip]. Chicago: Encyclopedia Britannica Educational Corp.; 1968; 7 filmstrips.
Gr. 4-8. Captioned filmstrips describe the parts of the human body and their function.

1535. Ward, Brian. FOOD AND DIGESTION. New York: Watts; 1982.
Gr. 5-7. Explains where ingested food goes and what happens to it along the way.

1536. Ward, Brian. TOUCH-TASTE-SMELL. New York: Watts; 1982.
Gr. 5-7. Explains the physiological process of each sensation.

1537. Yarbrough, Camille. CORNROWS. Illustrated by Carole Byard. New York: Coward, McCann & Geoghegan; 1979.
Gr. 2-6. Explains how the hair style of cornrows, a symbol in Africa since ancient times, can today in this country symbolize the courage of outstanding Afro-Americans.

YOUR SENSES AND HOW THEY HELP YOU [Filmstrip]. Washington, D.C.: National Geographic; 1977; 2 filmstrips; 2 cassettes; teachers' guide.
Gr. Preschool-3. See #903.

1538. Zim, Herbert Spencer. YOUR SKIN. Illustrated by Jean Zallinger. New York: Morrow; 1979.
Gr. 4-6. Discusses the composition of human skin, ways in which it protects the body and common skin problems.

1539. Zim, Herbert Spencer. YOUR STOMACH AND DICESIVE TRACT. Illustrated by Rene Martin. New York: Morrow; 1973.
Gr. 3-7. Describes the structure of the stomach and the digestive tract and the functions of each in the digestive process.

Humans: The Working Body: Health

1540. Adams, Barbara. LIKE IT IS: FACTS AND FEELINGS ABOUT HANDICAPS FROM KIDS WHO KNOW. Illustrated by James Stanfield. New York: Walker; 1979.
Gr. 4-6. Children with handicaps tell the facts about their lives as well as their feelings.

1541. Branscum, Robbie. FOR LOVE OF JODY. Illustrated by Allen Davis. New York: Lothrop; 1979.
Gr. 4-up. In the Arkansas hills during a calamity-filled summer of the Depression and Ma's third pregnancy, 12-year-old Frankie overcomes her bitterness toward her mother and jealousy over her younger, mentally retarded sister.

1542. Brindze, Ruth. LOOK HOW MANY PEOPLE WEAR GLASSES: THE MAGIC OF LENSES. Illustrated. New York: Atheneum; 1975.
Gr. 5-9. Traces the history of spectacles over seven hundred years and discusses how lenses are made, how eyes work, and how to choose the right glasses.

1543. Burnett, Frances. THE SECRET GARDEN. Pictures by Tasha Tudor. New York: Harper & Row; 1962.
Gr. 4-9. Colin is rescued from the life of a spoiled and incurable invalid by a young cousin and a neighbor boy who can "talk" to the birds. Other editions also available.

1544. Burns, Sheila. CANCER: UNDERSTANDING IT. Illustrated. New York: Messner; 1982.
Gr. 3-5. Uses a narrative story format to explain cancer, the latest developments in treatment.

1545. Carr, Rachel. RACHEL CARR'S CREATIVE YOGA EXERCISES FOR CHILDREN. Illustrated by Don Hedin and Edward Kimball. New York: Doubleday; 1973.
Gr. 1-5. Shows photographs of children in Yoga positions and drawings of the natural objects they emulate along with directions on how to do them.

1546. Clifton, Lucille. MY FRIEND JACOB. Illustrated by Thomas DiGrazia. New York: Dutton; 1980.
Gr. K-2. A young boy tells about Jacob, who, though older and mentally slower, helps him a lot and is his very best friend.

1547. Cobb, Vicki. HOW THE DOCTOR KNOWS YOU'RE FINE. Illustrated by Anthony Ravielli. New York: Harper & Row; 1973.
Gr. 2-4. Shows the procedures done in a physical check-up.

1548. Fassler, Joan. HOWIE HELPS HIMSELF. Illustrated by Joe Laker, Chicago: Whitman; 1975.
Gr. 1-3. Howie, a child with cerebral palsy, wants more than anything else to be able to operate his wheelchair by himself.

1549. Fleischman, Paul. THE HALF-A-MOON INN. Illustrated by Kathy Jacobi. New York: Harper & Row; 1980.
Gr. 5-up. A mute boy is held captive by the strange proprietress of an inn.

1550. Gilbert, Sara. YOU ARE WHAT YOU EAT: A COMMON SENSE GUIDE TO THE MODERN AMERICAN DIET. New York: Macmillan; 1977.
Gr. 5-7. Discusses nutrition, diseases and allergies and the impact of processed foods on American dietary habits.

1551. Harries, Joan. THEY TRIUMPHED OVER THEIR HANDICAPS. Illustrated. New York: Watts; 1981.
Gr. 6-up. Profiles the lives and achievements of six severely handicapped people who triumphed over blindness, deafness, missing limbs, and brain damage to excel in sports, music, jobs, and living optimistically.

1552. Henriod, Lorraine. GRANDMA'S WHEELCHAIR. Illustrated by Christa Chevalier. Chicago: Whitman; 1981.
Gr. Preschool-1. Four-year old Thomas spends his mornings helping his grandmother who is in a wheelchair.

1553. Jones, Rebecca. ANGIE AND ME. New York: Macmillan; 1981.
Gr. 5-9. During her stay at a children's hospital where she is treated for juvenile rheumatoid arthritis, twelve-year-old Jenna comes to terms with her illness.

1554. Kamien, Janet. WHAT IF YOU COULDN'T: A BOOK ABOUT SPECIAL NEEDS. Illustrated by Signe Hanson. New York: Scribner; 1979.

Gr. 4-6. Explains handicaps and includes games and experiments to help you understand them.

Litchfield, Ada B. A BUTTON IN HER EAR. Pictures by Eleanor Mill. Chicago, Whitman; 1976.
Gr. 2-4. See #890.

Litchfield, Ada B. WORDS IN OUR HANDS. Pictures by Helen Cogancherry. Chicago: Whitman; 1980.
Gr. 2-6. See #891.

1555. MacLachlan, Patricia. THROUGH GRANDPA'S EYES. Pictures by Deborah Ray. New York: Harper & Row; 1980.
Gr. 2-4. A young boy learns a different way of seeing the world from his blind grandfather.

1556. Marcus, Rebecca. BEING BLIND. New York: Hastings House; 1981.
Gr. 4-6. A history of attitudes toward blindness as well as discussion of problems ot blindness.

1557. Marino, Barbara Pavis. ERIC NEEDS STITCHES. Illustrated by Richard Rudinski. Reading, MA: Addison-Wesley; 1979.
Gr. K-3. Eric is taken to the emergency room for stitches after a fall from his bike.

1558. Moeri, Louise. THE GIRL WHO LIVED ON THE FERRIS WHEEL. New York: Dutton; 1979.
Gr. 5-9. Til realizes with increasing urgency that her divorced mother's violently abusive behavior is getting more and more out of control.

1559. Morgenroth, Barbara. DEMONS AT MY DOOR. New York: Atheneum; 1980.
Gr. 5-10. A young girl drives herself into a nervous breakdown by striving to live up to others' standards.

1560. NUTRITION: WHO CARES? YOU SHOULD [Filmstrip]. Mount Kisco, NY: Guidance Associates; 1982; 4 filmstrips; 4 cassettes; 1 teacher's guide.
Gr. K-3. Aims to help kids learn how to make food choices. Includes: Choosing Foods; What's in Food; What Your Body Does with Food; Choices from Breakfast to Dinner.

1561. Ominsky, Elaine. JON O: A SPECIAL BOY. Photographs by Dennis Simonetti. Englewood Cliffs, NJ: Prentice Hall; 1977.
Gr. 1-4. Photographs and text describe the life of a young boy with Down's Syndrome who has adjusted to being a very special child.

1562. Perl, Lila. JUNK FOOD, FAST FOOD, HEALTH FOOD: WHAT AMERICA EATS AND WHY. New York: Houghton Mifflin; 1980.
Gr. 4-up. Discusses the food industry, American reliance on sugar, salt and additives and convenience foods as well as recommending more nutritious possibilities.

Peter, Diana. CLAIRE AND EMMA. Photos by Jeremy Finlay, New York: John Day; 1977.
Gr. K-4. See #893.

Peterson, Jeanne. I HAVE A SISTER - MY SISTER IS DEAF. Illustrated by Deborah Ray. New York: Harper & Row; 1977.
Gr. 2-4. See #894.

1563. POISONING FROM COMMON HOUSEHOLD PRODUCTS [Filmstrip]. Falls Church VA: Enjoy Communicating; 1983; 1 filmstrip; 1 cassette.
Gr. 4-12. "Shows how common household products account for a large percentage of poisonings".

1564. Potter, Marian. THE SHARED ROOM. New York: Morrow; 1979.
Gr. 6-9. Despite her grandmother's opposition, a 10-year-old reestablishes contact with her long-institutionalized mother.

1565. Raskin, Ellen. SPECTACLES. New York: Atheneum; 1968.
Gr. K-4. Iris sees things other people can't. When she sees a huge green caterpillar and frightens the teacher, her mother takes her to a blue elephant who prescribes glasses.

1566. Robinet, Harriette. RIDE THE RED CYCLE. Illustrated by David Brown. Boston: Houghton-Mifflin; 1980.
Hr. 1-5. Jerome, crippled since the age of two, struggles to realize his dream of riding a cycle.

1567. Rounds, Glen. BLIND OUTLAW. Illustrated, New York: Holiday House; 1980.
Gr. 4-8. A blind outlaw horse is tamed by a boy who can not speak.

1568. Simon, Seymour. BODY SENSE/BODY NONSENSE. Illustrated by Dennis Kendrick. New York: Harper & Row; 1981.
Gr. 3-6. Uses folk sayings about the body to examine some of our ideas about health.

1569. SLIM GOODBODY'S HEALTH SERIES [Filmstrip]. Chicago: SVE; 4 filmstrips; 4 cassettes; 1 teacher's guide.
Gr. K-2. Intended to alleviate anxiety about health examinations, hospital and dental visits, etc.

1570. SLIM GOODBODY: GETTING SICK AND GETTING WELL [Filmstrip]. Chicago: SVE; 1979; 4 filmstrips: 4 cassettes; teacher's guide.
Gr. 4-6. Teaches kids about common ailments and how to correct them. Other Slim Goodbody kits also available from SVE.

1571. Smith, Lucia B. A SPECIAL KIND OF SISTER. Illustrated by Chuck Hall. New York: Holt, Rinehart & Winston; 1979.
Gr. 1-3. A young girl describes her relationship with her brain-damaged brother.

1572. Sobol, Harriet L. MY BROTHER STEVEN IS RETARDED. Illustrated by Patricia Agre. New York: Macmillan; 1977.
Gr. 3-5. Eleven-year-old Beth talks about her older brother who is retarded.

1573. Sobol, Harriet. JEFF'S HOSPITAL BOOK. Photographs by Patricia Agre. New York: Walck; 1975.
Gr. K-4. Describes a young boy's experience in the hospital as he undergoes surgery to correct crossed eyes.

1574. Trier, Carola B. EXERCISE - WHAT IT IS, WHAT IT DOES. Illustrated by Tom Huffman. New York: Greenwillow; 1982.
Gr. 1-3. An introduction to exercise for young readers including a selection of exercises to try.

1575. Wahl, Jan. BUTTON EYE'S ORANGE. Illustrated, New York: Warne; 1980.

Gr. K-3. Taken to the market to be sold, a toy dog tries to return with an orange to his boy who wears a leg brace.

1576. WHAT IS A HANDICAP? [Filmstrip]. Santa Monita, CA: BFA; 1975; 4 filmstrips; 4 cassettes; 24 duplicating masters; 1 guide.
Gr. 4-6. Shows how four handicapped children interact with their friends, teachers, and families in everyday situations.

1577. Wolf, Bernard. DON'T FEEL SORRY FOR PAUL. Illustrated. New York: Harper & Row; 1974.
Gr. 3-6. Seven-year-old Paul functions well with two artificial feet and an artificial hand.

1578. Yolen, Jane. THE SEEING STICK. Illustrated by Remy Charlip and DeMetra Maraslis. New York: Harper & Row; 1977.
Gr. 2-4. A blind Chinese princess "sees" the world through the stories carved on a stick for her by an old wood-carver.

1579. YOUR BODY FOR LIFE: ELEMENTARY GRADES 1-3 [Kit]. Orlando, FL: Tupperware Home Parties; 1979; 2 filmstrips; 2 cassettes; 1 game; 48 stick-ons with backdrop; 5 hand puppets; 2 teacher's guides.
Gr. 1-3. Describes the five senses and their relation to food choice. Introduces the nutrient groups.

1580. YOUR BODY FOR LIFE: ELEMENTARY GRADES 4-6 [Kit]. Orlando, FL: Tupperware Home Parties; 1979; 2 filmstrips; 2 cassettes; 8 transparencies; 1 game; 20 role-play cards; 2 teacher's guides.
Gr. 4-6. Describes the body systems. Shows how food provides necessary substances for the body.

1581. YOUR HEALTHY BODY [Filmstrip]. Chicago: Coronet; 1976; 6 filmstrips; 6 cassettes; filmstrip guide.
Gr. 1-4. Filmstrip characters investigate nutrition, exercise, rest, disease prevention and safety practices.

Humans: Time and Space

1582. Adoff, Arnold. ALL THE COLORS OF THE RACE. Illustrated by Jonn Steptoe. New York: Lothrop; 1982.

Gr. 5-up. A young girl shares her feelings about having a black mother and a white father.

1583. Aliki, MUMMIES MADE IN EGYPT. New York: Harper & Row; 1979.
Gr. 2-6. Describes the art of preparing and wrapping bodies for burial in ancient Egypt.

1584. Ancona, George. GROWING OLDER, Illustrated, New York: Dutton; 1978.
Gr. 4-6. Thirteen portraits of older people with their discussion of their childhoods and feelings about aging.

1585. Ancona, George. IT'S A BABY. New York: Dutton; 1979.
Gr. K-2. Black-and-white photographs show a boy baby's life to age one.

Caveney, Sylvia. INSIDE MOM: AN ILLUSTRATED ACCOUNT OF CONCEPTION, PREGNANCY AND CHILDBIRTH. Illustrated by Simon Stern. New York: St. Martin's Press; 1977.
Gr. 5-up. See #1498.

1586. Cleary, Beverly. MITCH AND AMY. Illustrated by George Porter. New York: Morrow; 1967.
Gr. 3-5. Twins Mitch and Amy struggle with the fourth grade.

1587. Cohen, Robert. THE COLOR OF MAN: WHAT IT IS ALL ABOUT, WHY WE ARE CONFUSED AND CONCERNED ABOUT IT, HOW IT WILL AFFECT OUR FUTURE. Illustrated by Ken Heyman. New York: Random House; 1968.
Gr. 5-7. A survey of facts about race by scientists and thoughts on the development of prejudice.

1588. Conford, Ellen. ME AND THE TERRIBLE TWO. Illustrated by Charles Carroll. Boston: Little, Brown; 1974.
Gr. 3-6. Dorrie is bothered by the identical-twin boys next door.

1589. Farber, Norma. HOW DOES IT FEEL TO BE OLD? Illustrated by Trina Schaart Hyman. New York: Dutton; 1979.
Gr. 2-4. Poetic monologues of an older woman about aging, her past and loneliness.

1590. Herzig, Alison, and Jane Mali. OH BOY! BABIES. Boston: Little, Brown; 1980.
Gr. 5-up. A group of fifth and sixth grade boys take an infant care course.

1591. Krementz, Jill. HOW IT FEELS WHEN A PARENT DIES. Illustrated. New York: Knopf; 1981.
Gr. 4-8. Eighteen young people talk about how they have coped with the death of a parent.

1592. Lasky, Kathryn. MY ISLAND GRANDMA. Illustrated by Emily McCully. New York: Warne; 1979.
Gr. 1-4. Tells the pleasures Abbey and her grandmother share during summers on an island off the coast of Maine.

1593. Le Shan, Eda. LEARNING TO SAY GOODBYE: WHEN A PARENT DIES. Illustrated by Paul Giovanopauloz. New York: Macmillan; 1976.
Gr. 5-7. A direct discussion of questions, fears and problems young people face when a parent dies.

1594. McGowen, Tom. ALBUM OF PREHISTORIC MAN. Illustrated by Rod Rut. Chicago: Rand McNally; 1979.
Gr. 4-7. Life-like scenes from early humans - hunting, farming, use of fire, tools, etc.

1595. McHargue, Georgess. MUMMIES. New York: Harper & Row; 1972.
Gr. 5-7. Explains embalming and mummification process as well as discussing natural mummies.

1596. McKern, Sharon S. THE MANY FACES OF MAN. New York: Lothrop; 1972.
Gr. 5-7. A basic account of physical differences among human beings emphasizing that no one race or characteristic is superior to another.

1597. Pace, Mildred Mastin. WRAPPED FOR ETERNITY: THE STORY OF THE EGYPTIAN MUMMY. Illustrated by Tom Huffman. New York: McGraw Hill; 1974.
Gr. 5-7. Explains how the Egyptians preserved bodies and what they now reveal about life in that time.

1598. Pringle, Laurence. DEATH IS NATURAL. New York: Scholastic; 1977.
Gr. 3-5. A clear explanation, using the example of a rabbit, of what happens to living things when they die.

1599. Shanks, Ann Zane. OLD IS WHAT YOU GET: DIALOGUES ON AGING BY THE OLD AND YOUNG. Illustrated. New York: Viking; 1976.
Gr. 4-6. Old and young people discuss aging.

1600. Silverstein, Alvin. AGING. New York: Watts; 1979.
Gr. 5-7. A simple account of the aging process and of people's feelings about growing older.

1601. Spier, Peter. PEOPLE. Illustrated. New York: Doubleday; 1980.
Gr. 1-3. Emphasizes the differences among the four billion people on earth.

The Body in Art

1602. ANIMALS. In: SHOW ME A POEM [Filmstrip]. Chicago: Encyclopaedia Britannica Educational Corp.; 1975; 1 of a set of 6 filmstrips; 6 cassettes; 6 guides.
Gr. 1-6. Uses many examples of colorful images and figurative language.

1603. Barth, Edna. HEARTS, CUPIDS, AND RED ROSES: THE STORY OF THE VALENTINE SYMBOLS. Illustrated by Ursula Arndt, New York: Seabury; 1974.
Gr. 2-6. The history of Valentine's Day and the little known story behind it's symbols.

1604. Baskin, Leonard. HOSIE'S ZOO. Illustrated. New York: Viking Press; 1981.
Gr. 1-up. Watercolors depicting the familiar as well as the exotic in the world of animals.

1605. Baylor, Byrd. SOMETIMES I DANCE MOUNTAINS. Illustrated by Ken Longtemps. New York: Scribner; 1973.
Gr. K-3. A young dancer shows how she expresses emotions and creates concrete objects through dance.

1606. Brooke, L. Leslie. JOHNNY CROW'S GARDEN [Filmstrip]. Weston, Ct: Weston Woods; 1959; 1 filmstrip; 1 cassette.
Gr. K-2. Jonnny Crow's garden attracts a number of playful animals.

1607. Brown, Marcia. LISTEN TO A SHAPE. Illustrated. New York: Watts; 1979.
Gr. 1-4. Color photos of natural objects emphasize shapes.

1608. Calder, Alexander. ANIMAL SKETCHING. Illustrated. New York: Dover; 1973.
Gr. 4-up. Helpful ideas and examples of animal sketches.

1609. De Brunhoff. BABAR AND FATHER CHRISTMAS [Filmstrip]. New York: Random House/Miller Brody; 1982; 1 filmstrip; 1 cassette.
Gr. K-4. Based on the book, Babar looks for Father Christmas to ask him to visit the elephants on his seasonal rounds.

1610. DeRegniers, Beatrice Schenk. THE SHADOW BOOK. Illustrated by Isabel Gordon. New York: Harcourt Brace; 1960.
Gr. Preschool-3. Black-and-white photos show children exploring the many things they can do with their shadows.

1611. Elston, Georgia. THE ANIMALS' ALPHABET PICNIC. Illustrated by Ted Hill. Ontario: Gage; 1977.
Gr. K-2. An alphabet book that matches the first letter of the animal's name to a type of food.

1612. Emberley, Ed. ED EMBERLEY'S DRAWING BOOK OF ANIMALS. New York: Scholastic; 1970.
Gr. K-6. Explains how to use a few simple shapes, letters, numbers, and symbols to draw almost any animal.

1613. Gabriel, Mike. GABRIEL'S FRIENDS: AN A TO Z GUIDE TO CARTOONING THE ANIMAL KINGDOM. Aurora, CO: Gregory; 1980.
Gr. 4-up. Step by step drawings illustrate how to draw animal caricatures.

1614. Gardner, John C. A CHILD'S BESTIARY: WITH ADDITIONAL POEMS BY LUCY GARDNER. Illustrated. New York: Knopf, distributed by Random House; 1977.
Gr. 4-up. A collection of humorous verses about animals friendly and otherwise.

Giblin, James. THE SCARECROW BOOK. Illustrated by Dale Ferguson. New York: Crown; 1980.
Gr. 2-4. See #1252.

1615. Glazer, Tom. EYE WINKER, TOM TINKER, CHIN CHOPPER: FIFTY MUSICAL FINGERPLAYS. Illustrated by Ron Himler. New York: Doubleday; 1973.
Gr. 1-7. Words and music to fifty songs with directions for accompanying finger play.

1616. Goor, Ron, and Nancy Goor. SHADOWS: HERE, THERE AND EVERYWHERE. Illustrated. New York: Crowell; 1981.
Gr. 1-2. Explains the causes and shapes of shadows.

Haldane, Suzanne. FACES ON PLACES: ABOUT GARGOYLES AND OTHER STONE CREATURES. New York: Viking; 1980.
Gr. 3-7. See #1253.

1617. Hilbok, Bruce. SILENT DANCER. Illustrated by Liz Glasgow. New York: Messner; 1981.
Gr. 2-5. A ten-year-old deaf girl studies ballet.

1618. Hoban, Tana. SHAPES AND THINGS. New York: Macmillan; 1970.
Gr. Preschool-3. A collection of silhouettes of objects to identify.

1619. Holme, Bryan. CREATURES OF PARADISE: PICTURES TO GROW UP WITH. New York: Oxford; 1980.
Gr. 4-8. A collection of classic paintings which depict animals.

Isadora, Rachel. MY BALLET CLASS. Illustrated. New York: Greenwillow; 1980.
Gr. K-3. See #122.

1620. Jones, Doris. ACTIVITY RHYTHMIC MOVEMENTS OF ZOO ANIMALS [Sound Recording]. New York: Folkways Records; 1976; 1 sound disc; pamphlet.
Gr. K-3. Contents: Lion Song; Monkies Jumping; Elephant Slow Walk; Kangaroo Hop; Hyena; Snake Glide; Hippo Hippopotamus; Flighty Deer; Seal Flapper; Big Bear; Walking Ostrich; Galloping Zebra.

Kitchen, Bert. ANIMAL ALPHABET. New York: Dial Books; 1984.
Gr. Preschool-up. See #958.

Krementz, Jill. A VERY YOUNG DANCER. Illustrated. New York: Knopf; 1976.
Gr. 4-up. See #123.

1621. Langstaff, John. OVER IN THE MEADOW [Filmstrip]. Pictures by Feodor Rojankovsky. Weston Wood, CT: Weston Woods; 1971; 1 filmstrip; 1 cassette; 1 booklet.
Gr. K-3. Based on the book of the same title. A counting verse in which animals and birds, mothers

and babes provide a lesson in numbers and nature with audience participation.

1622. Lasky, Kathryn. DOLLMAKER: THE EYELIGHT AND THE SHADOW. Illustrated by Christopher Knight. New York: Scribner; 1981.
Gr. 4-up. Illustrates one dollmaker practicing her craft.

1623. LITTLE ADVENTURES IN ART [Filmstrip]. By Jacqueline E. Wall. New York: Warren Schloat; 1968; 4 filmstrips; 4 discs; teacher's guide.
Gr. K-3. Focusing on animals, the world of art is explored from primitive cave paintings to modern art.

Low, Joseph. BEASTLY RIDDLES: FISHY, FLIGHTY, AND BUGGY, TOO. Illustrated. New York: Macmillan; 1983.
Gr. 1-3. See #1193.

A PEACEABLE KINGDOM: THE SHAKER ABECEDARIUS. Illustrated by Alice and Martin Provensen. New York: Viking; 1978.
Gr. K-3. See #964.

1624. Pene du Bois, William. LION. Illustrated. New York: Viking; 1981.
Gr. 5-8. In an animal factory in the sky, an artist invents a lion after a few false tries.

1625. Price, Christine. DANCE ON THE DUSTY EARTH. New York: Scribner; 1979.
Gr. 4-7. Discusses folk dance around the world, showing actions and traditions of the dance.

Price, Christine. DANCING MASKS OF AFRICA. New York: Scribner; 1975.
Gr. 2-6. See #1260.

Raskin, Ellen. WHO, SAID SUE, SAID WHOO? Illustrated. New York: Atheneum; 1973.
Gr. K-3. See #1000.

1626. Ryder, Joanne. INSIDE TURTLE SHELL. New York: Macmillan; 1985.
Gr. 3-8. A collection of poems that portray the meadow and its creatures from morning till night.

1627. Scarry, Richard. RICHARD SCARRY'S ANIMAL NURSERY TALES. New York: Golden Press; 1975.

Gr. Preschool-1. Eleven favorite nursery tales including Little Red Riding Hood, The Little Red Hen and The Three Little Pigs.

1628. Stadler, John. CAT AT BAT. Illustrated. New York: Dutton; 1979.
Gr. K-2. Presents 14 rhymed verses describing the activities of animals such as "A duck and his truck are stuck," etc.

1629. THE WIDE-MOUTHED FROG [Filmstrip]. Chicago: SVE; 1982; 1 filmstrip; 1 cassette.
Gr. K-5. Retelling of the book by Rex Schneider. The frog asks a succession of animals what's good to eat. One answers "a wide-mouthed frog."

PHYSICAL BODIES

Celestial

1630. Adler, David. HYPERSPACE! FACTS AND FUN. Illustrated by Fred Winkowski. New York: Viking; 1981.
Gr. 4-6. A collection of facts, puzzles, riddles, etc. about various astronomical phenomena.

1631. Adler, Irving. THE STARS: DECODING THEIR MESSAGES. New York: Crowell; 1980.
Gr. 6-up. Discusses the properties and behavior of stars, including their composition, brightness, distance from the earth, motion, size, and weight.

1632. Asimov, Isaac. ENVIRONMENTS OUT THERE. Illustrated with photographs. New York: Abelard-Schuman; 1967.
Gr. 5-up. From known facts and scientific probabilities a scientist fashions the environment of the moon and of distant planets.

1633. Asimov, Isaac. VENUS, NEAR NEIGHBOR OF THE SUN. Illustrated by Yukio Kondo. New York: Lothrop; 1981.
Gr. 5-up. Discusses astronomy and myths about space as well as presenting up-to-date information about Venus.

1634. Asimov, Isaac. WHAT MAKES THE SUN SHINE? Illustrated by Marc Brown. Boston: Little, Brown; 1971.
Gr. 4-6. An easy-to-read explanation of the chemical and physical nature of the sun.

1635. ASTRONOMY: STARS FOR ALL SEASONS [Microcomputer Program]. Freeport, NY: Educational Activities; 1983; 1 disk (Apple II); document.
Gr. 5-up. Provides practice in recognizing stars and constellations. Contents: Introduction (shows why stars change in the sky, how astronomers locate stars); Seasonal Skies; Constellations.

1636. Berger, Melvin. COMETS, METEORS AND ASTEROIDS. New York: Putnam; 1981.
Gr. 5-up. An explanation of what we know about the formation and makeup of these three celestial bodies.

1637. Berger, Melvin. QUASARS, PULSARS AND BLACK HOLES IN SPACE. New York: Putnam; 1977.
Gr. 4-6. Explores theories which explain the quasar, pulsar and black hole - recent and strange discoveries in space.

1638. Blumberg, Rhoda. FIRST TRAVEL GUIDE TO THE MOON: WHAT TO PACK, HOW TO GO, AND WHAT TO SEE WHEN YOU GET THERE. Illustrated by Ray Doty. New York: Four Winds; 1980.
Gr. 4-6. Explores the moon as if it were a tourist spot in the year 2000.

1639. Branley, Franklyn M. SATURN: THE SPECTACULAR PLANET. Illustrated by Leonard Kessler. New York: Crowell; 1983.
Gr. 3-6. Based on information from Voyager I and II.

1640. COMETS & PLANETS: A LOOK INTO OUR SOLAR SYSTEM [Filmstrip]. Burbank, CA: Walt Disney; 1982; 3 filmstrips; 3 cassettes; guide.
Gr. 5-12. Part 1 and 2 give a tour of the planets, Part 3 discusses comets as a possible source of information about the origin of our solar system.

1641. D'Ignazio, Fred. THE NEW ASTRONOMY: PROBING THE SECRETS OF SPACE. New York: Watts; 1982.
Gr. 4-up. Explains how astronomers are using new kinds of telescopes, computerized cameras, and space probes to generate new theories about the universe and its mysteries.

1642. Dayrell, Elphinstone. WHY THE SUN AND THE MOON LIVE IN THE SKY: AN AFRICAN FOLKTALE. Illustrated by Blair Lent. New York: Houghton Mifflin; 1977.

Gr. K-2. Sun and moon leave earth and find a home in the sky. Characters wear ceremonial masks.

1643. EARTH AND ITS NEIGHBORS IN SPACE [Filmstrip]. Chicago: Encyclopaedia Britannica Educational Corp.; 1977; 6 filmstrips; 6 cassettes; 1 teacher's guide.
Gr. 4-8. Summarizes the findings of moon probes, visits observatories devoted to sun study and speculates on the origins of galaxies beyond our solar system.

1644. THE ELEMENTARY PLANETARIUM [Model]. Saginaw, MI: Trippensee; 1968; 1 model; 1 guide.
Gr. 2-6. Demonstrates the relationsbips of the sun, moon, and earth, and their various positions and movements throughout the year.

1645. EXPLORER METRO. [Microcomputer Program]. Pleasantville, NY: Sunburst; 1982; 1 disk (Apple II, 48K, DOS3.3).
Gr. 4-9. A space simulation which provides opportunity to develop metric skills in highly motivated "encounters."

1646. Fields, Alice. STARS AND PLANETS. Illustrated by Michael Tregenza, New York: Watts; 1980.
Gr. 2-4. Describes the sun, the planets which orbit it, and other pheonomena of the universe, including asteroids, comets, meteors, and other stars and galaxies.

1647. FIRE OF LIFE: THE SMITHSONIAN BOOK OF THE SUN. Washington, D.C: Smithsonian Exposition Books, distributed by Norton; 1981.
Gr. 6-up. With words and images the book celebrates man's relationship to the sun.

1648. Ford, Adam. SPACESHIP EARTH. New York: Lothrop; 1981.
Gr. 3-6. Introduces the sun, stars, and other companions in our solar system, and explains light, gravity and the "big bang" theory of the creation of the universe.

1649. Fradin, Dennis B. ASTRONOMY. Illustrated, Chicago: Children's Press; 1983.
Gr. K-4. Presents basic information about the stars, constellations, galaxies, universe, Earth, and solar system and briefly discusses space travel and astronomers.

1650. Fradin, Dennis B. COMETS, ASTEROIDS, AND METEORS. Chicago: Children's Press; 1984.
Gr. 1-3. Describes in simple terms the meteors, comets, and asteroids that are part of our solar system. Also discusses the various theories concerning their origin and their effect on life on Earth.

1651. Friedman, Herbert. THE AMAZING UNIVERSE. Washington, D.C: National Geographic; 1975.
Gr. 6-up. An exploration of the science of astronomy, and of our universe.

1652. Gallant, Roy A. FIRES IN THE SKY: THE BIRTH AND DEATH OF STARS. Illustrated. New York: Four Winds; 1978.
Gr. 5-9. Discusses the characteristics of stars using the sun as an example, examining the composition of the sun, various theories about its energy production, differences among stars, and the birth and death of stars.

1653. Ginsburg, Mirra. WHERE DOES THE SUN GO AT NIGHT? Illustrated by Jose Aruego and Arlane Dewey. New York: Greenwillow; 1980.
Gr. K-3. A series of child's questions are asked by a collection of animals in a humorous picture book.

1654. Herbst, Judith. SKY ABOVE AND WORLDS BEYOND. Illustrated by Richard Rosenblum. Charts by George Lovi. New York: Atheneum; 1983.
Gr. 5-up. An introduction to astronomy, examining planetary and stellar motions, ancient concepts of the universe, the solar system, astronomy's wild goose chases, Einstein's mass/time relationships, stellar evolution, and the unexplained mysteries of space.

1655. INTRODUCTION TO SPACE SCIENCES [Filmstrip]. Stamford, CT: Educational Dimensions; 1977; 4 filmstrips; 4 cassettes; teacher's guide with script.
Gr. 6-up. "...presents some basic facts and simple-to-grasp concepts regarding tbe physical nature of tbe solar system, stars and galaxies." Contents: The Solar System; Sun and Moon; Stars and Galaxies; Cosmology.

1656. Jacobs, Joseph. THE STARS IN THE SKY: A SCOTTISH TALE. Pictures by Airdrie Amtmann. New York: Farrar, Straus, Giroux; 1979.

Gr. Preschool-3. Story retold of a tiny lassie who, wishing she could play with the stars, sets out to obtain them.

1657. Jobb, Jamie. THE NIGHT SKY BOOK: AN EVERYDAY GUIDE TO EVERY NIGHT. Boston: Little, Brown; 1977.
Gr. 4-7. Description of night sky with activities to help readers to understand space.

1658. Joseph, Joseph Maron, and Sarah Lee Lippincott. POINT TO THE STARS. Illustrated. New York: McGraw Hill; 1977.
Gr. 4-9. Includes diagrams and text to help the reader identify stars, planets, constellations, and artificial satellites as they vary their places in the heavens.

1659. Knight, David C. THE TINY PLANETS: ASTEROIDS OF OUR SOLAR SYSTEM. Illustrated with photos and diagrams. New York: Morrow; 1973.
Gr. 3-7. Discusses the origin, history, discovery, physical nature, and present and future uses of the asteroids, or minor planets.

1660. Lambert, David. THE EARTH AND SPACE. Illustrated by Tudor Art Agency. New York: Warwick; 1979.
Gr. 5-up. Discusses the origins of the Earth, its structure, and how it came to sustain life.

1661. Lauber, Patricia. JOURNEY TO THE PLANETS. New York: Crown; 1982.
Gr. 5-7. A survey of the planets, with information about recent space probes.

1662. Lurie, Alison. THE HEAVENLY ZOO; LEGENDS AND TALES OF THE STARS. Pictures by Monika Beisner. New York: Farrar, Straus, Giroux; 1979.
Gr. K-4. A retellimg of sixteen legends of the constellations and how they got their names, taken from such varied sources as ancient Greece, Babylon, Egypt, Sumeria, the Bible, Norway, the Balkans, Indonesia, and the American Indians.

1663. MATHEMATICS IN SCIENCE AND SOCIETY. Illustrated. Palo Alto, CA: Creative Publications; 1977.
Gr. 4-8. Materials for worksheets, calculator activities, games, puzzles, bulletin boards, etc. to provide practice with mathematics as it relates to astronomy, biology, environment, music, physics

and sports. Teacher's section includes discussion and teaching exercises.

1664. Moche, Dinah L. THE STAR WARS QUESTION AND ANSWER BOOK ABOUT SPACE. Illustrated by David Kawami. New York: Random House; 1979.
Gr. 3-6. Answers frequently asked questions about life on other planets, survival in outer space, astronomy, space, exploration and astronautics.

1665. Peltier, Leslie C. GUIDEPOSTS TO THE STARS: EXPLORING THE SKIES THROUGHOUT THE YEAR. New York: Macmillan; 1972.
Gr. 6-up. Uses fifteen of the brightest stars to point the way to all their neigbboring stars and constellations.

1666. THE PLANETS [Kit]. Washington, D.C: National Geographic; 1979; 1 filmstrip; 1 cassette; 30 copies of script; 5 duplicatlng masters; 3 study prints; teacher's guide.
Gr. 1-6. Helps improve readlng skills, increase reading and listening comprehension, and build vocabulary while teaching specific concepts. Discusses characteristics of the planets in our solar system, and the Viking mission to Mars.

1667. PROJECT PLANETARIUM [Model]. Northbrook, IL: Hubbard; 1964; 3 models; study guide.
Gr. 4-9. The small planetarium model and solar system chart can be adjusted to demonstrate day and night, seasons, and planetary positions for a given time.

1668. Radley, Gail. THE NIGHT STELLA HID THE STARS. Illustrated by John Wallner. New York: Crown; 1978.
Gr. K-3. After millions of years of dusting the stars all day to have them ready for the night sky, Stella decides she needs time to enjoy the day.

1669. Rey, H. A. FIND THE CONSTELLATIONS. Boston: Houghton Mifflin; 1976.
Gr. 3-7. Describes stars and constellations throughout the year and ways of indentifying them.

1670. Rutland, Jonathan. THE PLANETS. Illustrated. New York: Warwick; 1978.
Gr. 3-6. Describes the plants and their relationship to each other and discusses the technology which has made it possible for human beings to explore the rest of the solar system at a closer range.

1671. Schwartz, Julius. EARTHWATCH: SPACE-TIME INVESTIGATIONS WITH A GLOBE. Illustrated by Radu Vero. New York: McGraw Hill; 1977.
Gr. 5-9. Includes a variety of experiments with a globe to illustrate tbe movement of the earth and its satellites.

1672. Simon, Seymour. THE LONG JOURNEY FROM SPACE. New York: Crown; 1982.
Gr. 3-5. An introduction to comets and meteors and what we know about them.

1673. Simon, Seymour. THE LONG VIEW INTO SPACE. New York: Crown; 1979.
Gr. 4-6. Photos and descriptions of earth, solar system, Milky Way and beyond.

1674. Simon, Seymour. LOOK TO THE NIGHT SKY: AN INTRODUCTION TO STAR WATCHING. New York: Viking; 1977.
Gr. 5-12. Explains how to observe stars with the naked eye and how to understand what is seen. Discusses the difference between astronomy and astrology.

1675. SPACE SCIENCE: THE SOLAR SYSTEM [Study Print]. Chicago: Encyclopaedia Britannica Educational Corp.; 1977; 10 study prints; study guide.
Gr. 6-up. NASA photographs, explanatory diagrams and planetary models highlight a guided tour of our solar system.

1676. SUN AND MOON [Slide]. Stamford, CT: Educational Dimensions; 1976; 20 slides; guide.
Gr. 5-up. Shows the significance of the sun and the moon in the solar system.

1677. Traven, B. THE CREATION OF THE SUN AND THE MOON. Westport, CT: Lawrence Hill Books; 1977.
Gr. 5-7. Mexican Indian folklore - the gods of darkness steal the sun until a brave father and son create a new one.

1678. THE TRIPPENSEE TRANSPARENT CELESTIAL GLOBE [Model]. Saginaw, MI: Trippensee Planetarium; 1967; 1 model; guide; stand.
Gr. 4-up. Transparent shell represents the sky. The moon and earth can be rotated to see the constellations of any time of year.

1679. THE UNIVERSE [Filmstrip]. Stamford, CT: Educational Dimensions; 1978; 4 filmstrips; 4 cassettes; 1 teacher's guide.
Gr. 6-up. Introduces students to the nature of the cosmos, especially the stars. Contents: The Universe: What It Is; Stars and Motion; The Life and Death of Stars; Beginnings and Ends.

1680. Weiss, Malcolm E. SKY WATCHERS OF AGES PAST. Boston: Houghton Mifflin; 1982.
Gr. 5-8. Discusses how and why ancient peoples tracked the moments of the sun, moon, and stars.

1681. Whitney, Charlez Allen. WHITNEY'S STAR FINDER: A FIELD GUIDE TO THE HEAVENS. Illustrated. New York: Knopf. Distributed by Random House; 1981.
Gr. 6-up.

Geographic

1682. Amos, William H. LIFE IN PONDS AND STREAMS. Washington, D.C: National Geographic; 1981.
Gr. 1-3. An introduction to the animals that live in these bodies of water.

1683. Blassingame, Wyatt. THE EVERGLADES, FROM YESTERDAY TO TOMORROW. New York: Putnam; 1974.
Gr. 6-up. Describes the biology and geography of the Everglades, the history of this unique wilderness, and the need to conserve it for the future.

Freeman, Don. THE CHALK BOX STORY. Philadelphia: Lippincott; 1976.
Gr. Preschool-2. See #730.

1684. Gunston, Bill. WATER. Morristown, NJ: Silver Burdett; 1982.
Gr. 6-8. Discusses the many aspects of water, such as flotation, steam, the water cycle, ground water, oceans, etc.

1685. Henry, Marguerite. SEA STAR, ORPHAN OF CHINCOTEAGUE. Illustrated by Wesley Dennis. Chicago: Rand McNally; 1949.
Gr. 4-6. The award winning story of the island orphan colt.

1686. Henry, Marguerite. SEA STAR: ORPHAN OF CHINCOTEAGUE [Sound Recording]. New York: Miller-Brody; 1976; 1 cassette; teacher's notes.
Gr. 4-6. Based on the book of the same title.

Kellogg, Steven. THE ISLAND OF THE SKOG. Illustrated. New York: Dial Press; 1973
Gr. Preschool-3. See #741.

Kellogg, Steven. THE ISLAND OF THE SKOG [Filmstrip]. Weston, CT: Weston; 1976; 1 filmstrip; 1 cassette; 1 picture-cued text booklet.
Gr. Preschool-3. See #742.

Lederer, Chloe. DOWN THE HILL OF THE SEA. Illustrated by Ati Forberg. New York: Lothrop; 1971.
Gr. 4-6. See #745.

1687. McNulty, Faith. HOW TO DIG A HOLE TO THE OTHER SIDE OF THE WORLD. Illustrated by Marc Simont. New York: Harper & Row; 1979.
Gr. 1-3. An imaginary trip through the center of the earth which realistically details the geology of the core of the earth.

1688. RIVERS: ROOTS OF THE OCEAN [Filmstrip]. Burbank, CA: Walt Disney Educational Media; 1979; 5 filmstrips; 5 cassettes; teacher's guide.
Gr. 4-12. The Cousteaus explore the Mississippi, the Colorada, the Nile and the Thames rivers and discuss the stages in a river's development.

1689. Selsam, Millicent Ellis. LAND OF THE GIANT TORTOISE: THE STORY OF THE GALAPAGOS. Illustrated with photographs. New York: Four Winds; 1977.
Gr. 1-5. Describes two theories of the geological formation of the Galapagos Islands and explains the arrival and evolution of plant and animal life found there.

1690. Thackray, John. EARTH AND ITS WONDERS. New York: Larousse; 1980.
Gr. 5-up. Describes the geology of Earth, both past processes and current geological events.

1691. Thompson, Gerald, and Jennifer Coldrey. THE POND. Cambridge, MA: MIT Press; 1984.

Gr. 6-up. The pond and its inhabitants are revealed in all their extraordinary variety in over 400 superb colour photographs taken by Oxford Scientific Films and accompanied by an authoritative text.

Man-Made

1692. Arceneaux, Marc. PAPER AIRPLANES. Illustrated. San Francisco: Troubador Press; 1974.
Gr. 4-6. Directions, flying instructions, and suggestions for making twenty paper airplanes.

1693. Baker, A.J. GET OUT AND GET UNDER: AMERICANS AND THEIR AUTOMOBILES. Marlton, NJ: Periods and Commas; 1975.
Gr. 5-12. Describes in cartoon form the history of American automobiles and the American infatuation for them.

1694. Berliner, Don. HELICOPTERS. Minneapolis: Lerner; 1983.
Gr. 4-up. Traces the history of helicopters and discusses the many models and uses of this versatile flying machine which can take off and land vertically, hover in mid-air, and fly backwards and sideways.

Crews, Donald. SCHOOL BUS. New York: Greenwillow; 1984.
Gr. Preschool-2. See #251.

Crews, Donald. TRUCK. New York: Greenwillow; 1980.
Gr. Preschool-2. See #188.

1695. Crews, Donald. TRUCK [Filmstrip]. Somers, NY: Live Oak Media; 1981; 1 filmstrip; 1 cassette; guide.
Gr. Preschool-2. Based on the book of the same title.

1696. CUSTOM CARS [Filmstrip]. Written and photographed by Ed Radlauer. (Reading incentive language program). Los Angeles, CA: Bowmar/Noble; 1974; 1 filmstrip; 1 cassette; 7 books; 8 duplicating masters; teacher's guide.
Gr. 3-8. Introduces various types of custom cars from antiques to unusual models built for shows and discusses tbe criteria on which these cars are judged. Also issued in Spanish.

1697. De Vere, Nicholas. THE BOOK OF FANTASTIC PLANES. Illustrated by Roy Coombs. New York: Golden; 1974.

Gr. 4-8. A survey of some important developments in the history of powered airflight, from the first pair of mechanized wings through the supersonic transport plane, Concorde.

1698. Delear, Frank J. HELICOPTERS AND AIRPLANES OF THE U.S. ARMY. New York: Dodd, Mead; 1977.
Gr. 5-up. Gives a background of Army aviation and describes the purpose of the various types of aircraft used.

1699. Dorin, Patrick C. YESTERDAY'S TRAINS. Minneapolis: Lerner; 1981.
Gr. 4-up. Traces the development of trains from steam engines to diesel locomotives and recreates an overnight trip on a Pullman sleeper during the 1930's.

1700. Lenski, Lois. THE LITTLE AUTO. New York: Walck; 1962.
Gr. K-3. Mr. Small has a little red auto. The story and pictures show Mr. Small taking care of this little auto.

LISTENING, LOOKING AND FEELING [Filmstrip]. Santa Monica, CA: BFA; 1970; 4 filmstrips; 4 cassettes; 1 teacher's guide.
Gr. K-6. See #812.

1701. Marston, Hope Irvin. BIG RIGS. New York: Dodd, Mead; 1979.
Gr. 1-4. Describes various kinds of tractor-trailer combinations, the biggest trucks on the highway.

1702. Provensen, Alice, and Martin Provensen. THE GLORIOUS FLIGHT: ACROSS THE CHANNEL WITH LOUIS BLERIOT. New York: Viking; 1983.
Gr. 5-8. A biography of the man whose fascination with flying machines produced the Bleriot XI, which crossed the English Channel in thirty-seven minutes in the early 1900's.

Quackenbush, Robert. M. CITY TRUCKS. Illustrated. Chicago: Whitman; 1981.
Gr. 3-8. See #201.

1703. Siebert, Diane. TRUCK SONG. Pictures by Byron Barton. New York: Crowell; 1984.
Gr. K-3. Rhymed test and illustrations describe the journey of a transcontinental truck.

1704. Simon, Seymour. THE PAPER AIRPLANE BOOK. Illustrated by Byron Barton. New York: Viking; 1971.
Gr. 4-6. Step-by-step instructions for making paper.

1705. Spier, Peter. BORED--NOTHING TO DO! Illustrated. New York: Doubleday; 1978.
Gr. 1-3. On a lazy afternoon, two bored brothers keep themselves busy by building and flying an airplane.

1706. VW BUGS [Kit]. Written and photographed by Ed Radlauer, (Reading incentive program). Los Angeles, CA: Bowmar/Noble; 1974; 1 filmstrip; 1 cassette; 7 books; 8 duplicating masters; teacher's guide.
Gr. 3-8. Discusses the VW bug and some of its many custom variations. Also issued in Spanish.

1707. Walker, Sloan. THE ONE AND ONLY CRAZY CAR BOOK. Illustrated. New York: Walker; 1973.
Gr. 1-up. Presents a variety of unique cars, including the lunar rover, Hitler's car, and a car made from a telephone booth.

1708. Williams, Brian. AIRCRAFT. Illustrated. New York: Warwick; 1976.
Gr. 5-up. Discusses various kinds of aircraft including their history, design, and constructions.

1709. Zaffo, George. AIRPLANES AND TRUCKS AND TRAINS, FIRE ENGINES, BOATS AND SHIPS, AND BUILDING AND WRECKING MACHINES. New York: Grosset & Dunlap; 1968.
Gr. K-3. The contents of five books are combined into one volume describing the kinds, parts, operation and use of many common vehicles and machines.

Geometric

1710. GEOMETRIC FIGURES AND SOLIDS [Realia]. Springfield, MA: Milton Bradley; 22 geometric solids; 17 plane figures.
Gr. 2-6. Geometric figures and solids for use in studying elementary geometry.

1711. Harvey, Linda, and Ann Roper. PATTERN BLOCKS PROBLEMS FOR PRIMARY PEOPLE. Palo Alto, CA: Creative Publications; 1979.

Gr. Preschool-3. Activities to be done with pattern blocks.

1712. Heide, Florence Parry. THE SHRINKING OF TREEHORN. Drawings by Edward Gorey. New York: Holiday House; 1971.
Gr. 3-6. A boy discovers be is shrinking but does not know the cause or cure.

1713. Hoban, Tana. IS IT RED? IS IT YELLOW? IS IT BLUE? AN ADVENTURE IN COLOR. New York: Greenwillow; 1978.
Gr. K-3. Introduces colors and the concepts of shape, quantity, and direction.

1714. MATH LAB CARD GAMES [Game]. Springfield, MA: Milton Bradley; 1973; 1 game: 4 decks of 42 cards; 1 direction card; 1 plastic tray.
Gr. K-3. Games to develop basic math concepts. Contents: Attributes; Pattern Sequences; Number and Sets; Fractions.

1715. Newth, Philip. ROLY GOES EXPLORING: A BOOK FOR BLIND AND SIGHTED CHILDREN. Pictures to feel as well as see. New York: Philomel Books; 1981.
Gr. Preschool-4. Small, round, curious Roly explores the other geometric shapes in the the book in which he lives.

1716. PARQUETRY DESIGN BLOCKS [Realia]. Springfield, MA: Milton Bradley; 1977; 84 blocks; instruction sheet.
Gr. K-6. Designed to teach color and shape perception.

1717. Patent, Dorothy Hinshaw. SIZES AND SHAPES IN NATURE--WHAT THEY MEAN. Illustrated. New York: Holiday House; 1979.
Gr. 6-up. Examines the factors which influence the enormous variety of sizes and shapes in plants and animals.

1718. PATTERN BLOCKS AND MIRRORS [Realia]. Palo Alto, CA: Creative Publications; 250 hardwood blocks in various shapes and colors; 2 mirrors.
Gr. K-9. Provides experience in distinguishing forms and relatinonships, explores symmetry, congruence, angle measure and similarity.

1719. PATTERN CARDS FOR PARQUETRY DESIGN BLOCKS [Card]. Springfield, MA: Milton Bradley; 1977; 20 activity cards; instruction sheet.
Gr. K-6. Each card is design card for use with parquetry blocks. Designed to help children identify shapes of blocks and place them in appropriate positions.

1720. Porter, Albert W. SHAPE AND FORM. Illustrated. New York: Davis, distributed by Sterling Publishing; 1974.
Gr. 4-up. Explores the art elements of shape and form through observing the qualities of design and beauty of various shapes.

1721. RELATIONSHAPES [Kit]. By Teri Perl. New Rochelle, NY: Cuisenaire Company; 1973; 1 kit: 266 shapes; spinner; activity; manual.
Gr. 1-6. Provides activities involving geometric shapes to help in basic understanding of geometric attributes.

1722. SCIENCE PROCESSES SERIES. SET 1: OBSERVING AND DESCRIBING [Filmstrip]. New York: McGraw Hill; 1974; 6 filmstrips; 6 cassettes; guide.
Gr. 1-6. Designed to aid children in identifying shapes and distinguishing size. Contents: Color; Size and Shape; Similarities and Differences; Serial Ordering; Changes; To Communicate.

1723. Stevens, Peter S. PATTERNS IN NATURE. Illustrated. Boston: Little, Brown; 1974.
Gr. 2-6. An exploration of the universal patterns found in nature.

1724. TEACHER'S GUIDE FOR PATTERN BLOCKS. Developed by Elementary Science Study. New York: McGraw Hill; 1970.
Gr. 1-6. Activities for children to use pattern blocks for an aesthetic experience and an opportunity to manipulate shapes and patterns.

1725. Walter, Marion. MAKE A BIGGER PUDDLE, MAKE A SMALLER WORM. Illustrated. New York: Evans House; 1972.
Gr. Preschool-6. The mirror provided with the book can be used to make the illustrations shorter, fatter, longer, or double in number.

APPENDIXES

Appendix 1

Selected Lists of Subject Headings

(Taken from: LIBRARY OF CONGRESS SUBJECT HEADINGS, 9th Edition and SEARS LIST OF SUBJECT HEADINGS, 12th Edition)

These lists of subject headings are provided to aid in the search for more materials on the six topics covered in this book. In some cases the headings from Sears and the Library of Congress are identical, while in other cases there is a considerable difference in phrasing. Most school libraries and small public libraries use the SEARS LIST OF SUBJECT HEADINGS, while larger public libraries and academic libraries use the LIBRARY OF CONGRESS SUBJECT HEADINGS.

BODIES

Sears	LC
Figurative Bodies	
	Body and soul in literature
	Body, Human, in literature
	Body, Human (in religion, folklore, etc.)
	Islands in literature
Cabinet officers	Cabinet officers
Legislative bodies	Legislative bodies
United States Congress	United States Congress
Biological Bodies	
Animals	Animals
Animal communication	Animal mechanics
Animal locomotion	Animal navigation
Animal tracks	Animal sounds
	Animal migration

Sears	LC
Animals (s.a. types of animals, e.g., Birds, Mammals, etc.)	Animals - Infancy of
Animals - Hibernation - Infancy - Migration	
Birds - Eggs and nests Camouflage (Biology)	Body covering (Anatomy) Body size Feathers Fur Hair Hibernation Scales (Fishes) Shells Skin
Botany - Anatomy Fossils Plants - Collection and preservation	Botany - Anatomy Growth (Plants) Plants - Collection and preservation Paleontology
Anatomy, Human Blood Blood groups Bones Digestion Eye Heart Mentally handicapped Mentally ill Nonverbal communication Physically handicapped Physiology Sense-organs Senses and sensation Skin Vision	Anatomy, Human Blood Blood groups Body, Human Body-marking Body temperature Body weight Bones Digestion Eye Heart Mentally handicapped Mentally ill Nonverbal communication Physically handicapped Physiology Sense-organs Senses and sensation Skin Vision

Sears	LC
Aging	Aging
Child development	Child development
Child birth	Child study
Children-Growth	Child birth
Death	Children-Growth
Ethnology	Death
Growth	Ethnology
Infants	Growth
Life	Infants
Man, Prehistoric	Life
Mortality	Man, Prehistoric
Mummies	Mortality
Old age	Mummies
Race	Old age
	Race
Diet	Diet
Exercise	Exercise
Health	Health
Hygiene	Health education
Movement education	Human mechanics
Nutrition	Hygiene
Physical education and training	Movement education
Physical fitness	Nutrition
Posture	Physical education and training
Reducing	Physical fitness
Yoga	Posture
	Reducing
	Reducing exercises
	Yoga

The Body in Art

Sears	LC
Dancers	Dancers
Dancing (s.a. types of dances and dancing, e.g., Ballet, Modern dancing, Tap dancing)	Dancing (s.a. types of dances and dancing, e.g., Ballet, Modern dancing, Tap dancing)

Sears	LC
Anatomy, Artistic	Anatomy, Artistic
Animal painting and illustration	Animal painting and illustration
	Animal sculpture
	Animals in art
	Busts
	Children in art
	Face
Children in literature and art	Figure drawing
	Figure painting
Figure drawing	Figurative art
Figure painting	Human figure in art
	Masks (Sculpture)
	Nude in art
Masks (Sculpture)	Portrait painting
Portrait painting	Sculpture
Sculpture	

Physical Bodies

Sears	LC
Astronomy	Astronomy
Comets	Comets
Meteorites	Meteorites
Meteors	Meteors
Moon	Moon
Planets (s.a. names of planets, e.g., Saturn)	Planets (s.a. names of planets, e.g., Saturn)
	Satellites
	Solar system
Satellites	Stars
Solar system	Sun
Stars	
Sun	
Continents	Continents
Islands	Ice Islands
Lakes	Islands
Ocean	Lakes
Ponds	Ocean
Rivers	Ponds
	Rivers
	Water

Sears	LC
Dolls	Dolls
Size and shape	Form perception
Toys	Toys

CITIES

Sears	LC
Cities and towns	Cities and towns
City life	Cities and towns - planning
City planning	City and town life
Metropolitan areas	Local government
Villages	Metropolitan areas
	Sociology, urban
	Villages

The Cultural Context

Sears	LC
Ballet	Ballet
Bands (Music)	Bands (Music)
Conducting	Music - performance
Opera	Opera
Orchestra	Orchestra
	Street music and musicians
Cities and towns - Fiction	Cities and towns in literature
	Poetry of places
Archaeology	Archaeology
Art, Municipal	Art, Municipal
Folk art	Cities and towns in art
	Folk art
	Urban beautification

The Physical World

Sears	LC
Air-pollution	Air-pollution
Natural history	City noise
Plants	City sounds
Pollution	Natural history

Sears	LC
Trees	Plants
Weeds	Plants, Cultivated
	Pollution
	Traffic noise
	Trees in cities
	Urban fauna
	Weeds
Animals - Habitations	Animal colonies
Animals - Habits and behavior	Animal societies
Ants	Animals, Habitations of Animals, Habits and behavior of
Aquariums	Ants
Beavers	Aquariums
Bees	Beavers
Insects	Bees
Marine aquariums	Insect societies
Prairie dogs	Insects
Sponges	Marine aquariums
Terrariums	Prairie dogs
Whales	Sponges
	Terrariums
	Vivariums
	Whales
Architecture	Apartment houses
Architecture, Domestic	Architecture
Buildings	Architecture, Domestic
Houses	Buildings
Office buildings	Buildings - Conservation and restoration
Parks	Civic centers
Skyscrapers	Dwellings
Streets	Houses
Urban renewal	Municipal buildings
Zoological gardens	Office buildings
	Parks
	Plazas
	Public buildings
	Skyscrapers
	Street-names
	Street signs
	Streets
	Tall buildings
	Urban renewal
	Zoological gardens

Sears

Bridges
Buses
Cities and towns - Civic improvement
City traffic
Civil engineering
Excavation
Harbors
Heating
Local transit
Plumbing
Public utilities
Recycling (waste, etc.)
Refuse and refure disposal
Sanitation
Sewerage
Street railroads
Streets - lighting
Subways
Traffic engineering
Traffic regulations
Transportation
Tunnels
Urban renewal

LC

Bridges
City traffic
Civil engineering
Drainage
Electric railroads
Excavation
Harbors
Heating
Local transit
Motor buses
Municipal government
Municipal lighting
Omnibuses
Plumbing
Public utilities
Railroads, cable
Recycling (waste, etc.)
Refuse and refuse disposal
Sanitation
Sewage disposal
Sewerage
Snow removal
Street cleaning
Street - lighting
Street - railroads
Subways
Traffic engineering
Traffic regulations
Trolley buses
Tunnels
Urban renewal
Urban transportation

People

Cemeteries
City planning
Fire departments
Hospitals
Libraries
Local government
Police
Public health

Cemeteries
Cities and towns - planning
City planners
Fire departments
Hospital and community
Hygiene, public
Libraries
Libraries and community

Sears	LC
	Local government Police Public libraries
Occupations (s.a. names of type of occupations) Professions (s.a. names of types of professions, e.g., Teachers, or Teaching as a profession)	Occupations (s.a. names of types of occupations) Professions (s.a. names of types of professions, e.g., Teachers, or Teaching as a profession)
Department stores Factories Industrial buildings Mills and millwork Office buildings	Department stores Factories Industrial buildings Mercantile buildings Mills and millwork Office buildings Offices Skyscrapers
Family Family life Home Housing Social case work	Family Family life Family social work Home Housing Housing authorities Public housing Social case work
Community life Ethnic groups Race relations Religions Tenement houses	Community Community centers Community life Minorities Neighborhood Race problems Religion Slums Suburbs Tenement houses

Sears	LC
Comparisons and Contrasts	
Cities and towns (s.a. names of particular cities, e.g., Rome, etc.)	Cities and towns
Cliff dwellers and cliff dwellings	Cities and towns, Ancient
Ghost towns	Cities and towns, Medieval
	Cities and towns, Ruined, extinct, etc.
	Cliff dwellers
	Urbanization
MONSTERS	
Demonology	Demonology
Dreams	Dreams
Monsters	Monsters
Superstition	Nightmares
	Superstition
Real Monsters	
Dinosaurs	Dinosauria
Fossils (Prehistoric animals)	Paleontology
Reptiles, Fossil	Reptiles, Fossil
Mammals, Fossil	Mammals, Fossil
Mastodon	Mastodon
Sabre-tooth tiger	
See names of various animals, e.g.:	See names of various animals, e.g.:
Alligators	Alligators
Buzzards	Buzzards
Crocodiles	Crocodiles
Iguanas	Iguanas
Kimodo dragons	Kimodo dragons
Sharks	Sharks

Sears	LC
	Abnormalities (Animals) Deformities

Imaginary Monsters

Sears	LC
Dragons Fairies Folklore	Apparitions Centaurs
Monsters - Fiction	Ghosts in literature Heroes in literature Monsters in literature
Makeup, Theatrical Masks (Facial)	Animals, Mythical, in art Film make-up Ghosts in art Heroes in art Make-up, Theatrical Masks Monsters in art Mumming Witchcraft in art

MOUNTAINS

The Physical World

Sears	LC
Geology Mountains (s.a. names of specific mts. and ranges, e.g., Mt. Everest) Physical geography Volcanoes	Alpine regions Geology Mountains (s.a. names of specific mts. and ranges, e.g., Mt. Everest) Physical geography Volcanoes Watersheds
Man - Influence of environment	Acclimatization Altitude, Influence of Man - Influence of environment Mountain sickness

Sears	LC
	Plants, Effect of altitude on Weather, Influence of mountains on
Map drawing Topographical drawing	Map drawing Photography of mountains Topographical drawing
Camping Hiking Mountaineering Outdoor life Outdoor recreation Wilderness areas Wilderness survival	Camping Hiking Mountaineering Mountains - Recreational use Outdoor life Outdoor recreation Wilderness areas Wilderness survival
Natural Resources	Natural Resources
Conservation of natural resources	Conservation of natural resources Ecology Mountain ecology
Coal miners Coal mines and mining Miners Mines and mineral resources	Coal miners Coal mines and mining Miners Mines and mineral resources Ore-deposits
Forest products Forests and forestry Lumber and lumbering Wood	Clear-cutting Forest products Forests and forestry Lumber Lumbering Wood
See names of individual mountain animals, e.g.: Alpacas Alpine sheep Bighorn sheep Llamas Mountain goats	See names of individual mountain animals, e.g.: Alpacas Alpine sheep Bighorn sheep Llamas Mountain goats

Sears	LC
Mountain sheep Pumas Saint Bernard dogs etc.	Mountain sheep Pumas Saint Bernard dogs etc.
Alpine plants Herbs Plants - Collection and preservation Wildflowers	Alpine flora Food, Wild Herbs Mountain hemlock Mountain laurel Plants - Collection and preservation Wild flowers
United States - Description and Traval	

The Cultural Context

Sears	LC
Handicraft (s.a. names of specific crafts, e.g., Basketmaking) Arts and crafts Folksongs Folklore Mountains - Fiction	Handicraft (s.a. names of specific crafts, e.g., Basketmaking, Quilting) Folk-lore Folksongs Mountain-gods Mountains in art Mountains in literature Mountains (in religion, folk-lore, etc.)

OCEANS

Sears	LC
Ocean Oceanography	Ocean Oceanography

Sears	LC

Natural History

Sears	LC
Beaches	Beaches
Continental shelf	Coasts
Glaciers	Continental shelf
Icebergs	Deep-sea temperature
Islands	Glaciers
Ocean bottom	Ice-islands
Sand dunes	Icebergs
Seashort	Islands
Submarine geology	Manned undersea research stations
Undersea research stations	Marine caves
	Ocean bottom
	Ocean temperature
	Sand-dunes
	Sea ice
	Sea ice drift
	Seashort
	Submarine geology
	Tidal flats
	Underwater exploration
Hurricane	Gulf stream
Marine pollution	Hurricanes
Ocean waves	Marine pollution
Sea water	Ocean currents
Storms	Ocean waves
Tides	Saline waters
Typhoons	Sea breeze
Winds	Sea level
	Sea-water
	Sea-water, Distillation of
	Storms
	Tidal power
	Tidal waves
	Tides
	Typhoons
	Winds

Sears	LC
Marine biology Marine ecology	Marine biologists Marine biology Marine ecology Seashore biology Tide pool ecology
Algae Marine plants Seaweed	Algae Aquatic plants Coastal flora Marine algae Marine flora Marine phytoplankton Marine plants Seaweed
Coral reefs and islands Corals Crustaceans (s.a. specific types, e.g., Lobsters) Dolphins Eels Fishes (s.a. specific types, e.g., Shellfish) Lemmings Marine animals Mollusks Octopi Otters Seahorses	Aquarium fishes Aquatic animals Coral reef ecology Coral reef fauna Corals Crustaceans Dolphins Eels Fishes (s.a. specific types, e.g., Shellfish) Lemmings Marine animals Marine aquarium fishes Marine fauna Marine fishes Marine invertebrates Marine mammals Mollusks Octopi Sea birds Sea-horses Sea-otters Sea lions

Sears	LC
Seals (s.a. types, e.g., Elephant seals)	Seals (s.a. types, e.g., Elephant seals)
Sharks	Sharks
Shells	Shellfish
Starfish	Shells
Turtles	Snails
Water birds	Squids
Whales	Starfishes
	Turtles
	Whales

Human Endeavor

Sears	LC
Aquaculture	Aquaculture
Fish culture	Aquatic resources
Fisheries	Fish-culture
Marine resources	Fisheries
Ocean energy resources	Mariculture
Ocean mining	Marine mineral resources
Sea food	Marine resources
Sea water converwion	Nets
Whaling	Ocean engineering
	Sea food
	Sea-water, Distillation of
	Whaling
Marine ecology	Diving, Submarine
Oceanography	Marine ecology
Physical geography	Oceanographers
	Oceanography
	Physical geography
Fishing (s.a. types of fishing, e.g., Bass fishing, etc.)	Aquatic sports
Marine aquariums	Fishing (s.a. types of fishing, e.g., Bass fishing, etc.)
	Marine aquariums

Sears	LC
Sailing	Sailing
Shells	Salt-water fishing
Skin diving	Shells
Surfing	Skin diving
Water sports	Surfing
	Water skiing
	Water sports
Aquanauts	Aids to navigation
Icebergs	Beacons
Lighthouses	Buccaneers
Map drawing	Buoys
Maps	Collisions at sea
Maritime law	Icebergs
Military history	Lighthouses
Naval battles	Light-ships
Naval history	Map drawing
Navigation	Marine accidents
Ocean travel	Maritime law
Pilots and pilotage	Military history
Pirates	Nautical instruments
Privateering	Naval battles
Radar	Naval history
Sailing	Navigation
Sailors	Ocean-maps
Salvage	Ocean travel
Sea power	Oceanographic buoys
Seafaring life	Oceanography - Charts, diagrams, etc.
Shipping	Pilots and pilotage
	Pirates
	Privateering
	Radar
	Sailing
	Salvage
	Seamen
	Sea-power
	Seafaring life
	Shipping

Sears

Shipwrecks
Signals and signaling
Sonar
Tides
Underwater exploration
Vikings
Voyages around the world

Boat-building
Boats and boatings
Cables, Submarine
Clipper ships
Docks
Drilling platforms
Harbors
Marinas
Ocean engineering
Oil pollution of water
Oil spills
Oil well drilling,
submarine
Petroleum - Geology
Shipbuilding
Ships
Signals and signaling
Submarines
Submersibles
Tugboats
Yachts and yachting

LC

Shipwrecks
Signals and signaling
Sonar
Tides
Underwater exploration
Vikings
Voyages around the world

Boat-building
Boats and boatings
Breakwaters
Cables, Submarine
Clipper ships
Deep sea drilling ships
Dikes (engineering)
Docks
Drilling platforms
Fishing boats
Harbors
Jetties
Levees
Marinas
Marine engineering
Marine nuclear reactor plants
Marine pollution
Merchant ships
Naval architecture
Ocean engineering
Ocean liners
Ocean mining
Oceanographic submersibles
Oil pollution of rivers,
harbors, etc.
Oil pollution of the sea
Oil spills
Oil well drilling, Submarine
Petroleum - Geology
Petroleum pollution of water
Piers
Sailing ships
Sails
Sea-walls
Shipbuilding
Ships

Sears	LC
	Shore protection
	Signals and signaling
	Stemboat lines
	Submarine boats
	Tugboats
	Waste disposal in the ocean
	Whalers
	Wharves
	Yachts and yachting

The Arts

Sears	LC
Folklore	Folk-lore of the sea
Marine painting	Marine painting
Sea poetry	Ocean sounds
Sea songs	Ocean travel in literature
Sea stories	Oceana in art
	Oceana in literature
	Sailors' songs
	Sand sculpture
	Sandcastles
	Sea gods
	Sea gods in art
	Sea in art
	Sea in literature
	Sea monsters
	Sea poetry
	Sea songs
	Sea stories
	Seamen in literature
	Ships in art
	Storms (in religion, folk-lore, etc.)
	Water (in religion, folk-lore, etc.)

SOUND

Physics and Physiology of Sound

Sears	LC
Sonar Sound Sound waves Sounds Ultrasonics Vibration	Echo sounding Sonar Sound Sound-waves Sounding and soundings Sounds Ultrasonics Vibration
Animal communication Ocean waves Thunderstorms Ventriloquism Voice Water Winds	Acoustic phenomena in nature Animal communication Animal sounds Echo Insect sounds Nature sounds Sound production by animals Sound production by insects Storms Thunderstorms Underwater acoustics Ventriloquism Voice Water Waterfalls Winds
Noise Noise pollution	City noise Noise Noise pollution Shock waves Sonic booms Traffic noise
High-fidelity sound systems Intercommunication systems Magnetic recorders and recording Motion pictures	High-fidelity sound systems Loud speakers Magnetic recorders and recording Microphone Moving-picture, talking Phonograph

Sears	LC
Phonograph Radio Radio broadcasting Sound effects Sound - Recording and reproducing Sound recordings Stereophonic sound systems Telephone Television broadcasting	Phonorecords Phonotapes Public address systems Radio Radio broadcasting Radio broadcasting - sound effects Sound - Recording and reproducing Stereophonic sound systems Telephone Television Television broadcasting Television broadcasting - sound effects Theatres - Sound effects
Ear Hearing Senses and sensation	Ear Hearing Sense-organs Senses and sensation
Insulation (Sound) Noise Noise pollution Soundproofing	Absorption of sound Accoustical engineering City noise Noise Noise control Noise pollution Soundproofing Traffic noise
Deaf - Means of communication Deafness Hearing aids	Deaf - Means of communication Deafness Hearing aids

Sound and Meaning

Sears	LC
Communication	Communication
Language and languages Phonetics Speech	Conversation Elocution Language and languages

Sears	LC
Speech disorders	Linguistics
Vocabulary	Oral communication
Word Games	Phonetics
	Speech
	Speech, Disorders of
	Vocabulary
	Word Games
Alphabet	Alphabet
Alphabets	Alphabets
Calligraphy	Calligraphy
Ciphers	Ciphers
Crossword puzzles	Crossword puzzles
Cryptography	Cryptography
Deaf - Means of communication	Deaf - Means of communication
Graphology	Graphology
Handwriting	Hieroglyphics
Hieroglyphics	Indians of North America - Sign language
Indians of North America - Sign language	
Phonetics	Languages, Artificial
Picture writing	Penmanship
Programming Languages (Electronic Computers)	Petroglyphs
Shorthand	Phonemics
Symbols	Phonetics
Typewriting	Picture-writing
Writing	Programming Languages (Electronic Computers)
	Rock paintings
	Shorthand
	Sign language
	Signs and symbols
	Typewriting
	Writing
Animal communication	Animal communication
	Animal sounds
	Insect sounds
	Nature sounds
	Sounds produced by animals

Sears	LC
Ballet	Ballet
Bands (Music)	Bands (Music)
Bells	Bells
	Carillons
	Computer music
Instrumental music	Instrumental music
Music (s.a. types of music, e.g., Folk music, Church music, etc.)	Music (s.a. types of music, e.g., Folk music, Church music, etc.)
	Music - Acoustics and physics
Music, Popular (Songs, etc.)	Music, Popular (Songs, etc.)
Musical instruments (s.a. spec. instruments, e.g., piano)	Musical instruments (s.a. spec. instruments, e.g., piano)
Music notation	Musical notation
Opera	Opera
Operas	Operas
Orchestra	Orchestra
Orchestral music	Orchestral music
Percussion instruments (s.a. spec. instruments, e.g., drum)	Percussion instruments (s.a. spec. instruments, e.g., drum)
Rhythm	Rhythm
Songs	Songs
Songbooks	Songbooks
Vocal music	Vocal music
Ballads	Ballads
Poetics	Poetics
Poetry (s.a. spec. types, e.g., Free verse, Love poetry, etc.)	Poetry (s.a. spec. types, e.g., Free verse, Love poetry, etc.)
Rhyme	Rime
Rhythm	Rhythm
Versifications	Versifications

Appendix 2

Directory of Publishers and Producers

Abelard-Schuman, Ltd.
10 E. 53rd Street
New York, NY 10022
Orders to:
Harper & Row Publishers
Keystone Industrial Park
Scranton, PA 18512

Abingdon Press
201 8th Avenue, S.
Nashville, TN 37202

Abrams, Harry N., Inc.
Subsidiary of Times Mirror Co.
110 E. 59th Street
New York, NY 10022

Abt Associates, Inc.
55 Wheeler Street
Cambridge, MA 02138

Addison-Wesley Publishing Co.
Jacob Way
Reading, MA 01867

Aluminum Association
818 Connecticut Avenue, NW
Washington, D.C. 20006

Alva Museum Replicas
Education Division
140 Greenwich Avenue
Greenwich, CT 06830

American Bibliography Center/Clio Press
2040 Alameda Padre Serra
P. O. Box 4397
Santa Barbara, CA 93103

American Book Co.
135 W. 50th Street
New York, NY 10020

American Council on Education
1 Dupont Circle, NW
Washington, D.C. 20036

American Guidance Service, Inc.
Publishers Bldg.
Circle Pines, MN 55014

American Heritage Publishing Co.
10 Rockefeller Plaza
New York, NY 10020

American Library Association
50 E. Huron Street
Chicago, IL 60611

American Science & Engineering, Inc.
11 Carleton Street
Cambridge, MA 02142

Angel Records
1750 N. Vine Street
Hollywood, CA 90026

Appalshop
P.O. Box 743
Whitesburg, KY 41858

Apple Computer, Inc.
20525 Mariani Ave.
Cupertino, CA 95014

Arco Publishing, Inc.
219 Park Avenue, S.
New York, NY 10003

Argo Records
c/o Polygram Classics
810 7th Avenue
New York, NY 10019

Arista Records
6 West 57th Street
New York, NY 10019

Aristoplay
P. O. Box 7645
Ann Arbor, MI 48107

Aspect IV Educational Films
21 Charles Street
Westport, CT 06880

Atheneum Publishers
597 Fifth Avenue
New York, NY 10007

Audiotronics
7428 Bellaire Avenue
Hollywood, CA 91605

Austin Bilingual Language Editions
P. O. Box 3864
Austin, TX 78764

Avon Books
959 Eighth Avenue
New York, NY 10019

BFA Educational Media
2211 Michigan Avenue
Santa Monica, CA 90404

Bay Area Young Adult Librarians
345 D. Street
Fremont, CA 94536

Berkley Publishing Corp.
200 Madison Avenue
New York, NY 10016

Better Homes and Gardens Books
1716 Locust Street
Des Moines, IA 50336

Biological Sciences Curriculum Study
University of Colorado
Boulder, CO 80309

Bobbs-Merrill Co., Inc.
4300 W. 62nd Street
P. O. Box 7083
Indianapolis, IN 46206

Bowker, R. R., Co.
1180 Ave. of the Americas
New York, NY 10036
Orders to:
P. O. Box 1807
Ann Arbor, MI 48106

Bowmar/Noble Publishers, Inc.
4563 Colorado Blvd.
Los Angeles, CA 90039

Boy Scouts of America
1325 Walnut Hill Lane
Irving, TX 75062

Bradbury Press
2 Park Avenue
New York, NY 10016

Brain Bank, Inc.
Suite 408
220 Fifth Avenue
New York, NY 10001

Brodart Company
1609 Memorial Ave.
Williamsport, PA 17705
Orders to:
Order Dept.
500 Arch Street
Williamsport, PA 17705

Brumley & Sons
Camdenton, MO 65020

Burke, John Gordon, Publishers, Inc.
P. O. Box 1492
Evanston, IL 60204

CBS Records
51 West 52nd Street
New York, NY 10019

CMS Records
14 Warren Street
New York, NY 10007

CPI
P. O. Box 11409
Baltimore, MD 21239

Caedmon Records, Inc.
1995 Broadway
New York, NY 10023

California Polytechnic State University
Vocational Education Productions
San Luis Obispo, CA 93407

Caligani, Carl E.
P. O. Box 24228
Columbus, Ohio 43215

Cape, Jonathan, Ltd.
30 Bedford Square
London WC1B 3EL, EN, UK

Capitol Records, Inc.
1750 North Vine Street
Hollywood, CA 90028

Carolrhoda Books, Inc.
241 1st Avenue North
Minneapolis, MN 55401

Center for Language, Literature and Reading
College of Education
The Ohio State University
1945 North High Street
Columbus, Ohio 43210

Center for Science in the Public Interest
1501 16th Street, NW
Washington, D.C. 20036

Centre Productions, Inc.
1800 30th Street, #207
Boulder, CO 80301

Chalfonte Records
c/o Varese Sarabande Records
13006 Saticoy Street
N. Hollywood, CA 91605

Chartwell House, Inc.
P. O. Box 166,
Bowling Green Station
New York, NY 10004

Children's Book Council, Inc.
67 Irving Place
New York, NY 10003

Childrens Press, Inc.
1224 W. Van Buren Street
Chicago, IL 60607

Children's Television
Workshop
1 Lincoln Plaza
New York, NY 10023

Child's World
P. O. Box 989
Elgin, IL 60121

Clarion Books
52 Vanderbilt Avenue
New York, NY 10017

Collins Publishers
1165 Fifth Avenue
New York, NY 10016

Collins World
See Collins Publishers

Continental Can
Distributed by
Creative Teacher, Inc.

Cook, David C., Publishing
Co.
850 N. Grove Avenue
Elgin, IL 60120

Coronet Instructional
Media
65 East South Water St.
Chicago, IL 60601

Council on Interracial
Books for Children
1841 Broadway
New York, NY 10023

Coward, McCann &
Geoghegan
1050 W. Wall Street
Lyndhurst, NJ 07071

Cowley Publications
980 Memorial Drive
Cambridge, MA 02138

Crane Russak & Co., Inc.
3 E. 44th Street
New York, NY 10017

Creative Classroom
Activities
P. O. Box 1144
Sun Valley, CA 91352

Creative Education, Inc.
123 S. Broad Street
P. O. Box 227
Mankato, MN 56001

Creative Publications
3977 East Bayshore Road
Palo Alto, CA 94303

Creative Teacher, Inc.
P. O. Box 5187
Grand Central Station
New York, NY 10017

Creative Visuals, Inc.
P. O. Box 1862E
Big Spring, TX 79720

Crescent Books
A division of Crown
Publishers

Crestwood House
P. O. Box 3427
Mankato, MN 56001

Crowell-Collier
See MacMillan

Crowell Junior Books,
See Harper & Row
Publishers, Inc.

Crown Publishers, Inc.
1 Park Avenue
New York, NY 10016

Cuisenaire Co. of
America
12 Church Street
New Rochelle, NY 10805

Current Affairs
Box 426
Ridgefield, CT 06877

The Curtis Publishing,
Co.
1100 Waterway Blvd.
Indianapolis, IN 46206

Cypress Publishing
1763 Garden Avenue
Suite 100
Glendale, CA 91204

Dandelion Press
184 Fifth Avenue
New York, NY 10010

Davis Publications
Distributed by Sterling
Publishing Co.

Day, John, Co.
257 Park Ave. S.
New York, NY 10010

Day Publishing Co.
43-53 Eugene O'Neill
Drive
New London, CT 06320

Delacorte Press
245 East 47th Street
New York, NY 10017

Dell Publishing Co.
1 Dag Hammerskjold
Plaza
New York, NY 10017

Delta Education, Inc.
P. O. Box M
Nashua, NH 03061

Dennison, T.S., Co.,
Inc.
9601 Newton Ave., S.
Minneapolis, MN 55431

Denoyer-Geppert Co.
5235 Ravenwood Avenue
Chicago, IL 60640

Designware, Inc.
185 Berry Street
San Francisco, CA
94107

Developmental Learning
Materials
P. O. Box 400
Allen, TX 75002

Diagram Group
See St. Martin's
Press

Dial Books for Young
Readers
2 Park Avenue
New York, NY 10016

Dial Press
1 Dag Hammarskjold
Plaza
New York, NY 10017

Dillon Press, Inc.
500 S. 3rd Street
Minneapolis, MN 55415

Dodd Mead & Co.
79 Madison Avenue
New York, NY 10016

Doubleday & Co., Inc.
501 Franklin Avenue
Garden City, NY 11530

Dover Publications, Inc.
31 E. 2nd Street
Mineola, NY 11501

Duell, Sloan and Pierce
An affiliate of Meredith Press
See Better Homes and Garden Books

Dutton, E. P.
2 Park Avenue
New York, NY 10016

EMC Publishing
300 York Avenue
St. Paul, MN 55101

Earth Science Materials
A Division of Colorado Geological Industries, Inc.
P. O. Box 2121
1900 E. Lincoln Ave.
Fort Collins, CO 80522

Edu-Game
See Creative Classroom Activities

Educational Activities, Inc.
P. O. Box 392
Freeport, NY 11520

Educational Development Corporation
Learning Resources Division
202 Lake Miriam Drive
Lakeland, FL 33802

Educational Dimensions Group
Box 126
Stamford, CT 06904

Educational Enrichment Materials
357 Adams Street
Bedford Hills, NY 10507

Educational Images
P. O. Box 3456,
Westside Station
Elmira, NY 19405

Elsevier-Dutton Publishing Co., Inc.
2 Park Avenue
New York, NY 10016

Elsevier-Nelson
See Lodestar Books

Encyclopaedia Britannica Educational Corporation
425 N. Michigan Avenue
Chicago, IL 60611

Enjoy Communicating, Inc.
P. O. Box 1637
Falls Church, VA 22041

Enslow Publishers
Bloy Street & Ramsey Avenue
Hillside, NJ 07205

Evans, M., and Co.
Distributed by Lippincott, J. B., Co.

Eye Gate House
333 Elston Avenue
Chicago, IL 60618

Farrar, Straus & Giroux
19 Union Square
New York, NY 10003

Faxon Co.
15 Southwest Park
Westwood, MA 02090

Fell, Frederick, Inc.
386 Park Avenue S.
New York, NY 10016

Ferguson, J. G., Co.
111 E. Wacker Dr.,
Suite 500
Chicago, IL 60601

Films Incorporated
1213 Wilmette Avenue
Wilmette, IL 60091

Focus Media
135 Nassau Blvd.
Garden City, NY 11530

Fodor's and McKay
O'Neill Highway
Dunmore, PA 18512

Folkways Records
9th Fl. 632 Broadway
New York, NY 10012

Follett Publishing Co.
1010 W. Washington Blvd.
Chicago, IL 60607

Four Winds
703 W. Ninth
Austin, TX 78701

Four Winds
Imprint of Scholastic
Book Services

Franklin, Charles, Press
18409 90th Avenue, W.
Edmonds, WA 98020

Franklin Watts, Inc.
Subs of Grolier Inc.
387 Park Avenue, S.
New York, NY 10016

Front Row Experience
540 Discovery Bay Blvd.
Bryon, CA 94514

Funk & Wagnalls
53 East 77 Street
New York, NY 10021

GMG Publishing
25 W. 43 Street
New York, NY 10036

Gage Distributing Co.
164 Commander Blvd.
Agincourt, Ontario M1S
929, Canada

Gage Educational
Publishing Ltd.
P. O. Box 5000
Agincourt, Ontario M1S
3C7, Canada

Gale Research Co.
Penobscot Bldg.
Detroit, MI 48226

Gallaudet College Press
Kendall Green
Washington, D.C. 20002

Garrard Publishing Co.
1607 N. Market Street
Champaign, IL 61820

Gateway Editions, Ltd.
P. O. Box 207
South Bend, IN 46624

Gateway Press
111 Water Street
Baltimore, MD 21200

Gateway Publishing
Co., Ltd.
1825 Main Street
Winnipeg, Manitoba
R2V 2A4, Canada

Gingerbread House
A division of
Elsevier-Dutton

Globe Book Co.
50 W. 23rd Street
New York, NY 10010

Gloucester Press
Imprint of Franklin
Watts Inc.

Godine, David R.,
Publishers, Inc.
306 Dartmouth St.
Boston, MA 02116

Golden Press
Imprint of Western
Publishing Co.,
Inc.

Gospel Publishing
House
1445 Boonville Avenue
Springfield, MO 65802

The Great American Film
Factory
Box 9195
Sacramento, CA 95816

Greenwillow Division
of William Morrow
& Co.
Gateway Station,
Box 440950
Aurora, CO 80044

Grolier Educational
Corp.
Sherman Turnpike
Danbury, CT 06816

Grosset & Dunlap, Inc.
51 Madison Avenue
New Yor, NY 10010

Guidance Associates
Communications Park
P. O. Box 3000
Mount Kisco, NY 10549

Hagemeister, Michael
D-3550 Marburg
Bunter Kitzel 1,
GW/West Germany

Hanna-Barbera, Inc.
3400 Cahuenga Blvd.
Hollywood, CA 90068

Harcourt Brace
Jovanovich, Inc.
757 3rd Avenue
New York, NY 10017

Harper & Row Publishers,
Inc.
10 East 53rd Street
New York, NY 10022
Orders to:
Order Service Dept.
Keystone Industrial
Park
Scranton, PA 18512

Hart Brothers Publishing
P. O. Box 205
Williston, VT 05495

Hart Publishing Co.
24 Fifth Avenue
New York, NY 10011

Hart Publishing Co., Inc.
Correspondence Dept.
P. O. Box 1917
Denver, CO 80201

Harvard University Press
79 Garden Street
Cambridge, MA 02138

Harvey House
20 Waterside Plaza
New York, NY 10010

Harvey House
128 West River Street
Chippewa Falls, WI 54729

Hastings House Publishers, Inc.
10 East 40th Street
New York, NY 10016

Hawthorn Books, Inc.
2 Park Avenue
New York, NY 10016

Highlander Research and Education Center
Rte. 3, Box 370
New Market, TN 37820

Hill, Lawrence & Co., Inc.
520 Riverside Avenue
Westport, CT 06880

Hoctor Products for Education
159 Franklin Tpke
P. O. Box 38
Waldwick, NJ 07463

Hoctor Records
c/o Hoctor Products for Education
159 Franklin Turnpike
Waldwick, NJ 07463

Holiday House, Inc.
18 East 53rd Street
New York, NY 10022

Holt, Rinehart & Winston, Inc.
383 Madison Avenue
New York, NY 10017

Horn Book
Park Square Building
31 St. James Avenue
Boston, MA 02116

Houghton Mifflin Co.
One Beacon Street
Boston, MA 02108
Orders to:
Wayside Road
Burlington, MA 01803

Hubbard Scientific
P. O. Box 104
Northbrook, IL 60062

Human Sciences Press, Inc.
72 5th Avenue
New York, NY 10011

Ideal School Supply Co.
11000 S. Lavergne Ave.
Oak Lawn, IL 60453

Imperial Educational Resources
19 Marble Avenue
Pleasantville, NY 10570

Imperial Film Company, Inc.
See Educational Development Corp.

Indiana University Press
10th and Morton St.
Bloomington, IN 47401

Instructo Corp.
Cedar Hollow & Matthews Road
Paoli, PA 19301

Invicta
Order from Ideal School Supply Co.

Keyboard Publications
A division of American Book Co.

Knopf, Alfred A., Inc.
201 E. Fifth Avenue
New York, NY 10022
Orders to:
Order Dept.
400 Hahn Road
Westminster, MD 21157

Larousse & Co., Inc.
572 5th Avenue
New York, NY 10036

Learning Concepts/ University Associates
8517 Production Avenue
San Diego, CA 92126

Learning Corporation of America
1350 Avenue of the Americas
New York, NY 10019

Learning Tree
P. O. Box 4116
Englewood, CO 80155

Lerner Publications Co.
241 1st Avenue, N.
Minneapolis, MN 55401

Library of Congress
Information Office
Box A
Washington, D.C. 20540

Library Professional Publications
An imprint of the Shoe String Press
Hamden, CT 06514

Lippincott, J. B., Co.
A subsidiary of Harper & Row
East Washington Square
Philadelphia, PA 19105

Listening Library, Inc.
One Park Avenue
P. O. Box L
Old Greenwich, CT 06870

Little, Brown & Co.
34 Beacon Street
Boston, MA 02106

Littlefield, Adams & Co.
81 Adams Drive
P. O. Box 327
Totowa, NJ 07511

Live Oak Media
P. O. Box 34
Ancramdale, NY 12503

Lodestar Books
2 Park Avenue
New York, NY 10016

Lodestar Maps
P. O. Box 33
Nampa, ID 83651

Longman, Inc.
95 Church Street
White Plains, NY 10601

Longview Publications
See Madrona Publications, Inc.

Lothrop, Lee & Shepard Books
105 Madison Avenue
New York, NY 10016

MCA Music
445 Park Avenue
New York, NY 10022

MIT Press
28 Carlton Street
Cambridge, MA 02142

MacMillan Publishing Co., Inc.
866 3rd Avenue
New York, NY 10022

Madrona Publications, Inc.
P. O. Box 22667
Seattle, WA 98122

Marsh Film Enterprises, Inc.
P. O. Box 8082
Shawnee Mission, KS 66208

McClelland and Stewart Ltd.
25 Hollinger Road
Toronto, Ontario M4B 3G2, Canada

McGraw-Hill, Inc.
1221 Avenue of the Americas
New York, NY 10020

McKay, David, Co., Inc.
2 Park Avenue
New York, NY 10016
Orders to:
Fodor's and McKay
O'Neill Highway
Dunmore, PA 18512

Medical Books for Children
See Lerner Publications

Media Review
Education Funding Research Council
1611 N. Kent Street
Suite 508
Arlington, VA 22209

Merrill, Charles E., Publishing Co.
1300 Alum Creek Drive
Columbus, OH 43216

Messner, Julian
(A Simon & Schuster Division of Gulf & Western Corp.)
1230 Avenue of the Americas
New York, NY 10020

Michael Hardy
Productions
26 Dickinson Ave.
Nyack, NY 10960

Miller-Brody Productions,
Inc.
342 Madison Avenue
New York, NY 10017

Milliken Publishing
1100 Research Blvd.
St. Louis, MO 63132

Milton Bradley Co.
443 Shaker Road
Longmeadow, MA 01028

Morrow, William, &
Co., Inc.
105 Madison Avenue
New York, NY 10016
Orders to:
Wilmore Warehouse
6 Henderson Drive
West Caldwell, NJ
07006

Multi Dimensional
Communications, Inc.
7 Delano Drive
Bedford Hills, NY
10507

National Council of
Teachers of English
1111 Kenyon Road
Urbana, IL 61801

National Gallery of
Art
6th & Constitution
Ave., NW
Washington, D.C. 20565

National Geographic
Society
17th & 'M' Street, NW
P. O. Box 1100
Washington, D.C. 20036

National Society to
Prevent Blindness
79 Madison Avenue
New York, NY 10016

Neal-Schuman Publishers,
Inc.
23 Cornelia Street
New York, NY 10014

Nelson, Thomas
Publishers
P. O. Box 141000
Nelson Place at Elm
Hill Pike
Nashville, TN 37214

New American Library,
Inc.
1633 Broadway
New York, NY 10019

Newbery Award Records,
Inc.
342 Madison Avenue
New York, NY 10017

New York Public
Library
Fifth Ave. & 42nd St.
New York, NY 10018

Norton, W. W. & Co.,
Inc.
500 Fifth Avenue
New York, NY 10110

Nystrom
3333 N. Elston Avenue
Chicago, IL 60618

Octopus Books
Distributed by Crescent
Books

Ohio State University
College of Education
1945 N. High Street
Columbus, OH 43210

Optimum Resources
Distributed by Xerox
245 Long Hill Road
Middletown, CT 06457

Orange Cherry Media
7 Delano Avenue
Bedford Hills, NY
10507

Outdoor Biological
Instructional
Strategies
Lawrence Hall of
Science
University of
California
Berkeley, CA 94720

Oxford Films, Inc.
Lock Box #92170
Los Angeles, CA 90009

Oxford Scientific
Films
Distributed by Putnam
Publishing Co.

Oxford University
Press
200 Madison Avenue
New York, NY 10016

Pantheon Books
201 E. 50 Street
New York, NY 10022

Parents' Magazine
Press
52 Vanderbilt Avenue
New York, NY 10017

Parker Publishing Co.,
Inc.
Rte. 59 at Brookhill
Drive
West Nyack, NY 10995

Pendulum Press, Inc.
Académic Bldg.
Saw Mill Road
West Haven, CT 06516

Penguin Books, Inc.
40 W. 23rd Street
New York, NY 10010

Periods and Commas
Marlton, NJ 08053

Phillips Publishing
Co.
7315 Wisconsin Avenue
Suite 1200 N.
Bethesda, MD 20814

Phillips, S. G.
P. O. Box 83
Chatham, NY 12037

Philomel Books
200 Madison Avenue,
Room 1405
New York, NY 10016

Plays, Inc.
8 Arlington Street
Boston, MA 02116

Pocket Books, Inc.
1230 Avenue of the
Americas
New York, NY 10020

Pomfret House
P. O. Box 216
Pomfret Center, CT
06259

Prentice-Hall Media
150 White Plains Road
Tarrytown, NY 10591

Puffin Books
Imprint of Penguin
Books, Inc.

Putnam Publishing Co.
200 Madison Avenue
New York, NY 10016

RCA Corp.
P. O. Box 432
Princeton, NJ 08540

Raintree Publications,
Ltd.
205 W. Highland Avenue
Milwaukee, WI 53203

Rand McNally & Co.
P. O. Box 7600
Chicago, IL 60680

Random House, Inc.
201 E. 50th Street
New York, NY 10022

Routledge & Kegan Paul
Ltd.
9 Park Street
Boston, MA 02108

SVE
See Society for
Visual Education

Scarecrow Press, Inc.
52 Liberty Street
P. O. Box 656
Metuchen, NJ 08840

Schloat, Warren,
Productions
150 White Plains Road
Tarrytown, NY 10591

Schocken Books, Inc.
200 Madison Avenue
New York, NY 10016

Scholastic Book
Services
730 Broadway
New York, NY 10003

Scott, Foresman and
Co.
1900 East Lake Avenue
Glenview, IL 60025

Scott Publishing Co.
3 East 57th Street
New York, NY 10022

Scott, William R., Inc.
333 Avenue of the
Americas
New York, NY 10014

Scribner's, Charles,
Sons
597 Fifth Avenue
New York, NY 10017

Seabury Press
815 2nd Avenue
New York, NY 10017

Sierra Club Books
530 Bush Street
San Francisco, CA 94108

Silver Burdett Co.
250 James Street
Morristown, NJ 07960

Simon & Schuster, Inc.
1230 Avenue of the Americas
New York, NY 10020

Smithsonian Exposition Books
Box 10229
Des Moines, IA 50336

Smithsonian Exposition Books
Distributed by Norton, W. W. & Co.

Society for Visual Education
Department BH
1345 Diversey Parkway
Chicago, IL 60614

Spoken Arts, Inc.
310 N. Avenue
New Rochelle, NY 10801

St. Martins Press
175 5th Avenue
New York, NY 10010

Stanfield Film Associates
1044 19th Street
Suite 1000, Bin 600
P. O. Box 1983
Santa Monica, CA 90406

Steck-Vaughn Co.
P. O. Box 2028
Austin, TX 78768

Sterling Publishing Co., Inc.
2 Park Avenue
New York, NY 10016

Sunburst Communications
39 Washington Avenue
Pleasantville, NY 10570

Teaching Concepts
230 Park Avenue
New York, NY 10017

Thames and Hudson
500 Fifth Avenue
New York, NY 10110

Thomas Nelson, Inc.
P. O. Box 141000
Nashville, TN 37203

3 M Co.
3 M Center
St. Paul, MN 55144

Time-Life Books, Inc.
777 Duke Street
Alexandria, VA 22314

Trippensee Planetarium Co.
301 Cass Street
Saginaw, MI 48602

Troll Associates
320 Rte. 17
Mahwah, NJ 07430

Troubador Press
385 Fremont Street
San Francisco, CA 94105

Tundra Books of Northern New York
51 Clinton Street
P. O. Box 1030
Plattsburgh, NY 12901

Tupperware Home Parties
Tupperware Educational Services
P. O. Box 2353
Orlando, FL 32802

United Learning
6633 W. Howard Street
Box 718
Niles, IL 60648

University of California at Berkeley
Berkeley, CA 94720

University of Chicago Press
5801 Ellis Avenue
Chicago, IL 60637

University of Colorado
Coulder, CO 80309

University of Oregon
1587 Agate Street
Eugene, OR 97403

University Press, The
University of the South
Sewanee, TN 37375

University Press Books
Division of UPBS, Inc.
New York, NY 10001

Vanguard Books
P. O. Box 3566
Chicago, IL 60654

Vanguard Press, Inc.
424 Madison Avenue
New York, NY 10017

Van Nostrand Reinhold Co.
135 W. 50th Street
New York, NY 10020
Orders to:
Order Processing
7625 Empire Drive
Florence, KY 41042

Viking Press
40 W. 23rd Street
New York, NY 10010

Vocational Education Productions
California Polytechnic State University
San Luis Obispo, CA 93407

Walck, H. Z.
See McKay, David, Co., Inc.

Walker & Co.
720 5th Avenue
New York, NY 10019

Walt Disney Educational Media
500 South Buena Vista Street
Burbank, CA 91521

Ward's Modern Learning Aids
P. O. Box 1712
Rochester, NY 14603

Ward's Natural Science Establishment, Inc.
P. O. Box 1712
Rochester, NY 14603

Ward Ritchie Press
474 S. Arroyo Pkwy.
Pasadena, CA 91105

Warne, Frederick, &
Co., Inc.
2 Park Avenue
New York, NY 10016

Warwick Press
See Watts, Franklin,
Inc.

Watson-Guptill
Publications, Inc.
1695 Oak Street
Lakewood, NJ 08701

Watts, Franklin, Inc.
Subs. of Grolier, Inc.
387 Park Ave., South
New York, Ny 10019

Western Publishing
Co., Inc.
850 3rd Avenue
New York, NY 10022
Orders to:
Dept. M
1220 Mound Avenue
Racine, WI 53404

Westminster Press
925 Chestnut Street
Philadelphia, PA
19107

Weston Woods Studios,
Inc.
389 Newton Tpk.
Weston, CT 06883

Westwind Press
Rte. 1, Box 208
Farmington, WV 26571

White House Historical
Association
1600 Pennsylvania Ave.
Washington, D.C. 20500

Whitman, Albert, & Co.
5747 W. Howard Street
Niles, IL 60648

Whitman Publishing Co.
1220 Mound Avenue
Racine, WI 53404

Wilson, H. W.
950 University Avenue
Bronx New York, NY
10452

Windmill Books, Inc.
See Dutton, E. P.,
& Co., Inc.

Word Books
4800 West Waco Drive
Waco, TX 76701

World Book/Childcraft
International, Inc.
510 Merchandise Mart
Plaza
Chicago, IL 60654

Workman Publishing
1 West 39th Street
New York, NY 10018

Xerox Education
Publications
245 Long Hill Road
Middletown, CT 06457

Young People's Press
P. O. Box 1005
Avon, CT 06001

Young Scott Books
See Addison-Wesley
Publishing Co., Inc.

Zaner-Bloser, Inc.
823 Church Street
Honesdale, PA 43215
2500 W. Fifth Avenue
Columbus, OH 43216

INDEXES

Subject Index